Stefanie Van de Peer is Research Fellow at the University of Exeter. She has co-edited two books: *Art and Trauma in Africa* (I.B.Tauris, 2013) and *Film Festivals and the Middle East* (2014). She has also worked behind the scenes of several Arab and African film festivals around the world, including the Africa in Motion Film Festival, REEL Festivals, the Middle Eastern Film Festival, and the Boston Palestine Film Festival.

'For years the history of animation was understood as the history of the American animated cartoon. This eclectic, informative and insightful collection evidences lesser-known but significant traditions of production in the Middle East. It decodes and champions the aesthetic, creative and political distinctiveness in the region, and is an important contribution in revising assumptions about animation history and culture.'

– Paul Wells, Animation Academy, Loughborough University

ANIMATION IN THE MIDDLE EAST

PRACTICE AND AESTHETICS FROM BAGHDAD TO CASABLANCA

EDITOR

STEFANIE VAN DE PEER

BLOOMSBURY ACADEMIC

LONDON • NEW YORK • OXFORD • NEW DELHI • SYDNEY

This book is dedicated to Mari and Leon,
who love animation too

BLOOMSBURY ACADEMIC
Bloomsbury Publishing Plc
50 Bedford Square, London, WC1B 3DP, UK
1385 Broadway, New York, NY 10018, USA
29 Earlsfort Terrace, Dublin 2, Ireland

BLOOMSBURY, BLOOMSBURY ACADEMIC and the Diana logo
are trademarks of Bloomsbury Publishing Plc

First published by I. B. Tauris
This paperback edition published in 2021

Copyright Introduction, Chapter 5 and editorial selection © 2017 Stefanie Van de Peer
Copyright individual chapters © 2017 Maya Ben Ayed, Paula Callus,
Yael Friedman, Lina Ghaibeh, Mohamed Ghazala, Maryam Ghorbankarimi,
Colleen Jankovic, George Khoury (Jad), Nisrine Mansour, Omar Adam Sayfo,
Amber Shields, Başak Ürkmez

Stefanie Van de Peer has asserted their right under the Copyright,
Designs and Patents Act, 1988, to be identified as Author of this work.

For legal purposes the Acknowledgements on p. ix constitute
an extension of this copyright page.

All rights reserved. No part of this publication may be reproduced or
transmitted in any form or by any means, electronic or mechanical,
including photocopying, recording, or any information storage or retrieval
system, without prior permission in writing from the publishers.

Bloomsbury Publishing Plc does not have any control over, or responsibility for,
any third-party websites referred to or in this book. All internet addresses given
in this book were correct at the time of going to press. The author and publisher
regret any inconvenience caused if addresses have changed or sites have
ceased to exist, but can accept no responsibility for any such changes.

A catalogue record for this book is available from the British Library.

A catalog record for this book is available from the Library of Congress.

ISBN: HB: 978 1 78453 326 7
PB: 978 1 3502 4390 3
ePDF: 978 1 78673 171 5
eBook: 978 1 78672 171 6

Tauris World Cinema Series

To find out more about our authors and books visit
www.bloomsbury.com and sign up for our newsletters.

Contents

List of Illustrations	vii
Acknowledgements	ix
Contributors	xi
A Note on Referencing, Availability of the Films and Language	xv

Introduction: Modelling Local Content for
Animation in the Middle East   1
Stefanie Van de Peer

1   Restoring Cultural Historical Memories: Animating
Folktales to Form New Iraqi Identities   29
Amber Shields

2   The Key Frames: Milestones in the Institutional
History of Animation in Iran   51
Maryam Ghorbankarimi

3   Local Minds, Foreign Hands: Animation in Saudi
Arabia and the Gulf   69
Omar Adam Sayfo

4   Turkish Animation: A Contemporary Reflection of
the Karagöz Shadow Play   84
Başak Ürkmez

5   From Animated Cartoons to Suspended
Animation: A History of Syrian Animation   107
Stefanie Van de Peer

6   Cultivating an Arthouse Viewership: Lebanese
Animation Audiences Grow Up   129
Lina Ghaibeh and George Khoury (Jad)

7   Pixelated Intifada: Animating Palestine Under
Digital Occupation   150
Colleen Jankovic

Contents

8 Beyond the Burden of Representation: Israeli
Animation Between Escapism and Subversion   172
Yael Friedman

9 From the Pioneers to the Revolutionaries:
The Art of Animation in Egypt   196
Mohamed Ghazala

10 Animating Libya in Shorthand: The Skilful Art of
Visualising the Repressed Body   217
Nisrine Mansour

11 Cinema Against an Authoritarian Backdrop: A
History of Tunisian Animation   240
Maya Ben Ayed

12 Animation in Morocco: New Generations and
Emerging Communities   262
Paula Callus

Bibliography   **282**
Index   **298**

Illustrations

0.1 Still from *The Street Artist*, directed by Mahmoud Hindawi (2014) © Mahmoud Hindawi — 13

1.1 The Sa'luwa is reborn through 3D animation. Still from *Baghdad Night*, directed by Furat Al-Jamil (2013) © Furat Al-Jamil — 39

1.2 The resurrected city of Baghdad tells its own story. Still from *Baghdad Night*, directed by Furat Al-Jamil (2013) © Furat Al-Jamil — 42

2.1 Still from *The Mad Mad Mad World*, directed by Noureddin Zarrinkelk (1975) © Noureddin Zarrinkelk — 61

2.2 Still from *The Deception*, directed by Mahvash Tehrani and Hosseinali Ghorbankarimi (1982) © Bina Film — 64

3.1 Still from *Dream of the Olives* (2009), a Palestinian story in a Saudi interpretation © Usama Khalifa — 76

4.1 Still from *Don't Go*, directed by Turgut Akaçık (2010) © Turgut Akaçık — 101

4.2 Still from *Tornistan*, directed by Ayçe Kartal (2013) © Ayçe Kartal — 103

5.1 Still from *The General's Boot*, directed by Akram Agha (2008) © Akram Agha — 115

5.2 *Untitled* (2012), digital print by Sulafa Hijazi © Sulafa Hijazi — 120

6.1 Still from *Burj El-Mur: Tower of Bitterness*, directed by Lina Ghaibeh (2012) © Lina Ghaibeh — 134

7.1 'Proof of Concept' image from *Fatenah* (2009) created using 3D modelling and stylised photographs taken in Gaza © Ahmad Habash — 161

7.2 Sequence of stills from *The Wanted 18*, directed by Ahmad Habash and Paul Cowan (2014) © Ahmad Habash and Paul Cowan — 165

8.1 Still from *Hollow Land*, directed by Uri and Michelle Kranot (2013) © Uri and Michelle Kranot — 184

Illustrations

8.2 Still from *Sketches from Munich*, directed by Jack
TML (2013) © Jack TML 185

9.1 Still from *Honyan's Shoe*, directed by Mohamed
Ghazala (2010) © Mohamed Ghazala 209

10.1 Editorial cartoon by Mohamed Zwawi, showing members of
popular committees touting public health campaigns while
people are drowning in poor infrastructure (n.d.)
© Mohamed Zwawi 223

10.2 Still from *Boq'at Jaw*, directed by Mohamed Karwad
(2010) © Mohamed Karwad 229

11.1 Still from *L'mrayet (The Glasses)*, directed by Nadia Rais
(2011) © Nadia Rais 255

12.1 Sketch for the Tagine Character from blog
Harakatoon (2008) © Youssef El-Aakouchi 269

12.2 Still from *Rass Derb*, directed by Rachid Jadir (2010)
© Rachid Jadir 272

Acknowledgements

The filmmakers discussed in this volume often have to work in circumstances that are precarious and in a medium that does not usually get the financial support, critical recognition or academic attention it deserves. In this book all the contributors recognise the artists' passion and talent, and their unrelenting devotion to developing a platform for animation from the Middle East. We are grateful, above all, to the filmmakers. They make a powerful impact on an under-appreciated field inhabited by inspired and inspiring people.

I would like to thank the Film Studies editors at I.B.Tauris, Anna Coatman and Madeleine Hamey-Thomas, who have been encouraging in their dedication to the volume and in opening up avenues for its publication. I am very grateful to Cristina Johnston for the translation of the French language chapter on Tunisia. I also received tremendous help from two copy editors who really assisted in bringing the project to fruition. Without Stephen Blackey and Richie McCaffery this book would simply not be as good as it is.

The limited opportunities for exposure of Middle Eastern animated films and the dispersed nature of the network of people working in the field ensured a wide diversity of contributors. I thank the authors of the chapters in this volume: Maya Ben Ayed, Paula Callus, Yael Friedman, Lina Ghaibeh, Mohamed Ghazala, Maryam Ghorbankarimi, Colleen Jankovic, George Khoury (Jad), Nisrine Mansour, Omar Sayfo, Amber Shields and Başak Ürkmez, for having come on board at different stages of the project, and delivering materials of such excellent quality.

The limited availability of scholarship on animation from the Middle East has also made me explore sources from the Middle East in languages in which I am not fluent. I thank Ana Grgič and Sara Aguzzoni for helping me with the Italian writing on African animation, Öznur Karaça for

Acknowledgements

assistance with Turkish language sources and Silke Goijens and Helge Daniëls for help with some Arabic materials.

Other colleagues I am grateful to are Samia Chelbi, Florence Martin, Will Higbee, Guy Austin, Inès Jerray, Richard Neupert and Sébastien Denis for opening up their network of scholars of Tunisian cinema; Michael Marten, the members of the Middle East Caucus at SCMS, Dia' Azzeh and Amer Shomali for helping me find someone to write about animation in Palestine; Ann Davies for advice and guidance on being the editor of such a culturally diverse volume; and Nichola Dobson of the Society for Animation Studies and Malikka Bouaissa at *al.arte magazine* for letting me try out some of my initial ideas in their online publications.

Lastly, I want to thank family and friends for listening to me enthuse endlessly about animation, and allowing me to test arguments and analyses on them: Marjan Weyn and Dirk Van de Peer, Valerie Van de Peer and Geert Van Dosselaer, Emilie Van de Peer and Jan Peynsaert, Leen Maes and Lore Van Acker, Öznur Karaça, Ana Grgič, Kholoud Baher Hussein, Michael Marten, Helge Daniëls and Richie McCaffery – always my main source of inspiration.

Contributors

MAYA BEN AYED received her PhD from the Institut de Recherches et d'Etudes du Monde Arabe et Musulman (IREMAM) at the Université de Provence and at the University of Tunis. The title of her thesis is 'Le cinéma d'animation en Tunisie: Genèse et évolution (1964–2010)' [Animated Cinema in Tunisia: Origins and Development (1964–2010)]. She is the director of two experimental animation films: *In and On* (2001) and *Kashf* (2003).

PAULA CALLUS is Senior Lecturer at the National Centre of Computer Animation at Bournemouth University, UK. She holds a PhD in Sub-Saharan African Animation from SOAS, University of London, and is busy creating an archive of African animation. Previous experience in this field includes consultancy and training for UNESCO's 'Africa Animated' projects, and compiling animation programmes for various festivals, including Africa in Motion (Edinburgh), Cambridge African Film Festival, Meknès Animation Festival (Morocco) and Africa at the Pictures (London).

YAEL FRIEDMAN is Lecturer in Film Theory and Documentary Film Practice at the University of Portsmouth. Her research interests include Israeli and Palestinian cinemas, transnational film studies and documentary theory and practice. She has published in *South Cinema Notebooks – Cinema, Destruction & Trauma* (2007) (in Hebrew), in *Jewish Film & New Media* (2015) and in *Transnational Cinemas* (2015).

LINA GHAIBEH is a Syrian-Danish animation and comics artist living in Lebanon. She is Associate Professor of the Graphic Design Programme at the American University of Beirut (AUB). Her research interests include comics and illustration in the Arab world, illustration as a pedagogic tool and animation and motion graphics. Her animated shorts have been screened at international film festivals, including Oberhausen Film Festival, Angouleme Comics Festival, Annecy Animation Festival and festivals in Ottawa, Seoul, San Francisco, Copenhagen, Casablanca, Ismailia and Beirut.

MOHAMED GHAZALA is Assistant Professor at the Animation Department of Minia University in Egypt and Chair of the Visual & Digital Production Department at Effat University in Saudi Arabia. He has directed award-winning films, including *Honyan's Shoe* (2009), winning the Animation Prize at The African Movie Academy Awards in 2010. He is Vice President of ASIFA and the founder of ASIFA Egypt and has served on many international animation festival juries.

MARYAM GHORBANKARIMI is Teaching Fellow at the University of St Andrews. She studied at Toronto's Ryerson University and completed her PhD in film studies at the University of Edinburgh. Her book *A Colourful Presence: An Analysis of the Evolution in the Representation of Women in Iranian Cinema since 1990* is published with Cambridge Scholars Publishing. Her main research interest is the representation of sexuality and women in Middle Eastern cinema. She is also a filmmaker with award-winning shorts shown at festivals in Montreal, Beijing and Tehran. As a film editor she worked on Iranian-Canadian feature-length *The Desert Fish* (2013).

COLLEEN JANKOVIC is a researcher in Palestinian and Israeli film, visual culture and queer politics. She holds a PhD from the University of Pittsburgh where her thesis received an Eric O. Clarke Dissertation Award. Her work has been published in journals such as *The Canadian Journal of Film Studies* and *Camera Obscura*, and in the forthcoming *Homonationalism and Pinkwashing*. Her academic work engages Palestine solidarity activism, centring on the academic and cultural boycott and the role of cinema and queer/feminist politics in Israeli settler-colonialism and its resistance.

GEORGE KHOURY (JAD) is a faculty member at the Lebanese American University (LAU), where he introduced Digital Media and revamped the Advanced Computer Graphics and Animation courses. He has had a career in animation and comics since the 1980s and has served as Head of the Animation Department at Future Television since 1993. His work has

Contributors

been featured in exhibitions and festivals, and awarded with prizes internationally. He authored *A History of Arabic Comics* for the Research Centre of Comics in Angoulême, France. He is co-founder of the Lebanese Syndicate of Professional Graphic Designers, Illustrators and Animators, launched in 1999.

NISRINE MANSOUR is a researcher and documentary filmmaker based at the Arab Media Centre at the University of Westminster in London. She holds a PhD in Social Policy from the London School of Economics and an MA in Documentary Filmmaking from the University of the Arts in London. Her research and film interests include gender and family policies, civil society, forced migration, queer subcultures and mediated cultures among Arab children.

OMAR ADAM SAYFO is a PhD candidate at Utrecht University and a previous Visiting Scholar at the University of Cambridge. His main research field is media and political propaganda in the Arab world. He is currently engaged in research on identity and Arab animation.

AMBER SHIELDS is a PhD candidate in the Department of Film Studies, University of St Andrews. Her research project 'Inbetween Worlds: A Fantastic Approach to Trauma' explores fantasy as a mode of cultural trauma representation. Her main areas of interest are trauma studies, fantasy, cultural memories, collective identities and storytelling. She holds a BA in Latin American Studies from Carleton College and an MPhil in Screen Media and Cultures from the University of Cambridge.

BAŞAK ÜRKMEZ is an animator and lecturer in İstanbul. He completed his doctorate in Mimar Sinan University in 2011, where he works as Assistant Professor in the Graphic Design Department. He was granted a Turkish Graphic Design Society Award as the Best Exhibition Design in 2011 and 2012. He is a member of Grafist – the İstanbul Graphic Design Week Organisation Committee and is working towards the founding of the Turkish Society of Animation.

STEFANIE VAN DE PEER is Research Fellow at the University of Exeter. She holds a PhD in Postcolonial Cinema from the University of Stirling.

xiii

Contributors

She specialises in Arab and African women in cinema, with a particular interest in documentary and animation. She has worked as a programmer and director of film festivals such as MONA Film Festival in Antwerp, the Africa in Motion Film Festival, the Middle Eastern Film Festival and REEL Festivals in Edinburgh, and for the Boston Palestine Film Festival.

A Note on Referencing, Availability of the Films and Language

Film Titles

On first mention, all films are referenced in the following fashion: *Original title* (*English language title*, date); subsequent references are by the English language title.

Many of the films mentioned in this volume have original film titles in Arabic, French, Farsi or Turkish and even Japanese. Where possible, we provide the original title of the film first. However, not all films have titles that have been translated, and some have been made available with English titles only, with an eye on a large transnational audience. Where this is the case, we have used the most common translations and transliterations of the titles in question. If the films do not have an English title, we use the most common transliteration, or the French given title, and translate this into English. Where possible, we have included links to the online version of the films, in order to make the films as widely accessible as possible.

Names

Given names, transliterated from Arabic, Turkish, Farsi and Hebrew into English (or the Roman alphabet), often use el/El or al/Al, sometimes with a hyphen. As there are no firm rules on how the transliteration is to be rendered, for the sake of consistency, we have opted for capitalisation, with the hyphen.

Language

One of the chapters in this volume was originally written in French. This piece has been translated, as indicated.

Introduction: Modelling Local Content for Animation in the Middle East

Stefanie Van de Peer

Animated films from the Middle East and North Africa hardly ever make it into cinemas in the US or Europe, or onto the film festivals circuit, let alone into academic studies of the art form.[1] This is despite the West's continued gaze onto the area since 9/11 and the Arab Revolutions, which have no doubt increased the visibility of Middle Eastern media and cinema globally. Nevertheless, animation is an enormously popular art form that is widely practiced and exhibited in the Middle East. Animation is not only popular with local audiences, it is also a form through which artists could arguably attain on the one hand a more complex transnational Middle Eastern identity, and on the other hand a more expressive entrepreneurial outlook. With the rise of regional interests in the production, distribution and exhibition of local creative material, the fast developments in animation embody and reflect the cinema of the region's growing confidence and substance on a global scale. This volume therefore aims to reveal the significance of animators in Middle Eastern and North African film culture, while rooting the contemporary developments firmly in a local interpretation of, and experimentation with, the art form.

Firstly, though, some engagement with the geographical scope of this volume is required. The Middle East and North Africa are vast regions, and in this volume they are dealt with in their largest possible interpretation: we have not limited ourselves to the Arab world. As the title suggests,

1

it includes the westernmost country in North Africa's Maghreb, Morocco, as well as Iraq, the easternmost Arab country. In between, we discuss non-Arab countries such as Iran and Turkey. Likewise, and perhaps controversially, a chapter on Israel is included, not only because of the significance of *Vals Im Bashir* (*Waltz with Bashir*, Ari Folman, 2008), but also because animators there deal with territorial issues in parallel to how Palestinians animate their struggle for return and self-rule. I also fully acknowledge the problematic terminology of 'Arab', 'Middle East' and MENA ('Middle East and North Africa'): it remains necessary to diversify our understanding of the region and its cohesive nature through history, culture, language and religion.[2] This volume's geographical and political scope makes it transnational in its editorial approach – both artistic and academic – and offers the reader the opportunity to read chapters in relation to one another, as animators travel, co-produce, subcontract locally and regionally, exile themselves, and export their work throughout the region.

Beyond the Dichotomies

Instead of positing West versus East in a discourse that draws attention to the origins of cinema and animation in the West, and the East's insecurities regarding figurative arts, it is perhaps more useful to follow Laura Marks' stance on the infinite enfoldment of art and its influences, in both directions, from East to West and West to East. At the same time, the late arrival of animation in the Middle East, and the complex context within which it now blooms, need to be acknowledged. In some countries in the Middle East where Islamic law rules, the relationship between film and religion has been complex. Precisely because of its *animated* nature, animated film takes man as the creator a step further. While the basic form and aim of animation, of lending the illusion of movement and a soul to a drawn body for its supposed young audience, is arguably why it has not always been appreciated in the East, in areas in the Middle East this under-appreciation has been ascribed to its allegedly un-Islamic nature. As Islam declares that Allah is the only image-maker, the only creative and shaping being, for centuries Islamic artists faced insecurities about representational arts.[3]

In *Enfoldment and Infinity* (2010) Marks explores in detail how patterns of ancient Islamic art enfold digital media art infinitely. She constructs

Introduction

an Islamic archaeology of new media, and refuses to indulge in the dialectic between East and West, between Islamic and digital media, and between religious and secular art. She demonstrates the historical continuities between the ancient and the modern, as digital concepts such as algorithms, pixels and virtual reality are actually rooted in centuries-old Islamic art.[4] Both Arab artists and the Islamic body of thought have acutely influenced European and Western culture.

Marks shows how one of the most popular non-figurative Islamic arts – calligraphy – in many respects is itself animated: its written words or single letters encapsulate life and movement in their fluidity. Calligraphic artworks, while they do not depict living forms, do embody the movement of life itself. 'Watching calligraphic animation, we feel empathy with the letters as they swoop free of their symbolic constraints and become animated, take on (non-organic) life.'[5] This is illustrated by the Turkish film *Amentü Gemisi Nasıl Yürüdü* (*How the Ship of Creed Sailed*) by Tonguç Yaşar (1960s).[6] The animated calligraphy film shows how the letters of the title-poem are inherently animated: that movement is present in the aesthetics and the meaning of the letters. Calligraphy here reveals the movement and performance in poetry, but also in meaning, and as such it brings Islamic and secular art together. Marks further argues that, in the way calligraphy indexes the hand that created it, so too does 'computer-based animation [index] the software and hardware on which it was produced.'[7] Where the understanding of calligraphy as a performative and animated art may be significant for the more traditional forms of animation in the Middle East, ideas on Islamic art and enfolding pixels are noteworthy for animation as a digital art in the contemporary area. In this view, objects have inherent meaning, the way meaning is there behind the surface of the animated image, in the code. Objects and images as well as their meaning need to be unfolded, just as digital code can be decoded as non-figurative art. The idea of a performative code parallels Marks' insight into performative calligraphy in modern digital animation.

In some countries existing under dictatorships (Libya), with a rigorous censorship board (Saudi Arabia), or subject to constant political tensions (Algeria), there is no infrastructure for film, and cinemas are being closed down. Nevertheless, films are being made either clandestinely, slowly or in exile, and historically have had an enormous impact on the national identity formation of these countries. We can therefore not reduce film and its presence or absence in the Middle East to simple dichotomies. Before the Revolutions, enfolded meaning remained hidden from censors, only to be unfolded and appreciated by those who purposefully sought it out: a secret dialogue in plain sight between the art and the viewer.[8] Enfoldment can thus be employed as a tool of political subversion, and as we see in chapters on Syria and Libya in this volume, a secret dialogue in plain sight is exactly what has taken place historically and continues to do so (though not so secret any more) with intensifying vigour. Animation is increasingly a digital art form, certainly so since 2011, when the Revolutions in several Arab countries forced animators with revolutionary propensities onto the global online network, posting their films online in an expression of collective political and artistic dissent. While the Revolutions started in response to repressive regimes, Arab media now have perhaps the most nuanced views of, or influence on, artists' expressive empowerment.

As Marks shows, 'many artists are bringing Islamic textual aesthetics to contemporary media art, and are thus enriching this art's qualities of latency, performativity, and transformation.'[9] Perhaps this also works in the opposite direction: artists are equally bringing contemporary media art to conservative aesthetics and are again broadening horizons and enriching more traditional views of what art can and cannot do. The central thought here is the 'performance' of the tools, where pens as well as computers enable movement, and the index performs a transformative function. In animation, whether this is conservative or modern-liberal, as in all art forms, the popular and the artistic go hand in hand, and approach one another constantly. Likewise, artists and entrepreneurs collaborate, and aspects of both roles are present in one person simultaneously or over a period of time. Trends and developments in the art form change, and ensure that artists become entrepreneurs or move back to their more artistic side. Often, auteurs need to be entrepreneurs to make their art form a financially viable one. Entrepreneurs have turned into auteurs as they experience the revolutions (both digital and political) and liberate themselves from dominant morals and financial restrictions. More and more, on politically interactive and revolutionary platforms, artists as well as entrepreneurs have to consider their audiences and use art in a quest for a wider meaning. To achieve this, it becomes increasingly apparent in films, networks of artists and at festivals, that the basic search is for a common language in film: an Arab identity that can inspire a local audience and lead to a confident, more sustainable industry. All chapters in this volume engage with the quest for identity in and through animation, for a regionally inspired and produced body of work, whether this is entrepreneurial or artistic.

The Digital Age has made space for a young population in the Middle East and with this comes an increased spirit of entrepreneurship. Animation is now pervasive in commercial advertising, games, social networking and television, as well as artistic circles, where experimentation with the digital sometimes takes us back to ancient patterns. The computer and the possibilities offered by digital media have dramatically changed the relative neglect of animation and has ushered in a renewed interest in and favoured attention for animation and related techniques and practices in the cinema.[10] Critically, the impact of these technologies is felt through experimental practices, but also in the possibilities and economies these offer in production, dissemination and distribution to countries in the Middle East. We are looking, then, at the exchanges between the artistic and entrepreneurial impulses in Middle Eastern animation, in the artists' search for a common transnational animated identity.

The Scope of the Volume

This volume seeks to establish a multifaceted media-archaeology and a new history of animation in the Middle East and North Africa. Current film scholarship about the region and its cinema is dominated by Arab, Iranian *or* Turkish cinephile cinema that has been accessible in the West, at film festivals or in art house cinemas. Here, we take a more integrated look at the animation of the region. Both academics and artists, hailing from the Middle East and North Africa as well as from Europe and the US, have contributed to this volume, a spread in identities indicative of the transnational approach we take. With the rise of animation's popularity globally, its speedy development as edutainment, its current ubiquity and financial viability through advertising, its increasing political importance since the Revolutions and its slow recognition as a serious art form, scholarly interest in the history of the form in this region is also gaining momentum.[11]

As Egyptian cinema blossomed earlier and more confidently than other countries in the region, animation also first took shape here, in Alexandria, in the large and rich expat communities. From Alexandria in the 1930s to Ramallah and Damascus in the 2000s, animation has undergone periods of intense popularity and neglect, as well as spurts of distinctive innovations and applications. Looking at the popularity of the early Egyptian animations by the Frenkel Brothers in the 1930s and 1940s and the Moheeb Brothers in the 1950s; the parallel development of commercial animation in advertising studios and more experimental films in the 1960s in Turkey; the increasing popularity of television animation in the 1970s in Lebanon; the creation of feature length animations in Israel in the 1980s; the countless experimental Moroccan short animations of the 1990s; the astounding worldwide success of *Persepolis* and *Waltz with Bashir* in the 2000s; as well as the application of animation as a stand-in for the lost archive in Palestinian cinema in the 2010s and the animated response to the Arab Revolutions – animation has a much longer and intricate history than imagined. Chapters in this volume each provide an overview of a specific country's animation developments, taking into account cinematic and political circumstances and their influence on production, distribution and exhibition, while the volume as a whole establishes transnational links and overlaps between countries in the region.

The enormous success of *Persepolis* (Iran, 2007) and *Waltz with Bashir* (Israel, 2008) in the 2000s opened up an avenue into the history of animation in the Middle East, beyond the countries that are commonly associated with high production values such as Iran, Israel and Turkey. While these countries' amazing strides in animated cinema are explored and their influence on the region's work acknowledged, the Arab contingency of the Middle East and its animation's exponential rise in production and significance in world cinema needs to be addressed. Animation is a form that has never been absent from the region and one wonders exactly why the form travels less well than cinephile and festival films. Excluded from critical accounts, but often widely available on online platforms such as YouTube and Vimeo or the artists' websites, animation in the Middle East needs to be assessed beyond the big budget, high production value non-Arab films that have entered the Western consciousness.

Introduction

As Paul Wells shows, 'animation emerged in a range of developmental and experimental techniques, [each] new form suggesting another "modernity", aesthetically and socio-culturally progressive'. He asserts that 'virtually all forms of animation have been predicated on experimentation in one form or another and certainly have been in the continual embrace of technological progress.'[12] Perhaps for the Middle East it is more nuanced in that, as emerges from these chapters, animation often grew out of either an interest in cartoons or a love of Western or Asian popular animation, and due to a lack of funds and infrastructure, training took place in commercial and/or transnational circumstances. Learning the trade abroad, in an academic context or in more commercial circumstances, are the most obvious journeys for young Middle Eastern artists. As there have been few or no schools teaching animation in the Middle East, artists and entrepreneurs learned their craft in commercial studios and advertising agencies, abroad or locally. Of course there are those who develop their style through experimentation and video art, but that is mostly the case where there are schools, or where they are already established as producers of commercial and advertising materials. This is changing rapidly though, as universities with departments in animation and other digital arts are springing up. Lebanon for example is one of the forerunners in this respect, with a proportionally large number of training and education opportunities for young artists, and even Saudi Arabia has recently designed its first course in animation, at Effat University in Jeddah.[13]

With the positioning of the Gulf as the source of most funding opportunities and production money as well as being the nexus of distribution and exhibition of animated (and other) films in the Middle East, entrepreneurial trends in animation reveal three strands here: advertising, TV serialised edutainment and children's films. Perhaps the increasing need for local education, and the recent establishment of the animation courses in Jeddah, will inject Gulf animation with new, artistic tendencies. Certainly, the outsourcing of labour on children's serials and TV animation from the Gulf to Turkey, Syria and Lebanon has meant a level of regional transnationalism that has fed into the animated series and their potentially more wide-reaching audiences, but the local training opportunities and platforms springing up in the previously quasi-closed-off Gulf region will undoubtedly contribute to a local flavour, emancipation and self-confidence for artists and entrepreneurs alike.

The most persistent need the artists (both commercial and intellectual) identify in the region is for a confident local or regional identity in animation. From the first animators, the Frenkel Brothers from Egypt, improving their hero Mish Mish to become more relevant for large Arab audiences, over Turkish Tonguç Yaşar's *How the Ship of Creed Sailed* and its Ottoman calligraphy contributing to the aesthetic development of Turkish animation, to Lebanese animators' preoccupation with finding a local voice, the search for local style and form is ubiquitous. Perhaps then the overlaps between commercial and artistic animation reveal the need to strike new balances. Artists and entrepreneurs come together more productively in order to find an equilibrium, firstly, between developing local content versus outsourcing the labour globally and regionally; secondly between dealing with the high costs of setting up local infrastructure versus the continuing dominance of Western stories on Middle Eastern screens; and thirdly between Western stories being executive produced in the Middle East versus Middle Eastern stories being produced in the West. As Chris Newbould shows, for example, the recent *Postman Pat* film – a quintessentially English story – was produced by Jordanian animation development and production company Rubicon Group Holding (RGH) Entertainment,[14] while Islamic stories like *Muhammad: The Last Prophet* are produced by American Rich Animation Studios/RichCrest, and Disney films like *Aladdin* clearly remain influenced by Middle Eastern stories. While this touches on the potential of transnational work in the animated world, all three cited films show problematic representations of the characters.

In *The World History of Animation*, Steven Cavalier states that some of the origins of animation can be traced back to the Middle East, specifically ancient Egypt and Iran. He shows how some of the most popular Western animated films have been rooted in Middle Eastern stories and aesthetics. Orientalist usages of Arab folklore and stories such as *One Thousand and One Nights* inspired the world's first feature length animated film *Die Abenteuer des Prinzen Achmed* (*The Adventures of Prince Achmed*, 1926) by Lotte Reiniger. As well as being inspired by a Middle Eastern narrative (Andrew Lang's *The Blue Fairy Book* (1889)), this film 'has the feel of traditional Asian shadow puppets', thus also materially referencing the

Introduction

ancient Middle Eastern art form of puppetry.[15] This continued to be the case later on, as the *One Thousand and One Nights* has become integral to a repertoire of transnational storytelling. For example, the Fleischer Studios' 1936 film *Popeye the Saylor meets Sinbad the Sailor* also drew on one of *One Thousand and One Nights'* most famous stories. An even more obvious adaptation of *One Thousand and One Nights* was created in the period when the market for theatrical shorts collapsed and apart from TV the only potentially profitable path was feature animation: UPA produced the Mister Magoo vehicle *1001 Arabian Nights* in 1959, 'with the Mister Magoo character tacked on to a traditional Aladdin story.'[16] The phrasing here indicates the repeated usage of *One Thousand and One Nights* -inspired stories.

However, animators clearly did not tire of this source of inspiration, as Disney's *Aladdin* became an unprecedented box office success in 1991. In *Animating Difference*, the authors show how *Aladdin* was also one of the most controversial, perhaps even racist, films made by Disney, because it 'reiterated Orientalist clichés in the immediate aftermath of the First Gulf War'. They also show 'the efforts of the Arab-American Anti-Discrimination Committee (ADC) to educate the public about the stereotypes and misrepresentations central to the film', and the racist contents of some of the original songs, which 'allowed Disney and much of its audience to picture Arabs as barbaric others.'[17] Richard Williams' unfinished *The Thief and the Cobbler* (1993) is another adaptation of a *One Thousand and One Nights* story, with some of its staff ending up working on Disney's *Aladdin*. In *Reel Bad Arabs* Jack Shaheen has shown that these films are highly problematic in their depictions of 'Arabs' and more broadly people from the Middle East. He was of course not the only one to notice this. Artists from the region have continually strived to create homegrown, relevant and recognisable content in their films, in opposition to the exoticisation and racial stereotypes of Arabs and other Middle Eastern peoples.

While the transnational nature of animation, its inspiration and production, is part of a global tendency to collaborate on projects, what this volume aims to do is describe animated films as part of their specific local histories, while also revealing how regionalism came before the global industry it is developing into. While individual chapters have historical approaches, and cover a number of significant developments, the volume's emphasis on practice and aesthetics hopes to expose parallel developments

9

across space and time. While it is too early to speak of a coherent industry in any of the nations under discussion here, there are large, active transnational networks of auteurs and entrepreneurs that reveal the early developments of an industry. These need to be awarded the attention they deserve as they have the potential to renew the animation industry, while they also need to be rooted firmly in local and regional histories, and as such can start to reveal circuits and networks of artists in the Middle East and North Africa. The search for innovative practices and locally-relevant aesthetics go hand in hand on this quest.

Filling the Gaps

Mohamed Ghazala was the first artist-educator to address the gaps that have been left in discourses on world animation. His short study *Animation in the Arab World: A Glance on the Arabian Animated Films since 1936* (2011) is the first and only work dedicated to animated films from the Arab world so far. The impetus to publish this piece came precisely from the observation that while the Arabs and their folktales have inspired animated films from around the world, no published work has been dedicated to the study of Arab animated productions. Ghazala wrote the chapter on Egyptian animation for this volume, intending to expand on his own research and practice in the field. His groundwork has had to be complemented with archival research, interviews, accumulating online blog entries and articles, as well as original analyses of films, films that were made available either through contact established with the filmmakers or their studios, or through the ever-expanding network of videos on YouTube and Vimeo.

Online source materials go hand in hand with the online availability of the films, and the entrepreneurial and/or revolutionary nature of many of these artists. As the Gulf region in particular continues to raise its profile on the global market as a strong competitor for American and European production companies, film festivals and distribution channels, boosting their profiles with an active online presence, so do revolutionaries in Syria, Egypt, Libya and Tunisia use the internet as a platform to spread idealistic political messages. The digital revolution has enabled smaller scale productions, as the ever-increasing wealth of the Gulf States has attracted foreign

Introduction

investment and outsourced labour, but it also enabled the development of homegrown talent in films with high production values.

Historically there may have been a lack of indigenous feature-length experiments, due to high costs, lack of training facilities and infrastructure, a limited pool of production-ready talent and the complete absence of government support for local initiatives.[18] But in the contemporary world Abu Dhabi and Dubai are certainly at the forefront of film and animation production. In Dubai, the MBC group has developed local expertise and in Abu Dhabi the Cartoon Network Studios Arabia have equally supported local talent as they gain prominence and financial power thanks to their work on foreign productions.[19] While work used to be subcontracted abroad, production is now more often handled and developed in the Middle East. These channels have enabled local talent to mature, as distribution of these products slowly but surely reaches global audiences.

The revolutionaries of the last five years have increasingly claimed their space on online platforms. These artists might be the complementary section to the current entrepreneurial impetus in the Gulf, as producers are aware they require unique, interactive and relevant content beyond children's edutainment. Building on the historic pioneers as well as the current wave of politically and socially inspired content instils local artists with increased self-confidence.

The entrepreneurs, auteurs and revolutionaries of animation in the Middle East have in common a central interest in transnationalism and global reach. In the first place their inspiration and education in animation has been fed by the international scope of Disney and other major studios. Additionally, training and education has for the most part taken place abroad as well, in institutions in the UK, the US, Russia and Europe. This is changing rapidly, as Lebanese, Tunisian, Turkish and even Saudi Arabian universities and academies are now offering courses on animation and digital art. Local sources of inspiration are increasingly finding their audience, as the emphasis for auteurs lies on developing local content and styles. As the transnational nature of big-scale co-productions continues to inspire local entrepreneurs, so does the potential of global audiences inspire transnational distribution and exhibition, mainly through the many festival platforms.

The diversity in, and size of, the Middle East and North Africa determined the broad scope of this volume, which nevertheless necessarily lacks chapters on some countries. The first gap is the lack of engagement with Jordan, a country whose cinema culture is young but growing fast, both through the nurturing of homegrown talent and the Royal Film Commission's (RFC) efforts to attract foreign filmmakers to locations in Jordan.[20] As Anne Ciecko describes, Jordanian cinema started really in 2008, when Amin Matalqa, 'the first Jordanian graduate of the American Film Institute, [directed] *Captain Abu Raed* (2008), an Amman-set narrative', and received the World Cinema Audience Award.[21] In addition to homegrown talent, many regional filmmakers have gone into self-imposed exile in Amman, where they experience freedom of expression in a more liberal and stable political climate. Ciecko concludes that film professionals thriving in Jordan possess a true entrepreneurial spirit.[22]

Within this entrepreneurial spirit, young Jordanian animator Tariq Rimawi has created two important films. In 2010, he graduated with a Master's Degree in Animation from Newport Film School in the UK. His graduation stop-motion film *Missing* is about a child growing up in a war-torn area, longing for peacetime. The nostalgia embodied by this little child evokes acute sympathy, as his big eyes look perpetually sad, and he cannot find solace in the flowers and butterflies surrounding him. These flowers and butterflies return in Rimawi's later work. In 2013, his CG short animated film *Growing* again shows the pain of growing up with war, as a child finds a weapon and 'shoots' a red heart balloon and a butterfly. The tropes of beauty and childhood destroyed by violence are effective in their evocation of how children suffer as they experience adult cruelty. Rimawi's integrated auteurism and entrepreneurship are not only visible in his collaborations with local companies and his exploration of his own profile as the 'first' Jordanian animator, but also through his workshops, lectures and influence as a jury member at JoAnimate.[23]

Set up in 2012 under the more descriptive title Jordan Animation Festival, JoAnimate profiles itself as 'the MENA region's leading animation and creative arts and designs event'. The festival consists of a wide variety of components, including hands-on training and workshops with international industry experts. The festival also runs a competition for shorts, thus offering the opportunity to young, ambitious animators globally to get

Introduction

noticed. Mohammad Abusharif, one of the programmers for the festival, explained that for the competition JoAnimate only accepts short films by independent individual artists, not by production companies. The festival's focus is on auteurism and fostering local talent. The best-represented countries in 2015 were Egypt, Jordan, Lebanon, Syria and Palestine. Jordanian Mahmoud Hindawi's film *The Street Artist* (original title) won the main prize for Best Animated Film.[24]

The film, Hindawi's first, is a universal story that looks at the (mis-) adventures of an ageing street artist who is experiencing a creative block. It is not until a local florist approaches him with compassion that he regains his lust for drawing and fills the empty frames in his house with images of flowers, children and people. Hindawi is an animator and cartoonist, who has worked on promotional and advertising videos in Jordan and on the *Postman Pat* film, after receiving an MA from the University of South Wales in the UK. For *The Street Artist* he used himself as inspiration for the figure of the artist, thus also confirming his interest in the auteurist status of the animator (see image 0.1). The characters in the film and its locations are a mix of British and Arab-inspired elements: architecture in the film is distinctly British-European, while the characters carry a universal look, even if the models for the artist carry political undertones that suggest Arab stereotypes. Quite opposite to Tariq Rimawi's visualisation

0.1 Still from *The Street Artist*, directed by Mahmoud Hindawi (2014)

of war winning over beauty, Hindawi's film lets love triumph over loneliness and misunderstanding. This film is about looking at the surfaces of people versus really seeing their inner selves: where the artist is able to see and understand his models' inner truth, the models themselves are averse to being confronted with this. The artist practices his art not for money – another strong statement about Hindawi's auteurist status.[25]

Apart from JoAnimate's focus on local independent talent, the festival also holds a Regional Talents and Business Forum that showcases production companies, to offer independent animators the chance to network with local and regional companies. The festival does this with an eye to developing a 'regional animation ecosystem and industry.'[26] One of their main aims is to attract international players to meet local talent and develop further local opportunities, in the context of the speedily expanding role of Jordan in the world of Arab and Middle Eastern cinema, for entrepreneurs. The festival is interested first and foremost in their global reach benefiting local talent. The bulk of the talks and discussion panels moreover focus either on the practical side of the animation industry or on the Arab character of Middle Eastern animation, and how to develop that specific local flavour in animation. This trend, expressing a sense of dissidence in the phrasing of a local character for local animation, also expresses a continued and consistent opposition to the dominance of 'foreign' cultures in animation, while the festival and the animation industry at large attract foreign investment, either for location-shooting or for business opportunities. This two-pronged approach to animation as an industry *and* an auteurist art form looking for an identity specific to the region is visible in all chapters in this volume.

As the main goal of this volume is to start to draw a likeness of animation's history in the Middle East and North Africa, much of our time goes to the pioneers, the auteurs, the experimenters. This has also seemed to be the main movement forward for animation in Algeria. While in the early years of independence in Algeria, animation was used (as was the rest of cinema production) in a way that endorsed the FLN government, in a sense as a didactic tool in the formation of a national Algerian identity,[27] more recently Algeria has profiled itself as the country where 'the Arab world's first animation film festival' was held, in December 2012.[28,29] Organised by the Al-Jaahiziyya association, Algeria's foremost cultural association,

Introduction

this festival's programme shows an overall concern with auteur films, similarly to JoAnimate, screening films discussing social issues like unemployment and housing problems, or portraying the current political situation in the Arab world. As festival director Mustafa Kilani said, 'the festival is an attempt to open up new horizons for this unique genre, a genre that we love but neglect with the excuse that production costs are high'. He continues: 'new technologies have cut down these costs, enabling filmmakers to launch into animation, compete at international film festivals, and win prizes. The festival's goal is to introduce this genre into the Arab world, and to showcase our filmmakers' talent and potential'.[30] This again shows a major concern with the development of local talent, and with opportunities for these auteurs to showcase their art regionally.

Slightly more than a year after this inaugural animation festival focusing on Arab animation, Algeria also hosted its first International Animation Film Festival. This festival aimed to put Algiers on the map as a player on the international field of more commercial animation, and to help give the form a firmer place in the country's cinema culture. With attention paid to the role of Algeria in Arab and African cinema, it also held a number of round-table discussions with Arab and African experts in the field.[31] Once again, there is a clear focus on a confident development of local sources and resources, even at international animation festivals in the region.

While these initiatives to put Jordan and Algeria on the world map for animation are very recent, animation in Algeria is actually quite old, compared to the countries around it. In the spirit of national independence and a focus on local concerns, Mohamed Aram created short animated films for television, in opposition to colonial production. He has since the 1960s created more than 50 short films.[32] As an autodidact, he started work for Algerian TV in the early 1960s. In 1964 he was hired by the Centre National du Cinéma to become the director of the new animation department. His first animated short, *La fête de l'arbre* (*The Festival of the Tree*) came out in 1963. In black and white, the film deals with the necessity of reforestation after the war for independence. He also made *Ah, s'il savait lire* (*Oh, If He Knew How to Read*) and *Microbes des poubelles* (*Viruses in Bins*) in 1964, which dealt with illiteracy problems and health and hygiene for the local population respectively. For Aram, animation has a social function: his films are all essentially educational, infused with moral themes pertinent

15

to the contemporary problems of Algeria. He is passionate about the young population needing to see local, recognisable and relevant images on their television screens, in their own language, because for a long time the majority of Algerians have been illiterate.

But this clear path that he had set for himself as the educator of his audiences, as well as his self-taught passion for the art form and his prolific nature, did not solve any of his initial problems with finding support for his chosen art. Animation remained neglected by the cinema authorities in Algeria,[33] and when he was asked to retire and offered a bonus, the auteur used this gift once again in the service of his art: with the bonus he bought his own equipment which enabled him to continue to make his chosen type of films independently. Today, Aram testifies: 'the situation of Algerian animation is abysmal': only a few studios are making animation, and the insurmountable problems are caused mostly by the dominance of TV over cinema in Algeria, a historical problem with Islamism and the closure of cinemas, and a general lack of interest in and money for animated films. His social concerns and his concern for his young audiences do place him firmly within the general trend where local content and a relevant social background become central to the animated stories told on screen, reflecting a growing self-confidence. He is adamant that 'those responsible for finances need to realise that we need to develop Algerian children through images rooted in their own culture and language.'[34] As the development of local content is central to the growth of local audiences and funding, auteurs as well as entrepreneurs are taking on the task of acquiring and improving a self-conscious locally inspired content and design for films that become increasingly ambitious and accessible globally. It is within this context that animation in the Middle East is maturing quickly and becoming fully aware of its market and artistic potential.

Chronology of the Chapters

The order of the chapters in this volume is subject to three logics: chronological, geographical and aesthetic. Firstly, the nature of this volume is historical, and it re-writes or un-writes an existing canon. Through the strongest ideas in every chapter, we tease out an 'imagined' chronology: from an animation of folklore and tradition in Iraq, over twelve countries,

Introduction

we move to the animated internet communities in Morocco. This does not mean that the Iraqi film is not digital: it is entirely digital. And it does not mean that Moroccan animation does not refer to local folklore. On the contrary, it is strongly inspired by tradition and folklore. But the central argument of these chapters focuses, respectively, on Iraqi folktales rising out of the ashes of a destroyed city like a phoenix, and on Moroccan animators' social networking skills and the country's strong presence on the film festival circuit, another – often digital – network. These ideas of rebirth and accessibility are the beginning and end of the volume. Secondly, the geographical scope goes hand in hand with the chronological spread: from Baghdad to Casablanca means, literally, that the Middle East is a huge area, and that between the easternmost Arab city of Baghdad[35] and the westernmost city of Casablanca, the scope of the volume is diverse, multiple and wide. Thirdly, again, the aesthetic logic is inherently bound up with chronology and geography: in the Arabic and Persian scripts, the main scripts dominating the area under discussion, one writes from right to left, from Baghdad to Casablanca. As such, the volume 'reads' the region's geography and chronology from right to left. The central idea running through the volume is the development of local contents and styles, but the inspiration behind these is transnational. From Iraq and Iran, over Saudi Arabia and the Gulf, to Turkey, and Syria, Lebanon, Palestine, Israel, and North Africa with Egypt, Libya, Tunisia and Morocco, this volume offers an entirely new history of a place, an art form and artists who need to be recognised individually and, importantly, as a collective. Animation did not suddenly sprout out of nowhere. It is and has always been an inherent part of a transnational film history, where a language is created that goes beyond words – a language of art and images that speak from and to political, economic and artistic sensibilities all over the world.

In Chapter 1, Amber Shields theorises ideas of animated cultural historical memory in Iraq through an in-depth discussion of Furat Al-Jamil's *Baghdad Night* (2013), Iraq's first-ever digital animated film. We start with Iraq as Shields and Al-Jamil look upon Baghdad as a city that can, through art, rise up from its ashes like a phoenix. As protracted war and oppression have dominated Iraq's history, films have often been made *in* Iraq, but not necessarily *by* Iraqis. It is perhaps surprising but mostly inspirational that a proportionally large number of artists and filmmakers from Iraq are

17

women. Maysoon Pachachi plays an important role in the development of local talent in fiction and documentary, while Furat Al-Jamil is the first Iraqi woman to create an animation. Inspired by a local traditional folktale, the film was developed with a transnational team. The chapter explores how the film reconstructs a community narrative by rendering an old Iraqi folktale attractive to young audiences through animation. Committed to saving the tale from extinction, Al-Jamil's process of resurrecting the past through 3D animation also represents a commitment to the future. Appealing to young audiences who have grown up during conflict and suffered extreme disengagement with the past, this animation offers not only the possibility to reconnect them with their past but also provides a path towards the integration of past and present into a new future for the nation.

In Chapter 2 artist and scholar Maryam Ghorbankarimi describes the key stages of Iranian animation, through an integrated history of its institutions, Ministries and organisations. She highlights the slow development of the art form from a tool in education-related film and TV shows, to intellectual experimentation in the 1960s and 1970s and back to educational purposes post-1979. This chapter is also the first of many to acknowledge the tremendous influence advertising has had on the development of a local animated style. It shows how the first examples of modern animation were not seen until the late 1950s, coinciding with the broader intellectual art movements of the late 1950s and 1960s and the Iranian New Wave. After the Revolution, animation remained a celebrated artistic medium and continued through the same institutions, but under new leadership. Ghorbankarimi argues that animation appears never to have become entirely mainstream. Its exclusive nature has allowed for the subjects and stories portrayed to be critical of society and politically charged.

Chapter 3 describes the inherently transnational nature of animation import and co-production in Saudi Arabia and the Gulf region. Omar Sayfo shows, through an auteurist approach, how producers outsourced the labour-intensive process while there is a strong emphasis on the development of local Islamic and educational content. Early animation in the Gulf region was triggered by the one-way inward flow of foreign productions. A limited number of Saudi feature-length animated cartoons appeared in the early 1990s, but it took until the mid-2000s for animation production to experience significant growth. Economic, political, social and technological

Introduction

developments in the 1990s enabled a generation of young entrepreneurs to establish their own companies and build professional networks for animation production. The regional popularity and financial success of animation encouraged authors and producers from other Gulf countries to create their own productions, targeting local (national) audiences. Inspired by this, new local series from Kuwait, UAE, Saudi Arabia and Oman have been articulating national identities, by using local dialects and referring to local culture. Sayfo shows that, despite their assumed censored nature, animated cartoons from the Gulf are in fact inherently political, as they are largely involved in nation building and also in the reconstruction – and in a sense the production – of ideas like 'home', 'community' and 'locality'. In these homegrown films different understandings of nation, religion and identity are defined and redefined against rival imported formulas.

In Chapter 4, on Turkish animation as a contemporary reflection of the Karagöz shadow play, Turkish artist Başak Ürkmez roots animation firmly in a strong theatre and cinema tradition, while emphasising the development of the field through advertising and commercial animated ventures. Karagöz shadow theatre and caricature functioned as a source of inspiration historically, while recent developments in digital art and advertising have influenced contemporary animation. With the economic boom and the industrialisation process, animation experienced a rapid growth in the 1960s. Advertising companies established animation studios. With the social and political transformations of the 1990s, Turkish society once again became increasingly conservative. Ürkmez shows how the succession of military coups and political instability in Turkey continue to define cinema and animation production not only through its institutions, but also in its content and style.

In Chapter 5, Stefanie Van de Peer shows how Syrian animation has gone from a struggle to animate to a suspension of movement due to the Syrian civil war. From cartoonists, imported and television animation, animated features co-produced with the National Film Organisation in the 2000s and regional collaborative work with the Gulf Cooperation Council, to the eventual suspension of animation due to the impasse of the Syrian Revolution in a transnational network of online dissent, animators have had to deal with censorship and outright political danger. In spite of adverse political conditions, young people continuously find the courage and energy to create their art and animation. The chapter argues that it is the recent turmoil in the country that has pushed these animators, and specifically Sulafa Hijazi, out of Syria, and into different art forms. In exile, most Syrian animation has come to a full stop – a suspension or interruption – but their commitment to a politically outspoken, Arab aesthetic for their artwork is firmer than ever.

Lina Ghaibeh and George Khoury (Jad) describe, in Chapter 6, a rich Lebanese cartoon culture, developed within the relatively liberal nature of the country's position in the Middle East, where Khoury, as he set up Future TV, started to develop a productive manner of producing experimental and innovative animation. Khoury and Ghaibeh discuss the developing role of education in the Lebanese animated world, and the establishment of a specialised festival in Beirut. Collaborations of artists with educational institutions and film festivals further developed a distinctively artistic animation culture, fed by a fast-developing commercial sector employing animation in its approach to advertising. The chapter focuses on independent animators targeting an adult audience and goes into the production and making of animation shorts screened on various platforms. These new trends have ensured the start of a formation of a dedicated audience in spite of the lack of funding or support for animation films.

In Chapter 7, on animation in Palestine, Colleen Jankovic looks at the idea behind Amer Shomali's concept of the 'Pixelated Intifada', and at the contemporary reality of digital occupation. She discusses two very important films, *Fatenah* (2009) and *The Wanted 18* (2014), contextualised by the stunted growth of the idea of Palestinian cinema. A tendency to make use of training opportunities abroad, co-productions with NGOs, and digital collaborations characterise Palestinian films. Palestine may be seen by some as a transnational 'cause' but its films demand a shared point of view from inside Palestine. A close reading of *The Wanted 18* frames the discussion of Palestinian animation's multi-media political and cultural heritage, as well as Palestinian animation's formal diversity and its unique production challenges. A comparative reading with other films – such as Ahmed Habash's 3D short *Fatenah* and installation animation work by Dia' Azzeh provides further insight into a dissident national cultural project.

Chapter 8 looks at Israeli animation, and its burden of representation, or how it moves beyond this. Yael Friedman outlines how the

Introduction

entrepreneurial spirit inherent to animation globally also defined burgeoning Israeli animation in the 1970s. As Friedman shows, *Waltz with Bashir* by Ari Folman (2008) undoubtedly marks an important achievement, but by no means represents the breadth and diversity the form takes on in contemporary Israeli media and film industries. She questions the ways in which different animated works correspond with the multifaceted Israeli culture and the dominant discourse that informs its production. Some works share *Waltz's* political consciousness and delineate a particular 'Israeli' story, while the majority of works engage in more ahistorical and universal tales of human experience. In this way the animated form perhaps frees the cinematic medium from the constraints that govern much of the production of live-action films, enabling transnational audiences to transcend the political and historical specificities of Israel, and of the Middle East at large.

In Chapter 9, artist Mohamed Ghazala traces the art of animation in Egypt, the country in the Middle East and on the African continent with the oldest film industry. From the earliest experiments with form, style and Arab content in the 1930s by the famous Frenkel Brothers, over the commercial work of another pair, the Moheeb Brothers in the 1950s, it is clear that the search for an internal and national identity in animation is at the forefront of this confident nation. This moved to experimental works by Ihab Shaker 1960s and 1970s, and a golden era of production in the 1990s and 2000s, with female animator Mona Abu Al-Nasr, showing how the history of animation in Egypt is one that has evolved from prominent individuals to one that boasts rich regional collaborations and initiatives, among others by Ghazala himself. Ghazala delineates the current entrepreneurial spirit as well as the newly found political activism among Egypt's young populations. The artistic and dramatic changes and developments to the art of animation in the country, as well as the different values and quality between commercial works and artistic ones, culminates in an increasingly confident self-expression since the Egyptian Revolution.

In Chapter 10, Nisrine Mansour continues with the idea of revolution in/as animation. She destroys the common idea that Libya has no cinema *tout court*. She shows how – similarly to Syria – artists learned to function within a repressive regime. Mansour illustrates how political satire could function in a country where the media was completely dominated by one man. With the spark of the Libyan Revolution, social media websites buzzed with illustration and animation artwork by seasoned and emerging Libyan artists. This act of protest unveiled five decades of untapped illustrated satirical heritage that preceded, endured, and survived Gaddafi's rule, raising questions on the possibility of animated critique under oppressive censorship. Libyan cartoonist Mohamad Zwawi's legacy paved the way for a new generation of savvy animators who skilfully manoeuvred censorship to broadcast a satirical animated series, *Boq `at Jaw*, on national TV. With the fall of the Gaddafi regime, these artists had to reposition their artwork and seek new avenues of socio-political critique. Through the research for her own documentary, *The Morganti Rebels*, Mansour traces the changing representations of citizenship and governance, gender relations, familial and social dynamics, and political protest in pre and post-revolutionary Libya.

Chapter 11 deals with Tunisian animation, made and exhibited against an authoritarian backdrop. In this chapter, animation artist and scholar Maya Ben Ayed surveys Tunisian animation from the so-called pioneers to the more contemporary era, illustrating how animation is such a new artform in Tunisia that some of these pioneers have never left the scene. In studies of North African cinema, Tunisian cinema is a fairly well-covered topic, as it went through a Golden Age in the eighties and nineties. However, people only saw animated films at the famous Carthage Film Festival and on some of the many other alternative circuits of cinema in the North African country. Ben Ayed shows a circular movement, where the two authoritarian regimes Tunisia has known since independence limited production but also provided the inspiration for daring, politically outspoken, artistic and metaphoric animated short films.

In the last chapter, focusing on Moroccan animation, Paula Callus unravels the converging networks and communities that developed after Moroccan cinema flourished in the 1990s, and after digital artists discovered and started exploiting the internet. As was the case in mainstream cinema, individual artists started with experimentation in diverse digital art forms, developing their skills in commercial ventures, only to return to their origins in fine arts and experimental, innovative animation. Moroccan animation is hardly visible at European animation festivals, but its presence online, the audiences it has garnered and the number of specialist social network groups for animation artists, suggest that there is a new generation of digital artists afoot. This chapter focuses on these emergent animators who are capitalising on the use of the computer to create moving images that straddle different aesthetic practices as they mobilise themselves transnationally through expert use of web-based technologies.

Conclusion: Transnational Connections and Identities

Animation is beautiful and addictive, but expensive, arduous and undervalued. Most chapters therefore draw attention to the artists' inspirations but also to the institutions necessary to keep the artists going. Each country has its own specific organisations dedicated to animation, whether this is through festivals or associations that look into and promote the rights of artists, such as SPGIL, the Syndicate of Professional Graphic Designers and Illustrators in Lebanon (since 1996), IAC, Israeli Animation Centre (since 2000), FICAM, the Meknès International Animation Festival (since 2000) and AMCA, L'Association Marocaine du Cinema d'Animation (since 2014), and the Guild of Egyptian Animators (since 2011). Undoubtedly one of the most important and well-established organisations for animation in the Middle East (and globally) is ASIFA, the Association Internationale du Film d'Animation (International Association for the Animated Film). It was founded in 1960 in Annecy (France, where the animation film festival is still held) by the most influential animation artists of that time.

Today the association has more than 30 chapters, and it runs the International Animation Day as well as various ASIFA workshops all over the world. As the pre-eminent transnational animation organisation, ASIFA is a collection of national and regional groups, and individual members across the globe, aiming to 'share information, preserve the rights of animators, and promote progress towards peace and understanding through a unified interest in the art of animation.'[36] The ASIFA website shows that Iran, Israel and Egypt are official chapters of the organisation, with Noureddin Zarrinkelk, Tsvika Oren and Mohamed Ghazala respectively as representatives. Iran joined as the first Middle Eastern group: unofficially in 1978 and officially in 1986. Next came Israel in 1985, and Egypt, as the first Arab country to join, did so in 2008.

23

Zarrinkelk (whose work is discussed in Chapter 2) was the founder of the Iranian chapter of ASIFA in 1986, which today boasts several hundred members. The work of ASIFA-Israel, though it was established early on, became more consistent in the 1990s, and included the launch of an annual bulletin in 1991 and, since 2001, showcases an annual Animix competition of Israeli animation. In Egypt, Ihab Shaker (mentioned in Chapter 9) worked with the French pioneer Paul Grimault, who was the head of ASIFA at that time. As Ghazala testifies, Shaker joined ASIFA as its first Arab and African member. Ghazala himself, as the contemporary Egyptian representative on the ASIFA board, sees his task as an educational one, focusing on the Arab and African region, training local animation artists and providing workshops all over the continents, while he also promotes the work of Arab and African animators at animation festivals all over the world. Lastly, as Ürkmez says (in Chapter 4), Turkey is also a full member of ASIFA since 2012. Joining ASIFA is crucial for the smaller local organisations, as the aspirations of local artists can be represented with more influence and recognition by a transnational organisation with the calibre of ASIFA. It is organisations like these that provide artists, producers and scholars involved in animation with the support and acknowledgement they need.

This volume draws together the diverse and fragmented strands of local productions, regional co-productions, the influence of early pioneers, television and contemporary digital interventions as well as cinematic animated films. The internet is an archive of animated films, especially since the so-called 'Arab Spring'. Some of the earliest films have been unearthed and uploaded, while an increasing number of activists and artists upload their work in the spirit of availability and global reach. Some media archaeology is therefore undertaken in the chapters, and – where possible – links to online videos have been included in the notes, in an effort to increase the accessibility of these films. It is my hope that this volume will contribute to and influence the process of dissident canon formation through creating new audiences for Middle Eastern animated films, scholarly and otherwise. This volume wishes to contribute to the opening up to the world of animation from a region as rich, culturally diverse and inspiring as the Middle East.

Notes

1. Exceptions are Ari Folman's *Waltz with Bashir* and Vincent Paronnaud and Marjane Satrapi's *Persepolis*. Neither of these two popular films are Arab, but they have contributed to the opening up of the region's animated production.

2. I have written about this in more detail elsewhere, and continue to acknowledge the Euro-centric terminology, but need a term to conceptualise the book and give it a title. For these reasons I understand the Middle East to *include* the Maghreb. For my other writings on this problematic terminology, see: Stefanie Van de Peer, 'The Moderation of Creative Dissidence in Syria: Reem Ali's Documentary Zabad', *Journal for Cultural Research*, 16, 2&3 (2012), pp. 297–317 & 'Introduction', Dina Iordanova and Stefanie Van de Peer (eds), *Film Festival Yearbook 6: Film Festivals and the Middle East* (St Andrews, 2014), pp. xxi-lvi.

3. An unpublished thesis by Tariq Rimawi at Loughborough University in the UK in 2014, entitled *Issues of representation in Arab animation cinema: practice, history and theory*, supervised by Paul Wells, discusses in great detail the concerns of artists and censorship boards regarding the depiction of the human form in general, and the Prophet Muhammad in particular.

4. Laura Marks, *Enfoldment and Infinity. An Islamic Genealogy of New Media Art* (Cambridge, MA, 2010).

5. Laura Marks, 'Calligraphic Animation: Documenting the Invisible', *Animation: An Interdisciplinary Journal*, 6, 3 (2011), pp. 307–23: 310.

6. *How the Ship of Creed Sailed* is on YouTube. Available at https://www.youtube.com/watch?v=pX3KXXZA6gI (accessed 30 March 2015).

7. Marks, 2011, p. 309.

8. Kathleen Scott, 'Review of *Enfoldment and Infinity: an Islamic Genealogy of New Media Art*', *Screen*, 52, 4, (Winter 2011), pp. 553–6.

9. Marks, 2011, p. 321.

10. Lev Manovich, *The Language of New Media* (Cambridge, MA, 2001).

11. See for example a book-length study and countless articles and chapters on *Waltz with Bashir*, many articles and chapters on *Persepolis* and the growing interest in the earliest Egyptian, Iranian and Turkish animated experiments, visible from the Society for Animation Studies' 2015 conference programme. Available at http://www.sasbeyondtheframe.com/schedule.html (accessed 10 March 2015).

12. Paul Wells, *Animation. Genre and Authorship* (London, 2002), pp. 30–1.

13. Mohamed Ghazala, Egyptian artist and educator who has written one of the chapters for this book, has contributed to the design of this course. Available at http://www.effatuniversity.edu.sa/Academics/CollegeOfArchitectureAndDesign/Pages/About-Visual-and-Digital-Production.aspx (accessed 10 May 2015).

14. Chris Newbould, 'Middle East animation on the map at *Postman Pat's* London premiere', *The National* (21 May 2014). Available at http://www.thenational. ae/blogs/scene-heard/middle-east-animation-on-the-map-at-postman-pats-london-premiere (accessed 22 March 2015).
15. Stephen Cavalier, *The World History of Animation* (London, 2011), p. 88.
16. Cavalier, *The World History of Animation*, p. 186.
17. King, C. Richard, Lugo-Lugo, Carmen R. and Bloodsworth-Lugo, Mary K. *Animating Difference: Race, Gender and Sexuality in Contemporary Films for Children* (Lanham, MD, 2010), pp. 141–2.
18. Badar Salem, 'Experts worry over high regional costs of animation production', *Variety Arabia* (September 2012). Previously available at http://www.variet-yarabia.com/Docs.Viewer/1ce464b6-8869-4eec-bc80-b151781e5a7b/default. aspx (accessed 8 December 2012).
19. Aparna Shivpuri Arya, 'Growth of animation industry in the Middle East', *SME Advisor* (4 September 2011). Available at http://www.smeadvisor.com/2011/ 09/growth-of-animation-industry-in-the-middle-east/ (accessed 22 March 2015).
20. Films made (partly) in Jordan include *Lawrence of Arabia*, directed by David Lean (1961); *Indiana Jones and the Last Crusade*, directed by Steven Spielberg (1989); *The Hurt Locker*, directed by Kathryn Bigelow (2008).
21. Anne Ciecko, 'Digital Territories and States of Independence: Jordan's Film Scenes', *Afterimage: The Journal of Media Arts and Cultural Criticism*, 36, 5 (March/April, 2009), pp. 3–6.
22. Anne Ciecko, 'Digital Territories and States of Independence: Jordan's Film Scenes', pp. 3–6.
23. Tariq Rimawi's website. Available at http://www.tariqrimawi.com (accessed April 2015).
24. It also won Best Story, Best Director, Best Art Director, Best Short Film and the People's Choice Award. The film went on to win Best Film prizes at the Cairo International Cinema and Arts Festival for Children, at FECICAM (Festival de Cine de Castilla la Mancha) in Spain, at the International Short Film Festival of India and was a finalist at the Zayed University Middle East Film Festival, Abu Dhabi, UAE 2015.
25. A showreel of Hindawi's work and character design on *The Street Artist* can be found online. Available at https://vimeo.com/76206929 (accessed 30 March 2015).
26. For more information on JoAnimate, see their website. Available at http:// joanimate.com (accessed 13 May 2015).
27. For an in-depth study of Algerian cinema as a tool for national identity forma-tion, see Guy Austin, *Algerian National Cinema* (Manchester, 2012).
28. 'Arab world's first animation film fest held in Algiers', *Euromed Audiovisual* (27 December 2012). Available at http://euromedaudiovisuel.net/p.aspx?t=news& mid=21&l=en&did=1125 (accessed 24 March 2015).

Introduction

29. This idea of being the 'first' to organise or create something within the history of animation returns throughout the book, but need not be taken at face value. As JoAnimate was also established in 2012, and takes place in November, we might presume that Jordan was in fact the 'first' to organise a festival dedicated to animation in the Arab world.

30. 'Arab world's first animation film fest held in Algiers'.

31. O. Hind, 'Festival international du film d'animation à l'Oref. Des films, ateliers et conférences au programme', L'Expression DZ (9 January 2014). Available at http://www.lexpressiondz.com/culture/187555-des-films-ateliers-et-conferences-au-programme.html (accessed 24 March 2015).

32. Abdelhakim Meziani, 'Mohamed Aram, ovvero la solitudine di un autore di disegni animati. Incontro con Mohamed Aram', Bazzoli, Maria Silvia (ed.), African cartoon. Il cinema di animazione in Africa (Milan, 2003), pp. 63–6.

33. Giannalberto Bendazzi, 'African cinema animation', translated from the Italian by Emilia Ippolito with Paula Burnett, EnterText, 4, 1 (2004), p. 24. Available at http://giannalbertobendazzi.com/wp-content/uploads/2013/08/Giannalberto-Bendazzi-African-Cinema-Animation.pdf (accessed 27 August 2014).

34. Meziani, p. 66.

35. Tehran is further East, but as the majority of this book focuses on the Arab world, I hope the reader may overlook this creative imprecision.

36. ASIFA website. Available at http://asifa.net/about/asifa-target-goals/ (accessed 11 May 2015).

Filmography

1001 Arabian Nights, directed by Jack Kinney (1959).

Ah, s'il savait lire (*Oh, If He Knew How to Read*), directed by Mohamed Aram (1964).

Aladdin, directed by Ron Clements and John Musker (1992).

Amentü Gemisi Nasıl Yürüdü (*How the Ship of Creed Sailed*), directed by Tonguç Yaşar (1960s).

Baghdad Night, directed by Furat Al-Jamil (2013).

Boq`at Jaw (*Chilling Spot*), directed by Mohamad Karwad (2010).

Burj El-Mur: Tower of Bitterness, directed by Lina Ghaibeh (2012).

Captain Abu Raed, directed by Amin Matalqa (2008).

Die Abenteuer des Prinzen Achmed (*The Adventures of Prince Achmed*), directed by Lotte Reiniger (1926).

Fatenah, directed by Ahmed Habash (2009).

Growing, directed by Tariq Rimawi (2013).

La fete de l'arbre (*The Festival of the Tree*), directed by Mohamed Aram (1963).

Microbes des poubelles (*Viruses in Bins*), directed by Mohamed Aram (1964).

Missing, directed by Tariq Rimawi (2010).

Muhammad: The Last Prophet, directed by Richard Rich (2002).

Persepolis, directed by Marjane Satrapi and Vincent Paronnaud (2007).

Popeye the Saylor meets Sinbad the Sailor, directed by David Fleischer (1936).

Postman Pat, directed by Mike Disa (2014).

The Morganti Rebels, directed by Nisrine Mansour and Mohamed Mesrati (forthcoming).

The Street Artist, directed by Mahmud Hindawi (2015).

The Thief and The Cobbler, directed by Richard Williams (1993).

The Wanted 18, directed by Amer Shomali (2014).

Valz im Bashir (*Waltz with Bashir*), directed by Ari Folman (2008).

1

Restoring Cultural Historical Memories: Animating Folktales to Form New Iraqi Identities

Amber Shields[1]

'Always a Phoenix': The Rebirth of the Past

> … always a phoenix …
>
> Because I have seen many wars and much violence, discrimination and abuse, my vision is to build life affirming compositions drawing from history and nature, ingrained with life, rebirth, compassion and healing, juxtaposing destruction and reconstruction to create works of hope in humanity and life.
>
> Furat Al-Jamil[2]

At the top of her blog, Iraqi-German artist Furat Al-Jamil has placed the three words 'always a phoenix'. Bookended by ellipses, it is a line with no defined story preceding or following from it. Yet despite these uncertainties, one thing is clear: the mythical phoenix symbolises the hope that out of the ashes of its unknown past it will be reborn and fly into a new future.

Al-Jamil's short animation *Baghdad Night* (2013) exemplifies this myth. Drawing on Iraqi folklore, her work retells the story of the Sa'luwa, a succubus who bewitches men. An enduring figure, she appears in works ranging from oral folktales to *The One Thousand and One Nights*. Intertwined with, and working to preserve, this evidence of a rich cultural heritage,

Al-Jamil's animation is a rebirth of the traditional tale. Her modern version unfolds in a noir-styled rendition of Baghdad where, over the course of three nights, the Sa'luwa seduces a young taxi driver. The choice to reanimate this cultural historical memory through animation is intriguing, for though Iraq has played a part in transnational animation projects in the past, an industry or even a notable trajectory for animation has yet to develop in a country where a lack of history, infrastructure and trained specialists forestall this industry's growth.

Iraqi cinema history has been dependent on the drastic historical shifts the country has undergone since the 1920s. Cinematic activity started to take shape during that decade, but it took until the 1940s, with British and French investment, before any significant filmmaking initiatives began. The Baghdad Studio was set up in 1948, to be replaced in 1959 by the Cinema and Theatre General that, under the auspices of the Ministry of Culture and Guidance, aimed to espouse the political goals of the regime. Insurgencies, war and autocratic rule further shaped cinema development as grand film projects were limited to propagandistic productions and audiences avoided public spaces like cinemas because of the dangers of war. It was not until 1968 that Norman Emberson Hoy was sent to Baghdad by UNESCO to explore the possibility of setting up a viable animation studio in the country. As he reported: 'There has never been any cartoon animation in Iraq, so the "development" was in fact a beginning.'[3] Hoy was there to 'establish the mechanics to enable cartoon animation' while 'investigating the sources of talent for its creation'. Though he found the country under-equipped, Hoy noted a considerable interest in the art form. Working with enthusiastic and versatile technicians enabled him to set up a nascent studio to create basic animated films.

The Iraqi Baath Party came to power during Hoy's stay in Iraq. The films he was requested to facilitate were 'largely connected with information, education and culture', in line with the Baath Party's developing power and its position towards film. Apart from a televised animation initiative in the 1980s (described below), it was not until 2005 that any information regarding developing animation initiatives could be found related to Iraq or Iraqi artists. In 2005 Iraqi theatre and television director Thamer Al-Zaidi directed the feature-length *Ibn Al-Ghabah* (*The Jungle Kid*) in exile. This Kuwait-based production featured a pan-Arab cast and was based

Restoring Cultural Historical Memories

on a story from the book *Hai bin Yaqzan* by twelfth-century Andalusian scholar Ibn Toufyl.

The country's limited animation history, as well as the contemporary working conditions in Iraq which added great complications to the creation of Al-Jamil's technologically advanced piece, raise questions as to the decision to use animation in *Baghdad Night*. This chapter explores the contributions of animation to this film and how this particular form of representation adds another layer of rebirth to traditional storytelling as it transitions to new media platforms.

The legend of the phoenix parallels the turmoil and actual fire that the Sa'luwa story endured in order to be reborn into its current state. As an Iraqi animation project, it was shaped by the recent decades of external and civil conflict that continue to physically, politically, economically and culturally devastate the country. One casualty of these ongoing conflicts has been the link to the past from which the tale originates. Lina Khatib proposes that one of the questions to be investigated as Iraq looks to move forward is how the country can address the relics of the past.[4] Though cultural heritage projects may not seem as the most pressing concern in a country still grappling with re-establishing basic amenities, quelling violent uprisings and forming a stable government, they offer a way of restoring ties to a unifying cultural heritage that are essential as Iraq struggles to build a new identity and a more peaceful future.

Furat Al-Jamil's *Baghdad Night* is one of these projects. Central to this essay is an exploration of how one folktale's rebirth through animation contributes to the restoration of Iraq's ruptured connection to its past. It proposes what is termed here 'cultural historical memory' as playing a part in re-establishing links to the past to aid in the healing process after dramatic historical ruptures. The case of Al-Jamil's animated folktale is an example of how cultural heritage is reinvented in and for the present context, serving as a cultural historical memory that seeks to unify people according to cultural affinities rather than national or religious dictates. Furthermore, it underscores how animation appeals to the younger generations who, most dramatically split from the past, must necessarily be included in this reconciliation process as they offer the hope for the future.

This chapter explores the creation and conveyance of cultural historical memories, as well as identity formation, through the arts and cinema generally, and through animation specifically. Firstly it presents an examination of Iraq's use of historical memory in creating a collective identity,[5] followed by an exploration of how projects relating to folklore, like Al-Jamil's, play a role in collective identity formation through cultural historical memory. Secondly it proposes *Baghdad Night* as critically engaged with the examined issues and the process of restoring a collective Iraqi identity. In its examination of the specifics of Al-Jamil's project and its use of folklore and animation, this chapter shows the importance of cultural heritage restoration in national reconstruction processes. As Iraq still struggles to reconnect with the past, establish itself in the present and envision its future, projects like *Baghdad Night* will play a significant role in shaping what is reborn out of the ashes.

Preserving Cultural Heritage through Cultural Historical Memory

Iraq's present struggle to restore its ruptured links to the past is not just a response to recent conflicts, but is an issue Iraq has been acutely aware of since its emergence as a nation-state in 1921.[6] This connection to the past is important for emerging states looking to define themselves as historical memory can be a tool of legitimation. Focusing on the Baath Party's reign from 1968 to 2003, political scientist Eric Davis examines how history, memory and culture were used to shape an Iraqi national identity to reflect the Party's values and legitimise its rule.[7] This effort included a promotion of folklore, with the state sponsoring folklore centres, journals and formal studies, as a means for the Baath Party to, according to Tareq Y. Ismael and Max Fuller, secularise and instil a 'sense of Iraqi nationhood or "Iraqi-ness" […] that progressively supplanted one's identity as Sunni, Shiite, Christian.'[8] These undertakings reinforced a common Iraqi identity centred on a proud heritage.

Film also served to reinforce this sense of identity and the Party's political decisions. Cinema was heavily controlled and censored by the Baathist state, leading to the production of several nationalist films. These films would often call upon historical memories to justify current political actions. For example, *Al-Qadisiya* (Salah Abu Sayf, 1981) portrayed the conquest of Iraq by the Sasanians to garner support for the war against Iran, while *Al-Malik Ghazi* (*King Ghazi*, Muhammad Shurki Jamil, 1993) was an epic film created to justify the invasion of Kuwait. Cinema also contributed to modern mythologising of Iraq's recent past in *Al-Ayyam Al-Tawila* (*The Long Days*, Salih Tawfiq, 1980) with its re-imagining of Saddam Hussein's position in the country's history. During this period, Iraq produced its first animation for television, which contributed to this fascination with historical memory. In 1982, Iraqi Television and The Arabic Centre for Animation Films funded the international co-production *Al-Amira Wal-Nahr* (*The Princess and the River*, Faisal Al-Yassiri), portraying a long ago, if not necessarily far away, fairytale story. However, the strict impositions that the Baath Party put on cinematic production crippled the industry. The problem was compounded by the trade boycott against Iraq making shooting materials scarce, and resulted in a fall in production after 1991, limiting animation to a few TV series.[9]

While the state did indeed succeed in cultivating some sense of 'Iraqiness', the Baath Party's association with this identity proved unfavourable after their removal from power. The disintegration of the Baathist state had two major consequences: the country's physical destruction as well as the intangible destruction of Iraq's national identity and cultural heritage. According to Al-Jamil, a lack of cultural references in Iraq's education curriculum, combined with increased religious fanaticism, materialism and corruption, 'has led Iraq's population to become alienated from their country's rich cultural heritage.'[10] As resources are directed towards rebuilding more concrete facets of society and with the alienation that sectarian violence promotes, these parts of cultural heritage are at risk of being lost forever.

The tangible ramifications of this threat can already be seen in the destruction of physical symbols of the country's cultural heritage. Since the 2003 Coalition forces' invasion and the fall of Saddam Hussein, there has been a widespread movement on both official and unofficial levels to rid the nation of all cultural symbols erected by his party and, consequently, the national identity constructed under the Baathists.[11] This process of 'de-Baathification' or 'de-culturalisation' has resulted in the loss of not only markers of the more recent past, but of Iraq's Mesopotamian legacy as well, overall threatening the sense of identity built around cultural historical memories.[12] Here, the deliberate destruction in disproportionately violent campaigns against symbolic and everyday landmarks of the built environment can lead to the more intangible foundations of a society that can, in turn, lead to further physical destruction. The waves of sectarian fighting that have erupted in Iraq since the 2003 invasion exemplify the physical violence created and perpetuated by cultural violence.[13]

One recourse to address the fissions created by cultural violence is a reversion to historical or cultural memory. Davis and historian Maria Todorova use the term 'historical memory' in their emphasis on political and social fusion through reversion to the past.[14] These memories can also be used to create identity in the social realm, especially when emphasising cultural aspects. Cultural theorists such as Marita Sturken and Svetlana Boym have emphasised how the cultural sides of memory can be crucial to understanding collective identity especially during times of political and social change.[15] In all these cases, memory is explored as a force that brings people together in a common sense of identity, instilling it with a commanding power that can be used to influence collectives.

Al-Jamil's animation incorporates these aspects of memory in a project of 'cultural historical memory'. Emphasising the historical, the folktale fulfils the purposes of Davis' and Todorova's historical memory by evoking interpretations of the past to establish a common history and by serving as an example for the present. However, the memory of the folktale, more than just being seen as a socially defined historical memory, also highlights its cultural aspects. Sturken stresses how culture can instil an identity that serves as a political tool, especially in building and defining national identities. Finally, the term 'cultural historical memory' is used in this chapter to separate it from the political connotations that historical memory has in Iraq. Folklore has been used both politically and socially as a foundation for memories and identities, forming its own past that contributes to Al-Jamil's use of folklore as a cultural historical memory.

Creating National Identities through Folk Culture

Constructing a palatable national identity based on historical memory during times when the immediate past is controversial necessitates an evocation of a more distant past. Folk culture serves as an ideal approach to escaping current divides by resurrecting what Boym refers to as the 'potential space of cultural experience' where – free of national and religious affiliations – human relations are developed and culturalisation of new members into society occurs.[16] In his studies on collective memory, Maurice Halbwachs points out how memories passed through collective frameworks perpetuate traditions, yet change to reflect current collective contexts,[17] combining past and present to shape the individual and society. As part of this process, cultural heritage is passed on through traditions like folktales and serves as a foundation for shared cultural historical memory, as well as for its potential to create societal relationships and foster unity.

Cultural historical memory is often used by political and social groups to create national identity. This is especially true after turbulent disruptions make the familiarity and stability offered by these memories most appealing. Folk culture is one powerful means of evoking cultural historical memories. Folktales often serve the purpose of uniting groups, as they teach about the society's governing moral code and support societal bonding. They further the sense of collectivity by representing a common past and tradition that appeals to a wide range of people who in other ways might be divided over the past. This creates a feeling of a collective, stable identity in which the present is linked to the past through folk culture that can establish a political or social group's legitimacy.[18]

For Al-Jamil, folk culture's heritage can contribute to a post-Baathist, unified Iraqi identity. Speaking about folktales surrounding the Sa'luwa she emphasises their role in 'bringing communities together, ensuring exchange, dialogue and understanding'. This in turn 'can keep communities connected to their traditions and will help reboot our collective memory of all the good things that we share', thereby contributing to the country's reconciliation by bringing people together in a 'pleasant, familiar dialogue'[19] around a shared cultural identity.

Folklore also serves to project cultural identity abroad. A group's distinct history and attendant cultural symbols, like folklore, simultaneously establish cultural recognition and legitimacy while garnering local and international respect. The need for positive cultural depictions is especially pressing in Iraq, as its image abroad has been mostly associated with violence,[20] doing little to foster understanding, much less aid in rebuilding the nation. Furthermore, Al-Jamil believes that focusing on negative images produces an incomplete picture of Iraq and an overabundance of melodramatic representations that can actually trivialise the important issues of violence and suffering.[21] She would rather create positive productions using an alternative means to address some of the problems caused by negativity in and about Iraq. She asserts her desire to 'give audiences inside and outside Iraq an enjoyable film that makes them listen and take something home with them even if it is only the magic of a small fairy tale'. She hopes that her work will 'make Iraqis feel proud about their heritage and the ability of their artists' creation.'[22] Her work represents how the cultural historical memory of folk culture recalls positive illustrations of heritage and unification to dispel prophecies of perpetual factionalism.

The use of folk culture as an uplifting, unifying and legitimising agent has been an important recourse for modern Iraq as the country has struggled to solidify a national identity. The Baath Party used folk culture to serve as a source of foundational myths for constructing a national identity and support its legitimacy.[23] This led the government to sponsor a special section of Folk Culture and Arts in the Ministry of Information. Museums, the establishment of the Iraqi Folklore Centre, journal and book publications, as well as university departments devoted to folkloric studies, such as The Centre for the Study of Folklore at Basra University, further served this revival. At this time folk culture was also embraced by a society facing the rapid changes of modernity, ensuring its continuation on the popular level as well.

Since the fall of the Baath Party, folklore has continued to play an important role in Iraq. Projects like Al-Jamil's are reclaiming stories to address the country's changing situation. However, while Al-Jamil sees the great potential in folk culture for bringing Iraqis together, pieces of folk culture like the Sa'luwa's tale are endangered by modernity and by the current fighting and displacement reshaping the cultural landscape.[24] All of this threatens the potential space of cultural experience and has a profound impact, particularly on the younger generation who are further severed from local cultures and traditions.[25] While the Sa'luwa in *Baghdad Night* comments that she does not need to learn of the past from her ancestors because she sees 'all times and ages', her connection to the history of Iraq and Baghdad stands in sharp contrast to that of the young taxi driver from the suburbs, who is disengaged from the old quarters he drives through to make a living.

The loss of space compounds a serious problem threatening the country's present and future. An estimated 60 percent of the Iraqi population is under the age of 24,[26] having come of age under the spectre of instability and violence. A 2007 *Newsweek* report on Iraqi youth painted a bleak picture: a large percentage of youth were out of school, suffering PTSD and being not only exposed to, but recruited to join, the continued fighting. As youths lose education and employment opportunities they become more vulnerable to recruitment by militias and insurgent groups; a situation magnified by the loss of stable community structures. Baghdad neighbourhoods have transformed from diverse spaces of support into places reshaped by displacement and new sectarian divisions, where strangers are 'thrown together by sect and defended by militias.'[27]

The rupture with normalcy, education, place and culture makes the younger generation especially susceptible to destructive rather than constructive tendencies and must be mended if these young people are to bring about peace and reconstruction as adults. By recalling a shared cultural historical memory of Iraq's past, folk culture reinforces a renewed shared and stable national identity that can contribute to easing such divisions. This process, however, does not simply involve a contemporary re-narration, but instead requires a rebirth of this memory for the next generation that is reflective of current situations and sensibilities. Working within a new historical context, Furat Al-Jamil seeks imaginative forms to revive the cultural historical memory of the Sa'luwa character for contemporary audiences. How, in *Baghdad Night*, she has updated this story through both a retelling of the traditional tale and a remediation of the story through animation – and how that reflects the present and creates hope for the future – is examined in the final section.

Animating Iraq's Past, Present and Future

In *Baghdad Night*, Al-Jamil modernises the Sa'luwa's story by setting it in present-day Iraq where a taxi driver encounters the succubus traversing Baghdad's recognisable landscape. In this retelling, the tale is mediated through a short 3D animation that incorporates music, radio, voices and images to (re)create the city's distinct atmosphere. Animation is an appealing medium for the reinvention of the cultural historical memory of folklore as it allows for both the preservation and transformation of cultural heritage. This form of retelling the story creates a place to embrace several aspects of cultural heritage, including music, place, art, voice and oral culture. Al-Jamil's use of animation not only facilitates the rendering of the folktale and the memory of the city and its people, but also creates a more robust cultural historical memory that generates greater reflection on the specific present context of Iraq.

While there is a lack of local animation history in Iraq specifically, animation's strong relationship with folklore globally displays the form's appeal. Noting the popularity of animated fairy tales, Paul Wells highlights how the use of illustrations in children's fairytale books lend themselves to screen illustrations and that the tales' fantastic elements can benefit from animation's more imaginative resources.[28] The connection between animation and folklore has also served political purposes, as exemplified by the acclaimed animation industries of the former USSR and former Czechoslovakia, in which animators employed 'innocent' folktales to convey subversive messages.[29]

Animation can also function as a unique link to the past and play an important part in accessing and shaping memory and, consequently, identity. Annabelle Honess Roe examines the use of animation for these purposes and their implications for animated documentaries. For her, animation contributes to the documentary genre by 'bringing the temporally distal into closer proximity by allowing filmmakers to aesthetically weave themselves into the past', as well as by offering 'insight into the processes of remembering and forgetting that are integral to the formation of personal identity.'[30] Honess Roe maintains that animation also provides a means by which an individual's memories can connect to collective memories and shape worldviews.[31] Animation thus provides a way to access and represent the personal, while simultaneously intertwining personal cultural memories that can be integrated into the larger collective memory.

This confluence of personal and collective memories is evident in Al-Jamil's fascination with the Sa'luwa. Her rendition of the tale is inspired by personal memories of her grandfather telling his version of the story in which he followed a strange woman towards the Sheikh Omar graveyard near the Qambar Ali neighbourhood where Al-Jamil's family lived for

Restoring Cultural Historical Memories

centuries. Further research led to her mother's diaries, where she read versions of this and other stories. Al-Jamil's personal connections demonstrate a continuity between generations and also those links to location provided by folktales. She perpetuates these various connections and breathes life into them again by retelling the tale, thus re-establishing a new generation's link with this cultural historical memory.

The rebirth of this story through 3D animation offers particular appeal to the large Iraqi youth demographic, who are most dramatically cut off from the past. The style of *Baghdad Night* resembles the aesthetic of video and computer games and other new media with which this demographic is familiar (see image 1.1). As Honess Roe says, the visual appeal of animation can inspire interest in a film's subject,[32] and is especially effective in capturing a younger generation's attention.[33]

Al-Jamil originally planned to complete the project using 2D animation, but when her collaborator received an immigration visa and left Iraq, she began working with two young animators experienced in 3D computer animation. Ghaith Mohammed Showqi and Haidder Abdul Rahim Yassir both graduated from the College of Arts, University of Baghdad in 2007 and are among the new generation of artists and filmmakers being trained in Iraqi institutions. This turn of events highlights 3D animation's current

1.1 The Sa'luwa is reborn through 3D animation. Still from *Baghdad Night*, directed by Furat Al-Jamil (2013)

popularity and a growing trend in training opportunities in the Middle East, even in Iraq. The use of 3D animation in sharing a piece of cultural heritage with a younger generation already aware of and attracted to this style comes to reflect less a story of chance than one acutely shaped by the present.

Stylistically blending old and new, *Baghdad Night* also establishes links between the past and present by relying on the familiarity of place. This is rare in the telling of folktales, as part of folklore's appeal is its ability to transcend time and place. The story of the Sa'luwa, for example, has been passed down in time through generations and, while she is clearly recognisable in Iraqi tales, she also appears in different forms in stories across the Gulf region. In *The One Thousand and One Nights* and in Baghdadi folklore, and now in *Baghdad Night*, the Sa'luwa is a woman of bewitching beauty; in the south of Iraq she lives in the waters and appears as a mermaid; and in the north she is a grotesque witch who abducts children.[34] Despite this character's emergence in various locations, Al-Jamil recalls her in a very specific locality in *Baghdad Night*, a fact underscored in the Sa'luwa's very firm assertion in the film of her Baghdad origins.

As a key element of cultural heritage, the city of Baghdad is itself an indispensable character in Al-Jamil's work. One problematising aspect of including this city as a character is the already irreparable damage it has incurred. One of animation's strengths is that it can represent those things impossible to depict using realist methods. That may mean the representation of emotions, fantasies or, as in this case, a reality that no longer exists.[35] Here, animation not only provides access to this idea of place that forms part of the cultural heritage that Al-Jamil fears is on the brink of being lost forever,[36] but counters the destruction by recalling a recognisable geographic reality forming the base of a cultural historical memory. The animation opens with Baghdad's rivers glittering in the moonlight. As the shot sweeps over the serene water and stately bridges, it enters into the dark city, equally silent and calm, empty of its inhabitants yet structurally restored. As part of a collective landscape, these physical spaces can potentially reinforce unity: even as neighbourhoods change and possibly come under the control of contentious factions, the face of the city is still a shared part of the culture.

40

Not only can the city be resurrected through animation, it can also tell its own story. While the film takes place in the city that Al-Jamil grew up in and forms part of her personal memory, the shadow cast upon the location by the film's noir elements – the city as a character is chief among these – captures the emotional reality of a place whose current form is about to be eclipsed (see image 1.2). Its deserted streets add to this haunting feeling, especially as the only hint of other occupants aside from the protagonists is a news report of people killed in a bombing heard over the radio. The animation captures those elements of the city that only exist in memory while simultaneously telling the story of recent and contemporary losses that this city is experiencing and how it is preparing for its rebirth.

By reconstructing the urban landscape through animation, Al-Jamil is counteracting the destruction with the recreation of an area that is a shared space for healing. This reconnection reinstitutes a history of coexistence not only between people but also between people and their culture, or, more concretely, between people and the culture represented by their physical environment. Furthermore, this tie to a physical space reinforces the folktale's legitimacy and its links with the culture dwelling within this topography by showing that it physically occupies its culture rather than being part of the imaginary. This restoration of physical symbols through animation is complemented by the re-imagination of intangible symbols through the folktale. The Sa'luwa comes to serve as a connection not only between the imaginary and the physicality of the space, but also between time and place.

The Sa'luwa character has appeared in specific locations throughout time and generations. Her ability to reappear in the same place, even if it has changed or been destroyed, signifies an ability to connect time and place despite the transformations. By transmitting the history, aspirations and morals of a community, folklore highlights easily identifiable cultural bonds that bring people together independent of particular affinities. In a present where political, religious, ethnic and other factions are vying for power, these connections offer to restore the legitimacy of an inclusive Iraqi national identity.

Al-Jamil's struggle to complete this project despite the very tangible challenges she faced is a testament to her commitment to preserving culture and incorporating it into Iraq's redevelopment. She is not alone in her

1.2 The resurrected city of Baghdad tells its own story. Still from *Baghdad Night*, directed by Furat Al-Jamil (2013)

emphasis on this crucial aspect of national rebuilding. The work of other artists, foundations and cultural institutions is placing growing emphasis on revitalising Iraqi culture. Film production had become stagnant in the last years of Hussein's rule, and his overthrow resulted in a greater freedom of expression that reinvigorated film production in Iraq. Iraqis living in exile returned and made films about rediscovering their place of origin and their new perspectives. This is exemplified in films such as *Return to the Land of Wonders* (Maysoon Pachachi, 2004), *16 Hours in Baghdad* (Tarek Hashim, 2004), *Where is Iraq?* (Baz Sham'un, 2005), and *Hayat ma baad Al-suqoot* (*Life after the Fall*, Qasim 'Abid, 2008).[37]

A new generation of filmmakers started making independent and school productions to document the changing cultural landscape, as well as the continued difficulties of everyday reality following the Coalition invasion. Oday Rasheed, part of *Al-Najin* ('the survivors'), a group of artists, writers, poets and directors who grew up under war and sanctions and commented on contemporary life in Iraq, made his first feature film, and the first post-invasion feature, *Underexposure* (2005) and followed it up with *Qarantina* (2010). Al-Jamil was heavily involved in both films, serving as executive producer for the first and producer for the second. Rasheed, like Al-Jamil, emphasises the importance of reviving culture as part of the nation's rebuilding process, commenting that 'after 30 years of dictatorship, three wars, 13 years of sanctions, we need to rebuild our minds, not just the buildings.'[38] Concerned about the future of cinema in his country, Rasheed began working with Al-Jamil and fellow director Mohamed Al-Daradji to start the Iraqi Independent Film Production Centre, which holds workshops for young Iraqi filmmakers and encourages the development of local production.

The founding of this centre builds on the work begun soon after the 2003 overthrow of Hussein to train new filmmakers who subsequently began documenting the life and changes they observed in Iraq. The Independent Film and Television College of Baghdad was founded in 2004 to offer free filmmaking courses that encouraged the development of Iraqi voices after the years of imposed silence. In its first year, it produced four short documentaries portraying the stories and struggles of Iraqis negotiating their quests for individual and cultural progress amid the difficulties of everyday realities.[39] Despite its continual moves and disruptions, including closure between 2007–08, the school continues its mission by offering courses run by filmmakers Maysoon Pachachi and Kasim Abid and producing short films and documentaries by new filmmakers. These projects, like Al-Jamil's, show the resilience of a group of people committed to renewing the rich Iraqi culture as part of the nation's rebuilding and, importantly, incorporating the younger generation in this process.

Festivals and cultural institutions have also contributed to this cultural reinvigoration process. The Ruya Foundation for Contemporary Culture in Iraq, a funder of *Baghdad Night*, is committed to not only supporting the redevelopment of Iraqi culture, but also to using the country's rich culture to build global cultural connections. The Baghdad International Film Festival, which held festivals in 2005, 2007 and 2011–15, also focuses on showcasing local artists within a wider international discourse, all the while strengthening local community connections. As part of a larger commitment to fostering the younger generation, in 2012 and 2013, the festival organised workshops for Iraqi orphans that aimed to assist the re-socialisation of this vulnerable population. Still relatively new, these cultural institutions represent the growing emphasis on culture's role in rebuilding society at home and strengthening the nation's cultural ties abroad.

How a nation's culture is viewed from abroad and how it takes part in global dialogues also influences national cultural identity. While *Baghdad Night* highlights a local story, animation provides a pathway to enter a global discourse. International ties are represented by a growing trend in Iraqi animation, starting with the country's first animated production in 1982, *The Princess and the River*. Financed by Iraqi sources, this project included designs and drawings from East German artists and was produced by an Australian animation crew. In terms of production, such global exchange has become more localised as the animation industry experiences an upsurge in the Middle East. Large investments from the Gulf States, especially the United Arab Emirates, into media infrastructure and training represent an effort to create state of the art facilities and artists who appeal to the region's young, media savvy population.[40]

With its all-Iraqi cast and crew and its local development, *Baghdad Night* stands out as an extremely localised production. It nevertheless also enters an international dialogue. To begin with, Al-Jamil herself, being of Iraqi-German descent and with professional experience in the Middle East, Europe, and North and South America, represents the international cosmopolitanism at the centre of these dialogues. In addition, it was a post-production grant from Dubai Film Market's Enjaaz Film Fund that paved the film's way to enter global circulation;[41] it premiered at the 10th Dubai International Film Festival in 2013. With no local animation industry, other young Iraqi animators are following a similar path by inserting their work into a transnational market through the film festival circuit.

Art can create bridges to transnational artistic communities and rise above cultural differences (especially the negative stereotypes cultivated during war periods) while simultaneously encouraging greater cultural understanding.[42] These contributions offer counter-narratives to the misconception of Iraq propagated by a news media whose coverage is mainly limited to repetitive storylines that display general breadth but little depth. In contrast, Al-Jamil's film offers a positive alternative, not only in its resurrection of cultural heritage, but in the artist's choice of animation as an artistic creation. Animation for Al-Jamil offers the ability to combine the art forms she enjoys and to create aesthetically appealing artwork that viewers can admire for its beauty, thereby instilling local audiences with a sense of pride and foreign audiences with a sense of admiration. These aspects solidify the creative potentialities and positive attributes of cultural heritage that Al-Jamil and others are trying to revive and share with the local community and the world.

Baghdad Night is an example of the bond between past and present that needs to be reconstituted in order to rebuild Iraq's identity. By bringing this story to a new generation through animation, Al-Jamil's work restores the collective unity between generations that cultural historical memory can provide. Further, the collective process required to complete this work serves as a living example of how diverse people can come together in difficult times to create something beautiful. The distribution of this film within a global context gives the Iraqi collective something to be proud of as it succeeds in reintroducing Iraq as an equal within a larger global collective. The project's importance thus rests not only in its reunification of the Iraqi people through cultural historical memories at home, but also in demonstrating this collective identity to the world.

'Always a Phoenix': Flight to the Future

One of the main priorities in forming a new Iraqi government following the 2003 Coalition forces' invasion has been finding a leader to unite a country that was threatened by, and later succumbed to, civil war. Violent outbreaks in 2014 showed that even after more than ten years, peace and unification remained an elusive goal. As the parliament looked to elect a new president and prime minister that year, the major debate surrounding the candidates was whether they would be able to bring together opposing Shiite, Sunni and Kurdish groups, and put an end to sectarian violence by reunifying the country under a common Iraqi identity. While this debate continues in politics, steps are being taken to address it in the cultural realm. The growing strength of cultural projects, exemplified by the success of independent artists, schools and supporting institutions, shows that this engagement continues. However, as Khatib points out, it is a process that must include reconciliation with the past.[43]

Furat Al-Jamil's *Baghdad Night* is a moving example of how this path to a new future can incorporate the past in a positive way through the creation of a cultural historical memory that can be extended to inspire a positive future. Retelling the Sa'luwa folktale through modern animation allows Al-Jamil to reconjure this positive unifying memory in a way that is untouched by sectarian politics and so bring it to a new generation. Also, her use of folklore continues a strong tradition, both locally and internationally, of employing folk culture to establish nationally and culturally unifying identities by creating a sense of continued and continuing history, coexistence and pride in a community. Finally, by using animation, Al-Jamil is able to represent an intangible cultural heritage (and those lost tangible aspects) in work that is appealing for its connection to and connecting of the new media aesthetics of the younger generation. Thus Al-Jamil not only saves this ancient tale for those older generations who can remember growing up and hearing folk stories, but also introduces the folktale as cultural historical memory to a new generation. This new generation has been cut off from the past through current continued violence, and works such as *Baghdad Night* carry hope, voiced by the character of the Sa'luwa, that good times will return to Baghdad.

Baghdad Night shows that the beauty of this particular piece of cultural historical memory is enduring and does not and should not have to exist merely in the past; that it can rise out of the ashes and soar, reborn, into the future. More importantly, it reveals how such cultural projects can be used to shape the national rebuilding process. By presenting a positive piece of cultural historical memory to the conflicted present, *Baghdad Night* recalls a shared history that can inspire hope for the emergence of similar stories of unification to inform a collective Iraqi identity that is about to be reborn.

Notes

1. I would like to thank Furat Al-Jamil for her generosity in sharing with me stories and material, including her beautiful film, and Stefanie Van de Peer for sharing her knowledge and passion for this topic with me.
2. Furat Al-Jamil, 'Furat Al-Jamil'. Available at http://furataljamil.webs.com/ (accessed 3 July 2014).
3. Norman Emberson Hoy, 1969, 'Report on Mission in Iraq, December 26th 1968 to February 24th 1969', UNESCO Document Archive. Available at http://unesdoc.unesco.org/images/0015/001582/158205eb.pdf (accessed 2 February 2015).
4. Lina Khatib, 'Iraq: Between the Present and the Future', *Middle East Journal of Culture and Communication*, 4 (2011), pp. 253–5, p. 253.
5. While this work will be referring to 'cultural memories' as opposed to 'collective memories', for reasons which will be explained in this chapter, it will still use the term 'collective identity' instead of 'cultural identity' as the identity being referred to here is both cultural and national and thus requires a more encompassing term to account for these two facets.
6. Following the collapse of the Ottoman Empire, Iraq was declared a nation, however it was still subjugated to foreign control and was ruled under the British mandate until 1932 when it was granted independence to self-rule.
7. Eric Davis, *Memories of State: Politics, History, and Collective Identity in Modern Iraq* (Berkeley, 2005).
8. Tareq Y. Ismael and Max Fuller, 'The disintegration of Iraq: the manufacturing and politicization of sectarianism', *International Journal of Contemporary Iraqi Studies*, 2, 3 (2008), pp. 443–73, p. 449.
9. Viola Shafik, *Arab Cinema: History and Cultural Identity* (Cairo, 2007), p. 43.
10. Furat Al-Jamil 'Interview', (2014).
11. Benjamin Isakhan, 'Targeting the symbolic dimension of Baathist Iraq: Cultural destruction, historical memory, and national identity', *Middle East Journal of Culture and Communication* 4 (2011), pp. 257–81.

Animation in the Middle East

12. For more on this, as well as the possible political intentions behind it, see Ismael and Fuller, 'The disintegration of Iraq', p. 450.

13. How this violence affects the everyday is a topic explored in several Iraqi films created since 2003, such as *Underexposure* (Oday Rasheed, 2005) and *Dreams* (Mohamed Al-Daradji, 2005).

14. Davis, *Memories of State*, p. 6 and Maria Todorova, 'Introduction: Learning memory, remembering identity', *Balkan Identities: Nation and Memory* (London, 2004). Davis is very particular in distinguishing this as 'historical memory' rather than the often substituted 'collective memory' in order to emphasize the directed collective understanding of the past shaped for a group as opposed to a Jungian collective consciousness that the latter term invokes.

15. Marita Sturken, *Tangled Memories: The Vietnam War, the AIDS epidemic, and the politics of remembering* (Berkeley, 1997). Svetlana Boym, *The Future of Nostalgia* (New York, 2001).

16. Ibid., p. 53.

17. Maurice Halbwachs, *On Collective Memory* (Chicago, 1992).

18. Péter Niedermüller, 'Ethnicity, nationality, and the myth of cultural heritage: a European view', *Journal of Folklore Research*, 36, 2–3 (1999), pp. 243–53, p. 251.

19. Al-Jamil, 'Interview', (2014).

20. Looking briefly at two critically acclaimed western portrayals of Iraq exemplifies this point. James Longley's documentary *Iraq in Fragments* (2006) focuses on the country's destruction during the Coalition invasion, reinforced by images of the country perpetually burning. Kathryn Bigelow's *The Hurt Locker* (2008) captures the terror that this threatening place represents for Western countries like the US.

21. Furat Al-Jamil, ' "Baghdad Night" Press Folder', p. 11.

22. Ibid., p.12.

23. Davis, *Memories of State*, p.207–208.

24. Paradoxically the threat to and salvation of folk culture in the Iraqi context has been dramatically affected by the influx of oil wealth during the Baath rule. Oil wealth led to rapid modernisation and lifestyle changes that threatened traditional ways of life and the folk culture that relied on these traditions. However the government used oil revenue to financially support many of the programmes that bolstered the interest, study and preservation of folk culture. For more on the connection of oil wealth and folk culture see Davis and Gavrielides 1991 and Al-Najjar 1991.

25. A concrete example of the younger generations' lost connections to folk traditions can be seen in the decreased use and production of new Iraqi children folk songs. Passed on orally between generations of children, these songs reflect national as well as local cultures. However this oral tradition is threatened by

Restoring Cultural Historical Memories

modern influences in children's play, such as the increased use of technology, as well as by the increasing violence damaging spaces for play, leading to a decrease in the popularity of these songs. For more on Iraqi children folk songs see Masliyah 2010.

26. This number is based on the United Nations' Department of Economic and Social Affairs *World Population Prospects: The 2012 Revision* for Iraq's population in 2010. They show this trend continuing in their 2015 population projections.

27. Christian Caryl, Michael Hastings, Scott Johnson, Ayad Obeidi, Ahmed Obeidi, Mohammed Sadeq, Christopher Dickey, Karen Fragala Smith, 'Iraq's young blood', *Newsweek*, 149, 4 (2007), pp. 24–34.

28. Paul Wells, *Animation: Genre and Authorship* (London, 2002).

29. See Jack Zipes, *The Enchanted Screen: The Unknown History of Fairy-tale Films* (London, 2011); and Natalie Kononenko, 'The Politics of innocence: Soviet and Post-Soviet animation on folklore topics', *Journal of American Folklore*, 124, 494 (2011), pp. 272–94.

30. Annabelle Honess Roe, *Animated Documentary* (Basingstoke, 2013), p. 16.

31. Ibid., p. 146.

32. Honess Roe develops this idea from Tom Gunning's claims that the cinema of attractions had a certain appeal that intrigued spectators.

33. Ibid., p. 69.

34. Al-Jamil, 'Press Folder', p. 13.

35. Honess Roe, *Animated Documentary*.

36. Al-Jamil, 'Interview'.

37. This return is also a subject of the 2013 documentary *Back to Iraq* (Anne Dilven) which follows Shaho Jabbari's return to his country 14 years after leaving. This film features some moving animation sequences.

38. Interview quoted in Lucia Sorbera, 'History and fiction in the new Iraqi cinema', Riccardo Bocco, Hamit Bozarslan, Peter Sluglett, and Jordi Tejel (eds), *Writing the Modern History of Iraq: Historiographical and Political Challenges* (Singapore, 2012), p. 431.

39. The films are: *Baghdad Days* (Hiba Bassem, 2005), *Hiwar* (Kifaya Saleh, 2005), *Omar is my Friend* (Mounaf Shaker, 2005), and *Let the Show Begin* (Dhafir Taleb, 2005).

40. The Abu Dhabi media and entertainment company twofour54 has teamed up with Cartoon Network to offer courses in animation and also runs its own course on 3D animation production as part of its efforts to position itself as the media and entertainment centre of the Arab world.

41. This funding support programme is designated for Arab filmmakers and Gulf State productions.

42. In a piece on Iraqi heavy metal music, Lisa Foster highlights how the transcendence of cultural, political and geographical boundaries through music

creates a space for exchange crucial at this juncture in Iraqi history. Lisa Foster, 'The Rhetoric of heavy metal resistance: musical modalities in Iraqi public life', *Middle East Journal of Culture and Communication*, 4 (2011), pp. 320–38.

43. Khatib, 'Iraq: Between the Present and the Future'.

Filmography

16 Hours in Baghdad, directed by Tarek Hashim (2004).

Ahlaam (Dreams), directed by Mohamed Al-Daradji (2005).

Al-Amira wal-nahr (The Princess and the River), directed by Faisal Al-Yassiri (1982).

Al-Ayyam al-Tawila (The Long Days), directed by Salih Tawfiq (1980).

Al-Malik Ghazi (King Ghazi), directed by Muhammad Shurki Jamil (1993).

Al-Qadisiya, directed by Salah Abu Sayf (1981).

Back to Iraq, directed by Anne Dilven (2013).

Baghdad Days, directed by Hiba Bassem (2005).

Baghdad Night, directed by Furat Al-Jamil (2013).

Hiwar, directed by Kifaya Saleh (2005).

Ibn Al-Ghabah (The Jungle Kid), directed by Thamer Al-Zaidi (2005).

Iraq in Fragments, directed by James Longley (2006).

Let the Show Begin, directed by Dhafir Taleb (2005).

Life after the Fall, directed by Qasim 'Abid (2008).

Omar is my Friend, directed by Mounaf Shaker (2005).

Qarantina, directed by Oday Rasheed (2010).

Return to the Land of Wonders, directed by Maysoon Pachachi (2004).

The Hurt Locker, directed by Kathryn Bigelow (2008).

Underexposure, directed by Oday Rasheed (2005).

Where is Iraq?, directed by Baz Sham'un (2005).

2

The Key Frames: Milestones in the Institutional History of Animation in Iran

Maryam Ghorbankarimi

Iranian cinema is one of the most successful and productive in the Middle East, and yet animation, while important, has not yet received much scholarly attention, and has not been acknowledged as an intrinsic part of Iranian cinema history. Due to its international success, first as a graphic novel and then as a film by a French-Iranian, *Persepolis* (Marjane Satrapi and Vincent Paronnaud, 2007) may come to mind when one thinks about animation and Iran. Moreover, while a considerable number of acclaimed short animation films are produced every year inside Iran, the number of feature length animations that pass beyond the regional and Asian markets to the Western world is still very low.

This chapter offers an overview of the emergence and early development of animation in Iran by introducing some of the institutions and artists that have played crucial roles in laying down the foundation of the animation industry. The 1960s, an important decade in Iranian film history, were a time that saw the country undergoing major changes reflecting a newly-adopted industrialisation policy and a strengthening of the role of the state in managing the economy. In addition, thanks to growing oil revenue, the government undertook major investments to build and improve the country's infrastructure, to import technologies and expertise, and to introduce modern media and telecommunications to the country. In what follows, I analyse the three chief institutions that collectively created the milieu from within which the animation industry gradually emerged, namely the Vezarat-e Farhang va Honar (Ministry of Art and Culture), the Kanun-e Parvaresh-e Fekri-ye Kudak va Nowjavan (the Centre for Intellectual Development of Children and Young Adults (CIDCYA)) and Sazman-e Radio va Television-e Melli-ye Iran (National Iranian Radio and Television (NIRT)).

Institutional Concerns and Pioneering Initiatives

As Lord and Sibley have shown, recognition of movement and animation is instinctive in humans, and this is evidenced in the artefacts of early humans who drew on cave walls depictions of spear-waving hunters in pursuit of wild game, conveying the illusion of movement by showing the beasts with multiple sets of legs.[1] Iranian wall paintings form part of the bas-reliefs found in the city of Persepolis (*c.* 500 BC), the ritual centre of the Achaemenid Kingdom (that contributed to the global conceptualisation of Iranian animation presented in *Persepolis*).[2] These bas-reliefs reached their stylistic peak in the depiction of the complex hunting scene in *Taq-e Bostan* (*Arch of the Garden*) referred to about a thousand years after Achaemenid, in the Sasanian era. Perhaps the earliest example of representative animation in Iran is from a clay bowl from *Shahr-e Sukhteh* (*The Burnt City*) located in the Southeast of Iran, that dates back more than 5,000 years. The bowl is decorated with successive images of a goat leaping to snatch a leaf from a tall tree and was discovered in the 1970s, although no one was to realise the significance of its decoration until much later.[3]

The histories of Iranian cinema and animation are intertwined, much like those of other world cinemas and animation. Solidly embedded in twentieth-century Iranian history, Iranian cinema has endured many changes and interruptions. It has veered off into different directions at different times throughout its history. In broad strokes, the paths Iranian cinema has followed include: its status as luxury entertainment for a small group of elites in the Royal Court of the Qajar shahs at the turn of the twentieth century; its introduction to the general public and the production of the first Iranian films outside Iran in the late 1920s; the introduction of tight censorship and state control of the film industry under Pahlavi rule in the 1930s and the Allies' occupation of Iran during World War II which caused the film industry to almost fade away. Strength was regained in the late 1940s and 1950s, by importing industry cultures from popular Hollywood cinema and the influential neighbouring Indian cinema.[4] Like these other film industries, albeit on a smaller scale, Iranian cinema began to fall into the hands of producers, leading to a focus on profit-making and commercial work above the aesthetic considerations it had at first favoured. The feature film industry conformed to the desire for this commercialised lowbrow entertainment and the product – films now known as *film farsi* – entered into the filmic language of Iranian cinema.[5] Despite the existence of highly developed abstract visual arts and artistic potential, and the warm reception given to cinema in the first half of the twentieth century, it is surprising that by the 1950s there had still been no concerted attempt to produce animated films in Iran. Prior to the emergence of Iranian animation in the late 1950s, the only opportunity people had to see animation was via the screening of US productions in Iranian cinemas.[6] This late blooming of animation in Iran has much to do with the nation's late institutionalisation and the lack of financial support for artists to explore new ways of artistic expression.

The birth of animation in Iran coincides with the emergence of Iranian New Wave cinema. It was a time when smaller independent groups of filmmakers and institutions began their activities alongside the Iranian mainstream cinema of the 1960s. The socio-political changes in the country reveal a history of animation divided into three periods. The first period, from the 1960s up to years after the Islamic revolution in the early 1980s, represents a period of the birth and flourishing of animation. The second period saw a stagnation of the form caused by the political uncertainty of the 1980s and a lack of resources during the eight year long war between Iran and Iraq. The third period has seen a rebirth of animation since the 1990s. It is a period during which animation – and the Iranian film industry as a whole – emerged into a new era of financial support by both the state and the private sectors.

Iranian society was on the verge of serious upheaval in the 1960s, and this was directly reflected in the films produced in that era. On the one hand, as Hamid Dabashi asserts, the socio-political changes in Iran were in part due to a shift in the Shiite clerical authority dating back to 1961.[7] On the other, the rejection of the uncritical adoption of foreign values by the foreign-educated intellectuals led to a shift in intellectual discourse, best represented by Jalal-e Al-e Ahmad's popular treatise *Gharb-Zadegi* (*Westoxication*), published in 1962. It was into this climate, in which the clergy had already started actively opposing the Shah's plans to modernise the country that many literary activists, poets, writers and filmmakers emerged. As Mehrnaz Saeed Vafa notes, 'their work was charged with political rebellion and existential despair, as well as a sceptical view of progress and development.'[8]

Among the intellectual literary leaders of this opposition were the fiction author Sadegh Hedayat, the poet Nima Yushij and the social critic Jalal-e Al-e Ahmad. The political changes of the 1960s also produced some ideologues, such as Ali Shariati, with strong Marxist-socialist and anti-colonial backgrounds. These intellectuals' 'embrace of Islam forced them to create a radically alternative form of revolutionary socialism',[9] in line with Ali Mirsepassi's assertion that the 'Iranian Revolution was not a simple clash between modernity and tradition but an attempt to accommodate modernity within a sense of authentic Islamic identity.'[10]

This intellectual movement was not confined to the literary and political realms, but also spread to other cultural outputs, including cinema. In the late 1960s and 1970s films became the subject of intellectual debates and began to exert some political charge.[11] Along with this intellectual movement, the formation of several independent and semi-independent institutions alongside mainstream cinema was a key development. Animation's development can rightly be considered the result of a flowering of some of these institutions, whose aim was to create a more meaningful, artistic and expressive cinema that was not under the same financial pressure as mainstream cinema.

In reaction to the profit-driven mainstream cinema of the 1960s, a group of foreign-educated intellectual filmmakers started their own film studios. In 1969, several key figures in Iranian cinema established a movement under the name Sinemaye āzād (Free Cinema),[12] which was endorsed by Ferydoon Rahnama, one of the three figures chiefly responsible for the inception of the Iranian New Wave. As part of its activities during the decade prior to the Islamic Revolution of 1979, Cinemaye Azad had an outreach programme that brought cinema to many people. By the end of the 1970s, film workshops had been held in more than twenty cities throughout the country.[13]

The 1960s were a crucial decade in the evolution of Iran's animation industry: its foundations were laid by the Ministry of Art and Culture which established an educational centre for the training of a new generation of talented Iranian animators. Moreover, a clear commitment by the authorities to promote documentary films and children's cinema and animation began to unfold.

It was in the spirit of such new ways of thinking that Esfandiar Ahmadieh (1929–2012), the pioneer of Iranian animation, reinvented the animation process using a 16mm Bolex camera to animate his drawings. Ahmadieh was a professional painter and a follower of the Kamal Al-Molk school of art: 'The culmination of a trend towards the adaptation of a European naturalistic style in Persian art,' usually called the Euro-Persian style of painting in Iran.[14] He made the very first Iranian animation film, entitled *Molla Nasreddin*, in 1957. This short experimental animation was only a few seconds long and, as he modestly describes it, 'it resembles animation.'[15] On white paper Ahmadieh had drawn a few images of the thirteenth century Muslim cleric Molla Nasreddin riding his donkey, which he shot consecutively with the semi-professional Cine-Kodak Special 16mm camera. Throughout his professional career working for the Ministry of Art and Culture, and later the NIRT, he continued to make animations. His final traditional animation project was an 80-minute animation feature film entitled *Rostam and Esfanidiar* (2002), an adaptation of a famous epic battle between Rostam and Esfandiar, two heroes from the Persian epic *Shahnameh* (*The Book of Kings*).

The Ministry of Art and Culture has been instrumental in fostering a range of artistic developments, and has played a significant role in founding and developing a local and independent animation industry in Iran. Asadollah Kaffafi, the author of a history of Iranian animation and an animator and photographer who was a product of the first Iranian animation centre, believes that one of the reasons for the rise of animation in Iran was the enthusiastic reception given to foreign animation films by Iranian children through the ministerial outreach programme. The Ministry of Art and Culture saw merit in these films for children, and shortly after

Ahmadieh's first animation and the return of director/producer Parviz Osanlu from two years of animation training in America, set up its own animation department in 1959.[16] The Ministry was keen to find and train animators who would be capable of reflecting aspects of social life in a country rapidly undergoing modernisation. Soon Nosratollah Karimi, who had studied puppet animation in Czechoslovakia, and the caricaturist Jafar Tejaratchi joined the department.[17,18]

Efforts towards creating a better cinema, one that contrasted with the dominant commercial film industry, were not limited to the filmmakers themselves. Some members of the ruling factions also lent a hand to this movement. For instance, the former Queen of Iran, Farah Diba, acted as the chief ambassador of the arts and culture in Iran, endorsing two other institutions that played a crucial role in the development of the Iranian animation industry: Kanun and NIRT.[19] Kanun was established in 1964 and, as cinema historiographer Mehrabi explains, was created as an avenue to produce films that, unlike popular cinema, steered clear of banality and the profit motive.[20] It was the first and largest artistic and cultural organisation focusing on children and young adults. It opened studios, invited artists and produced experimental and professional animated shorts.

Key figures in Iranian animation, such as Noureddin Zarrinkelk, Ali Akbar Sadeghi, and Farshid Mesghali, worked for Kanun and were supported by the institution. Kanun usually operated with a fixed group of employed filmmakers, but also occasionally invited guest filmmakers to work on its projects. Many significant films and animations were produced with Kanun's aid, and a large number of filmmakers found there the opportunity to make films they could not have made otherwise. Zarrinkelk emphasises the experimentation inherent in such an intellectual movement, and it was a freedom and lack of pressure that enabled the development of artists who may not have been discovered otherwise.[21] Directors such as Abbas Kiarostami and Naser Taghvai began their careers at Kanun, and some prominent directors of the time, Bahram Beizai and Masud Kimiai, for example, used this fertile environment to make short films.

Kanun was also responsible for the launch of the first International Film Festival for Children and Young Adults in Tehran in 1966, creating a platform for Iranian artists to familiarise themselves with the work of the greats of world animation.[22] Many brilliant films were screened, and Eastern

European and Western artists ranging from Norman McLaren, Raoul Servais and Bordo Dovnikovic to Frédéric Back, Fyodor Khitruk, Bruno Bozzetto and Břetislav Pojar had their works presented. For Zarrinkelk, it was in 'this way [that] Iran opened a panoramic vision of quality animation to young and eager talents inside the country who had no access to such advanced art at the time.'[23] Emerging from this success came a new wave of demand for high quality animation from both the cultural authorities and the inspirational artists of Iran. A colourful collection of educated designers, illustrators, graphic artists and painters, Farshid Mesghali, Ali Akbar Sadeghi, Nafiseh Riyahi and Morteza Momayez among them, joined forces to create homegrown animation. The formation of a film archive, which remains one of the most important treasures of the Iranian film industry, and includes many of the earliest animated films, is another of Kanun's legacies.

Noureddin Zarrinkelk, one of the most influential figures in Iranian animation, began a career in the arts working as a caricaturist and book illustrator for Kanun after completing his PhD in Pharmacology at the University of Tehran. In 1968, he was sent to Belgium for training in animation at the Royal Academy of Fine Arts, and he produced his first short animation films there. Upon his return in 1972, he made a few very successful short films, some of which will be discussed below. In addition to being a filmmaker, Zarrinkelk founded the first animation school in Iran in 1974 – through Kanun – and taught animation there. He also designed and established the postgraduate degree in animation at the Farabi University of Arts.[24] He was the founder of the Iranian chapter of the International Animated Film Association (ASIFA) in 1986 (Iran had been an unofficial member of ASIFA since 1978) that today boasts several hundred members.[25]

The other institute that provided significant assistance to the development of independent cinema and animation in Iran was Madrese-ye Ali-ye Television va Sinema (the College of Television and Cinema), established in 1968. This was a film school whose teaching philosophies were focused firmly on creating a better cinema under the flagship of the NIRT. It was established by Reza Ghotbi Gilani, a young intellectual politician who had been educated abroad and who acted as the head of NIRT from 1967 to 1979.

Ghotbi was of a similar ideological outlook as the filmmakers of the Iranian New Wave and helped create a more open, egalitarian environment, something very significant at a time when it was almost impossible to pursue a career in the film industry without any personal connections. In 1973, NIRT also launched an animation department that produced a few short films and mini-series before the revolution with the help of graduates.[26] The newly-established film school offered an entry exam in public media, newspapers and television. Anyone was eligible to take this exam, one of the first attempts to make Iranian cinema more widely accessible to the general public. Whereas most filmmakers in the Iranian film industry up to this point usually came only from those families wealthy enough to afford to send their children to Europe or the US to attend film school,[27] these students did not necessarily come from money.[28] It was only necessary that potential students who took the exam had a general interest in the arts, and more specifically, a keen interest in cinema. This was not a broadly held interest in Iran at the time as the clergy had rejected cinema. According to Mir-Hosseini, cinema was among those fields of art considered as forbidden; some religious families even deemed it a sin to enter a cinema.[29] Many of the graduates of this school are the most notable Iranian cinematographers, editors and filmmakers of today.

After the collapse of the Pahlavi regime and the establishment of the Islamic Republic of Iran in 1979, the country underwent vast cultural changes. Against all expectations, cinema was revived for its use as an educational tool. This direction is made explicit in a famous quotation by the Ayatollah Khomeini: 'Cinema is one of the manifestations of culture and it must be put to service of man and his education.'[30] Khomeini's declarations broadly laid down the culture, worldview and goals of the Islamic Republic of Iran, and consequently directed the basic responsibilities of Vezārat-e Farhang va Ershād-e Eslāmi (Ministry of Culture and Islamic Guidance (MCIG)), which supervised cultural activities in Iran. As a result, the objectives of the film industry shifted, and films became closely supervised by the religious authorities.

The MCIG was, for the most part, modelled on the previous Ministry of Art and Culture, which had been established in 1940, the biggest difference being that after the revolution there were no independent producers, and during the first few post-revolution years most of the funding for film production was only available through government agencies. Kanun continued its work after the revolution without significant changes to the way it was run. There was a large turnover in its administrative staff, but most of its creative personnel remained intact. Kanun was one of the first organisations to resume film production after the halt imposed by the revolution.

Although NIRT changed its name to Seda va Sima-ye Jomhuri-ye Islami-ye Iran (Islamic Republic of Iran Broadcasting (IRIB)) after the revolution, its operational goals remained the same. The College of Television and Cinema within NIRT continued its work after the revolution but was renamed IRIB University (Daneshkadeye Seda va Sima), and now offers several undergraduate and two graduate programmes in media, arts, animation and engineering subjects. What was once Telefilm, the feature film producing body of NIRT, now operates under the name Sima Film and works very much the same way as its predecessor did before the revolution. Very early on, IRIB began commissioning and producing educational animation films in accordance with the dictates of the revolution, for example the five-episode children's short animation series *Fereshte-ye nejāt* (*Guardian Angel*) in which a guardian angel rescues children from various dangerous situations, or the thirteen-episode short animation series *Pākizegi neshāne-ye imān ast* (*Cleanliness is a Sign of Faith* – a well-known variation of a universal Prophetic tradition regarding cleanliness), about a young boy who learns about aspects of personal hygiene, like brushing his teeth.

The Iran–Iraq War (1980–8) necessitated severe cuts to the subsidies given to all art forms, including animation. Many animators, as well as other artists, either changed their careers, or sought jobs or opened businesses abroad.[31] Within this period, the only school of animation that continued running was at Farabi University; all other universities and art schools, as well as the International Festival for Children and Young Adults, were shut down. However, in 1989, the Iranian government began a process of restructuring its economy and came to recognise the important function that mass media played in political stabilisation and the forming of public opinion. Consequently, that year saw the beginning of a policy that involved the trimming down of much of the Islamic rhetoric as well as the return to Iranian cultural and artistic heritage, recognising the fact that a growing youth population requires an elaborate cultural policy that is responsive to their social and intellectual needs. Yet again, animation was seen as an important means of promoting cultural and religious values. During these years, many governmental institutions became semi-privatised and branched out into more specialised divisions, producing films and animations. Like the Farabi Cinema Foundation, the executive section of MCIG, IRIB began two production companies: Sima Film focused on feature films and Sherkat-e Farhangi Honari-ye Saba (Saba Art and Culture Company) became the IRIB animation section. This was a period during which Kanun also increased its animation production and launched the Biannual International Animation Festival in 1999 in Tehran. Established to celebrate animated films made in Iran as well as to exhibit examples of international animation deemed appropriate for local audiences, it became the first portal of exchange in terms of Iranian animation production.[32]

In recent years a large number of private animation studios have been established in Iran and although numerous animators have moved to computer graphic animation, there are still many who work with more traditional and experimental methods. Despite an inflationary economy and low salaries, the pursuit of animation is still quite attractive to new generations of artists from the middle and lower classes. The ready availability of computers and the fact that animation production does not necessarily rely on large crews allows some artists to pursue a career in animation outside their main source of income. Zarrinkelk explains: 'Many animators are still running their studios under hard conditions and most artists are following their careers by spending their income from other arts (graphic, illustration, etc.). This way animation is surviving.'[33] Like elsewhere, a recent and more profitable avenue for animation is to be found in advertisement and television and cinema spots. The difference with other nations is that due to Iran's unique protectionist political and economic situation, almost all advertisements for domestic products are produced within the country. This has created a viable production outlet by which animation companies can survive financially. Innovation is driven, too, as various cutting edge animation techniques have been employed for commercials since the early 1990s. With increasing frequency, animators have been shifting from traditional cel animation methods to computer graphics techniques, in both 2D and 3D animation.

Political and Revolutionary Animated Films: Central Figures

Noureddin Zarrinkelk has created films preoccupied with global politics and social issues, addressing capitalism and the influence of super powers. His general interest lies in criticising consumerism. In 1975, he made the black and white cel animation film *Donyā-ye divāneh-ye divāneh* (*The Mad Mad Mad World*). As the title suggests, this film is a critique of the world in modern times. In this simple animation short the outlines of the continents and different countries come to life on a world map. Continents and countries turn into different animals attacking one another, barking, tearing and breaking their neighbours off the map. Image 2.1 shows Asia and North America engaged in a cockfight, pecking away bits and pieces of one another. This film toys with the idea of an ever-changing assemblage of super powers likening the continents to beasts released from their cages.[34]

In his later cel animation from 1980 *Yek, do, se, ...* (*One, Two, Three, ...*) Zarrinkelk depicts the plight of poor people in the capitalist world. He

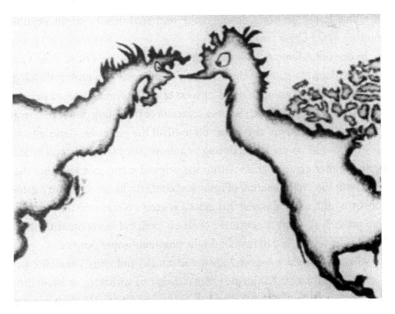

2.1 Still from *The Mad Mad Mad World*, directed by Noureddin Zarrinkelk (1975)

portrays a poor man who, over five episodes, becomes increasingly greedy and gains more and more weight. This short animation is a depiction of lust for power and of greed. An Iranian proverb comments, 'take the bread from the ones who have not eaten, and give it to the ones who have eaten' as the rich's appetite is insatiable. He continued this critique of socio-political issues in his later films and in 1987, during the Iran–Iraq War, made the minimalist film *Abar Ghodrathā* (*Super Powers*). In this short animation, the plus and minus signs become symbolic representations of two super powers that come to life as two monstrous characters with teeth and claws. They appear in an arena similar to a wrestling ring and fight to the death.

One must not overlook Ali Akbar Sadeghi's contribution to Iranian animation. After graduating from the College of Art in Tehran University, Sadeghi, one of Iran's most prolific artists and painters, began working as an illustrator and painter for Kanun. It was there that he became involved with the first group of animators in Iran and made a number of films in the 1970s. Although he did not pursue animation after the revolution, some of the films he made before the revolution are among the most notable animations made in Iran. He developed a style in Persian painting influenced by coffee house painting, iconography and traditional Iranian portrait painting in the Qajar tradition.

In one of his famous cel animation films made in 1974 titled *Rokh* (*The Rook*) he depicts a game of chess; the role of the rook is to protect the king. This metaphorical animation is a cartoon of an innocent game of chess on the surface, but can also be seen as a criticism of the ruling power in Iran at that time. This game of chess goes on until all the pieces are removed and only the two kings are left, resulting in a draw. The two kings then sit and begin another game of chess within the original game, in a sequence that plays with the cyclical nature of historical conflict; the game within a game conveying the endless power struggles between powers over an unattainable prize. It is a direct comment on Iran's political situation at the time both in the region and in relation to the dominant super powers.

Ahmad Arabani, a famous Iranian caricaturist and artist, joined the animation department at Kanun in 1973, collaborating with other artists in their productions until 1978 – the year before the revolution. He produced one of the most memorable revolution-themed cel animation films, *Tabar* (*The Axe*), in 1981. This short simple film, which is still aired on Iran's national television regularly, is a story about protecting natural resources, but also tells how unity can destroy the reign of a tyrant. The villain protagonist of the film is an axe that cuts any tree it comes across in the forest. The trees fear extinction and come to the conclusion that if they all pull together and create one giant tree they can stand against the axe. In the end, the trees successfully tie up the axe and defeat it. This is a film that lauds unification, the very notion celebrated each year at the Islamic Revolution's anniversary in Iran.

Mahvash Tehrani and Hosseinali Ghorbankarimi, two graduates from the first group of students at the College of Radio and Television, began their professional work in animation at NIRT and continued working for IRIB. They produced a large number of short films and a mini-series for IRIB in the late 1980s, before establishing their own animation company, Bina Film, which focused on the production of television spots and commercials. After early work with traditional animation methods they moved on to computer animation in the late 1980s, producing through IRIB in 1982 the cel animation short *Hileh* (*The Deception*), an adaptation of one of the short stories from the classic collection of fables *Kelile and Demne*. In this, yet another revolution-themed metaphorical film, a sea gull has deceived the fish in a small pond by telling them that on the other side of a nearby hill lies a bigger, much nicer lake. Every day the gull pretends to take a few fish to this new oasis. The hero is a crab who shares the pond with the fish. The crab becomes suspicious of the sea gull and one day requests to be taken to this new lake, too. The sea gull, happy about the change of menu, takes the crab. As they fly over the hill, the crab sees fish bones scattered on the ground and realises the gull's evil intentions (see image 2.2). The crab squeezes the sea gull's neck, making it fall and putting an end to its evil ways.[35]

Certainly, Iranian animation outside of *Persepolis* is not as well-known as Iranian cinema more generally, but the efforts and artistry that inform it are very impressive. The roles played by the state and its institutions in the development of an Iranian animation industry, the struggle many of these animators underwent to make films and how they managed to keep the pace with modern technology, can provide fascinating and fruitful insights into modern-day Iranian animation. In 1989, for example, small companies began experimenting with computer animation using Commodore 64 systems to produce short TV spots and commercials. In 1991, the private company Bina Film produced the first 40-minute long medium-length

2.2 Still from *The Deception*, directed by Mahvash Tehrani and Hosseinali Ghorbankarimi (1982)

musical 3D animation produced in Iran entitled *Jangal-e Ārezuhā* (*The Jungle of Dreams*), directed by Tehrani and Ghorbankarimi and commissioned by Saba Film. This is another story from the classic collection of fables *Kelile and Demne* about a deceiving fox, a sick lion and a donkey. Likewise, both IRIB and Kanun produced many short and long animations and mini-series that have been screened throughout the Middle East and Asia. One of the most recent triumphs is the 3D feature film by Kianoush Dalvand, *Rostam o Sohrab* (*Battle of the Kings*, 2012), a tragic drama from one of the most famous stories of the epic *Book of Kings*. A heroic general (Rostam) falls in love with the daughter of a rival king. The pair have a son, Sohrab, who is taken from the couple by the rival king before he can meet his father. Sohrab is trained to be a great warrior and the first time father and son meet is on the battlefield, as enemies. Themes of heroism, honour and love in the face of destiny and glory collide in an epic story of action and intrigue. This is one of the most successful Iranian animation films produced in Iran and was screened both in the Middle East and elsewhere internationally, with beautifully modelled characters and having been dubbed for an international market in Canada.[36]

Conclusion

From a global perspective, then, the output of the Iranian animation industry may not seem significant, but as an art form, Iranian animation has a proud standing. Iranian animation has been well-represented at renowned international animation film festivals, such as the Annecy International Animation Festival and the Zagreb Animation Festival. The Iranian animation industry has survived many hardships thanks to the passion and commitment of the people involved in the industry and also, not least, through governmental budgeting and the support of numerous institutions. Because animation has never completely turned into a profit-driven medium in Iran it has stayed true to its ideals as a form of artistic expression.

Through the work of institutions such as the Ministry of Art and Culture, the Centre for Intellectual Development of Children and Young Adults and Kanun, and the National Iranian Radio and Television, as well as of pioneering animators such as Zarrinkelk, Ali Akbar Sadeghi, Ahmad Arabani and Mahvash Tehrani and Hosseinali Ghorbankarimi, a solid foundation was laid for the enduring development of Iranian animation. The result has been, in parallel with the flourishing of a hugely successful cinema industry, the global success of transnational feature-length animation films such as *Persepolis* and *Battle of the Kings*. It is hoped that this chapter's brief examination of these early examples of Iranian cel animation films may serve as groundwork for more comprehensive study of the history of animation in Iran, and of the distinct features that characterise Iranian animation within contemporary Iranian cinema.

Notes

1. Peter Lord and Brian Sibley, *Cracking Animation, The Aardman Book of 3D Animation* (London, 1998), p. 17.
2. Honour Hugh and John Fleming, *The Visual Arts: A History* (New Jersey, 1992), p. 96.
3. The Heritage Trust, 'World's Oldest Animation?' (25 July 2012), *The Heritage Trust*. Available at http://theheritagetrust.wordpress.com/2012/07/25/worlds-oldest-animation/ (accessed 3 March 2015).
4. Shahla Mirbakhtyar, *Iranian Cinema and the Islamic Revolution* (Jefferson, NC, 2006), p. 140.

Animation in the Middle East

5. Hamid Reza Sadr, *Iranian Cinema: A Political History* (London, 2006), p. 90; Saeed Zeydabadi-Nejad, 'Iranian intellectuals and contact with the West: The case of Iranian cinema', *British Journal of Middle Eastern Studies*, 34, 3 (2007), p. 377.

6. Mohammad Ali Issari, *Cinema in Iran, 1900–1979* (New York, NY, 1990), p. 126.

7. Hamid Dabashi, *Close-up: Iranian Cinema: Past, Present and Future* (London, 2001), p. 25.

8. Mehrnaz Saeed-Vafa, 'Ebrahim Golestan: Treasure of pre-revolutionary Iranian cinema', *Rouge* (2007). Available at http://www.rouge.com.au/11/golestan.html (accessed January 2012).

9. Ali Mirsepassi, *Intellectual Discourse and Politics of Modernization* (Cambridge, 2000), p. 155.

10. Ibid., p. 1.

11. Sadr, *Iranian Cinema*, p. 111; Dabashi, *Close-up*.

12. Masoud Mehrabi, *Tarikh-i sinima-yi Iran, az aghaz ta sal-i 1357* (Tehran, 1984), p. 194.

13. Cinemaye Azad, 'Karnameh', *Cinemaye Azad*. Available at http://www.cinemaye-azad.com/karnameh/karnameh.html (accessed January 2008).

14. Encyclopaedia Iranica, 'Kamāl-al-molk, Moḥammad Gaffāri', *Iranica Online*. Available at http://www.iranicaonline.org/articles/kamal-al-molk-mohammad-gaffari (accessed 3 March 2015).

15. Mahin Javaharian, *Short History of Animation in Iran* (Tehran, 1999), p. 28.

16. Assaddollah Kaphafe, *The Background of Animation in Iran, Vision of Wakefulness* (Tehran, 1999), p. 315.

17. Nosratollah Karimi made many short animation films between 1959 and 1966, and worked on several other later animation projects too, but he mostly focused his career on live-action cinema and acting. For more information on Karimi, see Javaharian, *Short History of Animation in Iran*, pp. 31–2.

18. Javaharian, *Short History of Animation in Iran*, p. 27.

19. I do not wish to enter into a political discussion of whether or not her decisions with regards to the bigger picture of Iran were sound or not; I am merely observing the results of some of her actions with regards to the Iranian film industry.

20. Mehrabi, *Tarikh-i sinima-yi Iran*, p. 400.

21. Ibid., pp. 403–404.

22. Encyclopaedia Iranica, 'Noḵostin festivāl-e bayn-al-melali-e filmhā-ye kudakān o nowjavānān', *Iranica Online*. Available at http://www.iranicaonline.org/articles/kanun-e-parvares-e-fekri-e-kudakan-va-nowjavanan-international-film-festival (accessed 3 March 2015). This festival ran annually for 12 years until 1978. Kanun started the festival again under the same title in 1999 and it has been running continuously ever since. For more information on the history of this festival, see: Mohamma Reza Karimi Saremi, 'History of Tehran

International Animation Festival', *Tehran International Animation Festival*. Available at http://tehran-animafest.ir/first_fest/about_pg/about_history_first_fest_en.htm (accessed 25 February 2015).

23. Noureddin Zarrinkelk, 'History of animation' (n.d.) [Noureddin Zarrinkelk]. Available at http://www.zarrinkelk.com/eng/animation.html (accessed July 2014).

24. Javaharian, *Short History of Animation in Iran*, p. 47; and Zarrinkelk, 'History of animation.'

25. Zarrinkelk, 'History of animation.'

26. Javaharian, *Short History of Animation in Iran*, p. 87.

27. Hamid Dabashi, *Mohsen Makhmalbaf at Large: The Making of a Rebel Filmmaker* (London, 2007), p. 47.

28. Mahvash Tehrani and Hosseinali Ghorbankarimi, Personal interviews. September 2009. Toronto, Canada.

29. Ziba Mir-Hosseini, 'Iranian cinema: Art, society and the state', *Middle East Report*, 219 (2001), p. 2.

30. Khomeini qtd. in Richard Tapper (ed.), 'Introduction', *The New Iranian Cinema: Politics, Representation and Identity* (London, 2002), p. 6.

31. Zarrinkelk, 'History of animation.'

32. Mohamma Reza Karimi Saremi, 'History of Tehran International Animation Festival', Tehran International Animation Festival. Available at http://tehran-animafest.ir/first_fest/about_pg/about_history_first_fest_en.htm (accessed 3 March 2015).

33. Zarrinkelk, 'History of animation.'

34. For a clip of this film, see: https://www.youtube.com/watch?v=q9OkrNQk0AI

35. For more information on *The Deception* and its directors, in Persian, see the DEFC website. Available at http://www.defc.ir/fa/AnimationDetails.php?animationId=1734 (accessed 25 February 2015).

36. For more information on *Battle of the Kings* by Kianoush Dalvand, see the Fantastic Films International website. Available at http://www.fantasticfilms-international.com/screeners/#battle_of_the_kings (accessed 3 March 2015). The announcement of the international distribution of the film can be found here: 'Persian epic animation to go on US, UAE screens', *Press TV* (13 April 2013). Available at http://www.presstv.com/detail/2013/04/13/297984/us-uae-to-host-iran-3d-animation/ (accessed 3 March 2015).

Filmography

Abar Ghodrathā (Super Powers), directed by Noureddin Zarrinkelk (1987).

Donyā-ye divāneh-ye divāneh (The Mad Mad Mad World), directed by Noureddin Zarrinkelk (1975).

Animation in the Middle East

Fereshte-ye nejāt (Guardian Angel), produced by IRIB.

Hileh (The Deception), directed by Mahvash Tehrani and Hosseinali Ghorbankarimi (1982).

Jangal-e ārezuhā (The Jungle of Dreams), directed by Mahvash Tehrani and Hosseinali Ghorbankarimi (1991).

Molla Nasreddin, directed by Esfandiar Ahmadieh (1957).

Pākizegi Neshāne-ye Imān Ast (Cleanliness is a Sign of Faith), produced by IRIB.

Persepolis, directed by Marjane Satrapi and Vincent Paronnaud (2007).

Rokh (The Rook), directed by Ali Akbar Sadeghi (1974).

Rostam and Esfanidiar, directed by Esfandiar Ahmadieh (2002).

Rostam o Sohrab (Battle of the Kings), directed by Kianoush Dalvand (2012).

Tabar (The Axe), directed by Ahmad Arabani (1981).

Yek, do, se, ... (One, Two, Three, ...), directed by Noureddin Zarrinkelk (1980).

3

Local Minds, Foreign Hands: Animation in Saudi Arabia and the Gulf

Omar Adam Sayfo

Defining Animation in Saudi Arabia and the Gulf

Saudi Arabia and the Gulf States are latecomers to animation production. Developing a national animation industry requires, among many other things, two fundamental components: trained artists and technological infrastructure. Visual arts in Saudi Arabia and the Gulf have been dominated largely by non-figurative and calligraphic images; figurative illustrations have been rare.[1] While these nations are by and large the most financially successful through film festivals (the Gulf) established in the late 2000s and the largest entertainment company in the Arab world, Rotana, (Saudi Arabia) in the region, there are transnational myths about for example Saudi Arabia that there is no cinema, or that there is a ban on cinema. Anne Ciekco explains that 'contrary to conventional wisdom that views KSA as a cinema-less nation since commercial film theaters are banned, films are being made (and watched – albeit ones that cannot be widely exhibited in public contexts within the country.'[2] In addition, 'although cinema activity in the Arabian Peninsula has been limited compared with other parts of the Arab world, countries like [...] Saudi Arabia have historical status as an important market for Arab films within the

United Arab Republic.[3] Likewise, for potential animators it has been relatively hard to gain inspiration from local art forms. Animation production is also largely tied to modern artistic heritage, including cinematic and television production. Unlike traditional centres of Arab cinema, such as Egypt and Lebanon, the Gulf Countries were very late to establish and develop competitive television and media industries. Saudi Arabia has however played an important role in the funding of Egyptian productions since the 1970s.[4]

From the beginning of the establishment of national television channels in the Gulf in the 1960s and 1970s, creating local content was an important goal for national authorities, especially in Saudi Arabia where a particularly conservative society and elite demanded a similarly conservative content.[5] However, as children were not always regarded as a primary audience, the task of government-run channels was to fill the slots dedicated to children with the cheapest and fastest-produced content possible, mainly shows recorded with live participants. As animated cartoon was regarded as a childish medium, there was little effort to invest in establishing local animation studios. Therefore, local television channels relied on imports from Europe, Japan and the United States, dubbed over and made appropriate for the moral values of local traditions. After the introduction of television to the Gulf, many generations of Arab children grew up watching dubbed foreign animations. Choosing the sources of imported animations before the 1990s was often a political decision, as – unlike socialist countries such as Syria, Libya and Iraq who favoured the products of France and Eastern Europe – the more capitalist-focused Gulf countries tended to import American products, mainly Disney serials and Japanese Anime.[6]

The lack of artists and developed cinema and media industries were serious obstacles to the organisation of local animation production. In Egypt, well-developed media and film industries and a large number of trained artists facilitated the establishment of local workshops of celluloid animation and, later, computer generated imagery (CGI) studios, but this was certainly not an option in Saudi Arabia and the Gulf. While CGI and other technologies central to animation were developed in the 1960s and 1970s, there is no record of animated films produced using celluloid technology or with CGI in the region until the first fully locally-produced animated films were released soon after the global spread of 3D animation in the late 1990s.[7]

However, such absence of trained personnel and lack of infrastructure did completely prevent producers from creating homegrown animation productions. From the 1970s until very recently, producers of animated films and television programmes in Saudi Arabia and the Gulf preferred to outsource the labour-intensive animation phases, or even the entire production process, to foreign animation studios, while still claiming creative authority over the texts. In order to maintain continuous control over their productions, a number of producers and directors also chose to set up their headquarters abroad and supervise the animators personally.[8] Such involvement of foreign artists hindered the formation of a unique visual characteristic and style for Saudi and Gulf animation.

These particular circumstances of animation production in Saudi Arabia and the Gulf States raise the question as to whether or not it is actually appropriate to talk about Saudi or Gulf animation production at all. Considering that animation production from these countries has included a large proportion of non-national workforces, it is perhaps more appropriate to define the 'Saudiness', 'Kuwaitiness', 'Emirateness', 'Omaniness', etc., of a particular production not by the nationality of the participants or the homeland of the production industries, but by the nationality of its author. Therefore, a definition of authorship in animation will be applied here, following the approach of British animation scholar Paul Wells. Being aware of the number of available methods and models of animated film production, Wells counts eleven so-called 'textual' and sixteen 'extra-textual' definitions to describe the author in animation production.[9] Employing such ideas reveals that those definitions marked as 'textual' tend to overlap the functions of director, concept artists or animator, while definitions marked as 'extra-textual' describe the functions of the producer. In what follows I explore productions whose producers and/or directors hail from Saudi Arabia and the Gulf countries. I look at some pioneering individuals and production avenues, as well the inspiration for feature-length films and animated sitcom cartoons, in order to establish a preliminary history of animation in the region.

Animation Production of the Gulf Cooperation Council (GCC)

The very first recorded animation from the Gulf was produced in 1979; one- to two-minute spots designed to teach children about Arabic letters and numbers, produced on celluloid for *Iftah ya Simsim* (*Open Sesame*), the Arab adaptation of the globally successful formula *Sesame Street*. Like *Sesame Street*, *Open Sesame* had clear pedagogical goals, adapted to account for local didactic moral systems. The show was produced by the GCC's Joint Program Production Institution (JPPI), a transnational organisation established in Abu Dhabi on 4 January 1976 by the Ministers of Information of Bahrain, Kuwait, Oman, Qatar, Saudi Arabia and the United Arab Emirates (UAE).[10] The Institution is now based in Kuwait and its broad aims are the building of wider media cooperation and the integration of the media policies of member states.[11] *Open Sesame* ran in many Arab countries until 1990 and can be considered a milestone in Arab children's television programming. As the Gulf at that time lacked animation infrastructure, the animated spots of *Open Sesame* were produced in Japan and France. Following JPPI's partnership with the Hungarian DANA Film Studio, the production process was outsourced to Hungary. This co-production has been very successful, due in large part to DANA's Iraqi owners, animator Bassam Faraj and director Thamer Al-Zaidi, who recruited Hungarian professionals to supply their partners from the Gulf States with their commissioned works.[12]

Though initially JPPI largely focused on documentary productions, until recently its animation production was also an on-going concern. Productions were primarily presented on national television channels of the JPPI member states although, unfortunately, there is no complete list of the productions available. The document listing the official titles of animated productions on the JPPI's official website does not gather together all productions, i.e. all those that include the logo of JPPI in their opening scenes.[13] This incompleteness in registration can probably be ascribed to the large number of pilots and unfinished projects undertaken, and also to the fact that in many cases JPPI acted only as the financial donor for other Arab productions – chiefly from Syria and Egypt. While JPPI productions involved different Arab nationals, the majority of authors, particularly those heading these projects, were Kuwaitis. One of their most notable animated productions was a 15 episode series of 10-minute shorts recounting the adventures of a small donkey and his human friends: *Za'toor*, released in 1995. Although the show was the product of the Kuwaiti director Hashim Zaatari and executive producer Abdel Wahab Sultan, the animation process was again outsourced to the Hungarian DANA Animation Studio.

In 2005, an edutainment series, *Sunna' Al-Hadarah* (*The Makers of Civilisation*), was released with a declared goal to teach children the biographies and achievements of notable Arab scientists of the past. This scientific/historical impulse developed into a more religious drive a year later, when the series was followed by a feature-length production entitled *Ibn Al-Ghaba* (*Son of the Forest*) directed by Thamer Al-Zaidi. It relates a story based on Ibn Tufayl's *Hajj Ibn Yaqzan*, an eleventh century philosophical *Jungle Book*-style romance about a boy brought up by a gazelle on a deserted island who reaches belief in God on a purely logical basis. As in the case of *Za'toor*, animation was outsourced to Hungary. In 2009, a new 3D series called *Ahmad wa Kanaan* was released. For the first time, the project was entirely locally produced. Not only were producer Habib Hussein and director Faysal Al-Ibrahimi both of Kuwaiti origin, so were the executive animation studios, Ustudio and Cable Vision.[14] The series has a clear edifying mission, as the majority of the episodes revolve around moralistic issues, showing Kanaan, a fat, simple-minded, selfish boy receiving moral lessons from Ahmad, his slim, smart, generous friend.

Islamic Animation

Beginning in the mid-1990s, a number of private companies and religious institutions from Saudi Arabia and the Gulf became involved in the production of Islamic-themed animated cartoons. These were feature-length films, with plots recounting events from Muslim history or adapted from Arabic literature, although a significant number of original stories were also produced.

Though a number of companies (usually registered as foundations) became involved in this animation production, most ended their animation activities after merely releasing trailers or completing only a single project. A case in point is Arasoft, a creative company in Saudi Arabia (established in Riyadh in 1996) that dropped animation production entirely shortly after releasing *Al-Naser Salahulddin* (*The Victorious Saladin*), an animated adaptation of Youssef Chahine's masterpiece from 1963. The company decided instead to focus on computer software production.

The most active production company with regards to both quantity and quality of productions was Muassasat Alla' lil Intag Al-Fanniyy (The Ella Endowment for Art Production), established as a non-profit-oriented project in 1992 by Saudi animation producer Usama Ahmad Khalifa. Khalifa was born in 1956 and educated in the Saudi city of Medina, before studying biology at the King Abdul Aziz University in Jeddah. He worked in a number of governmental positions until he moved to the United States where he studied management and worked with the Canadian Islamic Congress. It was during this time that he became enchanted by the booming Canadian animation industry and decided to develop a similar industry in his homeland. His company in Saudi Arabia produced around ten feature-length productions before being rebranded and renamed as OK Toon in 2011.[15] The financial backing of the productions came in the form of donations from private individuals and institutions, with a significant amount of money also being invested by Khalifa himself.[16] After a failed attempt to find Arab animation studios with which to cooperate, Khalifa recruited Turkish professionals, establishing his headquarters in İstanbul in order to supervise the animation process. Later on, he exchanged his Turkish crew for Syrian studios. Most of Khalifa's feature-length films are based either on the stories of characters from Muslim history or stories adapted from Arabic literature, with a small number of original stories developed by the artists. According to Khalifa, his ultimate goal has been to mediate Islamic messages through his productions, and to create productions that act as alternatives to the popular American animated cartoons.[17]

Ella's first feature-length film, *Muhammad Al-Fatih* (*Mohammad the Conqueror*), came out in 1995. The animated epic on the life of Ottoman Sultan Mehmet II is nearly two hours long, and was released on VHS before being presented on different television channels.[18] In the same year, in cooperation with the Syrian Al-Zahra Studio (also called Venus Studio), Khalifa produced *Al-Ashbal*, an adventure TV series involving three young schoolboys who, guided by their teacher, visit a number of Muslim countries in Africa and Asia. Ella's second feature-length production was *Rihlat*

Local Minds, Foreign Hands

Al-Kholoud (*The Boy and the King*), released in 1996. This was an Arab-Turkish co-production directed by Dervis Pasin and produced by Usama Khalifa. The basic idea of the story was inspired by a *hadith* (a narration on the life and deeds of the Prophet Muhammad) that explores a reference to 'the people of the ditch' that appears in a verse of the *Surat Al-Burooj* (*Sura of the Bridges*) in the Quran (85:4). That same year also saw the release of *Ali Baba wal-Arba'ena Lissan* (*Ali Baba and the Forty Thieves*), again by Khalifa. This is a relatively unchanged re-telling of the famous story of Ali Baba, known from *The Arabian Nights*.

Two years later, in 1998, a new historical film, *Asad Ayn Jalout* came out. It told the story of the life of Sayf Al-Qutuz, the Mamluk Sultan of Egypt (1254–60) from his childhood in Central Asia to his death in the Battle of Ain Jalut. In the same year, *Al Qarasina wa Kanz Al-Dhahab* (*The Pirates and the Gold Treasure*), a Sinbad-inspired original work was released, telling the story of a brave young captain facing pirates and other foes. Also in 1998 came the release of *Masrur fi Jazirat Al-Lu'lu'* (*Masrur on the Pearl Island*), another Sinbad-inspired film of a young boy called Masrur who, together with his uncle, takes a journey to an island full of treasures. In 1999, *Fath Al-Andalus – Tareq ibn Ziyad* (*The Conquest of Andalusia – Tareq ibn Ziyad*) was released recounting the story of the Muslim conqueror of Andalusia. Finally, in 1999, Khalifa also produced three episodes of *Hikayat Al-'Amm Al-Hakim* (*Stories of the Wise Uncle*), an animated adaptation of *Kalila wa Dimna*, the fable of two jackals originally translated from the Persian by Muslim author Ibn Al-Muqaffa (d. 756).[19] These adventure stories were still firmly based in Arab culture and Arabic literature, but a shift away from traditional Islamic materials is also apparent.

This pan-Arab interest in history and culture was reflected in Khalifa's next big project. Like many filmmakers in the Arab world, Usama Khalifa was also very interested in the Palestinian situation. In 2003, he produced *Shahid Al-'Alam* (*The Martyr of the World*), a 3D film telling the story of a Palestinian child, Muhammad Al-Durra, who was shot by an Israeli soldier in 2000. However, a much grander project on the Palestinian case – in terms of budget, quality and distribution reach – was *Hilm Al-Zaytoon* (*Dream of the Olives*).

This feature-length production by Khalifa from 2009, tells the life-story of a girl called Miryam, who is forced out of her home in Ain Al-Karem

Animation in the Middle East

3.1 Still from *Dream of the Olives* (2009), a Palestinian story in a Saudi interpretation

by Zionist militias in 1948, but in a happy ending, achieves the collective Palestinian dream of a return home (see image 3.1). An optimistic tale, this film expresses the ambition of the Arab National project to accompanying music from Lebanese musician Elias El-Rahabani. Edited in Khalifa's studios in Turkey and Saudi Arabia, it became a truly transnational project that moved beyond the literary and religious inspirations for other animated stories coming from Saudi Arabia by presenting a story of concern to contemporary Arab identity throughout the region.

Animated Sitcoms

Since the mid-2000s, animated sitcoms have become an increasingly appreciated genre in Saudi Arabia and the Gulf. By that time nearly all countries in the region had their own productions, mediating national culture and revolving around locally relevant issues.[20] This growth in sitcom animation production was facilitated by four main factors.[21] First there is the significant impact of global trends towards animation technology. After the critical success of Walt Disney's *Toy Story* in 1995, 3D technologies replaced CGI animation on a global scale. Compared to traditional CGI animation, 3D is less labour-intensive and also a less talent-intensive process. During the production process of 3D computer animation, a distinction is generally drawn between mechanical and creative work. Creative work such as character ideas, script and direction, can be done in a geographical location separate from the labour-intensive drawing, colouring and animating.[22] With the support of ever-cheapening means of communication, outsourcing of the animation process to other countries no longer requires the personal presence of the authors.[23] A second factor is the proliferation of Arab television's satellite channels in the mid-1990s, which opened up new sources of funding while also providing a platform for the presentation of new media productions. The foundation of media zones across the Gulf is the third factor exercising fundamental impact on the growth of media production in the region overall.[24] The fourth and final factor that has increased the popularity and production of cartoons is the appearance of a new generation of globalised intellectuals who have grown up watching American animated sitcom cartoons such as *The Simpsons, South Park* and *Family Guy*, and who decided to create locally relevant productions within this genre.[25] These four factors intersected and were a significant boost for animation production both in Saudi Arabia and the Gulf.

The very first animated sitcom from the Gulf was *Qut'a 13* (*Block 13*), produced by Nawaf Salem Al-Shammari's Farooha Media Productions and premiered on Kuwaiti Al-Watan TV in 2000. As a Kuwaiti copycat of *South Park, Block 13* largely followed the American original's early cut-out style. However, instead of Cartman, Kyle, Stan and Kenny, the Arab version features Abboud, Azzouz, Hammoud and Salloum, who retained some of the original characters' traits, but were subtly redesigned in order to fit into the Kuwaiti moral context and environment. Also, considering the conservative local milieu, the series avoided addressing sensitive issues such as sexuality or deep engagement in political and religious affairs.

Although *Block 13* was a success, it took six years for the first quality Arab animated sitcom series to appear. *Freej* (*The Neighbourhood*), the brainchild of Mohammed Saeed Harib, a US-educated Emirati producer, debuted on Sama Dubai in 2006. Harib's company, Lammtara Pictures, was funded by Sheikh Mohammed Bin Rashid's Establishment for Young Business Leaders. Lammtara had been established in September 2005, with around 3 million Dirhams being provided by the Mohammed Bin Rashid Establishment. While the creative work was led by an international group based in Dubai supervised by Harib himself, the labour-intensive animation phases were outsourced to India.[26] The story of *Freej* involves four grandmothers, living in a traditional suburb of the modern UAE, and deals with the challenges faced by these elderly ladies in a rapidly modernising city. Very quickly, *Freej* became a success story on air and, via brand extension, through the sales of DVDs, toys and even the building of a theme park, developed into a national icon in the UAE.[27]

Around the same time as *Freej*, another animated sitcom, *Sha'beyat Al-Cartoon* (*Cartoon of Neighbourhoods*) was launched on a channel called Sama Dubai. Producer Mohamed Haidar insisted that his main goal was to produce a comedic cartoon rather than to preserve Emirati identity, as had been the case with *Freej*.[28] This aim was reflected in *Cartoon of Neighbourhoods* being more critical in its dealings with contemporary social problems. Similarly, a third animated Emirati series of this genre, *Khousa Bousa*, which debuted in 2009 on Sama Dubai, expressed interest in tackling social issues. The show was directed by Emirati director Njla Al-Sahy, while the animation process was outsourced to the Egyptian Tarek Rashed Studio. As was the case with *Freej*, the show dealt with local social problems such as rising prices and controversies in education.

It is likely that the regional success of *Freej* inspired and impelled authors from other Gulf countries to create their own animated sitcoms. In 2007, the first season of *Youmeyyat Bou Qatada wa Bou Nabeel* (*The Diary of Bou Qatada and Bou Nabeel*) was aired on Kuwaiti Al-Watan TV. The series – originally an adaptation of comic strips from the *Al-Watan* newspaper – was directed by Faysal Al-Ibrahim. While the voices were recorded locally, animation work was again outsourced to the Egyptian Tarek Rashed Studio. Like the original cartoons, it was direct in its political commentary, featuring stereotyped characters representing different factions of the local political scene, such as Islamists, liberals and traditionalists, and tackled contemporary issues of local public discourse such as the economy, education, sports and even religion. Then, in 2008, another Kuwaiti production, *Umm Sa'f*, appeared on Alrai Channel. Unlike the *Al-Watan* TV production, this series focused more squarely on social matters, rather than engaging in politics; it continued for three seasons.

In 2011, *Youm wa Youm* (*Day and Day*) debuted on Omani TV. This animated series was based on *Youmiyyat 'Arif Al-Bardhul* (*Diaries of the Lazy*), a satirical cartoon series published by Sulayman Al-Muammari in the Omani newspaper *Al-Zaman* between 2008 and 2010. The animated adaptation was produced by Al-Munis Media Production & Distribution, which is owned by the Omani writer and political activist Nasser Al-Badri, while the labour-intensive and expensive animation was once again taken care of by the productive Tarek Rashed Studio in Egypt. The story, a social and political satire, tells of the daily life of Arif and his friends, who live in a traditional neighbourhood. In the Gulf States, then, we see a burst of production in animated sitcoms, based on comic strips, and with an increasingly political bent and social inspiration.

Saudi Arabia did not lag far behind the other Gulf States when it came to animated sitcom production, the lion's share of Saudi productions being produced by and presented on the Dubai-based Middle East Broadcasting Centre (MBC), a private free-to-air satellite broadcasting company. Established in London in 1991, the Centre moved its headquarters to Dubai in 2002 and is now owned by Saudi businessman Waleed Al-Ibrahim. The majority of Saudi sitcom animated cartoons could be best described as adaptations of popular real-life series with their attendant actors. In 2006, *Youmeyyat Mnahy* (*The Diaries of Mnahy*) appeared on MBC. In this 2D animated production the popular Saudi comedian Fayez Al-Malki satirises Western stereotypes and prejudices of Arabs. It was a co-production between Al-Malki's Al-Malki Production Media and Advertising and the Dubai-based Emiratoons Production House, with the animation process being done by the Indian Adeyes Animation Studio. In 2007, a series called *Muznah and Fami* debuted, directed by Ali Al-A'raj. The series presented a curved mirror to Saudi society and its ambivalent relation to modern technology by relating the story of a fictional family stuck at the technological level of 2007 while the world around them lives in the year 2100.

In 2011, *Lurans Al-'Arab fil-Shurba wa Khal* (*Lawrence of Arabia in Soup and Vinegar*) debuted as an animated adaptation by social comedians who protected themselves by only appearing online under the pen names of Lawrence and Al-Shaikh Al-Baltouk.[29] A year later, *Taish Eyal*, an animated adaptation of the satirical series *Tash ma Tash* debuted. The original series, *Tash ma Tash* debuted on Saudi TV Channel 1 in 1992 and is regarded as one of the pioneers of self-criticism in the Saudi media because its episodes often addressed sensitive, contemporary social issues such as culture, terrorism, marital relations and religion.[30] Though a large number of the *Tash ma Tash* crew participated in the animated production, *Taish Eyal* lacked the explicit humour of the original. The animation process was again outsourced to Adeyes Animation Studio in India, the same animation studio that worked on *The Diaries of Mnahy* six years earlier. Saudi Arabian made-for-television animation was thus clearly conducive to a flourishing of satire and self-awareness in that country.

Conclusion

Though the first animated cartoons in the Gulf appeared as early as the 1970s, it took Saudi Arabian and Gulf animation until the 2000s to really experience significant growth. Despite being latecomers to animation production, after being fuelled by 3D technologies, Saudi Arabia and the Gulf countries have now caught up with countries like Egypt and Syria, long-standing centres of media and cinema production. However, as has been shown, production still involves a large amount of outsourcing and foreign labour, with nationals chiefly represented at the helm of these projects. While clear development in the form of inspiration has been forthcoming from literature and religion, social and political issues and even satire, there is still a distinctive lack of a common, recognisably Saudi Arabian or Gulf style. This is most probably due to the large number of foreign nationals involved in the production and to a lack of infrastructure or local technical talent. Nevertheless, local producers and directors have proven to be successful in addressing national and regional audiences, thus joining more cinematically advanced nations in the production and direction of exciting, engaging short and feature films.

Notes

1. Anna Contadini, *Arab Painting: Text and Image in Illustrated Arabic Manuscripts* (Leiden, 2007).
2. Anne Ciecko, 'Cinema "Of" Yemen and Saudi Arabia: Narrative strategies, cultural challenges, contemporary features', *Wide Screen*, 3, 1 (2011), p. 5.
3. Idem, p. 4.
4. Viola Shafik, *Arab Cinema: History and Cultural Identity* (Cairo, 2007), p. 27.

Local Minds, Foreign Hands

5. National television channels were established in the following years: Kuwait (1957), Saudi Arabia (1964), United Arab Emirates (1969), Qatar (1970), Bahrain (1973), Oman (1974).

6. Japanese Anime was also popular in Socialist Arab countries.

7. CGI (computer generated imagery) generates animated images by using computer graphics. It was developed in the 1960s, while the first film using the technology, *Westworld* (US, Michael Crichton), was released in 1973.

8. Omar Sayfo, 'Arab animation: between business and politics', T. Sabry, N. Sakr and J. Steemers (eds), *Children's Television and Digital Media in the Arab World* (London, 2015).

9. Paul Wells, *Animation Genre and Authorship* (London, 2002), pp. 74–76.

10. See on the official webpage of JPPI, http://www.gccopen.com/institution.html.

11. Ibid.

12. Personal interview with Bassam Faraj, Budapest, 8 August 2013.

13. An Arabic list of JPPI productions can be found at http://www.gccopen.com/SArb.pdf and an English version at http://www.gccopen.com/SEng.pdf.

14. 'abd Al-Muhsin Al-Banay, 'Jadeeduna Al-Musalsal Al-Kartouniyy «Ahmad wa Kan'aan»', *Al-Qabas* (25 December 2009). Available at http://www.alqabas.com.kw/node/562436_9.

15. The titles of the productions were discovered in a document, sent to me by Usama Khalifa on the 1 December 2012.

16. Phone interview, Usama Khalifa, 15 May 2014.

17. Ibid.

18. Ibid.

19. Carl Brockelmann, 'Kalila wa-Dimna', *The Encyclopaedia of Islam* 2 (1978), pp. 503–506.

20. Omar Sayfo, 'Arab sitcom animations as platforms of satire', S. de Leeuw (ed.), *The Power of Satire* (Amsterdam, 2015).

21. Omar Sayfo, 'The emergence of Arab children's televisions and animation industry in the Gulf States', M. Al-zo'oby and B. Baskan (eds), *State-society Relations in the Arab Gulf States* (Berlin, 2014), pp. 77–101.

22. Alexander Cole, 'Distant neighbours: the new geography of animated film production in Europe', *Regional Studies*, 42 (2008), pp. 891–904.

23. Hyejin Yoon and Edward J Malecki, 'Cartoon planet: worlds of production and global production networks in the animation industry', *Industrial and Corporate Change*, 19, 1 (2009), p. 240.

24. David McGlennon, *Building Research Capacity in the Gulf Cooperation Council Countries: Strategy, Funding and Engagement*', Zayed University Dubai, UAE.

25. Omar Sayfo, 'Arab sitcom animations as platforms of satire'.

26. Joe Khalil and Marwan M. Kraidy, *Arab Television Industries* (London, 2009), p. 51.

Animation in the Middle East

27. Dubai Press Club, *Arab Media Outlook 2009–2013* (Dubai, 2010), p. 178. Available at http://fas.org/irp/eprint/arabmedia.pdf (accessed 2 April 2015).
28. Sultan Sood Al-Qassemi, 'Our cartoon heroes: now that they are really our own', *Arab News* (7 September 2009).
29. Nagm "al-baltouk" fil-sa'udiyya yakshif ismuhu wa waghuhu ba'd sanawat min al-ghumud (11 June 2011). Available at http://www.alarabiya.net/articles/2011/06/11/152835.html (accessed 20 November 2014).
30. Eric Jensen, 'Mediating social change in authoritarian and democratic states – irony, hybridity and corporate censorship', B. Wagoner, E. Jensen and J. A. Oldmeadow (eds), *Culture and Social Change: Transforming Society Through the Power of Ideas* (US, 2012), pp. 212–17.

Filmography

Ahmad wa Kanaan (*Ahmad and Kanaan*), directed by Faysal Al-Ibrahimi (2009).
Al Qarasina wa Kanz Al-Dhahab (*The Pirates and the Gold Treasure*), directed by Usama Ahmad Khalifa (1998).
Al-Ashbal, directed by Usama Ahmad Khalifa (1995).
Al-Naser Salahulddin (*The Victorious Saladin*), produced by Arasoft (1990s).
Ali Baba wal-Arba'ena Lissan (*Ali Baba and the Forty Thieves*), directed by Usama Ahmad Khalifa (1996).
Asad Ayn Jalout, directed by Usama Ahmad Khalifa (1998).
Fath Al-Andalus – Tareq ibn Ziyad (*The Conquest of Andalusia – Tareq ibn Ziyad*), directed by Usama Ahmad Khalifa (1999).
Freej (*The Neighbourhood*), directed by Mohammed Saeed Harib (2006).
Hikayat Al-'Amm Al-Hakim (*Stories of the Wise Uncle*), directed by Usama Ahmad Khalifa (1999).
Hilm Al-Zaytoon (*Dream of the Olives*), directed by Usama Ahmad Khalifa (2009).
Ibn Al-Ghaba (*Son of the Forest*), directed by Thamer Al-Zaidi (2006).
Iftah ya Simsim (*Open Sesame*), produced by Gulf Cooperation Council (1979).
Khousa Bousa, directed by Njla Al-Sahy (2009).
Lurans Al-'Arab fil-Shurba wa Khal (*Lawrence of Arabia in Soup and Vinegar*), directed by Lawrence and Al-Shaikh Al-Baltouk (2011).
Masrur fi Jazirat al-Lu'lu' (*Masrur on the Pearl Island*), directed by Usama Ahmad Khalifa (1998).
Muhammad Al-Fatih (*Mohammad the Conqueror*), directed by Usama Ahmad Khalifa (1995).
Muznah and Fami, directed by Ali Al-A'raj (2007).
Qut'a 13 (*Block 13*), produced by Nawaf Salem Al-Shammari (2000).
Rihlat Al-Kholoud (*The Boy and the King*), directed by Dervis Pasin (1996).

Sha'beyat Al-Cartoon (*Cartoon of Neighbourhoods*), produced by Mohamed Haidar (2006).

Shahid Al-'Alam (*The Martyr of the World*), directed by Usama Ahmad Khalifa (2003).

Umm Sa'f, produced by Alrai Channel (2008).

Youm wa Youm (*Day and Day*), produced by Nasser Al-Badri (2011).

Youmeyyat Mnahy (*The Diaries of Mnahy*), produced by Al-Malki (2006).

Youmeyyat bou Qatada wa Bou Nabeel (*The Diary of Bou Qatada and Bou Nabeel*), directed by Faysal Al-Ibrahim (2007).

Za'toor, directed by Hashim Zaatari (1995).

4

Turkish Animation: A Contemporary Reflection of the Karagöz Shadow Play

Başak Ürkmez

The journey of Turkish animation cannot be viewed in isolation from the history of Turkey itself – it is closely intertwined with politics, change in society, superstition, fears, and with the loss of the countryside through migration: art reflects reality at almost every turn. Turkey has encouraged the growth of animation in parallel with its society – the political upheavals, the financial difficulties, the issues of migration, identity and gender are all reflected in the films produced. Turkish animated cinema continues to evolve and to discover new filmmakers. This chapter provides a framework to what contemporary Turkish animation offers. Like the country that is its source, it is a feast for those willing to partake.

Shadow Theatre and Caricature: Turkish Precursors to Animation

Cinema arrived in Turkey just a year after its invention, on the occasion of a visit to İstanbul by camera operators who had worked alongside the Lumière Brothers and who intended to capture images of the city. The first public screening was staged on 16 January 1897, and the new technology quickly attracted a wide circle of interest. One important reason for its gaining such enormous popularity at such a fast pace was the technical similarities to the popular traditional Turkish shadow play *Karagöz and Hacivat*, a form of puppet theatre based on impersonations, songs and banter between two main characters with several supporting roles, all represented two-dimensionally on a flat screen illuminated from behind. The puppets themselves have jointed limbs and are made from the hide of a camel or water buffalo. The hide is worked until it is semi-transparent; then it is coloured, resulting in multi-hued projections and 'making the figures look like stained glass.'[1] Although rudimentary in its technology, this particular form of performance art is based on the same principles – light and shade – as cinema; it also displays similarities in terms of its social function, acting as the 'spokesman for the people.'[2] *Karagöz and Hacivat* has origins as far back as the 1700s and remained extremely popular until the 1950s. Its growing popularity saw performances throughout the entire Ottoman Empire, and its own development through the ages. Simple and easily transportable equipment allowed mobility for the puppeteers *cum* animators who toured the country. Illustrating the traditional shadow plays' enduring links with animation, Güdükbay, Erol and Erdogan in 2014 'designed a software program that would digitally animate Karagöz characters', attempting to revive the long-neglected tradition in a modern framework.[3] Indeed, as they show, Karagöz's artistic features and means of expression are not yet exhausted but are open to further explorations.[4] As Canan Balan shows, the show has long been recognised as one of the original sources of cinema in Turkey,[5] yet, she says, 'Karagöz does not resemble Aristotelian narrative cinema so much as early animated or even surrealist films.'[6]

The Ottoman answer to the Lumière Brothers were the Manaki Brothers, Yanaki and Milton. Born in the Greek village of Avdella in 1878 and 1882 respectively, their cinematic venture to document the Ottoman lands was supported and authorised by the Empire's officials and the Supreme Ruler, Sultan Reşat, in 1911. The films they shot between 1905 and the early 1930s are widely regarded as the first of their kind in the history of Turkish, Macedonian and Greek cinemas. Still, historians usually herald Fuat Özkınay's 1914 film *Demolition of the Russian Monument in Ayastefanos*, made during the Ottoman Empire's entry into World War I, as the very first Turkish film. Under an initiative of the Central Army Cinema Office, founded with the support of both the military and the State, a great many documentary movies were produced in this period, but the number of full-length films was a mere seven. The first fiction film, *Pençe* (*Claw*), was shot in 1917 by Sedat Simavi.

The production of documentaries, newsreels, propaganda films and thematic movies continued throughout those war-torn years until the establishment of the Republic in October 1923. In 1921, during the height of the War of Independence being fought on the lands of Anatolia, Kemal Film, the first private film company was set up in İstanbul. The collapse of the Ottoman State and the founding of the Republic of Turkey affected, amongst many other things, activities in the field of cinema. The declaration of the Republic marked a critical turning point in the nation's social structure. The change of regime and the reformative steps taken by the new parliament had a revolutionary effect on all segments of society. Intellectuals and artists began to produce works inspired by the founding ideology and values of the new regime. Having found initial expression through the support of both the Turkish State and the military, cinema continued on an independent path in the period of the single party regime without any official support, being funded instead by free and private capital. It reached the most remote parts of the country and attracted the interest of the Turkish people who enjoyed locally-produced films.

During the 1930s, when animated feature films by Disney and others began to be shown in Turkey, local filmmakers and caricature artists expressed an interest in the field. It is important to highlight the fact that it was actually caricaturists who laid the foundations of animation in Turkey, and even traditional *Karagöz* contains central elements of caricature and satire. Famous caricaturist Cemal Nadir Güler for example started preparations for a film featuring one of the period's most famous caricature characters Amcabey. Güler worked for the newspaper *Aksam*, and invented the figure in 1929 in order to attract a larger readership for the newspaper. Amcabey became more famous than his inventor, the kind of popularity no other cartoon figure equalled in later years, and which elevated him to the level of popularity also enjoyed by Hacivat en Karagöz. In World War II Güler went to work for the newspaper *Cumhuriyet*, until his death in 1947. Güler never had the chance to finish his planned film.

Compared to the historical emergence of animation elsewhere in the world, the appearance of an animation sector in Turkish cinema arrived quite late, despite the obvious overlaps in aesthetics and sensibilities it shares with the popular shadow puppet theatre. For example, Karagöz has a loose episodic structure, has an inclination towards total theatre, and has a high degree of specialisation in presentational form.[7] Its caricaturistic, sarcastic, episodic nature as well as its specialisation and its inclination towards total performance, give Karagöz seemingly immediate links with modern animation. However, as we shall see, these obvious overlaps are not explored in much detail in historical or contemporary animation, apart from a few exceptional occasions, 'particularly after their disappearance following the institutionalisation of cinema in the early twentieth century.'[8]

The Pioneering Generations of Turkish Animation: Between Advertising and Art

Between 1939 and 1950, Turkish cinema experienced what has come to be regarded as a period of transition. Even though Turkey was not actively engaged in the War, the country still suffered its impacts, especially economically, which meant that the already minimal output of the cinema sector was further reduced. Moreover, the Censorship Law, which came into effect in 1939, further contributed to the deterioration of conditions in the industry. The most important development of the 1940s was the emergence of a new generation of directors interested in making films that touched on more diverse issues than had been the case in traditional theatre and film. Also important was the emergence of a number of businessmen who helped to introduce advertising into the medium of cinema, and animation into the medium of advertising, by commissioning film production companies to produce simple cinematic works for promotional purposes. Among these entrepreneurs were Güven Sigorta, Radyolin, Kerem Pertev and Rıdvan Umay. In particular the 1940s saw an increase in the number of advertising films made for pre-show screening at cinemas, which in turn led to a growing demand for the production of animated advertising films, among which a Fertek Rakı film, the first animated film in Turkey.[9] One of those who opened up space for advertising within the cinema sector was

Professor Vedat Ar of the Fine Arts Academy. Working with his team at Filmar Studios, he produced numerous two- to three-minute animations and stop-motion films.

With the end of World War II, Turkey entered a more democratic era, displayed by the acceptance of a multi-party system in 1946. This era was also reflected in the film and advertising industries. When the İstanbul Advertising Agency was set up in 1945, it became a gathering point for caricature artists, and the production of cartoon films followed. These simple films, made very quickly, attracted much popular interest. In the following years, more artists travelled abroad to study animation and, upon their return, led the way setting up numerous animation production studios in Turkey. Among these artists were Ferruh Doğan, Oğuz Aral, Tonguç Yaşar and Orhan Büyükdoğan.[10]

In 1947, Professor Vedat Ar launched the country's first education programme to focus on animation and began to produce short films with his students. The three-minute work *Zeybek Oyunu* (*The Zeybek Dance*) which he made with a group of 15 students, was the first purely artistic animation film produced by a team in Turkey. The film is based on a type of folkloric dance from the Turkish Aegean region. A member of this production team, Eflâtun Nuri Erkoç, was one of the most important proponents of Turkish caricature. He had turned to animation in 1942. His film *Dolmuş ve Şoförü* (*The Minivan and its Driver*) was made by drawing directly onto coventional filmstock. By evaluating traditional matters such as Zeybek, the artist shows the cross-generational, cross-cultural exchange between traditional and contemporary art.

With the introduction of tax regulations into the cinema sector in 1948, the number of films produced in one year increased from five to 15. A reduction in municipal taxes imposed on films, coupled with technological advancements, made film production more accessible and helped audiences develop a relationship with the art form. In 1950, the Democrat Party came into power under the leadership of Adnan Menderes. The consequent turn of affairs, such as the adoption of liberal economic principles, urbanisation, development initiatives and State policies encouraging consumption as well as production, produced a socio-cultural shift.

These changes in the country were reflected in its cinema. In this period marking the beginning of The Age of the Filmmakers Generation,[11] it is possible to observe a diversification of subject matter and an increase in the number of film productions. *Kanun Namına (In the Name of the Law)*, shot by influential director Lütfi Akad in 1952, was a work that signalled, through its narrative style and structure, the formation of a cinematic language particular to Turkish cinema. The regular publication of dedicated cinema pages in daily newspapers contributed to the formation of an informed audience. The changes observed in cinema by the late 1940s and early 1950s, and the increase in production, also inspired more investment in other cinematic genres.

The popularisation of, and investment in, genre production encouraged Turgut Demirağ, film director and owner of the And Film Production Company, to invest in an animation project in 1950. The first full-length animation film project *Evvel Zaman İçinde – Nasreddin Hoca, Keloğlan ve Gülderen Sultan (Once Upon A Time – Nasreddin Hodja, Kaloghlan and Gülderen Sultan)* was realised under the direction of Yüksel Ünsal. This film was based on the protagonists from humorous stories related in traditional Turkish fables. Nasreddin Hodja was an actual thirteenth century figure who gained legendary status as a man of humorous wisdom. Kaloghlan, on the other hand, was a fictional hero. A team of 50 worked on the film for nine years. As there were no facilities in Turkey to develop films, they were sent abroad. Films that had been sent to the United States for technical processing between 1951 and 1957 ended up getting lost. The only remaining part of Ünsal's film is a five-minute sequence, from the filmmaker's family archive, of a dancing woman shot in black and white. Producers no longer invested in animation because of the risks involved. There were no further attempts at making full-length animation films for a very long time.

In 1959, renowned caraciturist Eflâtun Nuri Erkoç was invited to London to hold a caricature exhibition. He ended up living there for a whole year, during which time his passion for animation resulted in a serendipitous meeting with the famous Hungarian animator John Halas who inspired him to launch a serialised animation project based on the comic strip *Çakaralmaz Hafiye (Çakaralmaz Detective)* originally published in the daily newspaper *Vatan*. This series, entitled *Gogo's*, was later completed by Halas studio. Erkoç returned to Turkey, while Halas continued with a similar character named *Foo Foo*.[12]

From the 1960s to the 1980s: Political and Cultural Upheaval in Animation

The Democrat Party remained in government in Turkey for 10 years. As the sole party in power, they adopted an intolerant stance against the opposition. Their policies were criticised by several sectors of society and provoked an especially adverse reaction from the army. So much so that, on 27 May 1960, a *coup d'état* was staged, the first of many to plague the country over the next thirty years. The military removed Adnan Menderes and his government from power. Trials were conducted, resulting in heavy sentences, even the death penalty in some cases. The libertarian approach of the Constitution of 1961 – composed and put into effect during these events – provided a comfort zone for certain sections of society, especially intellectuals. This environment was also conducive to film directors approaching social issues that had previously been impossible to tackle, and some noteworthy works came out of this wave. The number of films rose from 80 in 1960, to a record-breaking figure of 200 in 1965. Many new film production companies came into being, resulting in an increasing number of films aimed at a mass audience. Also important was the emergence in the 1960s of social realism. Films now dealt with matters pertaining to daily life as well as to social and economic issues with wider impact. This was also a period during which the sector imported Hollywood features to lure audiences to movie theatres. Religious story lines, music, dancing and sexuality were usually the most popular themes.

Meanwhile, the advertising sector continued to develop and many advertising companies set up dedicated animation studios. As the number of films kept increasing and different topics became thematised, many agencies and studios, such as Filmar, İstanbul Reklam, Kare Ajans, Karikatür Ajans, Radar Reklam, Stüdyo Çizgi, Canlı Karikatür, Ajans Bulu, Sinevizyon and Artnet used the money they earned from advertising to make both short and feature-length animated films. Oğuz Aral, Yalçın Çetin, Bedri Koraman, Orhan Özdemir and Ali Ulvi were just some of the master caricaturists who worked for these studios. *Koca Yusuf* (*Big Yusuf*) from 1966 and *Bu Şehri İstanbul* (*This City of İstanbul*) from 1968, both made at Kare cartoon studio by Oğuz Aral, Ferruh Doğan and Tekin Aral, are examples of such works from this period. 'Koca Yusuf' was the nickname of Turkey's first world famous wrestling champion. An animated biography, the film told of Koca Yusuf's extraordinary strength and his travels abroad. Wrestling was presented as a traditional combat sport with a central performative element, through the depiction of the life of the athlete on screen.

Between 1961 and 1964, the caricaturist Yalçın Çetin settled in Germany to a gain experience in animated cartoon production. He joined Insel Film in Munich. On his return to Turkey, he contributed to the development of production methods employed by the local animation studios of the time. He made two seven-minute films: *Boş Oda* (*The Empty Room*) and *Evliya Çelebi*. Evliya Çelebi was an important traveller and writer from the seventeenth century. For 40 years, he had travelled throughout the Ottoman lands and wrote *Seyahatname* (*The Book of Travels*). This figure inspired more films later on, as we will see. A personal quest for a national sense of aesthetics drove Çetin to take inspiration from, and make use of, the formal structure of *Karagöz*. The search for form and methods of fragmenting and halting movement to find a modern graphic system different to the Walt Disney approach and that of many European film cartoonists, carried Yalçın Çetin to experiment with adapting the line structure of Karagöz to cartoon.[13] An adaptation of Bedri Koraman's comic book, the 1962 production of *Cici Can*, became the first Turkish film to combine animation and live footage.[14] The animations were realised by Yalçın Çetin as a ghost story.

At And Film, Yüksel Ünsal became the first artist in Turkey to implement what was called the 'live picture' technique in animation. In 1960, he teamed up with Vedat Ar and Nihat Bali, and together the trio created many animated advertising films for the company Vog-Bali. During this productive period of the 1960s and 1970s, Ayla Seyhan, the first female Turkish animator who also worked under the mentorship of Vedat Ar, produced many films using the stop-motion technique and puppet animation. Women began their journey in Turkish animation in the 1960s, and according to Lent and Tunç were resigned to working closely with a male mentor, using traditional techniques, while other women studied animation at Anadolu University and later gravitated to computer animation as a pathway to work in the advertising sector.[15]

In 1961, the partnership of Yüksel Ünsal, Mehmet Muhtar and Kemal Baysal produced the first colour advertising films. Since there were no facilities in Turkey to develop colour film, the films were sent abroad for laboratory processing. The international transportation of undeveloped films required authorisation from the Council of Ministers. And yet, despite such difficulties, they were able to make successful advertising films for banks and companies. In 1962, Mehmet Muhtar and Yüksel Ünsal broke their partnership with Kemal Baysal and established Sintel Film, going on to produce films – in both live-action and animated format; in colour and in black-and-white – for businesses such as Unilever and the Turkish Commercial Bank. When the times changed and intuitive advertising gradually gave way to scientific advertising, a lone production company did not stand a chance within these modern parameters. Muhtar and Yüksel needed to collaborate with advertising agencies, so they closed Sintel Film. Muhtar joined the film department of Grafika Advertising Agency and Ünsal was appointed Chief of the Creative Office at Ankara Advertising Agency.

The years 1964 and 1965 were the most active for animated advertising films. Those caricaturists who had proved themselves while working in the press, or in And Film's animation projects, engaged in various activities in the field of advertising film production. Caricature Advertising, founded by the partnership of Ali Ulvi Ersoy, Bedri Koraman and Yalçın Tüzecan, did not last long due to a lack of decisive leadership and because of the inadequacies of the supporting team members. In the meantime, artists such as Ferruh Doğan, Yalçın Çetin, Eflatun Nuri and Tonguç Yaşar, continued to establish and dissolve many companies under a variety of names, all the while producing animated films.

In 1968, Oğuz Aral, Ferruh Doğan, Tekin Aral and Eflatun Nuri collaborated on an animation film entitled *Direklerarası*, a nostalgic depiction of the city of İstanbul and the theatrical centre of the 1700s, Direklerarası, a large trade and cultural market where theatres and cinemas were established. In this short film the last representative of the traditional Turkish improvisational theatre, İsmail Dümbüllü, talked about the period of the thriving Direklerarası. This was Turkey's very first documentary to use animation.[16]

Another significant innovation in the 1960s came with the founding of the Sinematek Society on 25 August 1965, during a time of political rejuvenation. By running activities in a number of places, the Society

Turkish Animation

soon increased its membership from 4,000 to 10,000. Screenings of films were programmed from the corpus of World Cinema not usually shown in Turkey. That writers, thinkers, and institutions like the Turkish Film Archive and Sinematek Society became engaged in the effort to introduce World Cinema at home, was a natural outcome. Inevitably, discussions on the subject of originality in cinema followed. *The New Cinema Magazine*, published by the Sinematek Society, was oriented towards discussing European cinema. A group of young people, including Yorgo Bozis, Jak Şalom, Artun Yeres, Veysel Ataman, Enis Rıza and Sezer Tansuğ aligned themselves with this New Cinema wave, making short films and documentaries with the financial and moral support of Bosphorus University's Cinema Club and the Sinematek Society. In 1967, the Hisar Short Film Competition was launched in İstanbul, which helped to create and solidify the concept of originality in animation films made in Turkey. The amateur stop-motion work of the semi-finalist Mehmet Celal Ülken, *Kibritler ve Böcü* (*Matchsticks and Maggots*) is considered to be the first experiment in stop-motion in Turkish cartoon film. This period produced the most brilliant examples of Turkish animation cinema.

One such work is Tan Oral's short film *Sansür* (*Censorship*), which won First Prize at the Turkish Radio and Television (TRT) Culture, Arts and Science Awards Short Film Competition in 1969, and the Grand Award at the Akşehir Nasreddin Hodja Animation Film Competition. Ironically enough, even though the film was awarded by state television, it was never broadcast, because of the taboo subject it addressed. During the 1970s, during the heat of political and artistic debates, caricature artist Tan Oral stood for this biting critical approach. Other important films by Oral include *Çizgi* (*Line*), in which he used the incision technique directly onto film and *The Good Soldier Schweik*, in which he explored the collage technique.

Seen by some as the most successful early example of Turkish animation cinema, Tonguç Yaşar's film *How the Ship of Creed Sailed* was also produced during this period. With this short animation film, which he co-wrote with Sezer Tansuğ, Yaşar won the Special Prize at the Third Altın Koza Film Festival. In this work, which was distinguished by its originality, a verse from the Quran figures as a galley in motion.[17] This experimental work explored the possibilities of animating symbols from Ottoman calligraphy and became the first Turkish animation to pass the pre-selection phase at the Ninth Annecy Cartoon Film Festival.[18] Tan Oral and Tonguç Yaşar's experimental works thus contributed greatly to the artistic and aesthetic development of the Turkish animation genre. Theirs was a statement declaring that animation was much more than advertising, and could and should include socio-political commentary in an attempt to renew the art form.

In the 1970s, Turkish feature film production reached a record-breaking high with between 200 and 300 films being made each year. However, quantity did not necessarily equate with quality. Eighty per cent of all films produced in this period were pornography, melodramas (known as arabesque films), religious films and second/third class adventure films. Both pornographic films and melodrama drove families away from the cinema. Another obstacle encountered by the sector was the rise of television. When the instability of the social, cultural and political environments forced people to withdraw into their homes, television gained the upper hand over cinema. With economic crises hitting the country, and with the rise of terrorist actions in the late 1970s, people began to prefer a private to a public life. And as the expansion of television broadcasting led to an increase in the sales of televisions, the new technology gradually usurped the place of cinema in people's lives. A new era opened up for workers in the cinema industry: a life in the television sector, making TV series and films, offered stability and a career path.

With this move away from cinema to television, in 1973 the production centre for animation moved to the state television body, TRT, which began broadcasting nationwide. This period saw the success of the first animated television commercials. Erim Gözen produced advertisements for Pirelli Tyres, Elmor and Mintax. In the turbulent climate of the 1970s, Emre Senan created experimental works such as *Gergeadam* (1975), *Hayatında Eğri Çizgiyi İlk Kez Keşfeden Adam* (*The Man Who Discovered The Curved Line For The Very First Time*, 1976), *Tabanca* (*Gun*, 1976) and *Kısasa Kısas* (*An Eye For An Eye*, 1979), all based on a socialist worldview. In 1979, he and Tan Oral presented a course in animation at the Applied Industrial Arts Vocational College, but had to stop after the government decided to merge the school with Mimar Sinan University.[19] While there was a rise in the politicisation of animation, taboo subjects were both directly and indirectly censored, and the independently-managed vocational college was converted into a state-sponsored art university. This ambiguous stance regarding freedom of expression was common in the Middle East in the 1970s, and created a complex dynamic for animators (and other filmmakers) to work within.

Nevertheless, animation artists creating works outside the Turkish cinema sector continued to participate in national and international festivals and to return home with prizes. Meral Erez, who studied animation in Italy, won First Prize in the 1978 Balkan Film Festival's National Film Competition with her animation *Il Gatto* (*The Cat*). She had been influenced in her style by Eastern European modalities and techniques, and her experimental animations were and are, as with those of other artists, sponsored by her more financially rewarding work in advertising. Equally successful outside Turkey was Ateş Benice, whose 1980 film *Stereo* was shown successfully at the Zagreb Animation Film Festival. In the following year, the same film received a special invitation to participate in a competition organised in the Portuguese city of Espinho. *Les Cordes* (*Ropes*), a completely unique film in terms of both its technique and use of cinematic language, made by Meral and Cemal Erez between 1981 and 1983, won an award at the Mary Le Roi Short Film Festival in 1988.

The 1980s began – just as the 1960s and 1970s had – with military upheaval. The *coup d'état* of 12 September 1980 marked the beginning of a very dark period in Turkey's history. Great social change was occurring nationwide and the effects became apparent in cinema. At first, the nation's artists and intellectuals failed to raise their voices against the brutal undermining of democratic rule, but after a brief period of stagnation, some filmmakers began to produce works that touched on the pressing issue of military intervention. The military government's policies following the *coup* initiated a process of depoliticisation that spread rapidly throughout society, affecting all sectors of the film industry. The video films that emerged in this period were made for purely commercial concerns and possess little artistic value.

In the second half of the 1980s, many studios such as Çizgi Advertising, Tunç İzberk Studio, Tele Çizgi, Animatek, Ajans Bulu and Artnet, began to make animation films commissioned by various state institutes, often based on traditional folktales. The 50-minute *Boğaçhan* (*Boğaç Khan*), adapted from the traditional stories in the *Book of Dede Korkut*,[20] was the first completed feature-length animation film produced and developed entirely in Turkey. Made in 1988 at the Pasin-Benice Studio, by Derviş Pasin and his team, it depicts the mythical story of a youth who stops a bull in his tracks with his fist alone. With roots in different but equally traditional stories, Derviş Pasin and Ateş Benice made films with the character Evliya Çelebi (who had also appeared in a film by Yalçın Çetin in the 1960s). It remains the best-remembered animation feature film in Turkish collective memory. The years between 1980 and 1988 can be seen as a time during which the nation once again underwent a fundamental transformation, as the government took steps towards producing equilibrium in the financial markets. The technical revolutions that took place as a result of the country's increased import trade also caused pronounced changes in visual communications. The media and advertising sectors developed further and vastly increased their influence.

The 1990s: Conservatism and Transnationalist Regionalism

Towards the end of the 1980s, ANAP – the centre-right nationalist Motherland Party – began its demise as the sole party in government. Politicians who had previously been banned from the political arena were pardoned, and they returned with greater conviction, quickly accumulating a voting public. In the meantime, the Islamic segment of society also grew in strength, expanding its circle of influence both politically and economically. This change was reflected in cinema. In an age when Turkish films were losing their audiences, Islamic films attained an unexpected level of success through advertising and promotional campaigns directed at this religious segment of society. The animation sector was also affected. Damla Animation, founded by Bahattin Alkaç in Ankara in 1988, made *Deli Dumrul* for the Ministry of Culture and other animation films commissioned by TRT. In *Deli Dumrul*, the eponymous protagonist builds a bridge over a dry river. He takes money from people who want to use the bridge. After one man dies on the bridge, God sends Azrail, the Angel of Death, to take Deli Dumrul's soul. Deli decides to fight Azrail, but fails. The film includes a transparently simple moral lesson, in line with the agenda of the more religiously-inspired films of the decade. Damla

Animation began to make animated films commissioned by TRT, the Ministry of Culture and the Office of Religious Affairs, and aimed at international markets in Germany and the Arab countries. These films were praised and reviewed positively by the right-wing and the Islamic sectors, but were sometimes ignored and often criticised in professional cinema circles.

During the early 1990s, Turkish cinema suffered its most challenging period. Living conditions became tougher, and the arrival of private television broadcasting companies at the cost of the video market saw the cinema sector begin to lose its audience. Failing to react to this situation in time, film production entered a period of decline. Concerns over the commercial success of some films meant that they were transferred to television before being given an opportunity for screening in cinemas. The annual volume of film production dropped from the hundreds to the forties. In 1990, a case of fraud took place in TRT that drove it to withdraw its support of the animation sector. Most studios could not withstand this loss of economic resources and had to close down. Factors such as the waning demand from the private sector for animation films intended for advertising, and the lack of consistent support from the Ministry of Culture and TRT, forced those artists with an interest in animation to seek training and career opportunities abroad. As a result, a number of Turkish animation artists found work in big international studios. Tahsin Özgür is one such name. Employed by Walt Disney Studios, Özgür worked as an animator on major productions such as *Tarzan* (1997), *Hercules* (1999) and *Asterix* (1994).[21] He gave courses and seminars throughout his career in many international educational institutions.

Ongoing social and political shifts resulted in Turkish society becoming more conservative in the 1990s, and the period saw the establishment of animation companies focusing solely on producing works with Islamic content. These companies – often run collaboratively with Arab partners – produced films and series intended for a specific section of society of the international market. As a result, hundreds of employment opportunities arose and the sector entered a period of rejuvenation. Evaluation of this state of affairs in relation to the political climate of its day reveals that the policies implemented by the Republican ideology towards the creation of a new nation, policies such as the abolition or transformation of Ottoman institutions and the consequent rejection of religious notions and figures deemed incapable of adapting to these changes, were reflected in the cinema of the period.

Another important development in Turkish cinema during the 1990s was the opening of local branch offices by many major Hollywood companies. Foreign companies signed deals with cinema enterprises in İstanbul and Anatolia, and shared most of the existing movie theatres among themselves. As the US cinema industry imposed its own rules on the local market, the Turkish cinema sector started to face rather unfair competition. The signing by local cinemas of exclusivity deals with foreign film companies meant that there remained very few if any available slots for the showing of Turkish films.

While Turkish cinema continued to battle with foreign films, the growing media and advertising businesses continued to look to the animation sector for positive results. The advertising sector had managed to achieve world standards and in the wave of fundamental change taking place in the country's economic structure, had accumulated a serious amount of capital. This funding served to improve the quality and coverage of the animation studios, laboratories and technical equipment. A few of the companies established in this period, like Anima İstanbul and Sinefekt, produced important works in the animation sector.

Anima İstanbul specialises in animation. Having started its journey in 1995 as a production company specialised in animation, it is now a fully integrated film company that can produce films using all available techniques (such as stop-motion, 2D, 3D, CGI, etc.) and offers post-production solutions through its own infrastructural facilities (such as editing, compositing and sound studios). Engaged in continuous development, in terms of both creativity and technology, Anima has claimed an undisputed place at the head of the advertising sector for many years. In time, it has also proven itself in the film sector, through its offering of artistic and technical support to Turkish cinema in the field of animation and special effects. Today, with the quality of its technological infrastructure and the creative strength of its artistically oriented team, Anima is one of the major companies in the European market.[22] Even though its production is predominantly geared towards advertising, the company also creates music videos, animated series, full-length films and special effects, participating in many national and international festivals. More recently, Anima has produced new film, *Kötü Kedi Şerafettin* (*Şerafettin the Bad Cat*). It is the biggest animation project in Turkey to date and is planned to come out towards the end of 2016.

Sinefekt is worth noting in its turn as it specialised in VFX for feature films and commercial animation films, and, importantly, because Lamia Karaali was the first women team director for Sinefekt. She trained in animation in Moscow. Her film *One* was awarded the T.A.R.U.S.A. best film award in 1998 and the Russian Anigraf 2D computer animation award in 1999 in Moscow. As an important female figure, of which there have been so few in animation, let alone in Turkey, she made a significant contribution to the industry with her film and became an example for the women in animation in Turkey today.

The 1990s also saw the intensifying development of training and education in animation, with the Anatolian University offering the first academic degree in animation in 1990. The course's aim was to train much-needed people for the visual communications sector (such as private television companies, video, animation and multimedia production companies and advertising agencies). Today, with the ongoing emergence of new technologies, the art of animation has expanded both its visual vocabulary and areas of functionality, the most significant development being the accessibility for the cartoon film artist of today to a professional career within the fast-changing contemporary media dynamics of Turkish society.

The Anadolu University's Animation Department founded by Erim Gözen has undertaken to provide not only the technical and aesthetic training required for this artistic discipline, but also the responsibility to develop it into a valid profession. The four-year long academic curriculum is prepared with the aim of producing artists who not only are well-versed in cinematic vocabulary across film, video, animation and multimedia techniques – and who are therefore employable in various sectors of the television, multimedia and education industries, but also artists who are well-equipped with expanded conceptual sensibilities and technical capabilities.[23]

The new century continued the domination of Hollywood movies in Turkish cinemas. However, the 9/11 terrorist attacks suffered in the US in 2001, the war in Afghanistan and Turkey's deployment of military troops in the region, all had a profound effect on the country's economy; uncertainty and armed conflict in the Middle East led to an economic crisis. The general elections held in 2002 resulted in the conservative Justice and Development Party (AKP) becoming the sole party in government with all other parties losing large proportions of their vote. The Republican People's Party (CHP) became the main opposition party and AKP took advantage of being the sole party in power by imposing various debilitating measures on the media sector.

Nevertheless, several individual efforts were made to keep the animation industry alive. In 2003, Efe Efeoğlu organised the inaugural İstanbul Animation Festival, a festival of animated films mostly for adults. The festival is still going strong and is one of the best-attended events in the region. Also, from 2008 onwards, the Turkish animation sector entered a new period of rejuvenation. On 1 November 2008, with Turkey's first children's television channel TRT Çocuk beginning its broadcasting life, the animation sector stepped into a new era. In 2009, Turkey's first 3D animation television series Keloğlan (Kaloghlan) was produced by Barış İslamoğlu at Animax Animation Studios for TRT Çocuk. The series' story is again rooted in folklore, a story that offers excellent opportunities for both moralistic and taboo-breaking tales.

Turgut Akaçık, a graduate of the Anatolian University's Animation Department with a professional history as a character animator, chief animator and director (in that order) at Anima, directed the short film Don't Go in 2010. This film won the Special Distinction Award, Junior Jury Award for a Short Film Winner and the Anima-J School Prize at the Annecy International Animation Film Festival in 2011. In the same year, at the Hiroshima International Animation Festival, Don't Go was presented with the Best of the World Selection award. In 2011 it won the Audience Award ages five to ten at the International Children's Film Festival in New York. This marked a period in which the animation sector's general tendency to attempt to satisfy audience expectations with technical finesse had caused a decline in the creation of interesting and unique characters. In this context, Turgut Akaçık's Don't Go was a break with the norm. Akaçık used familiar clichés that resonated with the audience, but at the same time created a unique, well-designed and considered character called Pinky (see image 4.1), a little creature that lives with a cat.[24]

Turkish Animation

4.1 Still from *Don't Go*, directed by Turgut Akaçık (2010)

Accompanying this trend of developing a unique characterisation, was a continued interest in religious subjects and characters. The animated film *Allah'ın Sadık Kulu* (*God's Loyal Subject*), based on the real life story of Muslim cleric Said Nursi, was the first full-length animation film made in Turkey using the motion capture technique. Directed by Esin Orhan, a female animator, it was screened in 2011 after a three and a half year production phase.[25] The biographical story shows Nursi's personal development into an inspirational cleric. Again, with a moralistic message at its core, this educational film is aimed at young children in the first instance, but its aesthetic appeal also attracts a more mature audience.

In 2011, a new law was passed pertaining to the Radio and Television Council and Broadcasting Services, according to which:

> In the case of television enterprises broadcasting general and thematic content, including cartoon films among their children's programmes, it is imperative that at least twenty percent of cartoon films, and at least forty percent of other children's programmes should be originally produced in the Turkish language and reflect the Turkish culture.[26]

With the introduction of this law came a new focus on local production in the local language, and the State also announced the re-introduction of generous funding for the production of local cartoon films. In addition to animation studios working for TRT Children's Channel, many other studios such as Raatsız Animation Studio, Gentlemen Visuals, Robotika Films, Düşyeri Animation Studio, Lighthouse Visual Effects, Cherrycherry Animation, Animanyam Animation and Arca Medya continue to be active in the animation sector. As part of the sustained economic recovery after the 2008 global financial crisis, this new injection of finances brought life to the animation industry and also saw the opening up of new animation studios producing local films, predominantly in 3D. The sector began to thrive once again both in terms of employment and production. Cordoba Animation Studio was set up in 2007 in İstanbul with the aim of producing local cartoon films for children and developing an innovative approach to animation. The series *Nane Limon* (*Mint and Lemon*) was the first Cordoba project to be aired. This studio, with its 80 employees, has become Turkey's foremost studio.

Within this productive atmosphere for animation, 'Canlandıranlar' ('Animators'), a string of ongoing projects, was developed in 2008 by Berat İlk in response to the needs and existing conditions of animation cinema in Turkey. It is now a full member of ASIFA, since 2012. Its projects are focused on people working in animation, both those actively engaged in productions and enthusiasts. This is a non-profit and technically non-discriminatory formation, with people aspiring to work in animation finding opportunities for training and active production in the free workshops İlk began to run in 2008.

Conclusion: Still Developing an Industry

At the time of writing, 2015, Turkey is a country that has been ruled by a conservative government for over 12 years. The ideological deadlock the nation is experiencing today is felt in all areas of life. Newly developing social movements are also inspiring the creation of divergent works in animation. In the aftermath of the Gezi Park Resistance in 2013, Ayçe Kartal's *Tornistan* (*Backward Run*, see image 4.2) was one such example. With mild echoes of Tan Oral's short film *Censorship*, this self-censored film criticised press censorship of the Gezi Park protests.

This is a time in which the majority of Turkish society lives in cities, in which rapid waves of communication encompass the country and physical

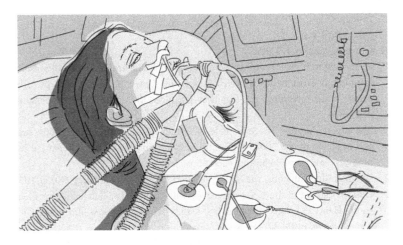

4.2 Still from *Tornistan*, directed by Ayçe Kartal (2013)

distance is no longer an issue. Despite the rate of growth observed in the animation sector, it is still not possible to talk about a Turkish animation industry that has reached corporate dimensions. The lack of cultural and economic policies addressing the sector, and the shortcomings of a legal system regulating production in the field, are important obstacles to the local animation industry's development. In some respects, animation in Turkey is still just like *Karagöz*. Like the shadow play, Turkish animation and its history show us some things and conceal others. By reflecting the history of the nation, the bright optimism and the dark shadow of oppression, it can interpret the memories that we have inherited in contemporary ways, giving them meanings for today. But there is always the real need for a guiding hand behind the screen to bring the industry's characters and story to new life.

Notes

1. Metin And, *Karagöz: Turkish Shadow Theatre* (Istanbul, 1987): n.p.
2. Ibid.
3. Ugur Güdükbay, Fatih Erol and Nezih Erdogan, 'Beyond Tradition and Modernity: Digital Shadow Theater', *Leonardo*, 33, 4 (2000), p. 264.
4. Ibid., p. 265.
5. Canan Balan, 'Transience, absurdity, dreams and other illusions: Turkish shadow play', *Early Popular Visual Culture*, 6, 2 (July 2008), pp. 171–85.

Animation in the Middle East

6. Ibid., p. 179.

7. Metin And, n.p.

8. Canan Balan, pp. 171–85.

9. According to filmmaker and cinematographer İlhan Arakon, who talks about the film advertisement for Fertek Rakı being shown at cinemas as a prelude to the main screening, the film was produced at Maçka Palas by persons unknown.

10. The advertising film *İzocam,* made by Orhan Büyükdoğan in the 1960s, was still available in the 2000s for commercial viewing on TV. It is regarded by many as a masterpiece among such films.

11. Scognamillo, Giovanni, *The History of Turkish Cinema* (Istanbul, 1990), p. 105.

12. Halas remained in the UK and created, with his wife Joy Batchelor (for their studio Halas and Batchelor), the first feature-length animated film in the UK, *Animal Farm,* in 1954.

13. Turgut Ceviker, 'Caricature and Karagöz', S. Koz (ed.), *Torn is the Curtain, Shattered is the Screen, the Stage all in Ruins* (Istanbul, 2004), p. 71.

14. Ege Görgün, 'Cici Can'. Available at www.tersninja.com (accessed 22 April 2014).

15. John A. Lent and Asli Tunç have written an insightful analysis of women in Turkish animation. Available at John A. Lent and Asli Tunç (1999) 'In a man's world: Turkish women animators', *Animation World Magazine,* 3, 11 (February 1999) http://www.awn.com/mag/issue3.11/3.11pages/lentturkey.php3

16. News, 'Live pictures', *The New Cinema Magazine,* 14 (1968), p. 6.

17. A. Serif Onaran, *Turkish Cinema* (Istanbul, 1999), p. 197.

18. This film is available on YouTube: https://www.youtube.com/watch?v= pX3KXXZA6gI (accessed 11 May 2015).

19. Aydin Engin, *This is the title of the book, Tan Oral book* (Istanbul, 2006), p. 557.

20. *The Book of Dede Korkut* is a collection of ancient moral tales and epic stories, part of the cultural heritage of the Turkic states.

21. Şahin Ersöz is another Turkish animator who worked on Disney's *Hercules* (1997) and on *Balto* (1995) as a storyboard artist.

22. Mehmet Kurtulus, 'Anima İstanbul'. Available at www.animaistanbul.com (accessed 30 June 2014).

23. Fethi Kaba, 'Department of Animation'. Available at www.anadolu.edu.tr/tr/ akademik (accessed 27 May 2014).

24. Basak Ürkmez, 'Interview: Turgut Akacik', *Grafist,* 16 (2012), pp. 99–111.

25. This film is available in its entirety on YouTube. Available at https://www.you-tube.com/watch?v=Vcetg2eQVtQ (accessed 11 May 2015).

26. Article 14 of Law, Radio and Television Council and Broadcasting Service Law in Republic of Turkey (2011).

Filmography

Allah'ın Sadık Kulu (God's Loyal Subject), directed by Esin Orhan (2011).

Amentü Gemisi Nasıl Yürüdü (How the Ship of Creed Sailed), directed by Tonguç Yaşar (1970s).

Boğaçhan (Boğaç Khan), directed by Derviş Pasin (1988).

Boş Oda (The Empty Room), directed by Yalçın Çetin (1964).

Cici Can, directed by Ertem Göreç (1962).

Çizgi (Line), directed by Tan Oral (1970s).

Deli Dumrul, directed by Bahattin Alkaç (1988).

Demolition of the Russian Monument in Ayastefanos, directed by Fuat Özkınay (1914).

Direklerarası, directed by Oğuz Aral, Ferruh Doğan, Tekin Aral and Eflatun Nuri (1968).

Dolmuş ve Şoförü (The Minivan and its Driver), directed by Eflâtun Nuri Erkoç (1942).

Don't Go, directed by Turgut Akaçık (2010).

Evliya Çelebi, directed by Yalçın Çetin (1964).

Evvel Zaman İçinde – Nasreddin Hoca, Keloğlan ve Gülderen Sultan (Once Upon A Time – Nasreddin Hodja, Kaloghlan and Gülderen Sultan), directed by Yüksel Ünsal (1950).

Gergeadam, directed by Emre Senan (1975).

Gogo's, directed by Eflâtun Nuri Erkoç (1959).

Hayatında Eğri Çizgiyi İlk Kez Keşfeden Adam (The Man Who Discovered The Curved Line For The Very First Time), directed by Emre Senan (1976).

II Gatto (The Cat), directed by Meral Erez (1978).

Kanun Namına (In the Name of the Law), directed by Lütfi Akad (1952).

Kebabaluba, directed by Tahsin Özgür (1995).

Keloğlan (Kaloghlan), produced by Barış İslamoğlu (2009).

Kibritler ve Böcü (Matchsticks and Maggots), directed by Mehmet Celal Ülken (1967).

Kısasa Kısas (An Eye For An Eye), directed by Emre Senan (1979).

Koca Yusuf (Big Yusuf), directed by Oğuz Aral, Ferruh Doğan and Tekin Aral (1966).

Les Cordes (Ropes), directed by Meral and Cemal Erez (1982).

Nane Limon (Mint and Lemon), directed by Gökhan Aşık, Çağrı Bayraklı and Özgün Zümrüt (2009).

One, directed by Lamia Karaali (1997).

Pençe (Claw), directed by Sedat Simavi (1917).

Sansür (Censorship), directed by Tan Oral (1969).

Tabanca (Gun), directed by Emre Senan (1976).

Animation in the Middle East

The Good Soldier Schweik, directed by Tan Oral (1970s).
Tornistan (Backward Run), directed by Ayçe Kartal (2013).
Zeybek Oyunu (The Zeybek Dance), directed by Vedat Ar (1947).
Kötü Kedi Şerafettin (Serafettin the Bad Cat), directed by Mehmet Kurtuluş, Ayşe
Ünal (2016)

5

From Animated Cartoons to Suspended Animation: A History of Syrian Animation

Stefanie Van de Peer

In the same way that cartoons formed the basis for animation's original development at the turn of the twentieth century, so too, though much later, has Syrian animation used cartoons as its inspiration. Still, just as there is no real Syrian film industry to speak of, there is also no animation industry. By the time animation achieved popularity in Syria, the Baath Party had made its mark on the creative output of the country and even though the digital age has enabled some studios to make names for themselves, with productions exported for satellite networks in the Gulf, there is no sense of a fully integrated network of artists. Moreover, with the escalation of civil war since 2011, many artists have dispersed, essentially exiling themselves, and almost all creative initiatives and organisations have been suspended. Through an historical overview of some of the earliest cartoonists/animators and a case study of one of the most prolific Syrian animators, Sulafa Hijazi, this chapter recounts how Syrian animation has come to a full stop: after 'giving life' to cartoons and other still images during the relatively stable era of the 1990s and early 2000s, animation artists have had to refocus their skills and bring their animated art back, full circle, to a standstill, in static images.

Cinema, Cartoons and Baath Tolerance

After centuries under Ottoman rule and decades of French mandate, Syria gained independence in 1936. It was prior to independence, under French rule, that the first film screening in Syria had taken place, in Aleppo in 1908. Film production proper began in 1928, with the silent film *Al-Muttaham Al-Baree'* (*The Innocent Suspect*) by Rashid Jalal. The first sound film, *Nur wa Thalam* (*Light and Darkness*) by Nazih Shahbandar, coincided with the arrival of Egyptian cinema, which catapulted Arab cinema as a whole in the direction of commercial ventures. Private financiers and producers dominated the film industry of the 1950s, with a focus on producing and distributing commercial genre cinema. This changed drastically with Baath.

The Baath Party instated a one-party system in 1963, simultaneously closing all private and independent newspapers and publications. The Syrian press was reshaped to mobilise the public in support of the Baath Party,[1] and the National Film Organisation (NFO) was created to regulate film production and distribution, thereby taking filmmaking out of the commercial sphere and placing it squarely into a nationalist discourse. The NFO functioned as a censorship board, and was established as an independent arm of the Ministry of Culture. It adhered systematically and rigidly to the prevailing Baathist ideology.[2]

Although there is a dearth of material treating Syrian cinema, what there is at least has critics in agreement as to its paradoxical nature. Lisa Wedeen (1999), Rasha Salti (2006) and Miriam Cooke (2007) depict Syrian cinema as a tale of two worlds: on the one hand the NFO was in control of filmmaking and distribution, dictating what was appropriate for a local audience; on the other, the organisation also sent its young filmmakers abroad to hone their craft (most often to the Soviet Union) and then back to Syria to work, for attractive salaries. In practice this meant that although films critical of the government were made – often as exercises in metaphor and allegory – NFO officials either did not grasp their non-conformity or did realise and shelved them without exhibition options. The central paradox of Syrian cinema then is that it is a 'state-sponsored cinema, whose most renowned filmmakers offered an alternative, critical and subversive narrative of the "national" lived experience of traumas that directly contested the official state-enforced discourse.'[3]

From Animated Cartoons to Suspended Animation

Miriam Cooke describes a state that silenced artists even while it needed them, using culture and cultural products to shape public opinion and to legitimise its power.[4] In spite of taboos on the discussion of politics, ideology, religion, society and economics, in the late 1960s Baath originally tolerated the publication and staging of works critical of the regime; in the 1970s, the party increased its censorship laws, but by the 1980s had again 'softened its autocratic image to deflect local revolutionary ambitions.'[5] Under a veneer of democracy, the state let up on some fronts and cracked down on others, resulting in a complicated cultural experience within a discourse that simultaneously emphasised cultural production while it stifled the atmosphere in which artists were permitted to function. Artists had to negotiate the 'permissible.'[6] Wedeen elucidates this complex reality somewhat when she compares what she terms 'tolerated parodies' to 'safety valves':[7] the controlled venting of dissatisfaction is allowed in order to displace or relieve tensions that otherwise might find expression in political actions.[8] She shows how, in film, authorised critical practices preserved the regime's repressive dominance rather than undermined it. As an example she uses the popularity of cartoon and comic-strip artists, who boasted access to a mass audience in the 1970s and 1980s.

Comic-strips had been a regular feature in official Baath Party children's magazines for decades. These were educational and moralistic in nature, so as to reach as wide an audience as possible with their family-friendly discourses. Since the 1970s, there has been a highly metaphorical editorial cartoon culture, too, best exemplified by Ali Ferzat, in the country's otherwise heavily-censored press.[9] When, in the 1970s, the country's official newspaper *Al-Thawra* (*The Revolution*) stopped publishing Ferzat's daily editorial cartoon, its circulation dropped by 35 per cent. The series was soon reinstated, but with a number of controls in place, and Ferzat functioned fairly well in this system.

In 2000, in what appeared to be the spirit of openness (the 'Damascus Spring') surrounding his new presidency, Bashar Al-Assad, who had succeeded his father Hafez, encouraged Ferzat to start his own satirical newspaper, *Al-Doumari* (*The Lamp Lighter*). Revealing the pervasiveness of censorship during the senior Assad's rule, as well as the hope embodied by the new young president, *Al-Doumari* was the first independent newspaper in 20 years; but it ran for only two years before being banned. For most of that time, Ferzat manipulated well the safety valves between censorship and tolerance, avoiding direct criticism of Assad, and creating instead metaphorical cartoons addressing wider issues facing the Middle East.[10] However, in 2011, during the initial stages of the Syrian revolution, Ferzat decided to move beyond the 'permissible' line by publishing two cartoons of Assad,[11] saying, 'If I am not prepared to take risks I have no right to call myself an artist.'[12] As a consequence of these cartoons Ferzat had both of his hands broken in a symbolic attack warning against criticism of the regime.[13] The assault itself is testament to his influence on the cultural scene in Damascus, as is the subsequent wave of solidarity he received.

Both cartoons and cinema had begun to enjoy immense popularity, and the fact that many cartoonists' work did not lead to more sustained collaborations with animation artists can be chiefly attributed to a lack of training opportunities and solid networks, and to the continuing control over culture by Baath. The political nature of cartoons did not mesh with the commercial nature of early animation. With Syrian animation's increasing politicisation since 2011, however, cartoons' inspiration of the form is unmistakeable.

Although the NFO maintained its monopoly over film production, it also suffered from meagre resources and limited success. While offering artists a steady, if limited, income and social security, it also drained their creative energies and stifled their voices. To address this, co-productions with private companies began to be permitted around 2000. A younger generation of artists, less daunted by the censor, began experimenting with new media and new forms, while at the same time independent studios offered training grounds, and co-productions became increasingly possible. The first feature-length animated film, *Khait Alhayaa* (*The Thread of Life*), saw the light of day, paving the way for a growing confidence in those Syrian animators to be found both in and outside of the country.

Early Animated Cartoons and the NFO

The 1980s had been a formative period for dissident filmmaking and cartooning; and television gained a mass audience. The convergence of these media resulted in the first real initiatives in Syrian animation, which – a decade later – were to bear fruit in the first studios popping up in

From Animated Cartoons to Suspended Animation

Damascus. Syria had, during this time, two national television channels, both controlled by the Syrian Arab Television and Radio Broadcasting Commission (SATRBC), intimately connected with the Ministry of Information, and each with very little interest in animation. As Ghazala points out, the enforced 'national identity' of these channels resulted in a lack of screening time for foreign animation and a lack of awareness of its domestic impetus.[14]

Syria's first short animated film for TV was made by Mwafaq Katt. His is an example of animation's tendency towards a suspended state of being. Having studied filmmaking and animation at the Gerasimov Institute of Cinematography (VGIK) in Moscow, on his return he became instrumental in the long process towards establishing a separate arm of television devoted to animation. His first film, *Juha fi Al-Mahkameh* (*Juha at Court*), was made in 1985, and he has, since then, made over 40 more. In 1991, he created the award-winning *Hikāya Mismāriya* (*A Tale of Two Nails: A Cuneiform Tale*),[15] a metaphorical tale that begins with two tall nails bickering, before calling in their armies of smaller nails, who proceed to exterminate each other completely. The film's ending shows the two large nails returning to the scene of the battle. They look at one another and then engage in a resounding kiss atop the mountain of dead, discarded nails who had battled on their behalf. Firstly, the film, of course, refers to the futility of war. Even the kiss at the end seems a brutal indictment of the notion of power for personal gain: only after they have destroyed each other's armies, after they have displayed their power to one another through senseless sacrifice that they did not partake in, do these two 'leaders' reach a truce. Their truce, while it crosses the dividing line, can be expressed only whilst standing on the bodies of the dead. It is thus a darkly sarcastic kiss, made obvious through the smacking echo in the sound design. Secondly, the film also draws attention to the universality of communication and the potential for eventual peace. It is interesting then to highlight the title. Cuneiform, being a mode of communication from the past, symbolises the old way of doing things. The film thereby emphasises that recognising contemporary trends in this film's ancient metaphor reveals the universal and timeless nature of conflict while it foregrounds the closing of the gap between the two nails, between past and present, and the urgency with which clearer communication has to be attained. By drawing attention to its 'cuneiformity', it foregrounds the power of communication rather than violence while its cynicism admits to the problematic nature of Syrian political reality.[16]

Failing communication and conflict are also central to Katt's latest film. *The Eleventh Commandment* (2011),[17] made just before the outbreak of the revolution, consists of a number of vignettes visualising the hallucinations of a hookah-smoking man. The vignettes combine mythological figures (Noah and Sisyphus, for example) as diverse embodiments of a suffering nation. Sisyphus represents endless toil, while Noah fails in his attempts to save the population from environmental and political disasters. The episodic nature and the style of Katt's drawings suggest an increasing suspension: the animation moves slowly, and like cartoons has a sarcastic bent. This intensified directness in his criticism of government resulted in Katt's self-exile. Because of increasingly menacing reactions to his growing political activism, he stopped animating and left the country. He has since become a cartoonist and, thus, his art has also come to a standstill.[18]

Syria's second animated film for TV was made by Samir Jabr[19] when, in 1987, he produced *Ishārat Al-Murur* (*The Traffic Signal*), a short that instructs children about negotiating traffic. Jabr became a technical consultant for Syrian Arab TV after also having studied film directing at VGIK in Moscow. He completed his PhD in Art Sciences (Cinematography) in 1984. During their studies, he and a group of other animators, among them Mwaffaq Katt, lobbied for the development of an animation department for Syrian TV. 'It was not easy,' he says. 'We tried between 1981 and 1984 to convince the Director-General, who did not give his okay until 1985.'[20] Syrian TV then formed a partnership with Neilson Hordell Ltd in London to import and export animation for television. Jabr's focus, however, was on creating homegrown short children's animations. In the early 1990s, Jabr became the chairman of the animation department of Syrian Arab TV, a position he held until 1998, after which he made no other animated films.[21]

No cinematic animations, that is animations made for cinema screening, were produced until the mid-1990s, when the NFO turned its hand to co-productions. The NFO's lack of interest in Syrian animation long remained debilitating for artists working outside television, until private companies began to garner global festival success. Moreover, formal training in animation remained unavailable. The craft of animation was learned

From Animated Cartoons to Suspended Animation

(or discovered) either abroad, or through advertising and other commercial uses, rather than by artistic experiment. It was these commercial avenues that provided training opportunities, internships and jobs for artists, cartoonists and filmmakers.

When the NFO decided to try its hand at animation in the early 1990s, two filmmakers stood out. Abdul-Mouein Oyoun Al-Soud, who created *Feeto* (*Veto*) in 1991 and *Pardon Me, Mr. X* in 1993.[22] Born in Homs in 1945, he studied theatre and film directing in Sofia, Bulgaria, at the Higher Institute for Dramatic Arts. Upon returning to Syria he found work as a teacher at the Higher Institute of Theatrical Arts in Damascus. He made films (not all animated) with the NFO, but drove his political critiques a little too far. The NFO neither approved of his treatment of 'non-permissible' topics, nor condoned his creative vision for a feature length film, and Al-Soud moved abroad to Kuwait.[23]

The other NFO filmmaker, Nasser Naasani, made *The Baton* in 1994 and *He and She* in 1995, the latter winning the Gold Award at the Damascus Film Festival in 1995. *He and She* uses as its inspiration the male and female symbols of toilet signs, and is an experimental short poking fun at the segregation of sexes, once again employing metaphor as a safety valve to avoid more serious political issues. A tragic personification of Syrian animation's spiral into stasis, Naasani died during the Syrian revolution. The abrupt end to his career leaves us with a small body of work by an artist who failed to reach his full potential, yet who still exerts a considerable impact on those animating in Syria today.[24]

In the mid-1990s, the NFO opened up to collaborations with small, independent studios. Star Animation and Tiger Production in particular stand out. The mission statements of these studios reveal a central preoccupation with education and children, and thus with family-friendly material.[25] Tiger Production, a privately-owned company headed by Mannaa Hijazi, produced educational cartoons encouraging social responsibility and reflecting Arab sensibilities, customs and culture.

But the first company to start independent activities in animation was Al Najm, or Star Animation, set up in 1995. As the first independent studio in Syria – and since there were no other facilities – Star Animation became the default training ground for animators, including Sulafa Hijazi. The company continues to produce children's animated media, still with an

Animation in the Middle East

eye on family values and cross-cultural awareness. They were the first studio to create an animated film of substantial length, producing a 52-minute film entitled *The Jar: A Tale from the East* in 1999, directed by Ammar Al-Shorbaji and produced by Tahsin Mzaik.[26] It is a moralistic tale, teaching its young audiences about the struggle between good and evil.

The Jar is an adaptation of an ancient Islamic story. Set in a rural village, the story begins when a poor family discovers a lost treasure, contained in a jar. A jealous neighbour thwarts their attempts to return the jar to its rightful owner. It is clear from the outset that the neighbour is going to cause problems: he is depicted as a typical villain, with green skin, a big wart on his nose, large crooked teeth and a high-pitched, mean voice, and he is abusive to his donkey. The family in possession of the jar, meanwhile, are depicted in colourful traditional clothes, with a healthy skin colour, and living in harmony with their animals on their farm. While a lot of care obviously went into the character design, criticism of *The Jar* has been aimed directly at the film's 'Western' point of view, criticism that is only sharpened by it being one of the few Arab animated films to have had a successful run in the US, through Fine Media Group.[27] In 2004, Star Animation changed its name to EmariToons and moved to the United Arab Emirates, to become one of the largest in-house animation studios in the region.[28]

These studios' emphasis on 'wholesome entertainment' and explicit adherence to particular moral values and educational tones, is directly related to continued NFO censorship. Animated films have been seen as agents of socialisation in that they may 'provide children with the necessary tools to reinforce expectations about normalized [...] dynamics.'[29] That studios were moved abroad due to a lack of freedom of expression in Syria, illustrates both the power of film and the Syrian government's difficulties facing criticism of any kind.[30]

A stand-out independent initiative in the early 2000s was the work of Akram Agha. One of the most visionary animators from Syria, Agha made two political shorts before the Arab Spring: *Intibah* (*Attention*) in 2005 and *Hidā Al-Jinrāl* (*The General's Boot*) in 2008.[31] His work is more activist-oriented than that of any Syrian animator to date. In *Attention* marching guns overrun golden children as an empty swing takes on the rhythm of the march. While not necessarily made for children, it shows a preoccupation with the young, denouncing how the children must endure endless

114

From Animated Cartoons to Suspended Animation

5.1 Still from *The General's Boot*, directed by Akram Agha (2008)

violence during wartime. A mix of pen-drawn and computer-generated images, this film – like Katt's *Tale of Two Nails* – laments the fate of all innocents in wartime.

The General's Boot is a 17-minute short and, like *Attention*, a one-man effort that took around a year to make. The film illustrates a narrative of dictatorship and freedom by once more utilising the safety valve of the metaphor, so convenient for Syrian cinema, through the use of animated footwear, as seen in image 5.1.[32] As the guns did in *Attention*, so here, black, shiny army boots take on the identity of the leader, becoming representative of authoritarianism while worn-out shoes are the oppressed. Agha considers history as a chain of repeating cycles, enabling him to predict the end of one cycle and the beginning of a new one.[33] Agha's timing with *The General's Boot* was both deliberate and serendipitous: he uploaded the film to YouTube in 2011 just as the Tunisian and Egyptian revolutions ended and only a few days before the Syrian revolution began. Agha says he wanted to send a message to his Arab audience that the success of a revolution does not necessarily mean the making of a civilised country.[34] Self-taught and now working in Cairo, he aspires to produce his first feature-length independent animated film about the Syrian revolution.[35]

As these works show, radical improvements in the animation industry and in the private sector arrived just before the revolution. And the same was true for the public sector: in the early 2000s the NFO expressed an interest in animation as well. As a result several co-productions between state and independent studios, including the first two feature-length animated films produced in Syria, saw the light of day: Razam Hijazi's *The Thread of Life* (2005) and Sulafa Hijazi's *Tujur Al-Yasmīn* (*The Jasmine Birds*, 2009) were co-produced by Tiger Production and the NFO.

The Hijazi Family: From Edutainment to Political Dissent

Born in Damascus, Sulafa Hijazi is a prolific visual artist, director and producer of animated films. She studied drama at the Higher Institute of the Dramatic Arts in Damascus, and art at the Städelschule Art Academy in Frankfurt Am Main, Germany.[36] Hijazi started her animation career in 1997 at the Al-Zahra Studio (Venus Studio) as a dubber of foreign animation, mostly Anime, but she became more interested in producing animation with a local flavour – so that children could see their own world reflected on the screen – and so set up the free-to-satellite channel SpaceToon.[37] She established her own company, Blue.Dar, in 2010, with the same aim of producing locally-relevant educational TV series, films and other media aimed at children.[38]

This inclination to create original, local content is the consistent thread through Hijazi's career, and she says she is most interested in discovering what an 'Arab identity on screen' means in terms of animation.[39] Most of the work she has created is in serial format, and co-produced by Blue.Dar and foreign production companies (in the Gulf). She has created a feature-length animation film for children, *The Jasmine Birds* (2009), and her second feature-length film, *The Foxy Rabbit*, is currently in pre-production. Now living and working in Frankfurt, she is also developing her first experimental animated short for adults, based on one of her drawings.

The first feature-length animated Syrian film was Hijazi's sister Razam's *The Thread of Life*, from 2005. It tells the story of a young boy, Alaa, who finds a magic thread that catapults him into the future. Mannaa Hijazi says Tiger Production's aim with this film was to create an animation firmly rooted in Middle Eastern and Arab culture, but with international appeal: 'It was crucial to the team that the environment, character traits and the language were recognisable to the local audiences'. Co-production with the NFO enabled the filmmakers to take advantage of public subsidies, thus ensuring that 'the cost of production was significantly lower than it would have been if the film had been produced outside Syria.'[40] The Hijazis decided to work with the NFO in response to its longer-term vision for the Syrian animation industry and continued to co-produce feature-length films, among them the award-winning *The Jasmine Birds* a few years later.[41]

This desire to reflect an Arab identity and creating a recognisably 'Arab look' for her work by combining tradition with education in animation drives her. She recognises the wide diversity of the Arab world but insists on finding common denominators and making her characters and their environments location-specific. In her quest to create homegrown Arab edutainment for children regionally, she has also produced serials such as *Data City* (2004): 22 episodes of 30 minutes each, with a mix of diverse animation styles and live-action, aimed at six to twelve year-olds.[42] In *Bayti Al-Arabi* (*My Arab House*), produced by Al-Jazeera Children's Channel,[43] puppets present different clips of animation with a view to educating children in politics and history, using various types of folk music recognisable to Al-Jazeera's Saudi audiences. Her latest series, *Malsoun.org* (2012) was also produced by the Gulf Cooperation Council, and explored puppet animation further.[44] This series is an ongoing success story, and deals with a creature living inside a website who explains the world to children who are home alone as their professional parents stay at work late. For the characterisation in *Malsoun.org*, Hijazi sought inspiration in photographs of kids from different regions of the Arab world. Likewise, for the backgrounds she took inspiration from local textures, traditional arts such as calligraphy, and furnishings and accessories typical in Gulf houses.

Hijazi's first feature-length animated film was the 2009 *The Jasmine Birds*. Like *The Thread of Life* it was co-produced by Tiger Production and the NFO. As a 2D low-budget production, it took a few more risks than *The Thread of Life* by attempting tentative political criticism. The story focuses on a settlement of Jasmine Birds, representing Damascus (historically known as the Jasmine City), where a young orphan bird wishes to complete his father's final quest to find the cure for his fellow-birds' mysterious disease. He learns that because his father's legacy lives on in him, he need not feel himself truly orphaned. At first glance it is typical Hijazi edutainment, with lessons about family values and heroism. But, as with the more subversive political live-action films of the late 1980s, this film uses its allegorical nature (birds), its medium (fictional animation) and its claimed intended audience (children) as safety valves in order to bypass the censor. The film contains a love story between two young birds, but it also contains some subtle political commentary: one of the communities of birds consists of 700 ministers and 7 citizens, reflecting Syria's proclivity for bureaucracy, empty political discourse and a lack of interest in its citizens.[45]

What Hijazi spent the most time on, and what she remains very interested in, is that the characterisation of her protagonists be recognisable as local and Arab by her young local Arab audience. She emphasises typical Arab physical characteristics such as thick brows for the male characters, while mascara and kohl eye-liner are used on the female characters' eyes. She also employs geometric, Islamic art as inspiration for her decorations, and the texture of the backgrounds is calligraphic. Fauna and flora are inspired by patterns known from Fatima's Hand, which she claims as an inclusive and universally recognisable symbol for Arabs everywhere.[46] This sensitivity towards the diversity in meaning of the symbols and signs used in her animated films reveals her concern with local identity formation, and displays the subtle impact her designs can have upon their narrative power.

Hijazi's most recent foray into feature-length animation has been titled *The Foxy Rabbit*.[47] The film is in its pre-production stages, but due to the on-going conflict, and her exile, the project has come to a standstill. It is projects such as these that have directly impacted on the power of Hijazi's own political outlook on animation. While there are some subversive, if allegorical elements to *The Jasmine Birds*, most of her work has indeed been child-friendly edutainment that has eschewed political commentary. But the revolution has radicalised her. In a 2012 interview with the DOHA Institute, she said:

> Animation is such a beautiful language, with vivid imagination, and it can translate creative ideas with endless options. There are lots of ideas that I'd like to express through this medium. I am currently working on an animation film for adults on the concept of freedom, reflecting on what we're going through at the moment. I have a lot to say in that regard.'[48]

While these ideas have not yet materialised due to exile and personal trauma, her artistic developments reveal that political activism is now central, with a clear shift in style and approach. Her anger is foregrounded, and became especially fervent in 2012, when her sister was imprisoned and her brother arrested. Hijazi is now an overt critic of the Assad government. Her illustrations attest to this. Whereas before the revolution she was obliged to work with the NFO, in exile she creates polemical and, in some cases, shocking images.[49] The conflict in Syria has arguably freed her from her inhibitions as well as from the censor, but it has also brought her animation both figuratively and literally to a standstill. Not only is *The Foxy Rabbit* on hold, but she now concentrates her artwork on the production of illustrations and cartoons. She told me: 'my work revolves around the impact of conflict on children, and the consequences of excessive exposure to violence, weapons and torture.'[50] However, children are now subjects, no longer the audience, and their plight elicits a deep affect in the spectator. That so much injustice is perpetrated on children in Syria is foremost on Hijazi's mind. Her artwork has lost its 'anima' – its life and its movement – and the still images demand reflection and mediation. This move from animated movement *for* children to still, frozen images *about* children is most evident in her illustrations of children in war on merry-go-rounds, in tanks and in pregnant guns (see image 5.2).

A new project, still in its pre-production stages, *Masturbation*, will be her first experimental short film for adults. The film continues from one of her illustrations, where an anonymous male figure is masturbating with a machine gun as his phallus. It is not only an indictment of the male-centred macho rule of Assad's wartime government, but also an exposure of that self-centred lust for power. The image is a direct reflection of the stasis of the revolution and the planned film a rehearsal for the reigniting of uncensored, independent animation in Syria. Hijazi treads in the footsteps of Samir Jabr, Mwaffaq Katt and other pioneers, who used this stasis to move beyond the power of the NFO. Having gone into exile, these animators have now either stopped animating, or have moved into un-animated art; into cartoons, caricatures, illustrations and other artwork. The national censorship and its delineation of what animation could contain has resulted in a transnational, uncontainable, but static depiction of the suffering of Syrians.

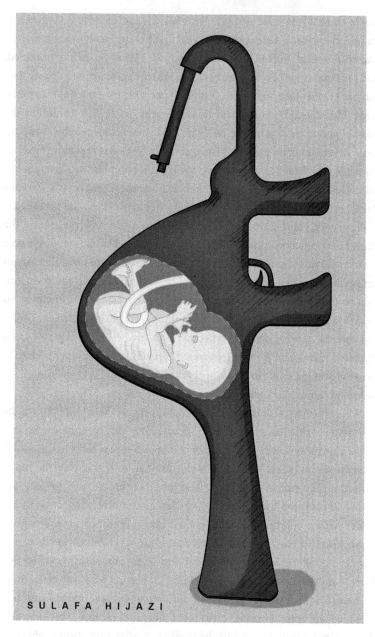

5.2 *Untitled* (2012), digital print by Sulafa Hijazi

The Syrian Revolution and Animated Suspension

The so-called 'Arab Spring' has had major consequences for artists' freedom of expression across the Middle East. Syrian artists in particular have found that it has resulted in a breaking free from censorship *if* they work outside Syria. Artists in exile have chosen to produce works expressing opposition to the government either anonymously, on online platforms, or boldly signing them, in defiance of past censorship. The recent wars and revolutions have pushed these animators out of Syria (and Tunisia and Egypt) and onto the world stage, and with the world's gaze now firmly focused on the area, the changes in and radicalisation of their styles are on display.

Agha's ability to 'predict' the revolution and its cyclical nature, has evidently influenced the revolutionary work of Syrians Wael Toubaji (now based in Lebanon) and Khaled Abdulwahed (now based in Turkey). In Abdulwahed's animated short *Rasāsa* (*Bullet*, 2014),[51] a painted figure on a wall transforms into a bullet, a woman gives birth to a gun (as in one of Hijazi's illustrations) and black and white figures cause a bloodbath when they squeeze a butterfly/red heart to bursting point, the latter a visual intertextual reference to Agha's *Attention* and the blood on the walls in *The General's Boot*. The visual motif of a blood-soaked wall also features in Toubaji's *Yad Wahida* (*One Hand*, 2010).[52] Agha's boots return, as Toubaji's tiny soldier wears enormous boots to stamp out any life that attempts to grow from Syria's soil. However, the soldier fails and the buds grow into a huge tree of unified buds. With its message of bright hope, this is a marked contrast to Agha's and Abdulwahed's work.

Toubaji started his career as an animator after interning with Tiger Production in 2003. He now lives in Beirut, Lebanon, where he set up his own production house and works on collective projects. He sees animation as a tool for documenting the revolution, and as a therapeutic medium that can bring solidarity and hope to young people in the region. One of his collective initiatives, The Youth Rally Against Oppression, has resulted in films addressing the context of conflict, and uses animation as a tool in therapy. For him, 'activists [are] becoming increasingly creative and innovative in their tactics of civil resistance.'[53] The result has been two animated films, *They Have Children* (2014) and *No Difference* (2014),[54] in which

Assad and the terrorist group ISIS are linked to each other. In spite of having to work with a small team and low budget, and with the need to share work quickly and widely, these are highly sophisticated films that are not only subversive in their content but also highly political in their look. Rana in *They Have Children* records a video message demanding from terrorists that they return her kidnapped father, so turning the medium of preference for terrorists into a medium of resistance and empowerment. In *No Difference* the military leaders of Syria are depicted as little green men and the leaders of ISIS as little grey men, both in a shape reminiscent of satirical series such as *South Park*, and the only sound they utter is 'blah blah blah', ridiculing the nonsensical discourse of both parties in the conflict.

More activist collectives have an engaged online presence, using animation as a tool for therapy. Estayqazat (Wake Up), a feminist association working on women's rights and the legislation for women in Syria (now based in Lebanon), has produced a trilogy of short animated documentaries entitled *Trilogy of Voice* (2014). The films give voice to women testifying about torture and trauma and use animation to visualise their emotions while allowing them to remain anonymous. The trilogy raises awareness of the violent actions that have taken place in the name of the regime, and depict (personal) acts of subversion and emancipation. Where for Annabelle Honess Roe, animation is often used as a substitute for something that is not or is no longer there, here animation is a way for these collectives to depict what *is* still there but has been denied depiction.

Conclusion: Exile and Transnational Suspension

To sum up, then, in Syria, as in other places in the region, animation and its broader appreciation arrived rather late. Even then, due to strict censorship laws and a lack of infrastructure, it was not until the 1980s that television became interested in the form, at a time when cartooning had enormous popular appeal. Using the safety valves of fiction, metaphor and a young intended audience, filmmakers have actively sought to avoid censorship proscriptions. The source of that censorship, the NFO, became increasingly interested in working with independent studios that had been successful in creating serials and formats exported to the Gulf States. A search for an inclusive yet heterogeneous Arab identity in animation was foremost on the agenda for some, and exports as well as serials made for a home audience found their own voice and look. While the first feature-length films were co-produced with the NFO, artists also carefully crossed lines into taboo subjects, and just before the revolution broke out in Syria animation had taken an innovative, confident route. Now animation artists (in exile) who have shaped strong transnational networks that exist across time and space, tracing intertextual references through their works and pioneering cross-border collaborations, whether individually or collectively, have brought their art to a standstill, evoking the stasis of the revolution and its aftermath by returning their art to its origins in static images.

A final case in point is Yasmeen Fenari who briefly worked as an animator at Star Animation and made her first independent film, *Shabab Souri* (*Syrian Youth*), in 2008.[55] *Syrian Youth* is an experiment visualising the dreams of a young man. The sequence pictures the frustrations of the figure as he tires of urban destruction and buzzing flies and runs into a dead-end street, where he slams into a wall; a quite literal abrupt end to youthful enthusiasm. Similarly, Fenari's work has come to a full stop. Like Hijazi she now creates illustrations and poster art. Her piece 'Vomit' shows men and women spewing forth words such as 'Lies' and 'Shame' into the form of the Syrian flag, an indictment of a government that has indoctrinated its people with lies and shame for the sake of a perceived national identity.

In her documentary *Comme si nous attrapions un cobra* (*As If We Were Catching a Cobra*, 2012), Hala Alabdallah studies the phenomenon of cartoonists and illustrators working across borders in order to comment on the 'Arab Spring'. She interviews Ali Ferzat about his 'permissible' work in the past, and invites him to reflect on how young Syrian artists have been unable to be politically outspoken. Ferzat himself suffered under attacks from the regime, and his healing process inspires younger generations to continue their work. While there was no 'rapport' between young artists and the press beforehand, since the revolution a thriving network of young caricaturists interested in practicing, and making it possible for others to practice their freedom of speech has sprung up.[56] If Agha's conception of history as cycles is correct, then with current animation artists' forays into poster art, illustrations, stencils and cartoons, perhaps we are witnessing in their 'suspended animation' a mere pause before a new, reinvigorated expression of dissent and subversion gets them and their work on the move again.

Notes

1. El-Mustafa Lahlali, *Contemporary Arab Broadcast Media* (Edinburgh, 2013), p. 23.
2. As is the case in many young post-colonial states, the Syrian NFO propagated a state-nationalism by having filmmakers document and hail the achievements of the state. This resulted in the initial production of many didactic documentaries, especially suitable for television, including a film by Syria's most hailed subversive documentarist, the late Omar Amiralay, who later regretted his involvement, as becomes clear in the dialogue between two of his films, *Film Essay on the Euphrates Dam* (1970) and *A Flood in Baath Country* (2003).
3. Rasha Salti, *Insights into Syrian Cinema. Essays and conversations with contemporary filmmakers* (New York, NY, 2006), p. 30.
4. Miriam Cooke, *Dissident Syria: Making Oppositional Arts Official* (Durham, NC, 2007), p. 5.
5. Cooke, *Dissident Syria*, p. 15.
6. Ibid., p. 17.
7. Lisa Wedeen, 'Tolerated Parodies of Politics in Syria', Josef Gugler (ed.), *Film in the Middle East and North Africa: Creative Dissidence* (Austin, TX, 2011 [1999]), p. 105.
8. Lisa Wedeen, 'Tolerated Parodies', p. 104.
9. Comic4Syria, 'Cocktail', Malu Halasa, Zaher Omareen and Nawara Mahfoud (eds), *Syria Speaks. Art and Culture from the Frontline* (London, 2014), p. 181.
10. For more information and interviews with Ferzat, see Hala Alabdallah's documentary *As If We Were Catching a Cobra* (2012).
11. A selection of his cartoons can be viewed in the Ali Ferzat gallery on *The Guardian* website. Available at http://www.theguardian.com/world/gallery/2013/aug/19/ali-ferzat-cartoons-in-pictures (accessed 3 May 2015).
12. Dave Stelfox, 'Ali Ferzat, cartoonist in exile', *The Guardian* (19 August 2013). Available at http://www.theguardian.com/world/2013/aug/19/ali-ferzat-cartoonist-exile-syria (accessed 3 May 2015).
13. Ali Ferzat, 'Two cartoons', *Syria Speaks*, pp. 169–70.
14. Mohamed Ghazala, *Animation in the Arab World* (Saarbrücken, 2011), p. 11.
15. *The Tale of Two Nails* is on YouTube. Available at https://www.youtube.com/watch?v=ZqxF5Cp9G_g (accessed 3 May 2015). Cuneiform is one of the earliest known systems of writing, distinguished by its wedge-shaped marks on clay tablets, reminiscent of nails in their shape. This film won the award of the Arab Film Critics and a Special Mention from the Jury at the Damascus Film Festival.
16. Another of Katt's animated shorts, *One Thousand and One Images* (1996), won the First Prize at the Cairo Film Festival for Children's Cinema, the Bronze Award for shorts at the Carthage Film Festival and the Golden Award in

Plastic Arts at the Festival in Tunis. A reference to this film can be found in Roy Armes' *Dictionary of Arab Filmmakers of the Middle East* (p. 96), a rare occasion on which an animated short film has made it into a popular encyclopedic overview of cinema.

17. *The Eleventh Commandment* is on Vimeo. Available at https://vimeo.com/50391263 (accessed 3 May 2015).

18. Katt posts a new political caricature on his Facebook page every day.

19. Samir Jabr's website and CV can be found online. Available at http://www.shaamfilm.com/index_e.html (accessed 3 May 2015).

20. Interview with Samir Jabr, 3 May 2015.

21. Since then, he has worked as a university lecturer at universities in Syria and Libya, and now works in the Department of Cinema & TV at the Al-Ahliyya University in Amman, Jordan. Interview, 19 February 2015.

22. *Pardon Me, Mr. X* was awarded the Certificate of Merit from the Hiroshima Festival in Japan, and a Special Jury Mention at the Damascus Film Festival. Al-Soud later received a certificate of appreciation from the Guild of Fine Arts for his efforts in the development of animation art in Syria.

23. When the Ministry of Higher Education of the State of Kuwait invited him, he moved there and now teaches in the Department of Acting and Directing Theater at the Higher Institute of Dramatic Art in Kuwait.

24. I spoke to Naasani's collaborators on *The Baton*, Marwan Alkarjousli and on *He & She*, Cumai Aboul Housn. Aboul Housn has dedicated a Facebook page to Naasani in order to bring together his work in animation and illustration, some of which has been lost in the NFO archives.

25. Stefanie Van de Peer, 'Fragments of War and Animation: Dahna Abourahme's *Kingdom of Women* and Soudade Kaadan's *Damascus Roofs*', *Middle East Journal of Culture and Communication*, 6 (2013), pp. 151–70.

26. *The Jar: A Tale from the East* is on YouTube. Available at https://www.youtube.com/watch?v=oWTEBdzf_cI (accessed 3 May 2015).

27. FMG has gone on to produce more animated films about aspects of Islam and the Arab world aimed at young US audiences, and with a clear agenda about educating them about Islam, with films such as *Before the Light* (2014), *Great Women of Islam* (2013), and *Muhammad, The Last Prophet* (2002).

28. EmariToons' motto is: Action without violence; Excitement without adult themes; Imagination without black magic'. Available at http://www.emaritoons.com (accessed 3 May 2015).

29. C. Richard King, Carmen R. Lugo-Lugo and Mary K. Bloodsworth-Lugo, *Animating Difference: Race, Gender and Sexuality in Contemporary Films for Children* (Lanham, MD, 2010), p. 11.

30. Newer studios Blue.Dar, Ox Animation, and ProAction Film were vibrant, young animation studios whose activities, due to the present conflict, have been suspended (Blue.Dar), are virtually non-existent (Tiger Productions

125

and ProAction Film), or have moved to safer countries, most notably the Gulf States (Star Animation became EmariToons and moved to the United Arab Emirates, as did Ox Animation). For an in-depth discussion of Ox Animation's work, see Van de Peer, 'Fragments of War and Animation.'

31. *Attention* (2005) and *The General's Boot* (2008) are on YouTube. Available at https://www.youtube.com/watch?v=KmQ8Oni1pIM and https://www.youtube.com/watch?v=eDyP2WWYRJY (accessed 3 May 2015).

32. The film was inspired by the 'Odessa Steps' sequence from *Battleship Potemkin* (Sergei Eisenstein, 1925).

33. Interview with Akram Agha, 22 February 2015.

34. Since *The General's Boot*, Akram has worked in commercial animation and television serials, as, he says, in the Arab world 'animation is about industry, not so much about art'. The most popular series he has made are *Haret Abu-Hudejan*, 2007, *Kractoon*, 2010 and *Um Hudyjan*, 2009–10 for Saudi TV.

35. Interview with Akram Agha, 22 February 2015. He says that animation projects are expensive and that all available funding now tends to go to documentaries about the revolution, not to animation.

36. Sulafa Hijazi, 'Biography' [Sulafa Hijazi Webpage.] Available at http://sulafahijazi.com/index.html (accessed 3 May 2015).

37. Venus Centre (set up in the 1990s) specialises in dubbing foreign animation, mostly Anime, for television. Their focus is on the correct pronunciation of Classical Arabic and their editing made films more appropriate for Arab children. The company sells these edited films to a variety of Arab television channels as materials that are 'safe', localised, and educational. See also Chapter 3 on Saudi and Gulf animation.

38. Blue.Dar's website. Available at http://bluedar.net (accessed 3 May 2015).

39. Sulafa Hijazi, 'AniFest Lecture in Czech Republic' (April 2012). Availbale at https://www.youtube.com/watch?v=kcC0SdL8qh0 (accessed 3 May 2015).

40. Reuters, 'Syrian director Razam Hijazi produces an award-winning animated film for Syrian and Arab children', *ITN Source* (2 September 2007). Available at http://www.itnsource.com/en/shotlist/RTV/2007/09/12/RTV1353807/?v=1 (accessed 3 May 2015).

41. Feature-length animation has been a family affair in Syria, as Bahraa Hijazi, the younger sister of the clan, was also assistant director at Tiger Production. She was involved in Arab TV serials such as *My Arab House* (produced by Al-Jazeera, 2007–09). She worked as a Project Manager for *Critical Messages*, another prominent project aimed at children, produced for SpaceToon, and she produced an experimental short documentary in stop-motion entitled *The Soft Mountains* (2012). A clip of *The Soft Mountains* can be found on YouTube. Available at https://www.youtube.com/watch?v=0clMuivRTpM (accessed 3 May 2015).

From Animated Cartoons to Suspended Animation

42. *Data City* is available at https://www.youtube.com/watch?v=sCK-tE5I_YA (accessed 3 May 2015).
43. *My Arab House* is available at https://www.youtube.com/watch?v=YrWUTL8Zrpk (accessed 3 May 2015).
44. *Malsoun.org* is available at https://www.youtube.com/watch?v=fdt4QfTLiyg (accessed 3 May 2015).
45. This reminds of the Ali Ferzat cartoon 'Leaders and Workers', nrs 20 & 28. Available at http://creativesyria.com/farzat.htm (accessed 3 May 2015).
46. The Shia people see it as the representation of the Prophet's daughter, the Sunni Muslims see Fatma's hand as a religious symbol and the Maghreb Berbers see Fatima's Hand as a the representation of the Goddess of the Moon, Hijazi said in our interview.
47. Artwork for *The Foxy Rabbit* can be found online. Available at http://bluedar. net/contacts.html (accessed 3 May 2015).
48. DOHA Film Institute, 'People in Film: Sulafa Hijazi' [DOHA Film Institute Blog] (17 january 2012). Available at http://www.dohafilminstitute.com/blog/ people-in-film-sulafa-hijazi (accessed 3 May 2015).
49. Stefanie Van de Peer, 'National animation in Syria' [*Animation Studies 2.0* Blog] (5 May 2014). Available at http://blog.animationstudies.org/?p=779 (accessed 3 May 2015).
50. Interview with Sulafa Hijazi, 17 February 2015.
51. *Bullet* is on Vimeo. Available at https://vimeo.com/61096027 (accessed 3 May 2015).
52. *One Hand* is on Vimeo. Available at https://vimeo.com/41392534 (accessed 3 May 2015).
53. Syria Untold, 'Animated films in the face of oppression', *Syria Untold* (28 March 2014). Available at http://www.syriauntold.com/en/2014/04/animated-films-in-the-face-of-oppression/ (accessed 3 May 2015).
54. *They Have Children* and *No Difference* are on YouTube. Available at https://www.youtube.com/watch?v=RuwF1jiTi2I#action=share and https://www.youtube.com/watch?v=aJ4W1AoAiCA#action=share (accessed 3 May 2015).
55. *Syrian Youth* is on YouTube. Available at https://www.youtube.com/watch?v=6gh8uywBZfw (accessed 3 May 2015).
56. Festival Dei Popoli, 'Interview with Hala Alabdallah' on YouTube. Available at https://www.youtube.com/watch?v=bvLWcvENQdU (accessed 3 May 2015).

Filmography

Al-Muttaham Al-Baree' (*The Innocent Suspect*), directed by Rashid Jalal (1928).
Battleship Potemkin, directed by Sergei Eisenstein (1925).
Bayti Al-Arabi (*My Arab House*), directed by Sulafa Hijazi (2007–09).

Animation in the Middle East

Before the Light, directed by Richard Rich (2014).

Comme si nous attrapions un cobra (*As If We Were Catching a Cobra*), directed by Hala Alabdallah (2011).

Data City, directed by Sulafa Hijazi (2004).

Domtom Salemeen (*Be Well*), directed by Sulafa Hijazi (2002).

Fables of Bah Ya Bah 2, produced by EmariToons (2004).

Fables of Bah Ya Bah, produced by Star Animation (2000).

Feeto (*Veto*), directed by Abdul-Mouein Oyoun Al-Soud (1991).

Great Women of Islam, directed by Richard Rich (2013).

Haret Abu-Hudejan, directed by Akram Agha (2007).

He and She, directed by Nasser Naasani (1995).

Hidā Al-Jinrāl (*The General's Boot*), directed by Akram Agha (2008).

Hikāya Mismāriya (*A Tale of Two Nails: A Cuneiform Tale*), directed by Mwaffaq Katt (1991).

Intibah (*Attention*), directed by Akram Agha (2005).

Ishārat Al-Murur (*The Traffic Signal*), directed by Samir Jabr (1987).

Juha fi Al-Mahkameh (*Juha at Court*), directed by Mwaffaq Katt (1985).

Khait Alhayaa (*The Thread of Life*), directed by Razam Hijazi (2005).

Kractoon, directed by Akram Agha (2010).

Malsoun.org, directed by Sulafa Hijazi (2012).

Masturbation, directed by Sulafa Hijazi (unfinished).

Muhammad, The Last Prophet, directed by Richard Rich (2002).

No Difference, directed by Wael Toubaji (2014).

Nur wa Thalam (*Light and Darkness*), directed by Nazih Shahbandar (1947).

One Thousand and One Images, directed by Mwaffaq Katt (1996).

Pardon Me, Mr. X, directed by Abdul-Mouein Oyoun Al-Soud (1993).

Shabab Souri (*Syrian Youth*), directed by Yasmeen Fenari (2008).

Slot in Memory, directed by Khaled Abdulwahed (2014).

The Baton, directed by Nasser Naasani (1994).

The Bullet, directed by Khaled Abdulwahed (2014).

The Eleventh Commandment, directed by Mwaffaq Katt (2011).

The Foxy Rabbit, directed by Sulafa Hijazi (unfinished).

The Jar: A Tale from the East, directed by Ammar Al-Shorbaji (1999).

The Soft Mountains, directed by Bahraa Hijazi (2012).

They Have Children, directed by Wael Toubaji (2014).

Trilogy of Voice, produced by Estayqazat (2014).

Tuj, directed by Khaled Abdulwahed (2014).

Tujur Al-Yasmīn (*The Jasmine Birds*), directed by Sulafa Hijazi (2009).

Um Hudejan, directed by Akram Agha (2009–10).

Yad Wahida (*One Hand*), directed by Wael Toubaji (2010).

6

Cultivating an Arthouse Viewership: Lebanese Animation Audiences Grow Up

Lina Ghaibeh and George Khoury (Jad)

Lebanon is no stranger to cultural experimentation, having throughout its modern history been exposed to Western political, social and cultural influences. From cars to printing presses, theatres to coffee houses, Beirutis have seen and absorbed it all, and adapted to the realities of their eclectic culture. So it is no wonder that they saw their first motion picture in the Fleur de la Syrie Theatre in 1899, just a few years after the medium came into being. Nor is it any wonder that what became known as 'Le Petit-Paris'[1] under the French mandate in the 1920s continued to promote its image as 'The Switzerland of the East'[2] for decades thereafter.

Since, as one observer puts it, 'until the mid-70s, the Lebanese were universally known to represent the avant-garde in the Arab World'[3] it comes as no surprise that from the earliest days of independence, members of the Lebanese (mainly Beiruti)[4] public were exposed to all types of foreign motion pictures, including cartoons. Some films even appeared on Lebanese screens simultaneously with their opening dates in European capitals, as a local newspaper advertisement for the premier of Walt Disney's *Cinderella* tells us: the film opened at the Capitole theatre in Beirut, Christmas 1950 – the same day as in the 'major cities of Europe.'[5]

If the city audience – limited at the time – was familiar with feature-length cartoons, that experience was not shared at a national level, since movie theatres in the early days existed exclusively in the capital. The wider public had to wait for the introduction of Lebanon's first television station Compagnie Libanaise de Télévision (CLT, Channels 7 and 9) in 1959 to enjoy cartoons.[6] Remarkably, the very first broadcast included a 15-minute foreign cartoon segment following the news slot, which was the opening sequence, and this pattern continued for years. Although one can only speculate about the number of viewers at the time (there being no statistics on the number of TV sets per household) it was considered quite normal to encounter gatherings in front of TV shop windows, with crowds watching the black and white screens.[7] The short cartoons broadcast on the local TV channels were included as part of the contracts with major Anglo-American companies such as ITC, NBC, Screen Gems and CBS.[8] Because Channel 7 broadcasts in Arabic, and subtitles and dubbing were not available for cartoons at this point, multilingual viewers enjoyed them, sometimes relying on children for help with translation; but the cartoons of the times could be said to be mostly self-explanatory.

On 2 May 1962, another TV station, Télé-Orient (Channels 5 & 11), entered the arena. Unlike its predecessor, the partnership was solely with the American giant ABC.[9] Equipped with advanced technical gear, a sophisticated organisational structure provided by ABC, and a wide range of contracts with regional, emerging state-run TV channels,[10] Télé-Orient followed a pan-Arab strategy. The Lebanese dialect was replaced by classical Arabic in all local productions, and Arabic subtitling was introduced to foreign shows. With the introduction of colour television in October 1967, cartoons for children became a main component of the broadcast schedule of all four of Lebanon's commercial channels. While colour TV sets were rare, it is estimated that the number of black and white TV sets had reached 250,000 by 1967.[11] The most popular cartoons at this time were those featuring *Mighty Mouse, Heckle and Jeckle, Tom & Jerry* and *The Flintstones*, as well as *Bugs Bunny* and other *Looney Tunes* characters.

In the early 1970s, Beirut began to shift its role from importer to importer/exporter of cartoons in the Middle Eastern media scene. It retained this role throughout the civil war,[12] during which the two existing TV stations were forced to merge into a single broadcaster, half-owned by the government, with 4 channels under the name of Télé-Liban.[13] With a continuing pan-Arab approach and the heavy demand from Arab-world markets for cartoons series, Lebanese distributors turned to the Japanese animation industry (known for its high productivity, high variety and low costs compared to those in the US or Europe) for import of animation.[14] However, there were still no Lebanese producers of cartoons at this time.

Mainly aimed at an audience of toddlers and school-aged children, coincidentally, the first selected themes by these Japanese productions were gleaned from Arab cultural or heritage sources, such as Nippon Animation's *Adventures of Sinbad*[15] from the *One Thousand and One Nights* tales. Because children of that age group have limited reading skills, subtitling was soon replaced with dubbing. Two specialised Lebanese dubbing studios, FILMALI Production SAL and Studio Baalbek, dominated the market, employing renowned actors from local television series to produce the voiceovers.[16] Opening sequences were remixed with Arabic lyrics by local singers, some of whose careers were launched in this way by the widespread audience of the cartoons in Arabic. Names of main characters were also changed to fit the regional audience, while twists in stories and free translation were common practices. Dubbed Japanese animated series renowned for their influence on the generation of the 1970s were such hits as *Moghamarat Sindibad* (*Adventures of Sinbad*, 1978), *UFO Grandizer* (*Robot Grandizer Raids*, 1979), *Zeina wa Nahhoul* (*Maya the Honey Bee*, 1978), *Jungar* (*Astroganga*, 1979), *Jazeerat Al-Kanz* (*Animal Treasure Island*) and *Adnan wa Lina* (*Future Boy Conan*, 1979) among others.

Two chief factors distinguished the era between the late 1970s and the end of the civil war in the early 1990s. Firstly, television became the major (if not exclusive) medium for the spread of cartoons to thousands of young viewers, since most cinemas had closed. In Greater Beirut a couple of theatres were irregularly operational for audiences made up mainly of members of militias, and cartoons were not their favourite shows. Furthermore, cartoons on VHS were restricted to affluent and influential members of the public. Secondly, cartoons became hugely prominent as independent shows in the weekly TV schedules, occupying prime time slots even on some of the illegal TV stations that flourished after 1985, which were led by LBC (Lebanese Broadcast Company). As a result, cartoon series became part of the collective memory of the civil war.[17]

Future Television: Local Production – A Turning Point

In Lebanon, cartoons had previously been marked by two major limitations: they were directed at a strictly juvenile audience, and the themes were limited to areas of education or entertainment. A new player, Future Television, however, changed this perception from its first national broadcasts, even as it developed into a pan-Arab satellite TV station.[18] Future Television is a private TV station founded in 1992 that started broadcasting nationally in February 1993. Aware of the influence of the genre, and as part of its strategy to target youth, the station started airing a weekly prime-time cartoon after the Saturday evening news (soon to become daily after the news), with its social-political content targeting an adult viewership. To secure long-term production capacities, the station (which broadcast 24 hours a day) created an in-house animation department, which is still unique among TV stations in the region.

Kalil wa Dimn (1993) was the first locally produced adult cartoon series in Lebanon (and probably in the Arab world). It entailed the adaptation of an Arabic folktale, its anthropomorphic characters tackling issues of political and social content, such as, for example, issues of sectarian strife. George Khoury (Jad), a journalist and renowned comics artist and animator, was approached by the executive director of Future Television and asked to produce a daily animation with a political edge.

Khoury's initial team hailed from various backgrounds of comics, graphic and interior design, and was comprised of cartoonists who later also created series of their own: Lina Ghaibeh and Edgar Aho were joined in the mid-1990s by Fulvio Codsi and Bahij Jaroudi.[19] Aided by two young scriptwriters, Rabih Mroué and Fadi Abi-Samra,[20] the team produced *Taaleek Al-Yaoum* (*The Daily Comment*, 1995), a daily political cartoon commentary in the format of a news broadcast with the main character a news anchor, shown directly after the evening news. Whereas this show was the result of teamwork, the later series *Roussoum Mutaharrira* (*Freed Drawings*, 2001 and still running) focused on a weekly theme and was directed by a single animator per week. That formula, imposed by the necessity of daily deliverables and the short length of individual cartoons, gave each animator the freedom to express him/herself, thus developing a wide variety of styles and content, a diversity that became the trademark of the department.

As well as its daily contribution, and based on the audience these adult cartoons attracted, the animation team became an essential contributor to the station's promotional campaigns. During the political turmoil of the early part of the new millennium, the team spearheaded the station's involvement in the presidential election controversy of 2004 with *Mouzakkarat Kursi* (*Diary of a Chair*, 2004). The *Istiklal 05* (*Independence 05*, 2005) series played an influential role in the popular movement against the Syrian presence in Lebanon, the Cedar Revolution, and was followed a year later by the series *Kafa* (*Enough*, 2006), which took a stand against the Israeli War of 2006.

What is remarkable is that the production of the department was not limited to 2D cel animation, but ventured into claymation with a series of promotion shorts entitled *Ata* (1997–present), but the high cost of the sets and production made it infrequent. With limited technical resources for that specific genre, the animation team had to rely on personal know-how, developing solutions from what was available. Based on humorous scripts, with sets related to popular landmarks in Beirut, *ATA*, the everyman clay character, entered the minds and hearts of thousands of viewers to such a point that he became synonymous with the TV station's identity. One cannot end the story of Future Television without mention of the short-lived series *Al-Watwat wa Al-Sununu* (*The Bat and the Robin*, 2004), a daily three-minute soap-opera parody, based on the Rotoscope technique, which ended after three months.[21]

The Future Television experience was a turning point for the regional production of cartoons. As has been noted, in addition to their work for television, animators from the team went on to create their own independent shorts or series: *Alf Yawm wa Yawm* (*1001 Days*, George Khoury, 2000) is considered the first short movie locally produced, and received regional and international critical recognition.[22] Tackling the issue of censorship in Lebanon under the Syrian occupation in the new millennium, the movie was inspired by the structure and the storytelling of the ever-popular *One Thousand and One Nights*, throwing its main character into daily hassles with the secret police. At the same time, Lina Ghaibeh began to tackle women's issues in animation. The first female animator in Lebanon, her *7 Days a Week* (2000) focuses on the problems a working mother faces in her daily life, while, with a more general concern for humanity, her *Sad Man* (2002) is a depiction of a re-occurring scene on different days with different problems and different outcomes. In *Ya Waladi* (*My Son*, 2006), Ghaibeh follows the daily route of a mother to the city centre holding the image of her missing son during the war. With a style that holds her signature sad cartoon-like characters, dwelling in a dark, yet somehow familiar urban setting, the short film acted as a catalyst in the public awareness regarding the cause of 'the disappeared'. Her most famous piece, *Burj El-Mur: Tower of Bitterness* (2012), is a departure from her cartoonlike-character style and linear narrative to a more serious, gritty and fragmented vision. A film about an abandoned landmark building in Beirut that was a notorious sniper hideout during the 15-year civil war, *Burj El-Mur* was inspired by Ghaibeh's daily view from her balcony of this unfinished and uninhabited building; and by her interest in the consequences of war not only for people but for buildings and the art of architecture. Ghaibeh made the movie as homage to those killed, tortured or disappeared during that war in Lebanon. Surreal events unfold in the spaces of *Burj El-Mur*, and its dark walls recall memories long forgotten with gritty lines and darkly textured scenes (see image 6.1). The

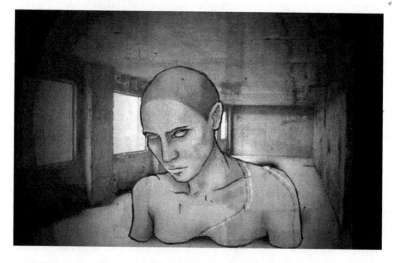

6.1 Still from *Burj El-Mur: Tower of Bitterness*, directed by Lina Ghaibeh (2012)

movie established her as a reference figure in the Beirut animation scene, and her shorts continue to be screened at international festivals.

Edgar Aho's series *The Dictator* (2003) similarly became a landmark in Lebanese animation. Although the subject matter is very serious, Aho manages through his animation and illustration skills, his aptitude for stylisation and his broad imagination, to make it funny and powerful.[23] A master of his craft and renowned for the surrealistic and Oriental influences in his work, he was an integral member and beloved and long-time friend of the Future Television team. His sudden death in 2003 was felt as a great loss by both the team and the wider Lebanese animation scene.

With the advent of a new millennium, Bahij Jaroudi joined the animation department at Future Television. As a young talented animator with an illustration and graphic design background, Jaroudi added new inspiration to the station's production. His work for TV and his independent shorts, *El-Toro Azul* (2008), *The Facts in the Case of Mr. Valdemar* (2009) and *Isabelle* (2010), introduced a distinctive style: his trademark peculiar characters influenced by 1950s cartoon aesthetics, his eerie landscapes and his fluid and detailed movements. Jaroudi's work is also well-known for its impeccable sound design, undoubtedly influenced by his extended conservatoire training and love of music.

Building an Infrastructure: Getting Academia on Board

Future Television's success story in making animation a major component of its branding, spread a signal to a post-civil war generation eager to venture into this new medium. The buzz that the short films created among the audience, opened wide the demand for skilled animators from other broadcasters and advertising companies. The animation experience of Future Television produced qualified animators who were ready to translate their practice into academic courses and training opportunities, answering the demand for skilled animators within Lebanon. The advancement of computers and the new relatively accessible animation tools provided by affordable and specialised software (as archaic as they may now seem) made this shift possible.

It was therefore no surprise that academic institutions (the main source of technicians who fuel the specialised market) began offering animation courses as part of their existing graphic design or audio-visual programmes. The American University of Beirut (AUB) took the lead, offering two courses on animation and motion graphics headed by Lina Ghaibeh. The graphic design programme in AUB started specialised courses in 1995 and over the years graduated a generation of TV graphic designers and animators who played a central role in the re-launch of pan-Arab TV stations across the Arab world, mainly in the Gulf region. The Lebanese American University (LAU) followed four years later, offering similarly tailored courses under the direction of George Khoury,[24] which later expanded to form part of a minor degree in Digital Media. The animation courses offered at these universities, however, are still to develop into fully-fledged programmes in animation.

It was not until the early 2000s that other universities took things further and developed their own programmes. Notre Dame University (NDU) established an animation programme in 2001, as part of the faculty of Sciences, naming it Computer Graphics & Animation (CGA),[25] and augmenting their visual arts and graphic design programme, which included courses in animation, with a three-year multimedia design focus.[26] Soon after, in 2003, the Lebanese Academy of Art (ALBA) started an animation degree and later introduced a Masters degree in animation under the direction of Alain Brenas, Michel Lamia and Emile Adaimy.[27] There were two streams offered at ALBA: 2D oriented animation at the School of Visual Arts, and 3D at the School of Advertising. The Université Saint Esprit at Kaslik (USEK) collaborated with the Institute of Technology in setting up their animation programme, offering it as part of their gamification and interactive media section. In addition to setting up the laboratories, DigiPen played an important role in providing training for the students and in offering employment to graduates. This formula worked quite well and developed an active group of game animators.[28] When DigiPen closed down in Lebanon, some employees left the country and joined the firm in the States, while others started their own gamification firms, such as Reine Abbas and Ziad Feghali, who opened Wixel Studios in Lebanon. In 2008, Abbas and Feghali wrote the curriculum for USEK's Master of Arts programme, which has been offered since 2009.[29] These collaborations

Cultivating an Arthouse Viewership

between professionals and academics, and a shift to the hiring of professionals as academics on university-level training courses, reveal the need for the further development of a broadening skillset in a rapidly expanding sector.

Animation d'auteur: Disorder and Reorganisation

Although the pioneering animation professionals in Lebanon were either self-taught or had studied animation abroad, most of the new generation arrived via local university programmes. Exploring the field to its fullest, animators ventured into a variety of animation genres and media: from music videos and TV commercials to awareness campaigns; from 2D classic cel animation to 3D modelling, stop-motion and video compositing. Of those who have ventured beyond the advertising and TV commercial stream, some have entered the category known as *animation d'auteur*, or auteur animator.

Ghassan Halwani's original style of depicting his own troubled inner world has marked out a difference among the newcomers. Halwani's *Jabal Tarek* (*Gibraltar*, 2005) is a combined pixilation and hand-drawn animation, revolving around a man with no roots or heritage in search of absolute freedom after a disappearance, while his *Takhabbot* (*Thrashing*, 2009) presents two lives lived side-by-side in Beirut, a city of perpetual mutation.[30] Lena Merhej's stark black and white *Drawing the War* (2002) reflects a vision of a whole generation affected by the civil war, as does her contribution to the roughly-drawn *Another Year* (2008), a series of animation spots for the day of solidarity with the Palestinian people.[31] This vision is also mirrored in her animated two-tone scenes using Naji Al-Ali's work in Dahna Abourahme's film *Ein El-Hilweh: Kingdom of Women*, a documentary about the women of the Ein El-Hilwe Palestinian refugee camp in southern Lebanon.

Others have chosen a more humorous approach to the war. Jad Sarout's *Zeid and Leila* (2009) stands out with its fast-paced animation, clean lines and modern love story. With daring nude scenes, Sarout depicts a bored couple who, having been killed in an explosion, begin a fierce race to heaven as ghosts. Jad Sarout and Chadi Aoun founded Yelostudio, an independent animation studio in 2009. Sarout's classmate at the Académie Libanaise des

137

Beaux-Arts, Chadi Aoun pays homage to his city, Beirut, through the fluid-action animation of a belly dancer in his short *Hawa* (*Wind*, 2007).

David Habchi, a multidisciplinary artist with a highly individualistic style, has made his name in the field of stop-motion and puppet animation in parallel with 2D cel animation. *Wehde* (*Loneliness*, 2011) is a 2D stop-motion play on the Arabic words 'loneliness' and 'unity', while his *Fouad* (2013) is an impressive short dedicated to the cause of the 17,000 people still missing as a result of the war. Habchi was one of the few artists to introduce animation as an exclusive component of music videos. His contribution to the hip-hop band Ashekman's media output was an essential component of their popular song *Ya Reit* (*I Wish*, 2013), illustrated in the signature high contrast dark and sombre style of Fouad Mezher, and directed by Michel Karshouny.

These animations are made doubly interesting by the fact that they were driven to completion by the auteurs'/animators' own passions and determination, in their own time and with self-procured sources of funding. The Lebanese government, suffering from enormous post-war national debt, did not consider the growth of an animation sector to be one of its priorities. Television stations follow their own agendas, driven by the supposed demands of large audiences, with short personal artistic cartoons being considered elitist. Indeed, to the broader audience, cartoons are generally perceived as a product for children. If anything could tempt the broadcasters, it would need to be based on a long-term, lucrative investment such as in an animated series or in feature-length movies. In Lebanon such projects lack the necessary manpower to accomplish all the steps required for their production, making the attraction of dubbed foreign cartoons the more lucrative option.

Auteur-animators, marked by their individualistic experimentations in style, genre and targeted audience, have played a major role in introducing diversified techniques and themes into local production. They have, in turn, been influenced by international trends in experimental and artistic cartoons produced for select audiences and closely monitor current innovations in the field. This is a process that started early during the civil war, with the organisation of periodic special screenings and workshops, led mainly by European cultural centres, before spreading to university campuses. These encounters motivated various groups of aficionados to attempt to inspire a gradual increase in public interest in animation through a variety of specialised events, workshops and screenings, including their own productions. Although many of these attempts were fleeting, with no continuity, one collective, Waraq, founded in 2013, has shown sustained and consistent activity as it aims to create and showcase multidisciplinary artistic projects in the Arab world. Waraq organises and hosts a multitude of animation workshops in Lebanon and the wider region, ranging from puppet-making and set design to puppet animation and stop motion. It also offers animation screenings, talks and other events. The group has successfully built a following and is inspiring many to work in the field.[32]

It is only natural that the scattered and individual activities have become channelled into a more unified forum, with professionals gathering to form an institutionalised body. The Syndicate of Professional Graphic Designers and Illustrators in Lebanon (SPGIL), which numbers animators and cartoonists among the range of professions it represents, began in 1996 as a joint effort by pioneers in these two fields.[33] Chiefly focusing on legal issues dealing with copyright laws, and with social and health insurance for artists, the SPGIL provides an important step towards protecting the rights of independent animators and in trying to stabilise (still with little success) prices in the market, by monopolising the legal representation of its members. Although the projects initiated by the syndicate have been geared more towards comics and illustration activities (workshops, festivals, etc.) it deserves credit for having launched the first animation festival in Lebanon. Still, European animations comprised the majority of this festival's screenings, and no local films were shown, and so it received none (or far less attention) of the attention it did garner at the more recent local festival: Beirut Animated.

Let's Get Serious: Beirut Animated

Launched in 2009[34] as an initiative of Metropolis Association (an organisation that convenes several film festivals and programmes at the Metropolis Empire Sofil Theater) in partnership with *Samandal* magazine, Beirut Animated could be considered the first serious animation festival in Lebanon. Evidence for such a conclusion is provided by the number of shows, the artists invited, the workshops and seminars accompanying

139

the event, the scope of categories covered (features movies, shorts, video clips) and the variety of techniques shown (2D cel animation, 3D and stop motion). Since its initiation, the festival has worked slowly but surely towards building a dedicated audience, as well as a steady increase in the number of its participants. Interestingly, the festival has been attracting a distinct audience of creative-professionals practising animation, illustration and design, as well as an audience that is younger than that typical of short film festivals.[35] Contrary to expectations, the festival did not attract a large number of families and children, illustrating Lebanese animation as an arthouse, auteur form aimed at mature viewers.

Applications to the second Animated festival more than doubled, from 23 in its first year, to 50 in the second; and twice that again sought entry to the third edition of 2013. Participants from the Arab world have increased seven-fold, from eight films in the first edition to sixty in the most recent.[36] In 2011, however, with the beginning of the 'Arab Spring' and the uprising of many Arab citizens against their respective totalitarian regimes, the festival – like so many other film festivals in the region – suffered a large fall in regional participants; only ten guests from the Arab world outside Lebanon attended. But this was to be expected, as the instability created chaos and most people were understandably concerned for their countries' political situations. It was also difficult for the festival team to reach possible participants, and challenging for animators and filmmakers to even submit on time let alone attend if invited. In 2013, a number of Syrian animators who had fled their own civil war to Lebanon, including Sawsan Nourallah and Ibrahim Ramadan, were able to participate with their work and to attend workshops and festival shows. Egyptian and North African filmmakers were, however, completely absent.[37]

A simple glance at the content of the programme reveals the extent to which the organisers of Beirut Animated have been eager to focus on non-commercial animations coming from small studios or independent animators rather than on blockbuster producers. Such little-known animators and their products have turned the festival into a forum and platform for professionals interested in alternative productions, and attract a sophisticated audience as well. The festival should also be credited for several other things: for a celebration of *Grandizer*, the dubbed Japanese cartoon phenomenon of the 1970s, during the first edition;[38] for screenings

Cultivating an Arthouse Viewership

of the earliest cartoons from the Arab region by showcasing the Frenkel Brothers' productions from 1930s Egypt during the second edition;[39] and for an homage to the Future Television experience also in the festival's second year. This all indicates an insistence on digging into the history of the genre in the Arab world in a conscious attempt to build a collective local (animated) memory and context.[40]

Commercial Sector: Not Quite an Industry Yet

Immediately following the fifteen-year civil war, all sectors of Lebanese society were recruited to rebuild the broken nation. The amount of reconstruction projects also led to an increase in TV channels[41] opening up to the world, resulting in advertising firms thriving and demanding professional TV graphics and animation professionals for their work. Graduates were hired fresh out of school and in turn specialised educational programmes were created to cater to the rising demand. Due to the high cost of specialised equipment and expertise, and the relatively low percentage of animations used in commercials, most advertising agencies did not have in-house animation departments. Animated sequences, therefore, were – and still are – almost exclusively outsourced, to post-production companies such as Hedgehog (in Lebanon), Cube (in France), Caustic (in Lebanon), and The Post Office (in The Netherlands), among others.

Nevertheless, during this time a few specialised animation studios did sprout, catering mostly to advertising firms. Two such studios stand out for their professionally animated commercials: Adaimy Studios, founded in 1994 by Emile Adaimy, and the similarly eponymous Hani Bayoun Studio, running since 1999. Each is continuing with its advertising work as well as with contributing animations to various TV channels, by including selective shorts and in some cases offering specialised services, such as Adaimy studio's 3D Projection Mapping.

The high cost of equipment and technology, however, along with a lack of sufficiently skilled manpower, has held back the development of small animation firms. Operating systems to run high-end moving graphics and animation software could cost $40,000 per unit, with annual software upgrades costing over $10,000,[42] thereby putting such equipment beyond the reach of smaller firms or individuals. Only institutions such as TV

141

stations, global advertising firms and specialised studios are able to purchase such prohibitively expensive technology.

Nevertheless, the last decade has seen an increase in the use of 2D and, especially, of 3D animation as alternatives to live-action in commercials. Advertising executives attest that shooting a live commercial is considered too expensive, while using animation cuts down on the expenses enormously and is therefore considered a viable choice for clients. Ten years ago, this had not been possible, as neither the professional talent nor the resultant technical quality required to convince clients was present.[43] Now though, with much lower-priced equipment, independent animators are no longer obliged to work at a large company, and have become more accessible and affordable as freelancers.[44] The increasing speed and volume of internet access has also made collaboration with animators from other countries possible, broadening the professional spectrum and enabling the display of a wider range of types and styles than ever before. Whereas more realistic or nonfictional ideas were popular previously, the new transnational and online working methods result in more fantastical and imaginative work, as collaborations face fewer technical limits. In this way, the possibility of integrating animation into advertising has broadened the horizons of creativity.

Today, between 15 and 20 per cent of advertising firms' commercial production in Lebanon is animation-based,[45] relying chiefly on 3D animation, no doubt due to the convincing style of hyper-realism it can create and the special effects it can produce. With the majority of animated commercials today targeting adult audiences, the genre cannot be considered a children's genre but rather one that speaks to a wide and diverse audience across ethnicities and generations.[46] The on-going global animation trend and years of accumulated exposure to and experiment with a variety of alternative styles, types and genres have positioned animation as a viable alternative medium of expression, bringing a broader acceptance of animation as an effective means for addressing adult issues. This has allowed animation to be used as a medium for the promotion of adult products and services, such as those recently developed for Bank Audi,[47] Balad and Pert shampoo, as well as public awareness campaigns addressing topics such as the stigma attached to mental health issues.[48]

The Future of Animation: Towards an Industry or a Developed Independent Scene?

Today, a multitude of platforms for showcasing short animated films exists in Lebanon: from cinemas and TV channels, to cultural centres, educational institutions and a robust film festival circuit. Various websites and social media pages also act as podiums for the local animation scene; the Lebanese Animation Foundation's social media page boasts over 300 members. Still in its infancy and uncertain of its sustainability, the dedicated animation festival Beirut Animated, in combination with various other platforms, provides hope that a modest growth in the animation sector is possible. But is that enough to sustain or even promote a fully-fledged industry?

Lebanon – with its multi-cultural identity, high rate of education, business acumen and greater freedom of expression permitted by the state than in other Arab countries – has often served as a hub for business and cultural activities, acting as a kind of service centre for the region. From the 1960s to the 1980s, Beirut was also the publishing hub of the Middle East,[49] catering to writers, intellectuals and thinkers of the region. It also produced experts who, fleeing Lebanon's instability in the 1980s and 1990s, went on to work in the Gulf States and other more stable countries in the region, to start their own successful businesses and work as independent contractors and consultants. Known for their entrepreneurship, resourcefulness and leadership qualities, the Lebanese have often taken the initiative, venturing into successful commercial ventures. Why, then, has this not produced an animation industry capable of creating feature length films?

Perhaps an analogy may be drawn with that of the closely related film industry, which suffers from a similar syndrome: there is evidence of strong individual experimentation, but no industry to speak of, as there is in Egypt.[50] Partly to blame is certainly the continued interruptions of war in Lebanon, and an continued lack of governmental and institutional funding available for cinema. By comparison, Egyptian state television and film associations are responsible for most of the films and the television shows produced in the country, resulting in the deserved reputation the country's film industry enjoys.

The lack of a strong film industry, one that would support and attract scriptwriters, production managers and complex, team-based pipelined processes that animation production requires, greatly affects the situation in Lebanon. And the local market is far too limited to justify the expensive production of animated series or feature films solely for domestic consumption; any such efforts must target the region, at the very least. The problem is that a fully commercial production capable of supplying animated films to the region requires two essential components: generous financing (absent in Lebanon) and the accommodation of political, cultural and religious morals.

Although the Lebanese are used to circumnavigating some of those religious and moral restrictions because of their complex sectarian composition, such a shift of focus to the wider Middle Eastern region would require abiding by the tougher regional rules of censorship, something they may find difficult to tolerate. A willingness has been shown to accommodate such restrictions in advertisements and commercial films, but there is a greater reluctance when it comes to broader questions of freedom of expression in art. The issue of language is also a concern, as pan-Arab productions tend to use Classical Arabic rather than local dialects so as to accommodate a wider audience. Used more frequently in official literature, newscasts or political speeches, this language option is not considered appropriate in cartoons, particularly as most television shows, movies and commercials are in colloquial Arabic. The very successful recent dubbing of Disney animations into the Egyptian dialect – as opposed to the Classical Arabic normally used – in order to attract younger audiences who are usually alienated by that form of expression is a good example.[51] But, the various factors that might coalesce in Lebanon in order to create a full-blown animated film industry have yet to appear. Things remain in their infancy: university animation programmes with strong ties to animation studios or production houses for the purpose of proper training remain tenuous, and a pool of scriptwriters, lighting and sound specialists, lead animators, project managers and directors is still lacking.

A number of factors contribute to the likelihood that Beirut continues to act as a field for experimentation: the relative freedom of expression; an openness to the West and what this brings in the way of new technologies and alternative perspectives; and universities acting as research hubs.

Add to these an already existing high level of motivation and expertise, components that are essential for exploration and experimentation, and it becomes clear that Beirut continues to have great potential for being the hub of animated experimentation.

It is difficult to foresee an expanded commercial future for feature-length animations in Lebanon, and it is not likely that the country will function as an outsourcing hub for animation similar to that in the Far East. Lebanon has neither the industrial foundations nor the infrastructure, governmental funding or market to support such an effort. It is likely that the production of more manageable short animated programmes will expand, as the demand already exists. Series that have appeared during the high season of Ramadan and have met with general approval make a comeback every year.[52] It is probable, then, that Lebanese cartoonists will continue to contribute to the independent animation production scene, exploring possibilities, pushing the boundaries of content, genre and quality, all the while providing the country and the region with ample talent.

Notes

1. Samir Kassir, *Beirut* (Berkley, CA, 2010), p. 251.
2. Ibid., p. 332.
3. Kamal Salibi, *Histoire du LIBAN du 18ème siècle à nos jours* (Paris, 1988); William Harris, *Lebanon: A History 600–2011* (New York, NY, 2012), p. 194.
4. In this chapter, Beirut is shown to be the centre of all film and animation production and distribution in Lebanon. The capital is therefore used as a metonym for the country.
5. Samir Kassir, *Beirut*, p. 382.
6. On 28 May 1959 the first images of the first commercial Arabic TV station were shown with La Compagnie Libanaise de Télévision broadcasting on Channel 7 (in Arabic), and Channel 9 (in French). The daily broadcast time was from 7:00pm until 10:00pm. See Jean-Claude Boulos, *La Télé Quelle Histoire!* (Beirut, 1997), p. 46.
7. Ibid.
8. Jean-Claude Boulos, *La Télé Quelle Histoire!* (Beirut, 1996), p. 51.
9. Ibid., p. 134
10. Abu Dhabi, Dubai, Jordan and Syria.
11. Jean-Claude Boulos, p. 98.
12. The Lebanese civil war lasted from 1975 until 1990.

13. The merger was effective in May 1977. Jean-Claude Boulos, *La Télé Quelle Histoire!*, p. 158.
14. The main companies were Nippon Animation Co. Ltd, TOEI Animation and Tokyo Movie Shinsha (TMS Entertainment).
15. *The Adventures of Sinbad*, a Japanese animated series directed by Fumio Kurokawa, produced by Nippon Animation, 1975, dubbed to Arabic in 1978.
16. FILMALI Production SAL and Studio Baalback are both located in Beirut. The first was founded by Nicolas Abou-Samah (already Director at Télé-Liban), who gathered lead actors from the Lebanese TV series that had ground to a halt due to limited budgets caused by the war conditions.
17. Interview with George Khoury (Jad), Head of Animation Department, Future Television since 1993, in June 2014.
18. Future Television was one of two Lebanese stations (with LBC) to occupy the space of the pan-Arab scene in the MENA region for almost a decade.
19. Interview with George Khoury (Jad).
20. Rabih Mroué is now a renowned playwright and performance artist. Fadi Abi-Samra developed a career in acting in feature-length movies.
21. Interview with George Khoury (Jad).
22. The film was selected for festivals such as Vidéaste recherché in Canada (2000), Casablanca Video Art Festival in Morocco (2000) and the Ismailiya Short Film Festival in Egypt (2001).
23. All these cartoons were subject to a broadcast ban, and the station stopped airing cartoons for three months.
24. Interview with George Khoury (Jad).
25. All information about the degree of Bachelor of Science in Computer Science and Computer Graphics & Animation (CGA) at NDU is available at http://www.ndu.edu.lb/academics/fnas/dcs/comp_gra_ani.htm (accessed 15 April 2015).
26. Information on the degree for Bachelor of Arts in Graphic Design at NDU is available at http://www.ndu.edu.lb/academics/faad/desdep/bagd.htm (accessed 15 April 2015).
27. Emile Adaimy founded one of the first commercial animation studios in Lebanon.
28. David Habchi is illustrator, animator and co-founder of the Waraq collective.
29. Interview with Reine Abbas.
30. For more information, see the Catalogue of the Beirut Animated Festival of 2009.
31. *Another Year*, directed by Maher Abi-Samra, animated by Merhej, Karim Farah and Maya Chami, 2008.
32. Waraq was founded in 2013 by four creative artists: David Habchi, Joan Bazz, Hussein Nakhal and Ashley Phebe Shoukair, who came together from

various fields, ranging from animation and illustration to graphic design and performing arts.

33. These include Lina Ghaibeh, George Khoury (Jad), Edgar Aho, Hani Baayoun and Emile Adaimy, all animators among the early founders of SPGIL, which is presided over by Rita Saab Mukarzel, a veteran comics artist herself.

34. The inaugural Beirut Animated took place between 16 and 19 November 2009, with the support of the Arab Fund for Arts and Culture, the French Embassy-Beirut and the Goethe Institute-Beirut.

35. Interview with Hania Mroueh, Founder and Director of Metropolis Art Cinema and Beirut Animated, July 2014.

36. Interview with Hania Mroueh.

37. For more information, see the catalogue of the third edition of Beirut Animated, 2013.

38. For more information, see the catalogue of the first edition of Beirut Animated, 2009.

39. Ibid.

40. For more information, see the catalogue of the second edition of Beirut Animated, 2011.

41. The Audiovisual Media Law of 1994 not only regulated the airwaves, but also ended the state's monopoly over broadcast television that had been in effect since 1977. Five licenses were granted to different broadcasters reflecting, more or less, the major political and sectarian communities: LBCI, MTV, NBN, Al-Manar and Future Television. Two years later they were accorded the rights to satellite broadcasting.

42. Interview with George Khoury (Jad).

43. Interview with Walid Kanaan, Chief Creative Officer at IMPACT BBDO Beirut (Advertising firm), July 2014.

44. Interview with Mahmoud Areej, Creative Director at H&C Leo Burnett advertising firm, July 2014.

45. Ibid.

46. Interview with Walid Kanaan.

47. *Clear all the way* is online. Available at http://youtu.be/mc47n-dl0dc (accessed 15 April 2015).

48. Mental Health Awareness campaign is by Embrace Fund, a support network for sufferers of mental health issues in Lebanon and the Middle East. For more information, see their website. Available at www.embracefund.org (accessed 15 April 2015).

49. William Harris, *Lebanon: A History 600–2011* (Oxford, 2012), p. 194.

50. David Livingston, in his article 'Lebanese Cinema', *Film Quarterly*, 62, 2(2008), pp. 34–43, draws a sustained comparison between Lebanese and Egyptian

cinema industries, and looks in more detail at the causes of the lack of a successful industry in Lebanon.

51. Elias Muhanna, 'Translating *Frozen* into Arabic', *The New Yorker* (30 May 2014). Available at http://www.newyorker.com/books/page-turner/translating-frozen-into-arabic (accessed November 2014).

52. *Nisaa' fil Quran*, for example, was a cartoon series broadcast on Future Television during the month of Ramadan in 2014.

Filmography

7 Days a Week, directed by Lina Ghaibeh (2000).

Adnan wa Lina (Future Boy Conan), produced by Nippon Animation (1979).

Alf Yawm wa Yawm (1001 Days), directed by George Khoury (Jad) (2000).

Al-Witwat wa Al-Sununu (The Bat and the Robin), produced by Future Television (2004).

Animal Treasure Island (Jazeerat Al-Kanz), produced by Toei Animation (1971).

Another Day, directed by Maher Abi-Samra (2008).

Astroganga (Jungar), produced by Knack Productions (1979).

Ata, produced by Future Television (1997).

Burj El-Mur: Tower of Bitterness, directed by Lina Ghaibeh (2012).

Clear all the Way, directed by H&C Leo Burnett (2012).

Drawing the War, directed by Lena Merhej (2002).

Ein El-Hilweh: Kingdom of Women, directed by Dahna Abourahme (2010).

El-Toro Azul, directed by Bahij Jaroudi (2008).

Enough, produced by Future Television (2006).

Fouad, directed by David Habchi (2013).

Grandizer (UFO Robot Grandizer Raids), produced by Toei Animation (1979).

Hawa (Wind), directed by Chadi Aoun (2007).

Isabelle, directed by directed by Bahij Jaroudi (2010).

Istiklal 05 (Independence 05), produced by Future Television (2005).

Jabral Tarek (Gibraltar), directed by Ghassan Halwani (2005).

Kalil wa Dimn, directed by George Khoury (Jad) (1993).

Maya the Honey Bee (Zeina wa Nahhoul), produced by Nippon Animation (1978).

Mouzakkarat Kursi (Diary of a Chair), produced by Future Television (2004).

Roussoum Mutaharrira (Freed Drawings), produced by Future Television (2001).

Sad Man, directed by Lina Ghaibeh (2002).

Taaleek Al-Yaoum (The Daily Comment), directed by George Khoury (Jad) (1995).

Takhabbot (Thrashing), directed by Ghassan Halwani (2009).

The Adventures of Sinbad, directed by Fumio Kurokawa (1975).

The Arabian Nights: Adventures of Sinbad (Moghamarat Sindibad), directed by Fumio Kurokawa and Kunihiko Okazaki (1978).

148

Cultivating an Arthouse Viewership

The Dictator, directed by Edgar Aho (2003).
The Facts in the Case of Mr. Valdemar, directed by Bahij Jaroudi (2009).
Wehde, directed by David Habchi (2011).
Ya Reit (I wish), directed by Michel Karshouny (2013).
Ya Waladi (My Son), directed by Lina Ghaibeh (2005).
Zeid and Leila, directed by Jad Sarout (2009).

7

Pixelated Intifada: Animating Palestine Under Digital Occupation[1]

Colleen Jankovic

The hybrid animated/live-action Palestinian documentary *The Wanted 18* (2014) opens with co-director and visual artist Amer Shomali's voice explaining how he grew up reading comics and how his parents told him about his Palestinian homeland through dramatically narrated stories. Later, Shomali explains that he had no equivalent to *Superman* as a kid, and it becomes clear that his cousin Anton, a young leader and fighter during the First Palestinian Intifada, took the place of such imaginary comic heroes. Similarly, in his short animation *Hide and Seek*, Dia' Azzeh, who is part of Ramallah-based Zan Studio with Shomali, uses a child-like minimalist crayon line-drawing illustration style to tell his own childhood story about his Uncle Nidal, held by Israel as a political prisoner, and who became Azzeh's superhero.

The famous political cartoon character Handalah provides another reference point for a culturally-specific Palestinian version of an unlikely and unconventional comic hero. Handalah is a line-drawn Palestinian refugee boy, created by political cartoonist Naji Al-Ali, who was murdered by Israeli authorities in 1987. Handalah always stands with his back to the viewer, mirroring how the world turned its back on the Palestinians during and since the Nakba, the catastrophe of Palestinian dispossession caused by the founding of the Israeli state and the subsequent Israeli military and

150

civilian occupation. Few Palestinians in Palestine or living abroad would be unaware of the political and cultural significance of Naji Al-Ali's political cartoons, especially as they inspired later political cartoonists and artists, as well as anti-occupation art and graffiti.[2]

However, according to young animator Azzeh, audiences in Palestine long referred to any animation as *Tom wa Jerry* (*Tom and Jerry*), the classic US cartoon, evidencing a widespread cultural assumption that animation is primarily Western and for children. As satellite television became more widespread, Azzeh notes, the notion of animation began to broaden, and this trend has only increased with the rise of the internet and easily accessible online animation serials.[3] Nevertheless, the examples of alternative Palestinian superheroes – resistance leaders, political prisoners and a refugee boy – suggest that for Palestinians, cartoons have a direct political history and a continuing relevance to the on-going political struggle; that it would be a mistake to dismiss Palestinian cartoons and animations simply as escapist or playful fantasy.[4] Although this viewpoint has been criticised by many, such a conventional or common sense notion of animation as mere cartoons persists, as does the idea that animation has a more intrinsic meaning than a simple semblance to anti- or hyper-realist fantasy. The popularity of *Tom wa Jerry* in Palestine suggests that the dismissive attitude towards animation as 'mere cartoons' is common, even despite the recent acclaim for Palestinian animated films, which rarely resemble their dominant Western counterparts in form or content, even when they are conceived, produced and funded abroad in Europe or North America. This idea of *Tom wa Jerry*, moreover, fails to capture the diversity of Palestinian commercially-produced children's animations, which more clearly warrant the title 'cartoons', yet frequently foreground historically and culturally specific stories related to Palestinian dispossession (such as life under occupation or in a refugee camp, or dealing with Israeli military destruction) and political struggle (such as understanding the Right of Return). One rarely finds a purely imaginative and playful Palestinian cartoon that does not reference Palestinian collective identity; or, if one views Palestinian cartoons from a Western perspective, perhaps looking to find a *Tom wa Jerry*, Palestinian cartoons look very unfamiliar.

Gaza's Zaitoon Studio, part of the Animation and Games Unit at the College of Applied Science, produced the children's educational/

edutainment animation *Why?*, which uses a basic colour 2D computer-animated style to depict a young Palestinian child's perspective of the Separation Barrier, Israel's massive internationally illegal wall that divides and fragments Palestinian society and was built on stolen Palestinian land. With cartoons like *Why?* and a forthcoming feature about occupation and stolen land called *Khayal Al-Haqil* (*Scarecrow*; the second or third film referred to as the 'first Palestinian animated film'), Zaitoon reportedly aims 'to instil a sense of pride and resilience among children facing adversity, making them aware of their culture and history, and connecting them with Palestinian children in the West Bank and internationally.'[5] This mission in part reflects the studio's foundational support for its productions, but it is, nevertheless, a serious mission for 'cartoons.'

With its alternative superheroes and serious children's cartoons, it is perhaps surprising that Palestinian animation has not yet been the subject of in-depth studies attuned to the cultural specificity of its production, aesthetic, politics and diversity of forms. Although Palestinian cinema itself is still a small field of study, it nevertheless seems remarkable that Palestinian animation has received almost no critical attention to date from film or other visual studies scholars. In many ways, Livia Alexander's (in)famous question 'Is there a Palestinian cinema?', continues, for better or worse, to shape the field of Palestinian cinema studies, and the question can surely be asked of Palestinian animation, too.[6] With no state or national film fund, limited local filmmaking resources and a lack of a strong local film audience, 'Palestinian cinema' labels an unstable and fragmented field; and 'Palestinian animation', perhaps, even more so.

Moreover, the on-going influence of Zionist settler-colonial occupation and Israeli military control on a variously dispersed, dispossessed, occupied and besieged Palestinian society, affects cinema and cultural production at every level of production, distribution, exhibition and cultural reception. As Alexander points out, Palestinian cinema underscores, perhaps more than other cinemas, the tension between the national and transnational in contemporary film production and critical studies.[7] Later in this chapter, I will discuss Palestinian animation's complex relationship with national/transnational forces. Yet, whereas Alexander emphasises the obstacles and challenges to Palestinian cinema's coherence as a field or industry, some recent Palestinian cinema studies attempt to cohere the development of

152

Palestinian cinema into a more intelligible, linear history, possessing a set of recurring themes and formal qualities. This is an important effort that can draw attention to Palestinian cinema, so that it receives the legitimate scholarly standing it deserves, by shaping its study to resemble other conventional studies of national cinema.[8] However, this effort also too quickly attempts to affirmatively and concretely respond to Alexander's challenging question from within.

It is tempting, then, with regard to Palestinian animated cinema, to simply answer 'yes' to Alexander's unsettling question 'Is there a Palestinian cinema?', especially given the recent attention to the award-winning *The Wanted 18*. However, Palestinian animation provides an occasion to reconsider why it may be advantageous to resist answering in the affirmative too quickly. Since so much of Palestinian animation explicitly references the context of Zionist settler-colonialism, Palestinian history and diaspora, Israeli occupation and siege, we should consider whether, and how, the field might itself remain unsettled, rather than pre-emptively and conventionally cohere. Otherwise, by packaging Palestinian cinema, including animated films, in the same way as other national cinemas, we may risk further obscuring how settler-colonialism, racism, and post-Oslo neoliberal economics and politics, profoundly shape the conditions of Palestinian stateless dispossession. We may miss, too, their impact on cinema's artistic and commercial production at every level, from narrative content to exhibition.

Although animated films have suffered some neglect in broader film studies, recent animation studies scholarship has sought to remind us of film studies concepts, including realism and narrative, that have always incorporated animation, but that have often been ignored in the attempt to draw clear lines between cinema and animation.[9] The variety of moving image works and media (2D and 3D computer animation, hand-drawn illustration and cel animation, stop-motion and many more) that tend to fall under the category of animation deserve further attention.

Since Palestinian animation is under-studied, this chapter can provide only a brief overview of it in its various forms – from international award-winning feature films to commercial shorts. I begin with the understanding that cartoons and animation have a specific historical and political relevance in the Palestinian context; this sets them apart from most Western

153

animated cinema, which informs Western animation theory, and which has tended to dominate the field of animation studies. Brief comparative readings of several animations—video and installation animation work by Dia' Azzeh; Ahmed Habash's 3D short *Fatenah* (2009); Amer Shomali's *The Wanted 18* (2014); and animated commercial educational, children's and political satire produced by Arabic satellite channels, online platforms, and Palestinian animation studios – provide a few concrete examples to elucidate a broad overview and critical discussion of the Palestinian animation industry. Ultimately, this chapter argues that Palestinian animation, especially the prevalence of documentary, political and serious animations, foregrounds a unique Palestinian realist aesthetic, one borne of conditions of occupation and visions of resistance, that confounds many definitions and theorisations of animation, and that both broadens and further unsettles the field of Palestinian cinema studies.

Animating Under Digital Occupation

Palestinian animators and other supporters of a developing Palestinian animation industry indicate that animation has a long way to go before it receives even the limited attention and acclaim of Palestinian non-animated cinema, which has gradually entered the global public sphere of world art cinema. The few recent animated films garnering attention on the international festival circuit faced countless funding and production obstacles. For instance, the internationally-exhibited and award-winning feature *The Wanted 18* (2014), directed by Shomali and co-directed by Canadian filmmaker Paul Cowan, faced a number of challenges over its lengthy five-year production, including securing funding and international co-producers, and that the co-directors worked and lived across the globe from one another.[10] Furthermore, many Palestinian animators, including Azzeh and Shomali, must travel abroad to study and train in their craft, since few Palestinian universities (or Israeli universities for those Palestinians with Israeli citizenship or a special permit to attend them) offer substantial training in either. Those universities that do offer animation courses focus more on the technical basics needed for commercial or consumer industries (and often only to a very limited degree), marginalizing animation as an artistic practice or conceptual field in its own right.

154

Palestinians' stateless and occupied condition also means that there are few local options for film fundraising and project subsidy through either foundation support, which is very limited in any case, or state funds, which are non-existent. Important existing local funding options include the Qattan Foundation, which coordinates local media production programs and which offered exhibition support to Ahmed Habash's *Fatenah*. Co-production, primarily with European but also with Arab countries, is a common film-funding model for Palestinian filmmakers, and animated films, like *The Wanted 18*, have followed suit. However, co-production brings its own set of specific challenges unique to the Palestinian context. For instance, since Israel's discriminatory anti-Palestinian policies extend into the arts and cultural context, Palestinians with Israeli citizenship are frequently declined support, are discouraged from referring to their projects or themselves as Palestinian, and/or have awarded support rescinded.[11] Many Palestinian artists deliberately avoid Israeli funding for these reasons, or because they see acceptance of Israeli state money as a form of complicity with occupation, as do artists who follow the Academic and Cultural Boycott guidelines of the call for Boycott, Divestment, and Sanctions of Israel. With few local state or independent funding options, Palestinian filmmakers often start their own production companies and seek out international funding.

In the mid- to late-1990s post-Oslo Accords Period, a large number of international NGOs flooded the West Bank and Gaza, promoting and financing projects that supported the Oslo Accords' frail notions of peace, but which more than anything only legitimated Israeli settler-colonialism and indefinitely delayed the question of Palestinian sovereignty and autonomy. As a broad field that crosses commercial and cultural sectors and audiences, animation may in some ways be more appealing to NGOs that offer creative and cultural project support. When, for instance, the British Council funds the Gaza College of Applied Science's Animation and Games Unit, or Zaitoon Studio, it achieves multiple humanitarian aims, such as supporting children's education and cultural heritage through creative projects, improving cultural understanding of Palestinian stories and building Palestinian cultural institutions; thus, it supports Palestinian civil society, while avoiding any challenge to Israeli occupation. Suggesting animation's appeal in this context, the Council held its own stop-motion animation workshop with deaf Palestinian children; the children hand-crafted characters and recorded movements that mimicked sign language.[12]

Local Palestinian funders and leaders in the Palestinian commercial and creative animation industries acknowledge the many current limitations to animation production, even those who are enthusiastic supporters of a Palestinian animation industry's capacity to create jobs and improve the Palestinian economy. For instance, although he characterises animation as an 'enabler' and as part of a larger 'borderless sector' of the information and computer technology industry, Palestinian Information and Computer Technology Incubator (PICTI) CEO Hassan Omar also underscores the many obstacles to the industry's success, including dependency on international funding agencies, limited funding, and the lack of training opportunities.[13] The small Palestinian animation sector includes satellite distributors and producers such as Al-Aqsa TV, Karameesh TV (Jordan), the Arab multi-channel network and YouTube broadcaster Kharabeesh.[14] Animation studios, many supported by PICTI's incubation programme, include: Dimensions Studio (Ramallah-based; claims itself as the first Palestinian animation company); Dragon FX (specialises in professional logos and commercial animated work); Zan Studio (co-founded by Amer Shomali), Johatoon (Gaza-based, women-owned and produces mostly children's cartoons); Afkartoon (a Gaza start-up founded by a former architect familiar with 3D imaging; produces children's cartoons and games); Shakhabeet Avatar (a Gaza start-up that produces children's cartoons and political satire); and Zaitoon.

Furthermore, as filmmaker Dia' Azzeh attests, while most efforts are individual and individualistic, rather than part of a coherent industry, there are also significant regional differences in style and format within Palestinian animation. He notes that animation from Gaza is markedly different from West Bank animation:

> [W]hile animation from Gaza consists mostly of direct messages in relation to the occupation and in some cases promoting the authorities in power and their ideology, the ones from the West Bank will have a wider artistic spectrum of subjects, varying from political issues and the occupation, to light humour for humour's sake.[15]

Artistic impetus also varies by location. West Bank animation foregrounds artistic form and experiments more with classical and handmade animation, while Gazan animation largely prioritises message, using more economical techniques of computer graphics and 3D. Not meaning to pigeonhole either location, these are valid generalisations, according to Azzeh, brought about by the respective political and social situations within which the artists in these regions function.

Further tempering the optimism suggested in the notion of animation as a part of a borderless sector, as PICTI CEO Omar called it, Helga Tawil-Souri has described how the post-Oslo Accords period has been marked by a neoliberal 'digital occupation' of territorial control (especially over Gaza) that extends into the high-tech realm and attends increasing privatisation and surveillance. Tawil-Souri describes how digital occupation is imposed by Israel, but also tacitly reinforced by the complicit Palestinian Authority and Hamas governments, as well as by the private sector, mainly the Palestine Telecommunications Company (PALTEL). Tawil-Souri notes that 'digital networks, too, are spaces of control' with 'material limitations,' despite our tendency to think of high technology as 'territory-less, boundless and inclusionary.'[16] In light of the concept of digital occupation, research into the Palestinian animation industry must acknowledge its subjection to Israeli legal and architectural limitations, including how digital occupation perpetuates Gazans' economic dependence and de-development, and hinders collaborations between animators in Gaza, the West Bank, Israel and elsewhere.

Moreover, the effects of digital occupation should moderate any tendency to characterise the Palestinian animation commercial and cultural industry (to the extent that it can be referred to as an industry) in utopian or liberatory terms. For instance, Tawil-Souri cautions against understanding Palestinian's increasing access to digital networks as part of a broader 'new media revolution' or 'virtual resistance' sparked by the Egyptian and Tunisian Arab uprisings. The audience for Palestinian animation includes those who can easily watch accessible Palestinian political and/or children's cartoons, but do not have the opportunity to see internationally-acclaimed Palestinian cinema and animated features. Thus, although the Palestinian commercial and creative animation sector ought to be further explored for its potential to expand Palestinian cultural expression and reach otherwise isolated audiences, optimism about the medium's potential must be balanced by further understandings of how it is shaped at every level by Palestinian dispossession and lack of social justice.

Animating Palestinian Forms of Realism and Resistance

Palestinian visual art is frequently discussed in terms of a Palestinian 'visibility' problem: all images, including cinematic images, are thought to carry the potential to resolve this problem. Israeli Prime Minister Benjamin Netanyahu's comment, 'they [Hamas] want to pile up as many civilian dead as they can... they use telegenically dead Palestinians for their cause. They want the more dead, the better [sic]'[17], made during an incredibly brutal, destructive and bloody military incursion into Gaza in 2014, is one example that demonstrates how the aim for representation and visibility has long been a double-edged sword for Palestinians and their advocates. Netanyahu's comment implied that news and documentary images of Palestinian suffering, including images of civilians who were directly killed by Israeli forces, should be considered with a high degree scepticism, as likely propagandistic sacrifices or simply false. Whereas an activist-oriented *cinema vérité* approach to revealing Palestinians' struggles and exposing Israeli abuses is common with Western activists, artists, journalists, and NGOs, it is rare in Palestinian cinema, which is marked by a more irreverent approach to conventions of documentation and narrative.[18]

Film scholar Hamid Dabashi has suggested the need for Palestinian cinema to find 'a way out of the *cul-de-sac* of representing the unrepresentable', positing cinematic representation as a potential reparative task, though an incredibly fraught one.[19] Similarly, although he advocates for Palestinian cinema's ability to respond to narrow and negative representations of Palestinians, Edward Said notes (in reference to written texts) that a Palestinian story precisely comprises the denial of a Palestinian story; consequently, its 'characteristic mode' is non-narrative and marked by formal instabilities.[20] Palestinian expressions are, as Said suggests, composed of failed attempts that reveal the contradictions and paradoxes structuring Palestinian life. Said elaborates on this mode of meaning-making when he writes that Palestinian creativity 'expresses itself in crossings-over, in clearing hurdles, activities that do not lessen the alienation, discontinuity and dispossession, but that dramatize and clarify them instead.'[21]

In its capacity to dramatise life through a supposedly less intrinsic commitment to the kind of semblance often seen as inherent to cinema's indexicality, animation may hold an especially unique set of relations for narrating Palestinian lives and stories. In *Understanding Animation*, Paul Wells posits that animation as a medium has an 'intrinsic capability to resist realism' and 'the intention to create "documentary" in animation is inhibited by the fact that the medium cannot be objective.'[22] Later, he implies that animation is thereby freed up to capture more of a subjective reality. In the case of Palestinian cinema, however, one finds a more cartoonish, absurdist version of reality in Elia Suleiman's live-action productions than in most Palestinian animation. By contrast, Palestinian animated films are largely serious, based in social reality, and lack the fantastic, playful, and imaginative quality frequently associated with animation.

The seriousness of Palestinian animation, particularly when compared to the cartoonishness of some Palestinian live-action cinema, begs the question as to whether or not animation affords a different kind of representation for Palestinians. In a scene in his 2004 film *Notre Musique*, French filmmaker Jean-Luc Godard uses two archival images – one of Jewish refugees arriving in Palestine, the other of Palestinian refugees forced to flee – to state that, with the founding of Israel and the Nakba, 'the Jews became the stuff of fiction; the Palestinians, of documentary.'[23] In this context, Godard's comment implies that, by remaining the 'stuff' of documentary, Palestinians lack a certain agency to make their own stories, or to become characters capable or worthy of audience identification. Although there are increasing examples of Palestinian films that do at least formally follow a more conventional narrative mode, while still maintaining a commitment to Palestinian stories, the 'characteristic mode' described by Said is still common, underscoring a complex and enduring representational and visibility struggle. If Palestinian films still largely take a more cautious approach to conventional forms of narrative and realism, perhaps animation allows Palestinians an alternative representational route. What would it mean for Palestinians to become the 'stuff' of animation or cartoons, given that these media seem to more easily accommodate an alternative version of realism that is unattainable or undesirable in Palestinian-produced indexical images? Perhaps since animation is already assumed to be non-representational, it makes space for a more realist (if unconventionally so) documentary approach, which has largely been avoided by Palestinian filmmakers (though still favored by many non-Palestinian solidarity activist filmmakers).

Palestinian cinema has been frequently characterised in terms of resistance and/or as an expression of Palestinian nationalism, which begs the question of the place animation takes up within this.[24] Since, by its very nature, animation more frequently crosses cinematic, commercial information technology, NGO industry, and artistic realms, animation could allow for new, more resilient modes of creative political and cultural resistance. Despite Béla Balázs' claim that 'where lines are drawn anything is possible', many Palestinian animations decline to simply visualise resistance and an end to occupation.[25] Rather, many use the medium to dramatise and clarify (as Said would put it) the many constraints on Palestinian lives and freedom that drawn lines cannot easily resolve. In Azzeh's animated installation work *The Line*, for instance, a model of resistance emerges precisely in the viewer becoming aware of the need to intervene in an act of violence depicted in a projected image of a line-drawn human figure being beaten by two other figures.[26] Only when the viewer crosses a red line in the gallery space does the assault stop; after the viewer steps forward, an alarm sounds and the attackers scatter. The suffering figure then rises up, multiplies, and overcomes the oppressive figures. In *The Line*, it is not enough to draw resistance, but rather to use lines to model a path toward resistance; such a path is shown to require intentional participation and engagement. According to much of popular Western animation (*Tom wa Jerry* being a prime example) and animation theory, animated figures rarely suffer, or die, since they are not bound by the rules of the non-animated world. Yet, in much Palestinian animation, as in Ahmad Habash's *Fatenah* (discussed next), figures suffer, die, and cannot (at least not on their own) defy or overcome oppression.

Fatenah (2009)

Animator and multimedia artist Ahmad Habash's nearly 30-minute 3D animated *Fatenah* is a very serious animation. Produced by Saed Andoni and DAR Films, in partnership with the World Health Organization (WHO) and Physicians for Human Rights (PHR), and with funding from the Sabreen Association for Artistic Development, the story follows a young Gazan woman's struggle with breast cancer, and her path through an impoverished local healthcare system and labyrinthine Israeli-imposed regulations and restrictions. Since there are few animators based in Palestine, and few resources to support animated productions, Habash animated the entire film on his own, using computer-animated 3D and 2D techniques. Photographs taken in Gaza enabled Habash to create quick 2D backgrounds, as illustrated in image 7.1, adding to the documentary feel of the film as they foreground the film's 3D characters, who drive the narrative. Screened in Palestine and abroad, the film is frequently referred to as 'the first' animated Palestinian film, though others have come to claim that title as well (*Scarecrow*, mentioned above, for instance, also circulated in the press as 'the first').

Fatenah is a young woman living in a Gaza refugee camp and working in a sewing shop. After she feels a lump in her breast, she visits several doctors in Gaza. The doctors give her absurdly bad advice, telling her that she merely needs to change her bra, or get married, to resolve the problem. Eventually referred to specialist care outside Gaza, she has to travel

7.1 'Proof of Concept' image from *Fatenah* (2009), created using 3D modelling and stylised photographs taken in Gaza

through Israeli bureaucracy and through an Israeli occupation checkpoint. She waits three months to gain access into Israel through the Erez crossing for medical treatments of her tumor, and at that point she has to undergo a mastectomy. The tumor spreads and becomes inoperable, and the now frail-looking character finally disappears into the white space from which she initially greeted us in the opening of the film (breaking the fourth wall, speaking to and looking directly at the viewer).

Fatenah was inspired by a short 2005 World Health Organization (WHO) and Physicians for Human Rights report titled 'Breast Cancer in the Gaza Strip: The Struggle for Survival of Fatma Bargouth.'[27] It is a character-driven animated film and story, mirroring the original report's intention to use one woman's struggle to elucidate the larger problem of access to healthcare for Gazan patients. Regarding animated characterisation, Suzanne Buchan discusses Jean Mitry's argument that the filmmaker's persona is more firmly embedded in the animated character than in the independent 'objective' filmic character-actor. Buchan explains that this is because 'the animated figure is not dissociated from creative imagination; it embodies just this, in that the figure's existence and character are defined entirely by the conceptual, stylistic and technical processes of its design, construction and animation.'[28] Put simply: an animated figure's interiority is that of its creator.

Although Habash did not conduct further research that might constitute *Fatenah* as an animated documentary, he did use photographs of Gazan interiors and exteriors to create stylised, realistic 2D backgrounds for the 3D figures of Fatenah and the other characters. As an NGO-funded, realistic, and serious animation, *Fatenah* disproves many of the conventions of traditional animation training, and much of animation theory as well. Habash describes how animators like himself are trained in Disney's 12 animation principles: formalist principles of motion that largely emphasise a playful, light, and exaggerated cartoon-like movement. *Fatenah*'s animation style underscores the narrative content's seriousness via slow, subdued character movements that seem designed to encourage careful attention to visual detail and emotional identification. For instance, the many close-ups on Fatenah's face invite viewers to study and interpret the subtle yet significant movements of her lips, eyes, and eyebrows. Habash's choice to give Fatenah slow movement and delicate facial expressions suits her worsening condition, and the seemingly hopeless position she is trapped in. A dream sequence, in which Fatenah imagines her tumor spreading inside and enveloping her body like a tentacled monster, provides the film's only (and devastating) moment of fantasy, taking advantage of animation's ability to create alternative worlds that defy the usual rules and expectations of live-action cinema.

As a film with documentary qualities, *Fatenah* perhaps surprisingly seems to quite aptly fit into Wells' distinction between animation and live-action cinema when it comes to their capacity to document. Wells argues that 'any aspiration towards suggesting reality in animation becomes difficult to execute' and, furthermore, 'the intention to create "documentary" in animation is inhibited by the fact that the medium cannot be objective'. Yet, despite this apparent inability of animation to document, Wells also notes, 'the medium does enable the film-maker to more persuasively show *subjective reality*.'[29] Thus, although *Fatenah* may well be understood as a work that 'aspires not only to naturalistic representation, but to the engagement with social reality' and thus may be usefully termed 'animation with *documentary tendency*', it may also be understood as one woman's subjective story filtered through a single animator's creative vision.[30] This notion of the film as arising from a singular artistic vision is complicated, however, by the fact that the film was produced for institutionalised humanitarian purposes (and funded by a humanitarian organisation), as well as by the fact that Habash felt constrained by what he described as a pressure to make serious, occupation-related work when he lived and worked in Palestine (he is now based in New Zealand). Thus, although Fatenah is based on a real woman, and can be said to embody her creator Habash to some extent, she is also the locus of other constraints and interests – including, specifically, post-Oslo NGO funding of creative humanitarian projects and the lack of resources for a longer or more technically complex animation.

Furthermore, as Habash notes, while animators usually exaggerate, both formally and conceptually, in *Fatenah* the real story's harshness was restrained and subdued. In a climactic scene, Israeli checkpoint soldiers force Fatenah to reveal her bare chest in order to prove that she needs to cross for medical reasons related to breast cancer. Habash positions the audience's perspective behind Fatenah, so that we see her open her gown and look away from the soldier's glare. We do not see what Habash pointed out would have been a harsher version of the scene, which would have located us behind the soldier's eyes and further emphasised the humiliating position she was put in.

Fatenah's illness and eventual death, as well as the violent occupation and poor infrastructure that attends it, positions *Fatenah* as a very different type of animation than that which Buchan describes when she writes that

> a defining feature of many animation films is that figures are often composed of a combination of physically incompatible elements, and in projection they and the spaces they are in can visually defy physical, optical and natural laws of gravity, electromagnetism, perspective and entropy.[31]

Rather than defy any natural or other laws (like those of occupation, checkpoint crossing or navigating complicated medical bureaucracies), Fatenah discovers she has cancer, struggles to receive care, undergoes humiliation and inhumane treatment at the checkpoint, and ultimately dies.

The Wanted 18 (2014)

Amer Shomali's *The Wanted 18* reflects the many talents of its director, whose background in both architecture and animation informs his work across formal media, including illustration and graphic design, cinema, and sculpture.[32] *The Wanted 18* is a hybrid documentary film that combines claymation, illustrations, live-action footage, interviews, and re-enactments (see for example in image 7.2), to tell the true story of a group of cows who were bought from an Israeli kibbutz and taken to a Bethlehem suburb where they play a surprising role in Palestinian resistance. Disparate pieces – semi-conventional talking-head interviews, ink-on-paper graphic novel style drawings, stop-motion animated clay cow figures, archival footage, and historic re-enactments of moments from the first Palestinian Intifada – are interwoven using voiceover narration, audio-bridges, dissolves between live-action and illustration, and a frame-dividing technique that allows these multiple forms and historical moments to appear side-by-side, as if in the frames of a graphic novel. *The Wanted 18* premiered at the 2014 Toronto International Film Festival and won the Abu Dhabi Best

7.2 Sequence of stills from *The Wanted 18*, directed by Ahmad Habash and Paul Cowan (2014)

Documentary in the Arab World prize, but it is also part of, or related to, several other projects by Shomali and his collaborators from Zan Studio, including an interactive graphic novel of the same name and a sculpture project entitled 'Pixelated Intifada'. As Mahmoud Abu Hashash notes on Shomali's website, Shomali's investment in pushing the artistic and conceptual limits of contemporary forms goes hand-in-hand with his critical concern for history and for engaging Palestinian collective consciousness.[33] As an innovative, highly-accessible and humor-laden documentary, *The Wanted 18* is also well-positioned to reach audiences worldwide, and perhaps to educate the less-informed about the recent history of Palestinians' struggle for justice and autonomy – all through the eyes of four cows.

The Wanted 18 is framed by a narrator's voice, that of director/illustrator/animator Shomali, who appears, as himself, at the beginning and the end of the film. Shomali describes growing up in a Syrian refugee camp and hearing from afar about his Palestinian homeland and the First Intifada in the late 1980s. He says he remembers a graphic novel he read about his hometown of Beit Sahour, a higher socio-economic suburb of Bethlehem.

The narrator's voice continually returns us to the perspective of four cows – Rivka, Ruth, Lola and Goldie – who some Palestinian men from Beit Sahour purchased from a nearby Israeli kibbutz, in part because they wanted to support the Palestinian boycott of Israeli products (such as milk from the Israeli co-operative Tnuva). This group of Beit Sahour men, who appear in the film in talking-head style interviews to relay their memories of that time, knew nothing about cows, but envisioned them as part of their resistance against Israeli occupation. They hoped to supply milk to their community, and so they discretely keep the cows and deliver milk, earning the title of 'lactivists' that the film bestows on them.

The cows themselves become a significant metaphor for the broader resistance, especially since Shomali's cousin – an apparently visionary young resistance leader – among others, used the cows' barn as a hiding place from Israeli forces. In the film, the cows have minds and personalities of their own, which are revealed in black and white stop-motion animated scenes. As Israeli cows, they are at first upset about being purchased by Palestinians, but over time they come to grow more sympathetic to the resistance cause. When the cows are deemed a 'threat to the national security of the State of Israel' and sought out by Israeli forces, the dramatic narrative takes up more screen time, and becomes increasingly comic and implausible (particularly when local families try to hide the cows in their homes), while the talking-head interviews continue throughout to remind the viewer that the illustrated and stop-motion animated figures depict real people and events, albeit with a thoroughly imaginative and irreverent re-enactment style.

As the Beit Sahour men speak in the recorded interviews, the occasional illustrated object (such as the cow truck) moves across the screen, disappearing or emerging from behind their backs. Because this overlapping and blending of form takes place throughout the film, few moments can be said to be purely live-action, illustrated, re-enactment, archival, or at all stylistically conventional for a documentary. In this way, *The Wanted 18* fully engages with the notion of animation as a term that applies broadly to moving images created via various means – no part of the film feels untouched by the hand of the animator, and no part of the film feels unsupported by a historically significant, culturally relevant story that the film's very contemporary style reminds us is an on-going conflict and struggle.

Lola, the 'sexy' pregnant cow, gives birth towards the end of the film, and the young calf escapes when the other cows' fates are uncertain. Shomali searches for the calf, perhaps now a cow, in the nearby rocky hills. In this sense, his animated footage, illustrations, and cow sculptures from the related project 'Pixelated Intifada' culminate in a wish for the next generation of resistance, one that finds ever-new and defiantly imaginative ways to animate resistance to occupation and its accompanying representational traps.

Conclusion: Political Animation as an Invitation to Engage

If traditional documentary modes fail Palestinians due to insurmountable representational and visibility problems like those described by Said – animated, hybrid, and experimental modes provide the world with a new way to engage with diverse Palestinian stories, the ongoing struggle against Israeli occupation, and the struggle for justice for Palestinians. Al-Ali's political cartoon refugee boy Handalah provides a model for Palestinian animation's relation to resistance. With his back turned, Handalah does not return our gaze, but rather invites us to follow. This invitation to engage, as with Azzeh's installation *The Line*, is perhaps a unique affordance of animation, in part due to its presumed low political, cultural, and aesthetic status. Animation's reputation as unrealistic children's cartoonery may in fact better equip it in the contemporary moment to reach and incite wider audiences into action. However, future studies must also remain attuned to those constraints, both immaterial and material, on Palestinian media production (such as funding, distribution, and exhibition) that also shape Palestinian animated productions. After all, as *The Line*, *Fatenah*, and *The Wanted 18* insist, while occupation kills and otherwise brutalises even line drawings, 3D characters, and stop-motion cows, it cannot stifle the resilient, creative imagination of Palestinian artists, lactivists, or their supporters.

Notes

1. The phrase 'Pixelated Intifada' is borrowed from the title of an installation produced by Amer Shomali, Dia' Azzeh, and others, which included the group

using 3D modelling software to build cow sculptures out of wooden blocks, referencing the same Intifada cows as in the feature animated *The Wanted 18* discussed in this chapter. For more information, see Amer Shomali, 'Pixelated Intifada', 2012. Available at http://www.amershomali.info/pixelated-intifada/ (accessed 23 February 2015).

2. In the field of animation see, for instance, Dahna Abourahme's film *Ein El-Hilweh/Kingdom of Women* (2010), which includes scenes that animate Naji Al-Ali cartoons.

3. Azzeh cites *Rosoum Motaherera*, an animated political humour series produced by Lebanese Future TV, as one of the first to be widely viewed in Palestine by adults.

4. Debates over utopian and dystopian possibilities have long been a part of animation studies, from Béla Balász' notion that where lines are drawn anything is possible, to widespread commonplace notions of cartoons as childish and/or propagandistic, to Judith/Jack Halberstam's reading of Pixar films as critiques of, not escape from, the fictions undergirding contemporary society. J. Halberstam, *The Queer Art of Failure* (Durham, NC, 2011).

5. For a video essay about this, see: Zaitoon, 'Gaza university student animation: the *Return* – video', *Guardian* (28 June 2012). Available at http://www.theguardian.com/global-development/video/2012/jun/08/gaza-university-student-animation-return-video (accessed 23 February 2015).

6. Livia Alexander asks this question in an essay, titled 'Is there a Palestinian cinema? The national and transnational in Palestinian film production' that, rather than offering a clear response, maps the many obstacles, the industrial and cultural context, as well as transnational, global and local national struggle influences that explain why this question arises so frequently in relation to Palestinian film studies. Alexander also identifies motifs such as land, the struggle for decolonisation and a 'complex notion of Palestinianness'. See Livia Alexander, 'Is there a Palestinian cinema? The national and transnational in Palestinian film production', R. Stein (ed.), *Palestine, Israel, and the Politics of Popular Culture*, (Durham, NC, 2005), pp. 151–72.

7. For instance, Alexander points out that Palestinian cinema is caught between national cinema modes and transnational or exilic modes; it is 'neither national nor transnational, but a hybrid cinema that offers a complex relationship between the two'; but many now question whether there is any cinema that maintains strict national boundaries or entirely surpasses them. For instance, see: Will Higbee and Song Hwee Lim, 'Concepts of transnational cinema: towards a critical transnationalism in film studies', *Transnational Cinema* 1:1 (2010); and Andrew Higson, 'The limiting imagination of national cinema', in E. Ezra and T. Rowden (eds), *Transnational Cinema: The Film Reader* (London and New York, 2006), pp. 15–25.

Pixelated Intifada

8. And, as I have argued, in some cases too neatly mirroring Israeli cinema studies' dominant historical narratives and teleology. For instance, in Nurith Gertz and George Khleifi, *Palestinian Cinema: Landscape, Trauma, and Memory* (Bloomington, IN, 2008), this implicit comparison (they are Israeli film scholars) leads to a kind of dismissal of Palestinian cinema's trajectory, given its seeming incapacity to emerge from what becomes seen as an anachronistic clinging to national politics. Thus, Khleifi and Gertz privilege a 'heterogeneous and open nature' that they describe Palestinian cinema as attempting to achieve since the 1980s. They prefer 'a new tendency to focus on conflicts and tensions within Palestinian society, leaving the Israeli-Palestinian conflict in the background' to the tendency of the films produced during political struggles in the 1960s, 1970s, and 1990s, described in terms of their 'tendency [...] to freeze time and preserve a united, militant, homogeneous nationality' (p. 197).

9. For example: Karen Beckman (ed.), *Animating Film Theory* (Durham, NC, 2014); Suzanne Buchan, *Pervasive Animation* (London, 2013).

10. *The Wanted 18* premiered at the Toronto International Film Festival in 2014, won the Best Documentary in the Arab World from the Abu Dhabi Film Festival (which also had awarded some funding for its production), played at the Rencontres Montréal International Documentary Film Festival, and was awarded the Golden Tanit for Best Documentary at the 2014 Carthage Film Festival in Tunisia.

11. See, for instance, Sarah Irving, 'Israel's movie-funders ban recipients from calling themselves Palestinian', *The Electronic Intefada* (30 January 2015). Available at http://electronicintifada.net/blogs/sarah-irving/israels-movie-funders-ban-recipients-calling-themselves-palestinian (accessed 23 February 2015).

12. A show reel of this initiative is available on YouTube, at https://www.youtube.com/watch?v=g1lrVlxQ7RE (accessed 23 February 2015).

13. See Hasan Omar, 'Entrepreneurial spirit and small businesses in Palestine: what is missing?', *This Week in Palestine*, 80 (April 2013). Available at http://archive.thisweekinpalestine.com/details.php?id=3990&ed=217&edid=217 (accessed 23 January 2015).

14. Available at http://www.kharabeesh.com/en (accessed 23 February 2015).

15. Personal correspondence with Dia' Azzeh, December 2014.

16. Helga Tawil-Souri, 'Digital occupation: Gaza's high-tech enclosure', *Journal of Palestine Studies* 41/2 (2012), pp. 27–43: p. 29.

17. See Sigal Samuel, 'Netanyahu: Hamas wants to pile up "telegenically dead Palestinians"', *The Jewish Daily Forward* (20 January 2014). Available at http://forward.com/articles/202436/netanyahu-hamas-wants-to-pile-up-telegenically/#ixzz3QjNw8kFg (accessed 23 February 2015).

18. See film scholar Terri Ginsberg's critique of North American Palestine solidarity film and video's reliance on *cinema vérité* conventions to document

169

Israeli violence in 'Radical rationalism as cinema aesthetics: the Palestinian-Israeli conflict in North American documentary and experimental film', *Situations: Project of the Radical Imagination* 4.1 (2011), pp. 92–3. Available at http://ojs.gc.cuny.edu/index.php/situations/article/view/767/1198 (accessed 2 December 2012).

19. Hamid Dabashi, *Dreams of a* Nation, p. 9 and 48.
20. For Said's writings on Palestinian cinema, see the preface to Hamid Dabashi's *Dreams of a Nation*; Edward Said, *After the Last Sky: Palestinian Lives* (New York, NY, 1986), p. 33.
21. Said, *After the Last Sky*, p. 41.
22. Paul Wells, *Understanding Animation* (London, 1998), p. 27.
23. Kamran Rastegar discusses *Notre Musique* and Godard's comments in: Kamran Rastegar, *Surviving Images: Cinema, War, and Cultural Memory in the Middle East* (Oxford, 2015), pp. 93–8.
24. Joseph Massad, discussing the importance of 'cultural resistance', argues that 'Palestinian cinema, along with other Palestinian cultural expressions more generally, has been integral to Palestinian resistance'. Joseph Massad, 'The weapon of culture: cinema in the Palestinian liberation struggle', Hamid Dabashi (ed.), *Dreams of a Nation*, p. 31.
25. Béla Balázs, 'The spirit of film', Erica Carter (ed.), *Bela Balázs: Early Film Theory*, trans. Rodney Livingstone (New York, NY, 2010), p. 174.
26. Dia' Azzeh, 'Installation' (2013), [Dia' Azzeh Blogspot]. Available at http://diaazzeh.blogspot.com/p/installation.html (accessed 23 February 2015).
27. WHO Office for Westbank and Gaza, 'Breast cancer in the Gaza Strip: the struggle for survival of Fatma Bargouth' (December 2005), [Israel's Occupation]. Available at http://www.israeloccupation.info/sites/default/files/Breast%20Cancer.pdf (accessed 23 February 2015).
28. Suzanne Buchan, 'Animation, in Theory', K. Beckman (ed.), *Animating Film Theory* (Durham, NC, 2014), p. 119.
29. Wells, *Understanding Animation*, p. 27.
30. Idem, p. 28.
31. Suzanne Buchan, *Pervasive Animation*, p. 120.
32. See Shomali's selected works on his website. Available at http://www.amershomali.info/ (accessed 23 February 2015).
33. Ibid.

Filmography

Ein El-Hilweh: Kingdom of Women, directed by Dahna Abourahme (2010).
Fatenah, directed by Ahmed Habash (2009).
Hide and Seek, directed by Dia' Azzeh (2013).

Khayal Al-Haqil (*Scarecrow*), directed by Khalil Almuzain (in production).

Notre Musique (*Our Music*), directed by Jean-Luc Godard (2004).

The Line, directed by Dia' Azzeh (2012).

The Wanted 18, directed by Amer Shomali and Paul Cowan (2014).

Why?, developed by Zaitoon Studio (2013).

8

Beyond the Burden of Representation: Israeli Animation Between Escapism and Subversion

Yael Friedman

With the recent upsurge in animated filmmaking around the world, and in the Middle East particularly, animation in Israel is equally entering the spotlight. It is without doubt the unprecedented success of Ari Folman's *Vals im Bashir* (*Waltz with Bashir*, 2008) that has brought about international and domestic awareness of Israeli animation. Most studies focused on the film's engagement with the political events it depicts, on its mediation of memory and on the meeting point between documentary and animation.[1] As significant as *Waltz with Bashir* may have been, the film's text and its animated style are far from representative of the history or the heterogeneity of Israeli animation. Little has been published thus far about the wider context of Israeli animation in general, and it is this gap in academic study that this chapter seeks to address. The aim here is to provide an historical overview of the development of animation in Israel – in its multiple contexts of production – and to place those animated films in the wider context of Israeli cinema.[2]

Animation in Israel was slow to develop and, until very recently, remained small in scale. In many ways, the catalysts for its development tended to come from media contexts other than cinema, primarily with the arrival of television in the 1970s, and later with the emergence of digital technologies and new media platforms. The vast majority of animation produced in Israel today is commercial and ranges across genres, from short series for television, children's entertainment and educational productions, to the advertising and music industries, and increasingly to mobile and internet-based media. Since the 1960s, the rate of production of animated films has been miniscule and confined to short formats, with few feature-length films being made. It is only in the last few years that the importance of animation as an autonomous form of artistic expression has been recognised by the Israeli film industry, *Waltz with Bashir* being both a catalyst of and testament to this shift.

As a marginal yet distinct form of cinema, animation was primarily adopted in Israel as a form of expression of the self: animated films expressed the individual, the personal, and transcended the specificities of Israeli or Middle Eastern contexts. As I argue, this tendency towards escapism is an important characteristic of the animated form, which in the context of an ultra-political society can take on a subversive dimension. Moreover, with the recent increase in production rates, animation has gradually taken on more political and social subject matters, becoming a more expressive voice in the Israeli public sphere.

The Pioneers of Israeli Animation: 1930s to 1970s

The origin of Israeli animation can be traced back to the pre-state period of the *Yishuv* (the organised Jewish population in Palestine) during the early decades of the twentieth century.[3] Cultural production in the *Yishuv* was entwined with the development of the Zionist enterprise, and the embryonic cinema that emerged was formed within the context of Zionist propaganda, whether commissioned by Zionist institutions or produced independently by filmmakers committed to the Zionist ideology.[4]

References to works of animation during this period cite a few animated commercials made during the 1930s for Jewish-owned businesses in the *Yishuv* and one animated short film, *Harpatkaotav shel Gadi Ben Sussi* (*The Adventures of Gadi Ben Sussi*, 1932), whose basic style betrays the primitive conditions of its production.[5,6] *The Adventures of Gadi Ben Sussi* was a rare and fairly unnoticed event in the cinematic landscape of its time. For all its rarity it was equally overlooked by subsequent studies of early Israeli cinema, despite being produced by prominent filmmaker

173

Baruch Agadati, whose newsreels and live-action films are often cited as seminal texts of Zionist cinema.[7] This is perhaps the first indication of animation's marginalised position in the Israeli cultural sphere. A closer look at the film's text reveals the idiosyncratic nature of Israeli animation, not only as a distinct film language, but also as a mode of expression that allows for the transgression of dominant discourses and codes of representation.

If in other parts of the world, including in the Middle East, animation was adopted as an expressive propaganda tool, especially during the two World Wars, propaganda cinema in the *Yishuv* comprised predominantly of non-fiction productions: promotional films, newsreels and documentaries. This was not only a consequence of the limited skills base, infrastructure and funds available at the time, but was also driven by the nature of the propaganda mission at hand. Seeking to convince audiences abroad and at home of the viability of the Zionist idea and to provide 'visible evidence' of its feasibility, early Zionist cinema prioritised a realist mode of representation, which relied on the mimetic qualities of the recorded image, notwithstanding the idealised construction of many of these images.[8] Filmmakers also adhered to strict codes of representation. Films engaged thematically with the highest ideals of Zionism and depicted heroic protagonists embodying the Zionist mythical ideal of the New Jew. In the context of the time this was the idealised image of the *Halutz* (the pioneer): *Ashkenazi* (European Jew), secular and modern, whose heroism was manifested in his ability to master the land and fight his enemies.[9]

In contrast, the narrative of *The Adventures of Gadi Ben Sussi* revolves around a newcomer Yemenite Jew and his attempts to find a way to make a living in the new country. The diminutive and traditional looking Gadi is the antithesis of the Zionist hero. At the opening of the film he takes shape as an invisible hand draws stereotypical features that serve to establish Gadi's traditionalism and ethnic origin. A caption informs the viewer that Gadi arrives in the Holy Land in response to religious sentiments of the kind that typified Jewish immigration for many decades prior to the advent of Zionism. Then follows a series of gags in which Gadi roams the urban centres of Tel Aviv in search of a future, all the while projecting imaginative scenarios upon the people and places he encounters. Gadi's fantasies are often derived from biblical stories: in one scene a rug turns into a lion in his mind and he becomes Samson fighting the beast; in another an almond

Beyond the Burden of Representation

vender turns into a whale and Gadi becomes Jonah. His fantasies, first presented in an explanatory caption then coming to life on screen, are the heart of the makers' experiments with the form – figures morph into others and bodies gain hyper-realistic elasticity.

While the film does not engage with overt Zionist propaganda, it is by no means a critique of Zionism. Rather, it allows for a playful escape into the realm of comedy. The fact that the escapism in this film takes the form of a story about a Yemenite Jew is significant because it reveals the Orientalist discourse that was, and still is, central to Zionism. In this Orientalist discourse the (European) Zionist enterprise was the driving force of modernity and progress in an area marked by decay and stagnated by traditionalist populations – Muslims and Jews alike. In *Gadi* this discourse is embedded in the comic structure of the cartoon. The gags derive their comic effect from Gadi's ill-fitting attempts to negotiate the realities of the modern city of Tel Aviv. His Yemenite origin and biblical reference points are ridiculed within the new context of the Zionist project. Interestingly, such comic portrayal of Arab Jews (or *Mizrahim*) only appears in Israeli live-action cinema several decades later, predominantly within the popular genre of the 'Bourekas' films during the 1960s and the 1970s.[10]

With the establishment of the State of Israel in 1948, the filmmaking infrastructure set up in the *Yishuv* became the Israeli film industry. During the first decades it was a small-scale and a largely commercial industry that enjoyed only very limited support from the state. Animation remained marginalised and was generally used during the 1950s and 1960s as a medium for public information and corporate films. Production was sporadic and led by a few auto-didact individuals, such as Yoram Gross, Joseph Bau, Barak Shekin and Yithak Yoresh, who often worked in isolation and from independent studios. State agencies such as the government's Information Office (Misrad Ha'hasbara) are known to have commissioned short animated films about tourism, health and safety, traffic control and similar issues. However, only a small number of the films have been preserved, mainly those made by Joseph Bau, whose daughters transformed his studio into a museum following his death.[11]

Very few self-funded independent films were made during this period, with the short experimental films made by Yoram Gross being perhaps the

175

most well-known. *Gadi's* idiosyncrasies were echoed in Gross' independent films. Israeli live-action cinema was still very much committed to the propaganda mission. Dominated by what Ella Shohat has called the nationalist-heroic genre, films continued to focus on mythic Israeli heroes, often within the context of the Israeli-Arab conflict. The character of the *Halutz* was substituted with those people who embodied the ideal of the new independent state: *Sabras* (Israeli born), *Kibbutzniks* (members of the Kibbutz) and soldiers.[12] Gross' shorts, in contrast, gave a voice to the diasporic Jewish heritage that was silenced by Zionism, as well as to more universal themes and artistic sensibilities. As was the case with *Gadi*, these animated shorts anticipated themes and trends that only began to appear in Israeli live-action cinema several decades later. For example, *Hava Nagilah* (1955) is a stop motion experimental film that celebrates Jewish *Hasidic* culture, a branch of Eastern European Jewish Ultra-Orthodoxy, which was conspicuously absent from the Israeli screen at that time. Similarly, *We Shall Never Die*[13] deals with the memory of the Holocaust through iconographic imagery that evoked a wider humanistic context, independent of Zionist signification, which tended to unify the representation of the Holocaust by subjecting it to the Zionist ideal of Jewish statehood.[14]

Gross *Shirim Le'lo Milim* (*Songs without Words*), which won a prize at the first Brussels Experimental Film Festival in 1958, bore no connection to the cultural context of its production. It is a prime example of the universal animism that typifies what is often thought of as pure animation.[15] It represents a form of animation that addresses the sensual, pre-rational and primordial conditions that precede the cognitive process of making meaning: the kind of animation that was established in the works of such artists as Len Lye, Oskar Fischinger and Norman McLaren; a non-objective and non-linear form of expression driven by the exploration of form, shape and movement 'beyond the obligation to narrate or make representational associations.'[16]

Following these experimental films, Gross ventured into the production of full-length animated film. In the early 1960s he self-funded the production of *Ba'al Hahalomot* (*Joseph the Dreamer*, 1962), a 60-minute puppetry stop-motion animation telling the biblical story of Joseph and his brothers. According to filmmaker and scholar Nathan Gross, this was also the first Israeli biblical film.[17] Biblical stories shot using the landscapes of the Holy Land were very much the domain of Classic Hollywood cinema. One or two expressions of interest to produce similar biblical films by Israeli filmmakers failed to materialise, and generally this was not a prominent thematic concern of Israeli cinema.[18]

While *Joseph* was screened at film festivals around the world, including Cannes, and won praise from contemporary Israeli film critics, it failed commercially. It was withdrawn from cinemas in Tel Aviv just two weeks after its release, and has never been screened commercially since. In 1964, Yoram Gross made a second attempt in the form of a feature-length comedy entitled *Rak Be'lira* (*One Pound Only*, 1964), combining live-action slapstick sketches with short, animated skits. While commercially more successful, it also failed to fully recover its production costs, causing Gross to leave Israel for Australia in 1968, where he still runs a successful production company.

The Emergence of an Israeli Animation Industry: 1970s to 1990s

The arrival of television in Israel in 1968 saw the dawning of a new era for animation. The animation department set up by the state-owned Israeli Broadcast Authority (IBA) became the principal producer of animation. Productions included chiefly animated title sequences and short animated segments for educational television, although some animation for adult audiences was produced. According to David (Dudu) Shalita, a veteran of Israeli animation, the IBA's animation division, headed by Yizhak Yoresh, was characterised in those early days by an innovative and entrepreneurial spirit. Freed from the commercial constraints of competition (IBA monopolised television broadcasts in Israel until the early 1990s), and with no local tradition of practice to shackle it (in animation or in television), it became a primary hub for animators to experiment with different formats and themes.[19]

An innovative spirit was evident, for example, in the animation created for the political satire show *Nikui Rosh* (*Clearing the Mind*, 1974–76) directed by Tzahi Ferber. The short-lived but immensely popular show was renowned for its unprecedented critical stance towards the state and its leaders, and was subsequently inscribed in the Israeli collective memory as

177

a marker of critical public discourse that emerged in the aftermath of the 1973 war. The show's format drew inspiration from *Monty Python's Flying Circus*, and the influence of that legendary British programme's surrealist psychedelic style of animated skits is evident, although the Israeli skits were shorter, black and white and were much less sophisticated. In hindsight, the animation in *Nikui Rosh*, which drew on a developed local tradition of caricature and comics, was the first indication of the popularity of animated satire in Israel, a genre of animation that has developed in the early years of the twenty-first century, especially on web-based platforms.

The optimism generated by television heralded the emergence of a local animation industry in the 1970s and 1980s, albeit on a very small scale. Several independent animation studios were set up, but most managed to operate only for a short time before being forced to close down or to move their production overseas due to their financial instability. This was the case, for example, with Ein Gedi Studios, the first professional animation studio in Israel, set up in 1978 by David (Dudu) Shalita in Kibbutz Ein-Gedi by the Dead Sea. The studio operated for almost a decade before its closure, and was succeeded by Anima Films in Tel Aviv in 1987, also instituted by Shalita.[20] Other prominent examples include Roni Oren's studio Frame by Frame, which was based in Tel Aviv from 1978 to 1984 (in 1988 Oren set up a studio in California), Hanan Kaminski's studios, based in Tel Aviv and Jerusalem between 1981 and 1989 (Kaminski later shifted production to Hungary), Sason Guweta's animation studio in Tel Aviv that operated between 1980 and 1991, and Yigal Doron's studio DAD that opened in 1979 in Tel Aviv; although both closed down, each later reopened as 3D studios.[21] Noam Meshulam's studio PitchiPoy, which opened in 1984 in Jaffa, is still in operation today and is one of Israel's biggest and most established animation studios.

At the same time, animation studies was gradually introduced into art schools and university departments.[22] An Animation Association was founded in 1977, and preliminary international links were forged as animators from Israel travelled to study and work abroad (primarily in Europe and North America) and Israeli animation films were presented in international festivals. These networks developed further with the establishment of the Israeli branch of the International Association of Animated Film (ASIFA) in 1985. The independent animation that developed in Israel

Beyond the Burden of Representation

at this time, shared the artistic sensibilities and humanistic (and Jewish) concerns of Yoram Gross' experimental films. Abstraction continued to be the key approach to much of the works produced, especially those that emerged from the animation departments in art schools, the most notable of which being the prestigious Bezalel School of Art. Works such as *Bitzbutz* (Gil Alkabetz, 1985)[23] and *Bitza* (*Egg*, Roni Oren, 1980)[24] share the pure artistic motivation to explore the performance of movement and metamorphosis itself. A similar approach was evident in 16 short films produced with assistance from the Israeli Film Centre.[25]

Other productions of the time included narrative-based children's films, such as the feature length *Ha'yayar Ha'kasum* (*The Enchanted Forest*, Shlomo Suriano, 1974), Dudu Shalita's *Orot* (*Lights: the Story of Chanukah*) and *Agada shel Hagada* (*The Animated Hagada*, Roni Oren, 1984). These animated films remain distinct and idiosyncratic in the cinematic landscape of the time, despite the rise of a more personal and politically critical cinema, insomuch as it largely avoided engaging with Israel's socio-cultural spheres, either thematically or aesthetically.[26]

An exception to this can be found in Hanan Kaminski's *Victory* (1987), possibly the first animated film to deal specifically with the Israeli-Arab conflict. Like *Waltz with Bashir*, this short cartoon was made in response to its director's military service during the 1982 war with Lebanon. It shows a cartoonish David and Goliath engaged in a succession of battles. The first scene sees the diminutive David sitting peacefully by his shack in the desert, surrounded by several trees and with two sheep. When an enraged Goliath approaches and threatens him, David drives him away with a stone. Encouraged by this victory he cuts down one of the trees to build a more sophisticated mechanism of defence. When Goliath returns, David is better prepared and hits him even harder. The cycle continues and escalates. With each battle David grows more powerful, utilising all he has (the trees, his sheep, his shack and eventually the line he is drawn with) to expand his war machine. Becoming obsessed with the machine itself, he fails to notice that his enemy has long been defeated and ends up bringing about his own destruction. While the version of the conflict's history suggested in this cartoon is highly contentious (as are the meanings attached to the allegorical use of David and Goliath), the critical stance towards Israeli aggression is clear. Such criticism – questioning the futility of the on-going conflict (though not necessarily its origins) – emerged in earnest after the 1982 war, increasing with the heavy presence of the Israeli army in the occupied territories during the first Palestinian Intifada. It was expressed in different ways in Israeli live-action cinema, as well as in more contemporary animated films that are discussed below.

Contemporary Israeli Animation: Coming Home

The important socio-political transformations of the 1990s brought with them significant changes to the media and film industries, changes that were crucial for animation and in many ways paved the way to its current expansion. A move from the monopoly of a single public service channel to multi-channel commercial television opened up new platforms, enabling and instigating the development of longer and more diverse animated formats. An influx of animators, most of them Russian immigrants, brought to the local animation scene a breadth of classical training and experience accompanied by a variety of techniques that transformed its competences.[27] And, as was the case elsewhere, the advent of digital technologies significantly changed the face of animation, making production not only more accessible and cheaper, but also creating new opportunities for exhibition and marketing.

Over the last two decades a growing number of animation studios of varying sizes have been set up. Many more animation studies programmes have been created, some within the traditional academic and art school contexts, others in the form of software training courses. In 2000, the Israeli Animation Centre (IAC) was inaugurated in collaboration with the Tel Aviv Cinémathèque and began hosting an annual international animation and comic festival, Animix. The work of ASIFA-Israel intensified, including the launch of an annual bulletin in 1991 and, since 2001, showcasing an annual Animix competition of Israeli animation. Another important landmark came with the establishment of a Trade Union for the Animation Professions in 2010, with the aim of promoting the particular interests of animation and animators within the Israeli visual and cultural industries.[28]

Although such institutional advances have been vital to the development of the industry, the entrepreneurial spirit of many young animation graduates was no less instrumental in pushing the field forward. The recent development of animation across the Middle East and North Africa was very much led by entrepreneurial and experimental young people.[29] While the demographics in Israel are somewhat different, and training institutions better-developed, parallels can still be drawn with the way in which young Israeli animators employ digital technologies, often bypassing traditional media gatekeepers by using social media sites. By doing so they can exhibit and promote their work while simultaneously using it as a tool for fundraising.

As the first decade of the new millennium drew to a close, the conditions for a viable Israeli animation industry, at least commercially, had finally come to fruition. Israeli animation today includes works in a variety of formats, techniques and styles, across various media and platforms, and is made both for the local market and for international clients. The lion's share of commercial work goes to music, advertising, games and mobile media industries, while television continues to play a key part in commissioning and featuring locally produced animation. The number of animation studios keeps growing, ranging from sizable and established studios such as PitchiPoy and Pil Animation, who produce independent films alongside their commercial work, to smaller and more innovative companies such as Yuval and Merav Nathan's Animation Home and Nir Gerber and Gali Edelbaum's Animation. Many other companies are solely producing commissioned work, specialising in visual effects, 3D animation and digital design. The largest of these, such as Gravity, Snowballs and Shortcut Playground, are based in Israel but operate on a global scale.[30]

The Israeli film industry has also seen significant transformations in the last two decades. The introduction of a new Cinema Law in 2000, together with a significant increase in state subsidies – distributed by several public film funds – and a growing Israeli participation in the expanding transnational co-production system, have all contributed to an unprecedented success for Israeli cinema in recent years, both at home and abroad.[31] However, the effect of these transformations on the production of animated films was slower. Certainly, public funding for animated films has increased to a degree, but this has only gone part way towards remedying the long-standing marginalisation of animation as a cinematic form. Moreover, support was given primarily to short films and so the production of feature-length animated films remains a considerable challenge. Since its establishment

36 years ago, the Israeli Film Fund has only supported three feature-length animated films, and only two of these – *$9.99* (Tatia Rozental, 2007) and *Waltz with Bashir* (Ari Folman, 2008) – have been completed. The third film, *Armon Ha'hol* (*The Sand Castle*, Noam Meshulam), a production of PitchiPoy, has yet to see production completed, despite the support given by the fund in 2011. Many feel that the current system of public funding does not take into account the particular timeframes and budgetary needs associated with animated productions, and that this hinders the chances of successful applications for subsidisation. Moreover, many feel badly equipped to operate strategically within the Israeli (and transnational) funding landscape, characterised as it is by decentralisation and diversity of sources.[32]

Nevertheless, the relationship between the Israeli film industry and the animated form may well see much-anticipated change in the near future, with growing recognition among animation institutions of the need to learn how to operate within the current funding climate. This comes alongside an acknowledgment on the part of the different film funds of the special needs of animation. Such a change in relationship is anticipated not only at the level of production. In the last few years, and particularly since the release of *Waltz with Bashir*, a growing number of Israeli animators are employing the distinct language of animation as a creative tool for social and political commentary, reflecting perhaps a more universal *zeitgeist*. Indeed, confirmation of this can be found in the programme showcased at Animix 2014, which was more 'Israeli' than ever, featuring, in addition to the annual programme of ASIF, three Israeli premieres – *Two Boys* (Joao Ternoirio and Coi Belluzzo, 2012), *Anafim Shvurim* (*Broken Branches*, Ayala Sharott, 2014) and *The Common Room Animated Project* (coordinated by Yael Ozsinay, 2014) – and two showcases of Israeli animation curated by Sharon Toval.

Certainly, the embedded abstraction, fantasy and escapism that have characterised Israeli animation since its inception continue to form an important part of contemporary production. Many films deal with universal topics such as ecology, parental and intergenerational relationships, technology, old age and so on. However, a closer look at this rather eclectic body of work reveals a shift towards an engagement with specifically Israeli issues. This is evidenced by the growing popularity of animated

Beyond the Burden of Representation

satire on YouTube in such animation productions as *Miflatzoni Ha'knesset* (*The Parliament's Monsters*) by the animator Michael Roznov, *Ahmed Ve Salim* (*Ahmed and Salim*) by Or Paz and Tom Trager (since 2009) of Ha' Srutonim, a web-based animation company, as well as *Pinat Lituf* (*Petting Corner*, 2014) by Nir Gerber and Gali Edelbaum. The latter began on the animators' YouTube channel and now features on television as part of the popular satire show *Eretz Nehederet* (*A Wonderful Land*, since 2003). This shift is also evident in the recent crop of independent animated films. A preliminary attempt to map this stylistically diverse body of work reveals some thematic commonalities.

Prominent among the shared themes are the tensions between the individual and society and between the private and the collective. Many of the films are consumed by questions of belonging and otherness, and portray subjective inner worlds and distorted exterior environments that are riddled with feelings of isolation, anxiety and displacement. Examples include films like Anat Costi's *Be' Petach Beiti* (*On My Door Step*, 2010), *The Red Suitcase* (Shaul Fried, 2008), *True Love Hotel* (Alon Ga'ash, 2008) *Be'deah Tzlula* (*In Clear Mind*, Ofra Kobliner and Eli Ben Dor, 2010) *Layla* (*Cut Me Off*, Luna Matar, 2013), *Café Babel* (Michal Rabinovich and Dafna Ben Ami, 2013). In these films – and many others like them – the narratives, characters and environments bear little connection to the concrete geographical or cultural context of Israel, thus rendering the stories and their social commentary universal.

A smaller number of significant works contain narratives and environments that reference the Israeli context overtly, so creating more direct interventions in the Israeli public discourse. Perhaps one of the most poignant examples is Uri and Michelle Kranot's *Hollow Land* (2013) in which the artists use a mix of materials and techniques (see image 8.1) to tell a multi-layered story about displacement and alienation.

The film's narrative revolves around a couple migrating to a new country where collective identity, signalled by the wearing of a plunger on one's head, is strictly policed by mechanisms of public surveillance. The couple's attempts to fit in, at the price of losing their individual identities, wishes and hopes, bring tension to their relationship. When they attempt to rebel, reasserting their individualism by taking the plunger off, they encounter, or imagine they encounter (the film is deliberately ambiguous on this point)

183

8.1 Still from *Hollow Land*, directed by Uri and Michelle Kranot (2013)

the tyranny of the masses demanding they conform. With the birth of their child they decide to leave, fleeing back to the sea in search of another future. The film's critical stance is articulated clearly in the final scene, which sees the couple at sea, floating in hope for a new home, surrounded by others – couples, individuals and small groups – who share a similar journey of displacement. The film's imagery shifts between the familiar and the strange, the real and the fantastic, the mundane and the dramatic. On one level its signifiers are fantastic, and thus universal; on another, the film subtly conjures up the particular Israeli context, as several signifiers of Israeli culture and geography are scattered throughout the film. For example, the plunger is referred to in the film by its colloquial name in Hebrew: *Pompa*. Likewise, the first image of the film, showing the couple standing on a sandy beach dressed in heavy coats, references archive photos of European-Jewish immigrants to Palestine at the turn of the twentieth century used by the animators as inspiration for the film's images.

In *Rishumim Me'Minchen* (*Sketches from Munich*, Jack TML, 2013) the Israeli context is made more explicit in the voiceover conveying feelings of displacement and dissent. The film is structured as an illustrated letter, written by a young Israeli artist on a visit to Munich to his lover back home. Black and white watercolour drawings make up the animated image track of

Beyond the Burden of Representation

8.2 Still from *Sketches from Munich*, directed by Jack TML

the film, while the content of the letter is read in voiceover (see image 8.2). The letter intimates the artist's desire to break out of what he calls the 'prison' of Israeli society. At the midpoint of the film the artist's panting voice relays to his lover:

> You are a prison. One big prison. Six million Jews cramped together, waiting for the Messiah to save them, and the borders of this prison are not made of enemies, no guards, no towers, and they are not made of heavy stones or fences or security cameras. The borders of this prison are made of collective memories of existential fears, which we carry from kindergarten to the time we take our vows in the army. Walls of Holocaust corpses and IDF [Israeli Defence Force] martyrs that, God forbid, anyone should say have died in vain. Electric fences from Grandpa's words, security cameras in mother's eyes.

This sense of imprisonment is here explicitly attributed to the Zionist narrative that substitutes the individual for the collective, and subjects contemporary Israeli realities to the mythical power of the historical trauma of the Holocaust.[33]

Likewise, *Adoni Melech* (*My Lord*, Ido Soliman, 2008) is the autobiographical monologue of a young man of Mizrahi origin, who *en route* to self-acceptance confronts the oppressive forces that have shaped his life: his father, the Israeli state and Jewish religion. The film overtly links patriarchal oppression at home to Orientalist oppression of Mizrahim by early Zionism, as well as to the role played by a religious institution that cynically capitalises on these feelings of oppression. Equally, *Altneuland* (*The Old New Land*, Sariel Keslasi, 2012) is a subjective interpretation of Theodor Herzl's utopian novel with the same title from 1902. According to Keslasi the film 'tries to deal with the collapse of Herzl's dream and seeks to emphasise the sense of absurdity and instability of my personal experience as an individual in the Israeli society.'[34] *Mechonat Yisrael* (*The Israel Machine*, Mysh and Moshko, 2011) and *Buka, Mabuka and Mabulka* (Ofek Shemer and Ada Rimon, 2014) deal with similar themes of collective identity, but in a more light-hearted way.

Issues of belonging and displacement are by no means unique to the Israeli context. All these films can be read as commenting on a universal, and in some ways ahistorical, human experience. Indeed, as the young animator Yael Ozsinay, who coordinated the *Common Room* project, explains: 'animators are often loners and introverted people, the animator works on his own, observing the world and communicating with it through "a screen." We often identify with the position of the outsider.'[35] Yet, in the specific context of Israeli society, where the relationship between individual expression and collective identity has always been an area rife with tension, such a thematic focus on questions of belonging and otherness can be read as acquiring a critical dimension, whether the films clearly reference the Israeli context or not.

While a unified Israeli identity, which was constructed by the once hegemonic Ashkenazi and secular Zionist discourse, has long been contested – from the left by the post-Zionist critique that emerged in the 1990s, and from the right by religious-nationalist ideologies that increasingly gain prominence – on-going struggles over the reshaping of a collective 'Israeli identity' take place in contemporary everyday discourse, as well as on the level of official politics. Competing sections of society divided along religious, ethnic, national, ideological and generational lines, take part in these struggles, and an assertion of individualism, informed by wider postmodern and transnational discourses is in itself politically contingent rather than simply escapist.

By commenting on the oppression of collective mechanisms of unification and by drawing attention to the other, the unique, the displaced and the individual, all these films can be seen as utterances that intervene in these on-going struggles over the very identity of Israeli society. Yael Munk has made a similar claim in relation to the so-called escapist live-action cinema that emerged in Israel during the 1990s. The retreat into the private domain and the avoidance of representing dramatic political events of the decade (such as the 1991 Gulf War, the Oslo Agreement, the assassination of Prime Minister Yitzhak Rabin) is read by Munk not as escapism but as a political reaction to the collapse of hegemonic narratives and the breakdown of Israeli collective identity.[36]

Another emerging theme, which impinges on a long-running preoccupation of live-action cinema, is that of war. *Waltz with Bashir* is by no means the only one. Several recent animated shorts have dealt with this subject matter and additional films are currently in production. While they all subscribe to a widely defined anti-war message, they differ from each other considerably in terms of their styles and techniques, their political standpoints, and the relationships they constitute between actuality, history and the animated image. Several films deal with mediating memory and trauma within the context of the Holocaust or of Israel's wars. For example, the shorts *Nyosha* (Yael Dekel and Liran Kapal, 2012), *Mut* (2013) and *Broken Branches* are based on fractions of memory of the filmmakers' grandparents' experiences during the Holocaust. Similarly, the collective project *Panim. Yom. Zikaron* (*Face. Day. Memory*, 2012–13), a commemorative project commissioned by the NGO Beit Avi Chai, consists of shorts that mediate momentary memories in the lives of war and terror attack casualties, as delineated by their loved ones.

These films fit comfortably within a definition of animated documentaries – audio-visual works either recorded or created frame-by-frame that deal with *the* world rather than *a* world wholly imagined by its creator, and that have been presented as a documentary by their producers or received as documentary by audiences, festivals or critics.[37] Moreover, Honess Roe's typology of the three ways in which animation functions in animated documentaries is useful in outlining the relationship between the actual events and the animated images in these films. She proposes that animation functions essentially as a substitute for some representational limitations of more conventional documentary devices, either in the form of mimetic substitution or non-mimetic substitution and evocation.[38]

187

Animation in the Middle East

In *Nyosha*, *Mut* and *Face. Day. Memory*, the animation functions as mimetic substitution, 'directly standing in for live-action footage' and attempting to mimic the look of reality.[39] *Krav E'had Yoter Midai* (*One Battle Too Many*, Yoel Sharon, Pil Animation, in production) recounts traumatic memories of veterans of the 1973 war. As a combination of live-action interviews with animated fragments visualising the war, the film's visual style resonates with that of *Waltz with Bashir*. The animation in *Broken Branches*, in contrast, is largely non-mimetic and evocative. Using multiple styles and techniques, it expands on live-action footage and visualises 'invisible' feelings and thoughts expressed by the protagonist.

Short films such as *Beton* (*Concrete*, Ariel Belinco and Michael Faust, 2007), *Eli* (Sagi Alter and Reut Elad, 2014) and to some extent *Libo Shel Amos Klein* (*The Heart of Amos Klein*, Michelle and Uri Kranot, 2008) and *Loof* (Daniel Sasson and David Rubin, 2011) engage in very different ways with the experience of occupation from the point of view of the Israeli soldier. While these films are not based on actual events, they do engage with actuality. Using the full potential of animated language by creating imaginative narratives and situations within the realities of the occupation, they destabilise ingrained perceptions and suggest new understandings.

Resonating with a scene from the Palestinian film *Yadon Ilaheyya* (*Divine Intervention*, Elia Suleiman, 2002), *Concrete* comments on the absurdity of the occupation when two Israeli soldiers are shown to wage an all-out war on a kite that 'refuses' to stay on the Palestinian side of the Separation Wall. In a more sombre tone, *Eli* creates a fantastic narrative about a lone soldier on guard in a Palestinian town who is tempted by a white rabbit (the reference to Alice in Wonderland is clear) into a 'hole' that leads to a role-reversal, or perhaps split-identity, situation. In the final scene of the film the soldier finds himself caught in his own hallucination, in the position of a Palestinian child and invaded by none other than himself.

Similarly, *The Heart of Amos Klein* creates a fabricated story, in cartoon style, about an IDF General named Amos Klein, who conceived the idea of the Separation Wall. The film, as is the case with most of Michelle and Uri Kranot's work, proves challenging to classify. The filmmakers often purposefully blur the actual (i.e. addressing *the* world) with the fabricated (i.e. creating *a* world) in order to offer new types of understanding and knowledge about *the* world. Amos Klein is a fabricated character, but his design

188

and biography clearly reference Ariel Sharon. The story was also inspired by the autobiographical elements of the filmmakers' lives. On the visual level, fragments of archive news footage and photographs of spaces and people are woven into the animated texture. These photographic elements are elaborated upon with animation, to varying degrees. They function as relics, traces, fossils of the reality upon which the animated story is built.

When discussing Syrian and Lebanese documentaries that contain animated fragments, Stefanie Van de Peer shows the push and pull dynamic of such hybrid texts, in which the animated fragments function partly to seduce and alter the spectatorial experience of documentary, even though the seduction is never complete. Such a dynamic leads, she claims, to a new awareness of the constructedness of reality.[40] We may think about films such as *Amos* as mirror cases – as animation with documentary fragments – in which the inherent subjectivity of animation, which constantly negotiates its ontological boundaries, and requires, when it engages with politically charged topics such as this, a kind of photographic ontology to push against in order to produce political commentary about reality.[41] Similar motivation led Ari Folman to include archive footage of the Sabra and Shatila Massacre in the final scene of *Waltz with Bashir*.

Finally, Uri and Michelle Kranot's films *God on Our Side* (2005), *White Tape* (2010), *Black Tape* (2014), as well as *Don Kishot Be'Yerushalim* (*Don Quixote in Jerusalem*, Dani Rosenberg, 2005), *Mi'Toch Sicha Ben Yeshayahu Leibowitch ve Israel Eldad* (*Debate Between Yeshayahu Leibowitz and Israel Eldad*, *1980*, Ofek Shemer and Ada Rimon, 2013) and *The Cabinet Decision* (Mayan Angelman, 2014), present more essayist commentary on the occupation. These films rely less on narratives and characterisation and more on drawing conceptual links and visual metaphors to provoke the viewer into considering new ideas.[42]

Conclusion: From Homecoming to Arriving in the Region

I have sought to show here how the historical marginality of animation within the Israeli film industry, and within the Israeli cultural sphere at large, has in many ways shaped it as an idiosyncratic art form. It was manifested not only in the distinct language of animation, a language

189

that forms a unique mode of expression, but also in the themes, subject matters and issues that animators have chosen to engage with. If dominant live-action cinema was often called upon to delineate the collective story of the nation, animated films seem to have escaped such a burden of representation. The inherent subjectivity of animated films, and their association with escapism freed many Israeli animators to eschew Israeli socio-political realities altogether and enabled them to transcend hegemonic codes of representation. The imaginative worlds they created were rooted in the personal and the private. In doing so they foreground, to use Sobchack's terminology, animation's own ontology, its own sufficient conditions for being 'what it is.'[43]

It is only in the last few years that Israeli animation has begun to take its place within the main body of Israeli cinema. Contemporary Israeli cinema is often hailed for its heterogeneity: speaking in many voices, comprising diverse genres and representing Israel's various, often competing, sectors, cultures and ideologies. Animated films, for their part, now increasingly engage with the social and political concerns of Israeli society. The inherent subjectivity and diversity of the form, as well as the universal appeal with which it addresses these issues, are no longer conspicuously alien to the Israeli cinematic landscape.

Such a shift in the thematic concerns and approach of animated films is not unique to the Israeli case. Animation has not only flourished all over the world, but it is becoming a visible mode of expressing political and social commentary. While Israel occupies a distinct place within the cultural and political sphere of the Middle East, the features of contemporary Israeli animation are not dissimilar to those of other countries in the region, especially in the ways in which it is produced and consumed by youth. As this chapter illustrates, Israeli animation engages with the Middle East predominantly, if at all, within the framework of the political conflict. While this is a result of the complex realities of the conflict, it remains an oddity worth noting, given the geographical position of Israel and its large Arab population of different faiths. Apart from a few initiatives and the Palestinian films that are produced inside Israel, Israeli cinema is still largely Eurocentric. Animation even more so; production is oriented towards the West, as is the majority of the cultural reference points. It took

Israeli animation nearly 70 years to 'come home'. Maybe one day, optimistic and idealistic as it may sound today, it might 'arrive' in the Middle East.

Notes

1. See for example: Raz Yosef, 'War fantasies: Memory, trauma and ethics in Ari Folman's *Waltz with Bashir*', *Journal of Modern Jewish Studies*, 9, 3 (2010), pp. 311–26; Garret Stewart, 'Screen memory in *Waltz with Bashir*', *Film Quarterly*, 63, 3 (2010), pp. 58–62; Katrina Schlunke, 'Animated documentary and the screen death: Experiencing *Waltz with Bashir*', *South Atlantic Quarterly*, 110, 4 (2011), pp. 949–62; Robert M, Peaslee, '"It's fine as long as you draw but don't film": *Waltz with Bashir* and the postmodern function of animated documentary', *Visual Communication Quarterly*, 18 (2011), pp. 223–35; Alice, Burgin 'Guilt, history and memory: Another perspective on *Waltz with Bashir*', *Metro Magazine: Media & Education Magazine*, 164 (2010), pp. 70–4; Natasha Mansfield, 'Loss and mourning cinema's "language" of trauma in *Waltz with Bashir*', *Wide Screen*, 1, 2 (2010), pp. 1–13.

2. Academic sources on animation in Israel are scarce and there is limited archival material to draw upon. In compiling the data for this chapter, I have relied on several short publications in Israeli journals, mainly by Zvika Oren, and on interviews with key practitioners in the field to whom I am grateful for sharing films, information and observations. As with any work of historiography, and particularly in such a short format, a degree of generalisation and selection is inevitable. There were many films and filmmakers I was unable to include and several points I would have liked to expand on. A comprehensive study of Israeli animation is yet to be written. For existing publications see: Zvika Oren, 'Animation in Israel – Summary 1982', *Cinematheque: Cinema Journal*, 13 (1983), pp. 18–19; 1999; Dana Arieli-Horowitz, 'Alive and kicking: Israeli animation – a conversation with Roni Oren, Head of the Screen Arts Department, Bezalel', *Bezalel – Proceedings on History and Theory*, 8 (2008), available at https://bezalel.secured.co.il/zope/home/he/1209439536 (Hebrew); and the ASIFA Israel bulletins published between 1991 and 1997. Interviewees for this chapter included: David (Dudu) Shalita (animation filmmaker, teacher and curator of Animix Festival Tel Aviv), Noam Meshulam (animation filmmaker and founder of Pitchipoy Studios), Sarah Hatooka (animation filmmaker and Head of Animation Studies at Minshar School of Art, Tel Aviv), Gilat Parag (animator and artistic director of Asif – the annual showcase of Israeli Animation); Uri and Michelle Kranot (animation filmmakers and teachers at The Animation Workshop, Viborg, Denmark) and young animation filmmakers such as Yael Ozsinay, Daniel Sasson and Sheli Hermon.

3. Oren, 'Animation in Israel – Summary 1982', pp. 18–19; Arieli-Horowitz, 'Alive and kicking'.
4. Hillel Tryster, *Israel Before Israel: Silent Cinema in the Holy Land* (Jerusalem, 1995). (Hebrew); Ella Shohat, *Israeli Cinema: East/West and the Politics of Representation* (London, 2010); Ariel Feldestein, *Cinema and Zionism: The Development of Nation Through Film* (Oregon, 2012).
5. Tryster, *Israel Before Israel*; Oren, '100 Years of Animation', pp. 13–22 and 'Animation in Israel'; Nathan Gross, *The Hebrew Film*.
6. Oren, 'Animation in Israel', cites a commercial for the shoe factory Keter-Yizhak that is stored in the Spielberg Film Archive. Tryster, in *Israel Before Israel*, mentions two Zionist animated propaganda films that were made in Germany in 1924.
7. Michal Goren, '*This is the Land*: Zionism, man and land – Cinematic aspects and poetic devices in the service of Zionism', pp. 40–50; Oren, 'Animation in Israel – Summary 1982', pp. 18–19; Feldestein, *Cinema and Zionism*; Gross, *The Hebrew Film*.
8. Scholarly studies of early Israeli cinema did not discuss animation production, but Shohat stresses that the focus on documentary was not only due to economic constraints, pp. 23–4. Feldestein, in his detailed historical account, provides several examples to the prioritising of 'realism'. See for example his discussion on realism and drama in *This is the Land*, pp. 101–102.
9. Ibid., p. xi.
10. This comic genre was named after the popular Sephardi pastry, and focused on the ethnic tensions between Mizrahim and Ashkenazim. For analysis of the Bourekas films see: Shohat, *Israeli Cinema*.
11. On Yosef Bau's work see: http://www.josephbau.com. For more on Gross' later work see: http://www.yoramgrossfilms.com.au (accessed 4 May 2015).
12. Shohat, *Israeli Cinema*, p. 53
13. A precise date for this film by Yoram Gross could not be ascertained, but we know it was produced around the same time as *Hava Nagila*, i.e. the mid-1950s.
14. Yosefa Loshitzky, *Identity politics on the Israeli Screen* (Texas, 2001), pp. 15–16.
15. Wells, *Understanding Animation*, pp. 30–2.
16. Ibid.
17. Gross, *The Hebrew Film*, pp. 247–8.
18. Ibid.
19. Phone interview, 18 September 2014.
20. For more information about Shalita's work see his web page (in Hebrew) at: http://www.dudushalita.com.
21. Oren, '100 Years of Animation', pp. 13–22; 'Animation in Israel'.
22. The first course opened in the College for Television Arts in Tel Aviv, in 1968, and was followed by the prestigious Bezalel Art School in 1971, and in 1972, by

the newly established Film and Television Department at Tel Aviv University. Additional animation courses opened in the years to come. For more detail see Oren, 'Animation in Israel'.

23. *Bitzbutz* is online. Available at https://www.youtube.com/watch?v= PqXTJ2GZc94 (accessed 4 May 2015).

24. *The Egg* is online. Available at https://www.youtube.com/watch?v= VUCG670NXOo (accessed 4 May 2015).

25. According to Oren, the Israeli Film Centre's low-budget Short Films Fund supported one animation production each year between 1968 and 1984, and several other films between 1989 and the mid-1990s (see '100 Years of Animation', pp. 13–22; 'Animation in Israel'). Not all of these films are available for viewing. According to Shalita, who curated several programmes dealing with the history of Israeli animation, these were predominantly abstract films.

26. On this wave of personal cinema see, for example: Ariel Schweitzer, *Ha'regisut Ha'hadasha: Israeli Modernist Cinema in the 1960 and 1970s* (Tel Aviv, 2003) (Hebrew).

27. Noam Meshulam, interview, Tel Aviv, 8 April 2014; Shalita, phone interview, 18 September 2014; Arieli-Horowitz, 'Alive and kicking'.

28. Oren, 'Animation in Israel'.

29. Stefanie Van de Peer, 'Fragments of war and animation: Dahna Abourahme's *Kingdom of Women* and Soudade Kaadan's *Damascus Roofs: Tales of Paradise*', *Middle East Journal of Culture and Communication*, 6, 2, p. 158.

30. For more information about these studios see their respective websites: http://pitchipoy.tv; http://pilanimation.com; http://galiedel.wix.com; http://www.animationhome.net; http://www.gravity.co.il,; http://www.snowballvfx.com, http://www.scpg.tv. A selection of recent animation from Israel is available for viewing on Yoni Salmon's Vemio channel *Moonfash* at https://vimeo.com/channels/israelimation (accessed 4 May 2015).

31. The new cinema law replaced the Encouragement of Israeli Film Law from 1954 that was concerned mainly with regulating broad commercial aspects of the industry. The new law is a more extensive legislation that defines the attributes of Israeli cinema as a national and cultural industry, ensures an increase in the level of public funding for cinema and sets guidelines for the allocation of public funds through the appointment of an advisory body – the Cinema Council. The law placed a new emphasis on the representation of Israel's diverse cultures and social groups.

32. Such sentiments were expressed in the interviews I conducted (see note 2) and in a talk about the funding of animation films given at the Animix festival in 2014.

33. On the centrality of the Holocaust in contemporary Israeli discourse see: Dalia Ofer 'The past that does not pass: Israelis and Holocaust memory', *Israel Studies*, 14, 1 (2009), pp. 1–35.

34. Taken from the artist's Vimeo page: http://vimeo.com/56648036 (accessed 4 May 2015).
35. Interview, Tel Aviv, 17 August 2014.
36. Yael Munk, *Israeli Cinema at the Turn of the Millennium* (Israel, 2012). (Hebrew), p. 12.
37. Annabelle Honess Roe, 'Absence, excess and epistemological expansion: Towards a framework for the study of animated documentary', *Animation: An Interdisciplinary Journal*, 6, 3 (2011), p. 217.
38. Ibid.
39. Ibid., p. 226.
40. Van de Peer, 'Fragments of War and Animation', pp. 151–77.
41. Ward, 'Animated realities.'
42. It is important to reiterate, before I conclude, that the list of films I discuss here, as well as the key thematic concerns I highlight, do not represent a comprehensive account of contemporary animation in Israel. There are additional films dealing with other aspects of Israeli society that I could not include, and which would make a fruitful case for further, and in my view, much needed scholarly writing on Israeli animation.
43. Sobchack, 'The line and the animorph', pp. 252–3.

Filmography

$9.99, directed by Tatia Rozental (2007).
Adoni Melech (*My Lord*), directed by Ido Soliman (2008).
Agada shel Hagada (*The Animated Hagada*), directed by Roni Oren (1984).
Ahmed ve Salim (*Ahmed and Salim*), directed by Or Paz and Tom Trager (2009-present).
Altneuland, directed by Sariel Keslasi (2012).
Anafim Shvurim (*Broken Branches*), directed by Ayala Sharott (2014).
Armon Ha'chol (*The Sand Castle*), directed by Noam Meshulam (in production).
Ba'al Hahalomot (*Joseph the Dreamer*), directed by Yoram Gross (1962).
Be'deah Tzlula (*In Clear Mind*), directed by Ofra Kobliner and Eli Ben Dor (2010).
Be'petach Beiti (*On my Door Step*), directed by Anat Costi (2010).
Beton (*Concrete*), directed by Ariel Belinco and Michael Faust (2007).
Bitza (*Egg*), directed by Roni Oren (1980).
Bitzbutz, directed by Gil Elkabetz (1985).
Black Tape, directed by Uri and Michelle Kranot (2014).
Buka, Mabuka and Mabulka, directed by Ofek Shemer and Ada Rimon (2014).
Café Babel, directed by Michal Rabinovich and Dafna Ben Ami (2013).
Don Kishot Be'Yerushalim (*Don Quixote in Jerusalem*), directed by Dani Rosenberg (2005).
Eli, directed by Sagi Alter & Reut Elad (2014).

Beyond the Burden of Representation

Eretz Nehederet (A Wonderful Land) (2003-present).

God on Our Side, directed by Uri and Michelle Kranot (2005).

Ha'yayar Ha'kasum (The Enchanted Forest), directed by Shlomo Suriano (1974).

Harpatkaotav shel Gadi Ben Sussi (The Adventures of Gadi Ben Sussi), directed by Baruch Agadati (1932).

Hava Nagilah, directed by Yoram Gross (1955).

Hollow Land, directed by Uri and Michelle Kranot (2013).

Kochav Katan (Little Star), directed by Dudu Geva (1978).

Krav E'had Yoter Midai (One Battle Too Many), directed by Yoel Sharon (in production).

Layla (Cut Me Off), directed by Luna Matar (2013).

Libo Shel Amos Klein (The Heart of Amos Klein), directed by Michelle and Uri Kranot (2008).

Loof, directed by Daniel Sasson and David Rubin (2011).

Mechonat Yisrael (The Israel Machine), directed by Mysh and Moshko (2011).

Miflatzoni Ha'kneset (The Parliament's Monsters), directed by Michael Roznov (n.d.).

Mi'Toch Sicha Ben Yeshayahu Leibowitch ve Israel Eldad (Debate between Yeshayahu Leibowitz and Israel Eldad, 1980), directed by Ofek Shemer and Ada Rimon (2013).

Monty Python's Flying Circus, directed by Ian MacNaughton and John Howard Davies (1969–74).

Mut, directed by Ayala Sharot (2013).

Nikui Rosh (Clearing the Mind), directed by Tzahi Ferber (1974–76).

Nyosha, directed by Yael Dekel and Liran Kapal (2012).

Orot (Lights: the story of Chanukah), directed by Dudu Shalita (1982).

Panim, Yom, Zikaron (Face. Day. Memory), commissioned by Beit Avi Chai (2012–13).

Pinat Lituf (Petting Corner), directed by Nir Gerber and Gali Edelbaum (2014).

Rak Be'lira (One Pound Only), directed by Yoram Gross (1964).

Rishumin me'minchen (Sketches from Munich), directed by Jack TML (2013).

Shirim Le'lo Milim (Songs without Words), directed by Yoram Gross (1958).

The Cabinet Decision, directed by Mayan Angelman (2014).

The Common Room Animated Project, coordinated by Yael Ozsinay (2014).

The Red Suitcase, directed by Shaul Fried (2008).

True Love Hotel, directed by Alon Ga'ash (2008).

Two Boys, directed by Joao Ternoirio and Coi Belluzzo (2012).

Vals im Bashir (Waltz with Bashir), directed by Ari Folman (2008).

Victory, directed by Hanan Kaminski (1987).

We Shall Never Die, directed by Yoram Gross (n.d., 1950s).

White Tape, directed by Uri and Michelle Kranot (2010).

Yadon Ilaheyya (Divine Intervention), directed by Elia Suleiman (2002).

Zot he ha'aretz (This is the Land) directed by Baruch Agadati (1935).

9

From the Pioneers to the Revolutionaries: The Art of Animation in Egypt

Mohamed Ghazala

With its long history in the arts dating back to the documentation and decoration of daily events in ancient murals during the time of the Pharaohs, it is unsurprising that Egypt was, more than 100 years ago, the first country in Africa and the Middle East to establish a successful film industry. The Egyptian film industry began within a year of the inception of cinema in France in late 1895. Film screenings of the works of the Lumière Brothers were held in Alexandria and Cairo as early as 1896. The rise to modernity in Egypt brought with it a tolerance of figurative representation. Figurative art has been traditionally regarded as an opposition to the central Islamic aesthetics and consequently is rarely practiced in the Middle East. In this chapter, I paint a picture of the beginnings and the diverse histories of animation in Egypt. This chapter highlights a couple of 'firsts' and continues with an evaluation of how history, particularly recent history, has influenced and to a certain degree also defined the most recent wave of popular political animation in Egypt specifically, and in the Arab world more generally.

Cinema Blooms on the Banks of the Nile

Prior to the independence movements in the 1960s, Africa and the Middle East were portrayed by Western colonialist filmmakers as ignorant lands

From the Pioneers to the Revolutionaries

lacking in culture or civilisation. French law in the colonies, for example, forbade Africans from making their own films or even using cameras. This form of prohibition, known as The Laval Decree,[1] arrested the growth of filmmaking as a way for many colonised African peoples to express themselves culturally, artistically and politically. Under British colonisation, Egypt became the only African and Middle Eastern country where the local population could produce newsreels and short films. This was due in large part to the international expat community in Alexandria, with their interest in the arts in general and film in particular. Kings Fouad and Farouk, the first monarchs of independent Egypt, were also interested in cinema. Geography, too, has played a crucial role in shaping Egypt's cultural history. Situated essentially at the centre of the world, between the East and the West, between Europe and Asia, Egypt has served as the essential link between Africa and Asia, and held together the eastern and western wings of the Arab world. In truth, Egypt was a meeting place of modernism and traditionalism at the beginning of the twentieth century. This access allowed Egyptian filmmakers to dominate the Arab and African cinematic world from the late 1920s to the 1990s.

The first record of Egyptian cinema production dates back to 20 June 1907, when, in Alexandria, a short documentary film about the visit of Khedive Abbas Hilmi II to Alexandria saw the light of day. Ten years later, in 1917, Mohamed Karim established the first Egyptian production company in Alexandria of which he was later to become director. The company produced two films, *Dead Flowers* and *Honour the Bedouin*, which were screened in Alexandria in early 1918. Although the following couple of years were turbulent, national infrastructures – among which cinema started to play an increasingly important role – were gradually set up after the country's formal independence in 1922. In 1925, nationalist entrepreneur Talaat Harb, founder of Misr Bank, set up the Misr Company for Acting and Cinema (Studio Misr) as one of many investment enterprises.[2] He also set up a film school, and has had an enormous impact on the industry. Gaining control over culture, education and economy was a core aim of the anti-colonial struggle in Egypt and so, while Egyptian cinema was a popular commercial venture from the beginning, it was within a context of nationalist narratives that cinema was balanced between the ruling elite and the censor on the one hand, and mass audiences on the other.

Many other innovators followed in Harb's footsteps. For instance, in 1923, Mohamed Bayyumi returned from Germany, where he had studied cinematography, bringing with him newly-acquired techniques.[3] He became the first Egyptian to produce and shoot a newsreel, entitled *Amun*, the only cinematic record of the nationalist leader Saad Zaghlul. In 1927, Aziza Amir became the first woman to produce a silent film, entitled *Laila*,[4] the first feature-length film to be financed by Egyptian capital. With the existing popularity of song and dance, the sudden arrival of sound technology in the early 1930s ensured that the Egyptian film industry became well established throughout the Arab world in a very short space of time. A notable contribution was Mohamed Karim's *Awlad Al-Zawat* (*Children of the Aristocracy*, 1932), the first Egyptian talkie. Karim also directed the first musical, *Al-Warda Al-Bayda* (*The White Rose*) in 1933. The industry enjoyed huge success, in large part due to its depiction of singers and dancers, and its appeal to large (and largely illiterate) audiences, and Egyptian cinema for a long time depended on and flourished through a studio-and-star system. In 1935, Misr Studio opened the doors of its own production facility and laboratory giving the local film industry a major boost. Following this success, Al-Ahram Studios opened, and was soon followed by a plethora of other, smaller studios.

These events represent the closing of the period during which Egyptian cinema found its voice. A new era began with *Widad* (1936), which marked a turning point in Egyptian cinema as the first long feature film made by Talaat Harb's Studio Misr. The film was written by Ahmed Badrakhan and featured the first on-screen performance of Egypt's famous and influential singer, Umm Kalthoum. The studio went on to produce some of the best Egyptian films over the next thirty years. Egyptian cinema had entered its Golden Age, with a genre cinema dependent on studios and stars, not only as actors, but also as singers and dancers. This was not the only type of cinema created in Egypt, but it was certainly the form that enabled the industry to mature and become profitable. The confidence that accompanied such success paved the way for the consideration of new, underexplored areas in the art of cinema, one of which was animation.

The Birth of Animation in Egypt

Accompanying the rapid growth of Egyptian cinema, bewitched by American animation (especially the short animated films *Felix the Cat*

From the Pioneers to the Revolutionaries

and Disney's *Mickey Mouse* screened between film programmes at the cinemas), the Frenkel Brothers – Herschel, Salomon and David – decided to make their own animated films. The brothers were born into a Jewish Belarusian family from Jaffa, Palestine, having emigrated to Egypt during World War I. They were interested in the arts, and cinema in particular, and attended films in Cairo's cinemas on a daily basis. The Frenkels decided to divert investment from their lacquered furniture business in Cairo towards the making of animated films like those they saw on the silver screen. This family of enthusiastic cinephiles saw Mickey Mouse for the first time in 1930 and, even though no one in the family knew anything about making films, after witnessing the rising local popularity of a foreign animated hero, decided to establish their own Egyptian version of the Walt Disney Studios.

In the course of 1936, the Frenkel Brothers re-invented the frame-by-frame technique, until they agreed on the development of their first character, Marco Monkey. The creation was roundly criticised because of the sketches' apparent similarity to Walt Disney's hero, Mickey Mouse, and the family was advised by friends to instead take inspiration from Egyptian culture and create a more traditional character in order to develop and address homegrown audiences. A daily newspaper, *Al-Ahram*, also pointed out that it might be necessary to explore more Egyptian or Arab-looking characters to ensure a market. Despite their initial successes, the brothers were continually compared to and had to compete with the powerful and prosperous American productions that were widely available in Egypt at the time.

One disappointing meeting with a potential producer elicited from a Frenkel brother the following complaint: 'After Mr. B. had listened to me, he said "Mafish fayda!" (No way out, dead end). As I insisted, he added, "Bokra fel mish-mish," which literally means something along the lines of 'tomorrow, there will be apricots'. This phrase is equivalent to the English 'When pigs fly'.[5] Rather than thwarting their aspirations, this initial setback led to a stronger determination, providing motivation for the Frenkels to come up with a new character quickly. As the title for their first episode they chose *Mish-Mish Effendi*, a slighting reference to the dismissive comment made by the producer. The eponymous character, Mish-Mish, was deliberately developed to be recognisable as a stereotypical Egyptian youngster wearing a fez. The Frenkels' next script, entitled *Mafish Fayda*

199

(*Nothing to Do*), was again an ironic tribute to the producer who failed to support their efforts. Animation historian Giannalberto Bendazzi notes that 'history is always in the making and new discoveries can contradict established certainties. But today I do believe that the first truly African animation was created by the Frenkel Brothers in the 1930s.'[6] *Mafish Fayda* was screened on 8 February 1936, at the Cosmograph cinema, in downtown Cairo. Legend has it that even though the film was not very well drawn, was roughly animated and had a naive script and character design, Mish-Mish's public appeal was immediately confirmed by loud laughter and applause that could be heard outside the cinema.[7]

In response to this first screening, on 24 May 1935 the daily newspaper *La Bourse Egyptienne* announced enthusiastically:

> Mickey Mouse has an Egyptian brother! The First Frenkel Brothers animated film. Egypt today got its national hero in *Mish-Mish Effendi*. He is the hero of the first Egyptian cartoon screened this week in the cinema Cosmograph.[8]

In fact, Mish-Mish and the Frenkels became so popular that the brothers were able to start a successful advertising agency from the proceeds of the screenings. They also succeeded in mixing live-action actors with the animated *Mish-Mish Effendi* shots via a rotoscoping technique that realised some short innovative sequences in which Mish-Mish dances in front of popular contemporary singers and belly dancers, such as Taheya Carioca.

Other productions based on the same character followed, including a 1937 film for the Ministry of Agriculture in which Mish-Mish encouraged farmers to eradicate cotton parasites, and the extremely popular war propaganda film *National Defence* (1939), which featured the playful Mish-Mish as a patriotic soldier pitted against a Nazi military occupation of Egypt in late 1939.[9] The film is obviously influenced by Disney's cartoons of the 1920s and 1930s which portrayed heroes with round body shapes and gloved hands, and closely resembles the Fleischer Brothers' animation style, but with plenty of local Egyptian colour.[10] The Frenkels shot the film using the traditional 2D technique, producing thousands of drawings. Capitalising on the immense contemporary successes of talkies and musicals, the soundtrack of the film includes popular Egyptian music of the time, played by local bands.

Around the same time, Antoine Selim Ibrahim (1911–89) made his first film, *Aziza and Youness* (1938). Even though the Frenkel Brothers' work was created in Egypt, the establishment considered them to be foreigners and expats living in Alexandria, and their films are still not considered inherently Egyptian. It is Ibrahim's film that is acknowledged as the first animated film entirely created by an Arab Egyptian. *Aziza and Youness* was followed by *Dokdok* (1940), but after that Ibrahim focused on producing commercials and live-action films. In 1972, he migrated to the US to work at the famous Hanna-Barbera Studio in Universal City, California, and from 1976 to 1980 he worked for the renowned American animation production company DePatie-Freleng based in Burbank, California. After his retirement, he devoted himself to painting.[11]

In 1952, Gamal Abdel Nasser led the Free Officers Movement that instigated military reform. This started the so-called 23 July Revolution, which abolished the monarchy and established a republic. A patriotic media resulted in an increased production of films, in a manner comparable to similar tendencies in other socialist states. The result was a continued penchant for nationalist films, usually educating the masses, and always censored. Even in the face of tremendous obstacles – a tendency to oversimplify; a favouring of quantity over quality and an oppressive censorship with three main taboos (politics, religion and sex) – this already remarkable industry began to grow quickly. Although foreign producers were allowed to shoot films on Egyptian soil, during this time, overshadowed as it was by the Middle East war with Israel, all so-called Zionist American filmmakers and their films were banned, including popular American animated films.

Between 1946 and 1951, the Frenkel Brothers made at least one film a year. *Bilhana Oushefa* (*Enjoy Your Food* or *Bon Appétit*) was released in 1947 featuring female figures, who appear as Orientalist versions of Betty Boop. But when the political strife in Egypt became too turbulent, the Jewish Frenkels, who were considered to represent an extension of Zionism, decided to leave the country. They took their films with them and started the process of reinventing their own work in France, substituting Mish-Mish's fez with a French beret and renaming him Mimiche. These new, French animated films were not distributed in theatres but sold as family shows. In 1964, they made *Le rêve du beau Danube blue* (*The Dream of the Beautiful Blue Danube*), an abstract, poetic fairy tale set to the music

201

of Strauss' famous waltz.[12] Yet, in spite of their unrivalled success in Egypt, this was to be their only major French production, unsurprising given not only the context of a popular and competitive French animation industry, but also because of the post-War sentiments towards Jews.

Back in Egypt in the 1960s, the film industry was gradually nationalised, and its Egyptian filmmakers gained international acclaim. The most famous actor for much of that period (in Egypt and elsewhere) was Omar Sharif, while Youssef Chahine was the most acclaimed Egyptian director, and his influence on Arab cinema cannot be exaggerated. However, the spread of television from early 1960s caused a dramatic decline in cinema. While the roots of animation in Egypt, with the Frenkel Brothers and Antoine Selim Ibrahim, lie in individualistic, independent, artistic and idealistic endeavours, the future of animation from this point is commercial.

Animation Production and National Television

With the Frenkels' migration, the development of animation in Egypt came to a standstill, and not much evidence of animation activity is to be found, the exception being a few unfinished experiments by cartoonists (among others Mostafa Hussein, Hassan Hakem, Al-Borgini). In the 1960s, with the emergence of Egyptian TV, there was a sudden development of a great market for animated film titles and advertisements. Animation truly became a commercial and innovative adventure.

Just a few years earlier, in 1958 and 1959, Ali Moheeb and his brother, Hossam El-Deen (1930–96) developed innovative rotoscoping techniques and managed to produce animated cartoons without the need of any external financial or technical help. The success ensured the selection of the Moheeb Brothers to run the Animation Department for Egypt's National Television by the Ministry of Media on its introduction in 1960. Bendazzi recounts how, in 1962, 'Ali Moheeb directed *The White Line*, a film animation plus twenty-five-minute live-action, which was a cross between a short musical and a documentary film [...] a lively and excellent film, which made fine use of the split-screen technique (unusual at that time).'[13]

Egyptian Television was established on 21 July 1960. During the 1960s, other great cartoonists worked in the Animation Department. Mohammed

From the Pioneers to the Revolutionaries

Hassib (1937–2001), Noshi Iskandar (1938–2009), Redha Goubran (1945–97), Ahmed Saad, Abdellaim Zaki (1939), Hassan Anbar, Adel Anwar, Raouf Abd El-Hameed, Fahmy Abd El-Hameed, Fayza Hussein and Shweikar Khalifa all contributed to the renaissance of animation in Egypt with popular short films, advertisements and television announcements. Abdel-Haleem Al-Borgainy, Hassan Hakem and Mostafa Hussein directed two Egyptian animated cartoons together: *Titi and Rashwan* and *Al Daynasor wa Al Namla* (*The Dinosaur and the Ant*) in 1962. Ahmed Saad produced *Narjes, Excellent, Abdulal* and – based on folkloric songs – *El-Goz Elhkeel, Abu Elfasad's Birthday*. Ahmed Saad also made famous television ads, such as that for Riri cereals, as well as the short *Omda*. Successful work of the time by the Moheeb Brothers includes a couple of popular television shows and introductions for a number of TV programmes, such as the *Nafeza Hawl Al-Alam* (*A Window Around the world*), *Ams Wal Youm* (*Yesterday and Today*), *Hekyat Sob'me't Masna* (*The Story of 700 Factories*), *Khamas Khamsat* (*Five Fives*) and *Nas Fo' We Nas Taht* (*People at the Top and Below*). While the Frenkel Brothers had been influenced by Western, specifically US styles, there is here an influence from the 1950s and 1960s animated films of the schools of Zagreb and the Soviet Union, with sharp lines and abstract designs for characters and backgrounds.

After Nasser's death in 1970, his successor Anwar El-Sadat implemented his famous Open Door Policy: economic reforms that encouraged domestic and foreign investments in private entrepreneurship. The cinema sector underwent *de facto* privatisation while TV remained state-owned. But privatisation resulted in a lack of indigenous funding, so very few films were actually made, and those that were completed displayed qualities that differed from those to which the Egyptian public was accustomed:

> As public-sector facilities decayed [...] directors were forced to become less reliant on studios. The city became the backdrop for many films, and astute directors [...] realised that getting out of the artificiality of the studios could be an advantage: their films achieved a level of realism never before seen in Egyptian cinema.[14]

However, these realistic films never reached a broad spectatorship and, like the funding, critical acclaim came mostly from abroad. Directors had taken the camera out on to the streets, shooting the urban lower middle class, but the theatregoers from this same urban lower middle class preferred escapist melodrama. Commercial interest in cinema drove animation as well. After his work at the Animation Department, where he had trained many young colleagues, Ali Moheeb switched to advertising. He created his own private studio and devoted some of his spare time to teaching animation in the Graphic Design Department in the Faculty of Fine Arts in Cairo, where some of the leading figures of the next generation of Egyptian animators (including Mona Abu El-Nasr, about whom more later) were studying.

Nevertheless, although the 1970s saw government rule and censorship become less restrictive, public production by the 1980s and 1990s was once again limited to TV and live-action film, and only sporadically distributed to cinemas. Private companies experienced difficulties getting their films on Egyptian screens and therefore started producing commercial films destined chiefly for the Gulf markets. In 1979, Ali Moheeb directed his first animated television series, entitled *Mishgias Sawah*, consisting of 30 episodes, for Saudi TV.

From another direction, came Ihab Shaker – described by Bendazzi as 'the most famous animation film director beyond the borders of his homeland'[15] – who had received his first lessons in art from the Italian Carlo Minotti[16] and graduated from the Cairo Faculty of Fine Arts in 1957. He had begun working in the press in 1953, and became a celebrated young caricaturist, being 'summoned by graphics designer Abdel-Salam El-Sherif to draw editorial caricatures for the newspaper *Al-Gomhouriya*.'[17] He later worked as a daily political caricaturist for *Sabah El-Kheir*. Wanting to 'paint music', in 1968 he directed *The Bottle*, a first experimental animated film which inspired his continued study of moving images and their relationship with music.[18] The film is a humorous exploration of how difficult it can be to open a bottle of wine with a corkscrew.

Shaker communicated by post with the Scottish-Canadian animator Norman McLaren (who was equally interested in blending sound and movement), asking him for a letter of recommendation to gain a grant from UNESCO to enable him to continue studying animation in France. McLaren supported him with the letter but due to Nasserist bureaucracy the grant never materialised.[19] Shaker did, however, move to Paris, where he worked with the French pioneer Paul Grimault, who was the head of ASIFA (International Association of Animated Films) at that time. Grimault helped Shaker to direct, in 1973, his *Un deux trois* (*One, Two, Three*), which earned Shaker the prestigious French Prix de Qualité from the Centre national du cinéma et de l'image animée (CNC).[20] The 'fact that it took him three years to complete, though, and the lack of any significant financial reward' meant that Shaker was reluctant to 'go through the experience again.'[21] Shaker joined ASIFA as its first Arab and African member. He found that his work with Grimault allowed him to contemplate the notion of music in art. He said:

> Cartoons taught me many things. The seven years in Paris were wonderful, causing me to think of how music and my art could work together. It influenced all my future work in terms of movement, and I marvelled at how [instruments], such as the piano, could yield so many varieties of music. Pondering how time can be translated into sound, action and then art [...] allowed me more freedom in the composition of bodies. I have no worries about adding an extra arm, but I ensure that whatever I draw is in accordance with the rest of the body in terms of motion and activity. I do not allow you a moment of hesitation or objection upon viewing these bodies.[22]

Shaker's ability to combine his painterly, cartoonist and caricaturist skills with a drive towards the development of new techniques and styles rooted in music and movement, make him a forerunner of the Golden Age of Egyptian animation.

As Rasha Al-Shafi'a argues in her brief overview, since the 1970s Egyptian animation has moved in three distinct directions: advertising, experimentation and credits.[23] But this neglects the more popular ventures into television animation. As El-Mustapha Lahlali shows, the cultural impact of Arab television, and of Egyptian television specifically, has been immense, both satellite and terrestrial. Because television in Egypt 'is designed to mobilise the public to support government policies and political ideas',[24] the creators of televised animation series must adhere to certain rules and sensibilities that result in animation mostly aimed at children and families. Still, such series have constituted the main success story underlying Egyptian animation of the 1990s and 2000s.

The Golden Era of Egyptian Animation (1990–2010)

In the 1990s, government funding for cinema and animation all but vanished, due to the continued Open Doors Policy, developed further by President Hosni Mubarak, and the continued privatisation of the cinema sector. In the face of all this, Egyptian cinema still managed to thrive. It continued to spread the Cairene dialect throughout the Arabic-speaking world and made a sizeable contribution to world cinema. With the new wave of Arab satellite TV in the early 1990s, animation and graphics became an essential component of mainstream Arabic broadcasting. The demand for original Arabic content fuelled more investment in an industry that was once looked upon as a space for children's entertainment, or experimental art, rather than as a commercial, cross-generational genre.

Mona Abu Al-Nasr (1952–2003) returned to Egypt after studying animation at the California Academy for Arts during 1987–8, where she produced her first cartoon film, *Al-Mountaser* (*The Survival*, 1988). This 10-minute piece, which was the fruit of a year and a half's study at the Academy, is an abstract piece of art conveying a message of international peace.[25] She established her own studio Cairo Cartoon in 1990 and started projects in cooperation with Egyptian TV, the aim being to produce cartoon series for children. In 2001, she recounted how 'we produced three series in the past 10 years: *Kani wi Mani*, *Sinbad*, and finally *Bakar*.'[26] Her company receives financial support from the Radio & Television Union and it was this collaboration which formalised the 1990s and 2000s as the Golden Age of Egyptian animation. Abu Al-Nasr's work is inspired by local folkloric stories and Arabian Nights fairy tales. She attributes *Bakar*'s success to the character's contemporary Egyptian context: 'a child from South Egypt, *Bakar* has been well-received by many people because he lives in our age.'[27] *Bakar* has become one of the most famous animated Egyptian series and is exported to other Arab countries. It tells the story of a child from southern Egypt (Nubia) who goes on adventures with his pet goat Rashida, and is broadcast annually on Egyptian TV during the month of Ramadan, when television consumption is at its highest in the Arab world. According to Abu Al-Nasr, 'it is easier to import foreign series but this would have a very negative effect on our children. Neither the content nor the characters

From the Pioneers to the Revolutionaries

reflect our cultural reality.'[28] The significance of Abu Al-Nasr's contribution to Egyptian animation lies precisely in her interest in local stories, characters and language.

Many episodes of *Bakar* didactically focus on raising children's awareness of their responsibilities towards others. One episode demonstrates sympathy for the disabled, others treat social issues, such as eliminating illiteracy and revenge crimes, and all carry a message of universal peace. The untimely death of Abu Al-Nasr in 2003 halted the production of her feature-length project *Bakar and the Search for King Tut's Heart*, which was destined to be the first Egyptian animated feature film. The project was supposed to depict both the Pharaonic and the Mediterranean civilisations through the adventures of Bakar. In any case, the TV series *Bakar* continued to be aired until 2007, still produced by her studio, which was managed by her son, Sherif Gamal.

The success of the Cairo Cartoon studio inspired many of its artists – as well as independent artists – to establish their own animation studios. During the 2000s, around 50 animation studios of varying sizes and capacities came into existence. About ten sizeable studios together provided more than 100 animated hours yearly, through series, episodes, adverts and short films. Al-Sahar Studio, established in 1992 is one such enterprise. It began work on what was a second attempt (after Abu Al-Nasr's early death) at creating the first Egyptian animated feature film, *Al-Fares Wa Al-Ameera* (*The Knight and the Princess*), in 1998; it is still to be completed due to a lack of funds.

While some larger studios began to dominate production by monopolising the Egyptian TV market, smaller studios sometimes took the opportunity of cooperating on their projects, or by getting co-productions off the ground with other Arab countries to make series or ads. The technologies used by these studios in Egypt were primarily 2D and clay animation, with studios such as Zamzam specialising in religious claymation series. However, new studios began working more with 3D, such as the Tarek Rashed Studio, and with Flash techniques, such as A+ Cartoon and Cartoonile.

Recruitment for the studios and production companies comes by and large from local academies and universities, such as the Cinema Institute, Helwan, South Valley, and Minia University. Every year, more than 200 graduate students study animation. Courses take at least two years, and half of these students continue to work in the field of animation. New studios recruit these graduates after the completion of their academic training.

Television is not the only dissemination route for Egyptian film, though. Various film festivals, such as the Cairo International Cinema Festival for Children, Alexandria Film Festival, Ismailia International Film Festival for Documentary and Short Films and the Luxor African Film Festival, for example, accept short animated films into their competitions. There are also local events, such as the Al-Sakia Animation Festival and the National Egyptian Animation Festival. The latter takes place each February to celebrate the anniversary of the first public animation show by the Frenkel Borthers on 8 February 1936.

In addition to these festivals, there exist communities for animators in Egypt, including the Egyptian Animation Association (since 2001), the Guild of Egyptian Animators (2011) and the regional chapter of ASIFA Egypt (2008). These communities hold public activities to celebrate the art of animation, organise tributes to the pioneers, promote young animators and local studios, and host gatherings of the artists to discuss their issues and to meet with international guests. Or to celebrate the International Animation Day on 28 October, held in collaboration with governmental venues such as the Cairo Opera House and Bibliotheca Alexandrina.

Apart from those artists producing organised commercial television and studio work, there is also a growing number of independent, freelance artists. I am one of these. As a Professor in Animation at Minia University and the Director of ASIFA Egypt, I am able to develop my skills through a wide network of African and Arab freelance artists. The department attracts students from all over Egypt to study animation and is considered a pioneer among animation departments in universities in the Arab world. It is from this context that I should like to share with the reader two of my own best-known works. Firstly, the 2D digital animation *Hm Hm* (*Hungry*, 2005), which was made as part of a video installation for the Youth Salon festival 2005 in Cairo where it was awarded a prize for the video art section.[29] As Paula Callus confirms, it is intended to be viewed in a gallery setting, projected on a screen facing upwards and placed as if it were the top of a table in a restaurant, set for dining. Its production process included drawings on the computer using rudimentary technology: drawing with the mouse rather than a graphics tablet. This gives the work an experimental, loose

From the Pioneers to the Revolutionaries

and erratic movement that suits well its humorous theme.[30] This humour is intended to be highlighted by the musical accompaniment, reminiscent of restaurant muzak 'Por una cabeza', by Argentine tango singer Carlos Gardel.

My film *Honyan's Shoe* (2010)[31] is a digitally animated work. More sophisticated and consistent in its techniques than *Hm Hm*, it is an allegorical tale of desire and loneliness in which the protagonist Honyan finds a single golden shoe in the desert, which his camel indicates he does not need (see image 9.1). Nevertheless, he goes in search of the second shoe, a quest during which he loses both his camel and his bearings, and is doomed to roam the desert, and later the globe, alone. Without dialogue, the soundtrack of the short film consists of 'Misirlou', an originally Greek/Ottoman composition from the 1920s whose title means 'Egypt'.[32] *Honyan's Shoe* uses this piece as a tool of re-appropriation, while it also functions as a hook, to gain the attention of global audiences. The short was awarded the coveted Animation Prize at The African Movie Academy Awards festival in Lagos, Nigeria in 2010.

With my films and my work for ASIFA, training local African and Arab animation artists and providing workshops for children all over the continent, I have been able to exert a modest impact on African and Arab

9.1 Still from *Honyan's Shoe*, directed by Mohamed Ghazala (2010)

animation, perhaps imbuing the popularity and perceived naivety of the medium with more political and cultural references. It is in just this way that animation has become such a powerful tool for the revolutionaries in the Arab Spring and its aftermath in Egypt.

Egyptian Animation and the 'Arab Spring'

Maureen Furniss tells us that in 'the context of considering a production, it is advisable to extend the analysis to at least ten years, the period during which a context was becoming established, before a production was made.'[33] This invites an examination of the last decade to see how animation has dealt with the lead-up to the 'Arab Spring' in Egypt, and with the post-Revolutionary atmosphere in the country. Prior to 2011, private producers in the feature film industry in Egypt faced the same bureaucratic hurdles as those which confronted the nationalised cinema sector in the 1960s. Despite approval from the censorship board, filmmakers needed a permit from the Filmmakers Syndicate in order to receive a shooting permit from the police. A Filmmakers Syndicate permit could cost anywhere between 10,000 and 25,000 USD. To maintain a permit, one had to be an official member of the Syndicate, which was possible only for those who studied cinema. Others had to pay exorbitant fees and even then the permit was not provided to all applicants. To top it all, theatrical release of a film needed the approval of the Censorship Board.[34]

For many years, Arab filmmakers and producers had been the censors of their own work in order to avoid trouble with the censorship board. The writers of cartoon shows were responsible for creating scripts free of problems. As Iridt Neidhart says, this self-censorship, which arose out of fear of the regime, created a set of unwritten rules for Arab filmmakers. Even so, producing films outside the official structure was often a more interesting route to take: while some simply ignored the regulations – feigning ignorance perhaps – others declared their dissent publicly. This rejection of, or sometimes revolt against, the control of the state goes hand-in-hand with a sense of emancipation and empowerment.

Online activity and creativity in Egypt has been galvanised by internet and mobile usage, affordable connections and cell phone services, and by lack of the censorship that traditional media outlets operate under. A large proportion of the world's 300 million Arabs are now tech-savvy youths who surf the Web for their content. As Tariq Rimawi observes, 'between 25–40% of the population in the Middle East and North Africa are watching YouTube daily, leading it to become one of the most active regions in the world for internet use.'[35] Further, he suggests that the

> importance of the internet for contemporary Arab civil society actors can be attributed to two factors: first, many groups were pushed online because other forms of political communication were prohibitively expensive and regulated by the state. Second, the internet allowed for content to be hosted on servers beyond the control of state censors and afforded anonymity to those who advanced political criticism.[36]

Social media provides Arab artists with a powerful platform for political self-expression. Silvia Cambie is careful to note that while the Arab people had been using social media for years prior to the revolution, the Arab Spring 'made people realise just how powerful these tools could be.'[37]

While the focus on Egyptian animation over the past few years has dropped compared to 20 years earlier (when there were long-term contracts with the governmental TV broadcasters), some animation filmmakers have managed to commission TV series for children's stories and religious-oriented content. However, in January 2011, it became obvious that the commercial and didactic tendencies of animation in Egypt were about to change radically. The Arab people's expectations of the success of the Arab Spring in North Africa and the Middle East were enhanced with the use of social media for posting numerous messages, opinions and criticisms addressing democracy and freedom. Animation artists came to work increasingly independently, posting their work on the Web either anonymously, as part of an activist collective or as individual artists. Thus, the 'Arab Spring' provided new hope for artists that 'a new era of artistic freedom and opportunity had finally arrived.'[38] In Egypt, young animators are among the first generation to have the means to freely experiment with digital media.

This has resulted in increased exposure of the Egyptian animators and their works in comparison to the limited opportunities and freedom of the past. With freely available social media technologies, it became easy to reach massive audiences in (and beyond) the Arab world. This exposure was much wider and timelier than those works shown via the slow-paced process of traditional media: newspapers, national television and cinema. Ashraf Hamdi, for example, who was active before the 'Arab Spring' as a caricature artist in newspapers and news websites, increased his activity and exposure and thus became ever more popular during and after the political uprising. Hamdi joined the small online Jordanian studio Kharabeesh in 2011 to produce social commentary animated videos using simple animation techniques, posting them on the internet. He participated in the creation of a satirical political animated series aimed pointedly at President Mubarak of Egypt and Colonel Gaddafi of Libya.

Egyptoon is another studio producing stylised animation with politically satirical dialogues. Their videos are created using a simple animation style with vector graphics via digital software, mainly Adobe Flash and Anime Studio, to make flat characters move, talk and change their facial expressions. The rapid political changes after the Egyptian Revolution inspired the speedy production of more clips and sketches which were uploaded to the Egyptoon channel on YouTube every few days.[39]

Conclusion: From Art to Commercial Ventures and Back Again

From the Frenkels' youthful enthusiasm, through Shaker's experimentation, to the more commercial and independent ventures of Abu Al-Nasr and Ghazala, Egyptian animation has not been complacent over the past nine decades. The Egyptian Revolution has pushed animators who may previously have suffered at the hands of state censorship and oppression out into the limelight as the use of online platforms develops. In animation, the increased prominence of Egyptian voices on the international ASIFA board, led on 4 March 2011 to the choice of Ihab Shaker to create the poster for the 10th International Animation Day on 28 October 2011; the first artist from Africa or the Arab world to achieve this honour. This occurred just a few weeks after the Egyptian Revolution, and inspired many animators to think anew and to exercise freedom of speech. Ashraf Hamdi, too, has carved a space with his videos from which he may criticise Egyptian public life, from political VIPs and singers to religious figures and everyday people interviewed in news reports. Shaker and Hamdi do not censor themselves, and they no longer face censorship. Their ability to express their vision is an important outcome of post-Revolutionary Egyptian cinema, which continues to renew its styles and methods, and to revolutionise the art from within.

Notes

1. Manthia Diawara, *African Cinema, Politics & Culture* (Bloomington, IN, 1992).
2. Viola Shafik, *Arab Cinema. History and Cultural Identity* (Cairo, 2005 [1988]), p. 14.
3. Mustafa Darwish, *Dream Makers on the Nile* (Cairo, 1998), p. 10.
4. Viola Shafik, *Popular Egyptian Cinema. Gender, Class and Nation* (Cairo, 2007), p. 137.
5. Historical Society of Jews from Egypt, 'Frenkel animated cartoons' (n.d.), [Historical Society of Jews from Egypt.] Available at http://www.hsje.org/mish_mish%20in_1935_files/mishmish.pdf (accessed 25 August 2014).
6. Personal communication with Giannalberto Bendazzi via email, 20 July 2009.
7. Historical Society of Jews from Egypt, 'Frenkel animated cartoons.'
8. Historical Society of Jews from Egypt, 'Frenkel animated cartoons.'
9. *National Defense* (1939) is on YouTube. Available at https://www.youtube.com/watch?v=pCDLfZAKQ_E (accessed 15 March 2015).
10. Jan-Christopher Horak, 'Animation symposium at FIAF', UCLA Film & Television Archive (May 2012). Available at https://www.cinema.ucla.edu/blogs/archival-spaces/2012/05/04/animation-symposium-fiaf (accessed 26 August 2014).
11. Giannalberto Bendazzi, *Cartoons: One Hundred Years of Cinema Animation* (London, 1994).
12. Tewfik Hakem, 'La fabuleuse histoire des momies animées du cinéma égyptien. Rétrospective de dessins animés égyptiens', *Liberation* (1 June 1996). Available at http://www.liberation.fr/culture/1996/06/01/la-fabuleuse-histoire-des-momies-animees-du-cinema-egyptien-retrospective-de-dessins-animes-egyptien_175533 (accessed 15 March 2015).
13. Giannalberto Bendazzi, 'African cinema animation', translated from the Italian by Emilia Ippolito with Paula Burnett, *EnterText*, 4, 1 (2004). Available at http://giannalbertobendazzi.com/wp-content/uploads/2013/08/Giannalberto-Bendazzi-African-Cinema-Animation.pdf (accessed 27 August 2014).
14. Walter Armbrust, 'New cinema, commercial cinema, and the modernist tradition in Egypt', *Alif: Journal of Comparative Poetics*, 15 (1995), pp. 81–129: 104.

Animation in the Middle East

15. Bendazzi, 'African Cinema Animation.'
16. Youssef Rakha, 'Inventing the wheel: Ihab Shaker profile', *Al-Ahram Weekly* (16 June 1999). Available at http://www.ihabshaker.com/news/Alahram/InvintingTheWeelF.html (accessed 13 March 2015).
17. Safar Khan Art Gallery, 'Ihab Shaker profile' (n.d.) [Safar Khan Art Gallery.] Available at http://safarkhan.com/Ex-ArtWork.aspx?artistid=161&Year=2009 &isartist=1&type=past&exid=296 (accessed 13 March 2015).
18. *The Bottle* (1968) is on YouTube. Available at: https://www.youtube.com/watch?v=dOjYT6gU5P0 (accessed 14 March 2015).
19. Youssef Rakha, 'Inventing the wheel: Ihab Shaker profile.'
20. *Un deux trois* (1973) is on YouTube. Available at: https://www.youtube.com/watch?v=2bB1ESRVB3Y (accessed 14 March 2015).
21. Youssef Rakha, 'Inventing the wheel: Ihab Shaker profile.'
22. Heba Elkayal, 'The musician artist', *Daily News Egypt* (18 March 2009). Available at http://www.masress.com/en/dailynews/108204 (accessed 1 September 2014).
23. Maria Silvia Bazzoli (ed.), *African Cartoon: il cinema di animazione in Africa* (Milan, 2003), p. 29.
24. El-Mustapha Lahlali, *Contemporary Arab Broadcast Media* (Edinburgh, 2011), p. 27.
25. It won the Silver Plaque prize for the best short animated film at the Chicago International Film Festival.
26. Rania Khallaf, 'One boy and his goat', *Al-Ahram Weekly Online*, 562 (29 November 2001). Available at http://weekly.ahram.org.eg/2001/562/fe3.htm (accessed 13 March 2015).
27. Rania Khallaf, 'One boy and his goat.'
28. Ibid.
29. *Hm Hm* (2005) is on YouTube. Available at: https://www.youtube.com/watch?v=R4PH5OozI4c (accessed 15 March 2015).
30. Paula Callus, 'Creative comment and critique: Animation filmmaking in Africa', Africa in Motion Blog (2008). Available at http://www.africa-in-motion.org.uk/2008/animation.html (accessed 15 March 2015).
31. *Honyan's Shoe* (2010) is on YouTube. Available on: https://www.youtube.com/watch?v=u4g5IuLF_C0 (accessed 15 March 2015).
32. The song was hugely popular in the Middle East and later introduced to Western audiences through Dick Dale's 1962 surf rock version (used by Quentin Tarantino for *Pulp Fiction* (1994)).
33. Maureen Furniss, *Art in Motion: Animation Aesthetics* (London, 1999).
34. *Irit Neidhardt*, 'Egyptian cinema-industry. A brief historical Overview', *MEC Film*, 2011. Available at http://www.mecfilm.com/de/media/z_regie/EgyptianCinemaIndustry_BriefHistory.pdf (accessed 13 March 2015).

From the Pioneers to the Revolutionaries

35. Tariq Rimawi, 'The Arab animation spring: How have Arab animation artists used the power of YouTube and social media in response to the recent Arab revolution?' Paper presented at CONFIA. Second International Conference on Illustration and Animation in Porto, Portugal (December 2013). Available at http://www.uop.edu.jo/download/Research/members/901_3179_T_Al.pdf (accessed 13 March 2015).
36. Tariq Rimawi, 'The Arab animation spring'.
37. Silvia Cambié, 'Lessons from the front line: The Arab Spring demonstrated the power of people and social media', *Communication World* (January–February 2012), pp. 28–32.
38. Silvia Cambié, 'Lessons from the front line'.
39. Egyptoon's YouTube channel is online. Available at: https://www.youtube.com/channel/UCJlsdBR7KYYAw1CjYN5msvg (accessed 13 March 2015).

Filmography

Abdulal, directed by Noshi Iskandar (1960s).

Abu Elfasad's Birthday, directed by Ahmed Saad (1960s).

Al Daynasor wa Al Namla (The Dinosaur and the Ant), directed by Abdel-Haleem Al-Borgainy, Hassan Hakem and Mostafa Hussein (1962).

Al-Fares Wa Al-Ameera (The Knight and the Princess), directed by Al-Sahar studio (unfinished).

Al-Mountaser (The Survival), directed by Mona Abu Al-Nasr (1988).

Al-Warda Al-Bayda (The White Rose), directed by Mohamed Karim (1933).

Ams Wal Youm (Yesterday and Today), directed by the Moheeb Brothers

Amun, directed by Mohamed Bayyumi (1923).

Awlad Al-Zawat (Children of the Aristocracy), directed by Mohamed Karim (1932).

Aziza and Youness, directed by Antoine Selim Ibrahim (1938).

Bakar and the Search for King Tut's Heart, directed by Mona Abu Al-Nasr (unfinished).

Bakar, directed by Mona Abu Al-Nasr (1990s).

Bilhana Oushefa (Enjoy your Food), directed by the Frenkel Brothers (1947).

Dead Flowers, directed by Mohamed Karim (1918).

Dokdok, directed by Antoine Selim Ibrahim (1940).

El Goz Elhkeel (Two Horses), directed by Ahmed Saad (1960s).

Hekyat Sob'me't Masna (The Story of 700 Factories), directed by the Moheeb Brothers (1970s).

Honor the Bedouin, directed by Mohamed Karim (1918).

Kani and Mani, directed by Mona Abu Al-Nasr (1990s).

Khamas Khamsat (Five Fives), directed by the Moheeb Brothers (1970s).

Laila, directed by Wadad Orfi (1927).

Le rêve du beau Danube bleu (*The Dream of the Beautiful Blue Danube*), directed by the Frenkel Brothers (1964).

Mafish Fayda (*Nothing to Do*), directed by the Frenkel Brothers (1939).

Marco Monkey, directed by the Frenkel Brothers (1936).

Mish-Mish Effendi, directed by the Frenkel Brothers (1936).

Mishgias Sawah, directed by Ali Moheeb (1979).

Mootaz (*Excellent*), directed by Noshi Iskandar (1960s).

Nafeza Hawl Al-Alam (*A Window around the World*), directed by the Moheeb Brothers (1970s).

Narjes, directed by Noshi Iskandar (1970s).

Nas Fo' We Nas Taht (*People at the Top and Below*), directed by the Moheeb Brothers (1970s).

National Defence, directed by the Frenkel Brothers (1939).

Omda, directed by Ahmed Saad (1970s).

Sinbad, directed by Mona Abu Al-Nasr (1990s).

The Bottle, directed by Ihab Shaker (1968).

The White Line, directed by Ali Moheeb (1962).

Titi and Rashwan, directed by Abdel-Haleem Al-Borgainy, Hassan Hakem and Mostafa Hussein (1962).

Un deux trois (*One, Two, Three*), directed by Ihab Shaker (1973).

Widad, directed by Fritz Kramp (1936).

10

Animating Libya in Shorthand: The Skilful Art of Visualising the Repressed Body

Nisrine Mansour

In what now seems a distant past, amidst the Arab revolutions, people briefly turned their attention to Benghazi. As the city fell to Libyan dissidents, Gaddafi's face popped up all over street walls. Colourful in design and content, graffiti ridiculed every eccentric shade of his public persona and spread like wildfire with every liberated city, right up to the fall of the dictator seven months later. These images broke the 42-year long national taboo of questioning the regime's apparatus or the pervasive and volatile censorship practices it enforced. They also revealed a glimpse of an existing Libyan dissident visual art scene that is little known across the Arab region. Both the Libyan population and its socio-cultural repertoire were kept under strict confinement and censorship. The latent movement of dissidence and visual art was promising. However, the Libyan revolution's legitimacy was soon questioned with Western foreign military intervention. Soon after, Libya's revolution returned to the back of people's minds, as did neighbouring Egypt and Tunisia's.

It was not until I was introduced to a group of Libyan artists, through the London-based writer Mo Mesrati, that vivid sketches of local dissident activist art and repression started to emerge. Mesrati's close circle of Libyan activists, writers, actors and animators were at the heart of the revolution in many ways. Among them was a group of activist artists who had

217

launched *Boq'at Jaw* (*Chilling Spot*), an animated cross-platform political satire series aired in Libya prior to, during and after the revolution.[1] The series went viral across the dissidents' social media platforms during the revolution.

Boq'at Jaw was a homegrown project undertaken in Misrata where the friends were based. The series used everyday street talk between two male Libyan characters to poke fun at collective – and often unspoken – anxieties in Libyans' daily lives. The series ran between 2010 and 2013 and spanned the three crucial transitional years preceding and following the regime change. It has a compelling visual design, polished craftsmanship and a sharp narrative that matches the growing independent political animation scene in the region. Thus, it opened up new avenues for exploring the possibilities and conditions for dissident animation to emerge and survive under the restrictive context of Gaddafi's Libya. We teamed up to film an independent documentary project on these dissident artists in Libya entitled *The Morganti Rebels*.[2] For, until now, as Opondo reminds us, 'the uprising in Libya has been spoken of in terms of regime change and democracy without demanding a revolution in the way people relate to and think about the people of Libya and the North African region as a whole.'[3]

It was with these concerns in mind that I travelled to Libya in the summer of 2013 to meet the *Boq'at Jaw* artists and record their experiences for my film *The Morganti Rebels*. The film's title seeks to capture the creators' involvement in starting Misrata's civilian protests, joining the dissident ranks until liberation, and realising their post-revolutionary dream of opening the first cultural café in the city, the Morganti, as a hub to keep the artists' post-revolutionary momentum going.

Visual Animation, Affect, and the Laughing Repressed Body

The viral online sharing of *Boq'at Jaw* during the revolution speaks of the value of visual political art as a medium of dissent. Across the Arab revolutions, dissident art was celebrated as a driving force for breaking the fear of repression.[4] Often, political humour is credited with empowering individuals with a sense of validation of their interpretations of repression and of driving their will for political change.[5] Historically, though, political satire has not been known in and of itself as the overthrower of repressive regimes. Drawing on the case of the Soviet Union, Oring criticises political humour for operating 'within the confines of the dynamics of repression. Thus it contribute[s] nothing at all to survival, adaptation, endurance or even equanimity in a repressive society.'[6] Yet, expecting regime change to come directly out of political satire presumes that mediated satire has a direct causal effect on populations. Audiences, including populations living under repressive regimes, engage with mediated satire as 'interpretive poetics', in that 'layers of meaning in narrative texts are interrogated and interpreted in a way that mirrors a sophisticated reading of a poem of which "languages of the unsayables and woven and torn signifiers" are key interpretation registers.'[7] Even more so in repressive contexts like Libya, laughing audiences engage in 'mnemonic performativity', in which they dialectically navigate through and between their own unspoken experiences of everyday life under repression, as well as their engagement with various actors and regime discourses. Thus they 'create a third meaning of self that lies at an intersection between the past, the present and the future, but which strategically embodies and champions the present and the future over the past.'[8]

Since political satire, including animation, has stood the test of time and gained audience appreciation across many contexts, it seems that the extent of its grand revolutionary usefulness is the wrong question to ask. Part of the popularity of the genre is its visceral and immediate effect on people. In political satire there 'lies a fundamental power that seems to say, even if you cannot overthrow tyranny, you can refuse to accept it at face value, and you are not totally vanquished if you can die laughing.'[9] In that sense, the repressed body is able to endure dictatorship through laughter. Political humour, then, is significant because of its uniqueness as

> a type of shorthand. In a joke or story attitudes and feelings are expressed in concentrated form and much of the impact of a particular episode derives from the collapsing of the complex into the simple. For the most part, political humor is also ephemeral and it loses much of its pungency outside the confines of delimited time and situation.[10]

The 'shorthand' of political satire repositions the specific temporal and situational restrictions within the everyday lives of artists and populations living under repressive regimes. With politically-targeted animation, this shorthand is enhanced by the power of visual illustration. Yet, unlike anonymous street art, authored animated satire filters out to audiences both through careful self-censorship and the regime's sanctioned dissent. Unable to pick on the regime directly, it focuses on the embodiment of repression within seemingly mundane and fictional visualisations of everyday situations through human(ised) illustrated characters.

The significance of laughing at such animated shorthand lies in Massumi's articulation of affect within the body, which, he says, 'doesn't just absorb pulses or discrete stimulations; it infolds contexts.'[11] Laughter reveals the power of the repressed body

> as poignant icon, viral meme and compelling metaphor for human agency, [that] fuels the peculiar aesthetics of insurrectionary media, cutting at once through the thick fog of raging propaganda wars between regimes and rebels and through the largely incompetent global media coverage.[12]

Exploring the affective power of animated satire can serve to redirect attention towards the politics of the body in assisting an understanding of current anxieties within post-revolutionary Libya. Opondo points to affective economies driving Gaddafi's longstanding repressive policies as well as his dissidents' revolutionary practices. Both sides discursively repressed the Libyan body, by contesting its composition, persisting in its violation while claiming its protection. Reading dissident animated satire as shorthand offers possibilities for understanding the 'processes that have made Libya and Gaddafi possible [and...] pay[ing] attention to the reproduction of values, exchanges, violences that characterise the passage to the "new".'[13]

In this chapter, I offer a reading of dissident animated satire as embodied 'shorthands' that are useful in chronicling everyday politics of the repressed Libyan body prior to and following regime change. While situational and ephemeral on their own, each clip, episode and joke is discursively pieced together, and when combined with contributors' recollections from an ethnographic filming process; they form an evolving timeline of everyday life during the crucial years bracketing the Libyan revolution.

Visualising Sanctioned Dissent in the Making of *The Morganti Rebels*

Summer 2013 was a crucial period in the unfolding of post-revolutionary Libya. As I landed in Tripoli airport, a general sense of victory was still going strong, despite uncertainty creeping in. Back then Libya knew it was on borrowed time. And the mood in Misrata was no different. When we first met, the creators of *Boq'at Jaw* were buzzing and busy establishing their new revolutionary cultural project, the Morganti Café.

They were all born and raised in Misrata. Mohammad Karwad, a graphic designer, is the creator of the show's concept. Jamal Sibai is a musician, actor and writer who lent his voice to one of the show's main characters. Ali Shahin is a writer and part of the scriptwriting team. Mesrati, who fled with his dissident parents to the UK in 2003, told me about their prominent positioning within the Libyan dissident landscape. They sketched the idiosyncrasies of an untold history of everyday repression informing their artwork and shaping their artistic experiences.

At the start of filming, we explored the scope and direction of the film. The group had the desire to let out all their uncensored experiences, thoughts or opinions. Yet, they felt tongue-tied by brewing local sensibilities and political uncertainty. We agreed on an ethnographic approach that combined informal situational filming, in addition to free-flowing formal interviews, with them having the option of claiming any conversations off-record.

Our main hangout was the newly-established Morganti Café. There I met many fellow artists and activists who contributed to the friends' accounts. In addition to the informal filming, we held free-flowing formal interviews that lasted for two hours each. Apart from the Morganti, there were very few public places where we could meet and talk freely. Our hangouts included cars, the offices of Karwad's graphic design company, or beach houses, commonly used by single men for private gatherings and scattered along the 6,000km of virgin coast. Three spaces were off-limits: their homes, the streets and any big, men-only gatherings or parties. Misrata's restrictive social context did not accommodate much mixed-gender socialising.

By the end of the summer, and as the film went into the editing phase, post-revolutionary Libya spiralled into conflict. The climate became increasingly threatening, and contributors felt uneasy about releasing the information they had initially approved on film. In particular, they were reluctant to be identified as 'rebels', as in the original film title. They sought to distance themselves from the then-growing controversy surrounding Misrati dissident groups who were keen on showcasing their city's crucial role in tipping the revolution to the dissidents' side and appropriated their status as 'rebels' to justify their refusal to disarm.

The changes in the narrative capitalised on the open-ended ethnographic approach to filming, revealing their personal stories as visual artists growing up in Gaddafi Libya. The chapter unfolds in an exploration of their artistic influences of visual satire, their efforts to manoeuver the minefields of regime and post-regime censorship, and their skills in crafting sanctioned dissent that spoke to a young dissident generation prior to, during and following the revolution.

The Birth of *Boq`at Jaw*: Local Inspirations

When I met the group for the first time, they were managing The Morganti. They ran the coffee bar, the remote for the muted pan-Arab satellite flat screen TV and their classic rock playlists on the sound system. A borrow-bookshelf lined one wall behind the cashier. On the other walls hung large portraits of iconic Libyan artists and intellectuals, men and women. As we talked about *Boq `at Jaw* Karwad pointed twice: once to a portrait and once to the TV, to illustrate his inspiration for creating the show.

The portrait was of Mohamed Zwawi, the godfather of Libyan satirical cartoons. His prolific artwork of thousands of editorial cartoons preceded, survived, and succeeded the 42 years of Gaddafi's rule. Zwawi's detailed work fascinated Karwad, who saw as its function the archiving of everyday life in Libya 'under a satirical microscope.'[14] Zwawi excelled at producing a shorthand of Libyan life. His poly-visual illustrations captured the lives of regular people in every possible social situation, as can be seen in image 10.1. Several others on the team were avid fans of Zwawi's comics and confirmed his central position in the national satirical psyche. Mesrati recalls how, as a child, he used to gather with his cousins around volumes of Zwawi's compiled editorial cartoon collections, and spend hours deciphering the hidden allusions to politics in the details of everyday life. Each

Animating Libya in Shorthand

10.1 Editorial cartoon by Mohamed Zwawi, showing members of popular committees touting public health campaigns while people are drowning in poor infrastructure (n.d.)

of Zwawi's illustrations condenses the political into the personal, and the complex into the simple, in effortless social situational tableaux (such as social occasions, weddings, funerals, family visits, neighbourhood fights). Without captions, they were filled with visual dissonances embodied in the characters' actions.

As they deciphered society behind closed doors, these artists spotted the idiosyncrasies that they, as children, saw in the lives of the adults around them as they 'got by' under dictatorship. Unlike their elders, the generation of the *Boq`at Jaw* artists did not live through Gaddafi's escalation from a promising post-colonial liberator to a staunch dictator. Nor did they experience first-hand the tightening grip of censorship along the way.

Zwawi and Gaddafi actually belonged to the same generation of disadvantaged Libyan post-colonial youth who sought change. Born into similar rural Bedouin settings under Italian occupation, they grew up to see, in 1951, the three historical governorates (Cyrenaica, Tripolitania and Fezzan) merge into the independent United Kingdom of Libya under King Idriss I.[15] Soon enough, the Nasserite pan-Arab revolutionary feeling emanating from Egypt reached Libya. Both Zwawi and Gaddafi gravitated to the centre of this revolutionary movement, along with many other Libyan thinkers, artists, activists and military officers who sought regime change.

Zwawi's first editorial cartoon was published in 1963, the year Gaddafi started his training at the military academy. Zwawi learned his craft from Egyptian illustrators,[16] while Gaddafi emulated Gamal Abdel Nasser by creating a critical mass around himself and establishing a Free Officers Movement that led to a successful coup in 1969. During that period, Zwawi established himself as a visual political satirist, publishing regularly in several papers and magazines under the watchful eye of the censor. Celebrating the revolutionary promise of the coup, Zwawi and his contemporaries began producing and assembling a rich intellectual and artistic repertoire. Yet in the span of one year, Zwawi, like many others, saw his artwork gradually funnelled from a pluralist mediascape into the regime's monolithic nationalism.

In 1970, Gaddafi initiated his longstanding crackdown on the press by establishing the state-run Libyan Broadcasting Division. The following year, in order to curb the then revolutionary zeal for critique, he banned public gatherings, closing down bars and cafes where intellectuals and artists met. In 1972, press codes were amended to enable the incrimination of political critique as treason. These amendments were enshrined in the Green Book in 1973, as all media and public institutions were put under the supervision of the newly-established Popular Committees.[17] Popular and Revolutionary Committees were Gaddafi's notorious apparatuses of governance and surveillance, operating under the slogan 'Partisanship is Treason'. Their role was crucial in implementing the regime's ruthless policies against leftist, pan-Arabist and, later, Islamist dissidents.[18] In 1980, Gaddafi fully nationalised the media and heavily funded it as the mouthpiece of the regime's propaganda.

Colonial rule and a brief independent monarchy did not grant Libya much of a tradition in film production. However, cinema going was popular and around 14 theatres in Tripoli and 10 in Benghazi were operating by the time Gaddafi took power.[19] In 1973, the General Foundation for Cinema, the GFC's planning department worked on erecting large cinema venues with a 400–1000 seat capacity.[20] In 1979, these venues were appropriated by the regime's political machine and were turned into popular committees' venues and cinemas as well as theatres and cultural venues, were completely shut down. Yet, Gaddafi used film to boost his expansionist strategy and heavily funded two iconic Hollywood-produced films by Syrian filmmaker Mostafa Al-Akkad. The first was *Al-Risala* (*The Message*, 1975–6), narrating the birth of Islam and the journey of Prophet Mohamad in spreading it. The second, *Omar Al-Mukhtar* (*The Lion of the Desert*, 1980) depicted the national leader in his battle against Italian colonial rule. Gaddafi used both films to assert his leadership over political Islam and nationalism. The oil-funded films were so lushly produced, that two versions of each film were made from scratch, one in English and one in Arabic, rather than using dubbing or subtitling. While these films were a flop at the western box offices, they became a staple screening across Libya and the Arab region, repeatedly aired on television during festivities.

During that time, Gaddafi also nationalised oil production and poured substantial revenues into funding over 20 anti-imperialist military groups around the world, including Palestinian factions and the ANC in apartheid South Africa. In 1980, he took over the press and slashed its budget in order to increase funding for his military allies to up to three-quarters of the national income. Nationalisation and military cuts, in addition to earlier property appropriation policies, left Libyans scraping for rations and dipping into a gruelling black market. By the end of the 1980s, the media sector had become insular and lagged behind the global technological changes taking place at the time.

Zwawi repositioned his artwork amidst these intense changes. Instead of critiquing the regime, his illustrations consisted of various situational shorthands of people's idiosyncrasies in manoeuvring through these stifling measures. Publishing in the only outlets available within the regime's press, he also chronicled the peak of Gaddafi's new era of African expansionism in the late 1980s, which witnessed the re-privatisation of the market, the Gaddafi International Prize for Human Rights offered to Nelson Mandela and the 1988 Lockerbie bombing.

Positioning Sanctioned Dissent

The team of *Boq'at Jaw* was born into this restrictive environment and, growing up in the 1990s, they grappled with the dissonance resulting from the regime's careful manoeuvring of technological liberalisation and political reconciliation with the West. In 1993, national media institutions suffered severe shortages after technological imports and basic printing materials were banned following the Lockerbie UN sanctions on Libya. Yet, thriving re-privatised and black markets still allowed for technological exposure. Karwad recounts how he liked drawing as a child and how thrilled he was when he discovered visual design software on a computer his father bought him.

During that period, the group's generation also saw the booming pan-Arab satellite channels make their way into Libyan homes. Likewise, in 1996, the first state satellite channel Al-Jamahiriya was launched. In order to prevent the growing Islamist surge, the regime freed all political prisoners (except Islamists) and increased the margin of critique by allowing local print and radio. Long-term dissidents became more vocal as they published in critical magazines such as *La* (*No*). Mobile communication was later introduced, followed by the internet in 2001. However, this technological boom also came with a state monopoly over providers and a huge budget to tightly monitor satellite content.[21]

Karwad considers *Boq`at Jaw* to be a natural extension of his experience as a graphic designer in Tripoli:

> In 2006, I got into the world of animation. I started with personal experiments that stayed on my computer. I had some modest work that was popular. I saw that I could do something different but I didn't have the final idea of *Boq`at Jaw*, I had just drawn one main character, Grande, and knew what he was about to say.[22]

Among the regional programmes, Karwad discovered a two-minute Lebanese political animated series *Rusum Mutaharrira* (*Liberated Illustrations*) that involved two characters engaging in political critique through regular exchanges on the street. Karwad was inspired by the situational concept and developed *Boq`at Jaw* around it. But the more permissive Lebanese political context did not resonate with Libya's restrictive environment. His real political inspiration came with a Syrian visual satire series: *Boq`at Daw* (*Spotlight*) was a (non-animated) visual satire series, popular regionally for carefully crafting its narrative through and around the restrictive political environment of Assad's Syria.[23]

By 2003 Mandela had brokered the removal of UN sanctions on Gaddafi's behalf.[24] Gaddafi's youngest son Saif El-Islam led the following period of normalisation and liberalisation. He gradually confirmed his position as heir apparent, and in order to ease into the transition, he took several steps to modernise the country. In 2006, he uttered his criticism of the regime's lack of media freedom. He launched Libya Al-Ghad (Tomorrow's Libya), a fully-fledged national reform project concerned with promises for a new constitution, political freedoms and media liberalisation.[25] Al-Ghad Media Group was established as the media branch of this reformist plan, including Al-Libiyya as its main TV channel, two newspapers and a press agency.[26]

In this volatile permissive media climate of heavy technological control, avenues for releasing underground dissident local art were non-existent. *Boq`at Jaw* found its only outlet through Saif Al-Islam's reformist media:

> Back then I was working in Tripoli. And the only available channels were state-owned. I linked with a body established by Saif Al-Islam. And I had to do it against my will because it was the only available option [...] When I met the manager's office that is linked directly to Libya Al-Ghad, he imposed harsh financial terms.[27]

Thus, Karwad carefully negotiated the regime's censorship in order to convey dissent in his show. *Boq`at Jaw* was meant to air during Ramadan, which is the prime season for new TV productions, however, that year the feast of Ramadan coincided with Eid Al-Fateh (The Liberator's Feast), the biggest annual celebration for Gaddafi's successful coup in 1969. As Karwad explained, this occasion was always an over-blown public celebration glorifying Gaddafi. Karwad wanted to take distance from the regime, and formed a team with his artist and activist friends to work on a proposal that would find its way into primetime Ramadan TV schedule without compromising the content. At the time, state censorship was struggling to manage the boom in local media and they cracked down on political content, leaving socio-economic or cultural critique to the journalists' everyday self-censorship in their production practices.[28]

Karwad spotted this opportunity as he explained: 'the supervising committee [of Al-Libya] was clueless so we got the proposal past them. Back then we wrote episodes that could get us in trouble with the regime. But we did it in an indirect way, not like we do now'. The creators of *Boq 'at Jaw* benefited from a momentary loophole in censorship resulting from Saif Al-Islam's temporarily growing margin of sanctioned dissent. The first series aired in the summer of 2010 on Al-Libya. However, soon after it was launched, one of Saif's media outlets criticised Gaddafi and, in retaliation, Gaddafi and his old guard closed it down and renationalised the media sector.

During the following months, more regional dissident political and cultural currents began to form. The group of friends followed events closely. As Karwad remembers, 'we were glued to the screens as the Tunisian and Egyptian uprisings sparked. We were in awe, dreaming of the same in Libya, yet scared of going on the internet to follow it because we knew it was monitored'. Abdulwahab Al-Haddad, the lead scriptwriter of the series, continues: 'Before the Revolution we used to meet frequently. Our convictions became closely aligned. We established a small cell, initially operating online'. As the population of Benghazi took to the streets, the group posted an invitation on Facebook to meet for civilian protest in Misrata on 19 February 2011. Around 20 young activists, including Karwad, Sibai and Al-Haddad, gathered before the regime arrested them and killed two in the crowd. Within two days, as Karwad and Sibai recall, their families took to the streets and the whole city followed, thus launching the start of the revolution in Misrata. After their release, the group established the media communications unit of the Misrata dissidents, and ran it while fighting on the frontline. In the following year, *Boq 'at Jaw* was finally produced in a liberated Misrata and aired on the dissidents' main TV channel Misrata Al-Horra (Free Misrata).

Animating the Libyan Street: Strings of Embodied Shorthands

Born out of these local and regional influences, *Boq 'at Jaw*, starting as a modest self-funded independent project, adopted the double-act structure and infused it with their own ethics and aesthetics, as well as a specific context of repression. Karwad explains that the show 'is a cartoon series about two characters [Zumba and Grande] who symbolise the Libyan archetype – the poor, neglected Libyan, in addition to an ambiguous silent third character, Al-Dhol (Shadow), who is open to interpretation.'[29] Al-Dhol

Animating Libya in Shorthand

is always just a few steps behind Zumba and Grande, leaning against a lamppost, and smoking away in the dark. As Al-Haddad, explains, 'he is always there but does nothing. He could be a regular youth hanging out on the street, or one of the many regime informers who used to be scattered around.'[30] As such, the set captured the national mood with elusive simplicity even while it intentionally repositioned the dialogue between the two main characters within the everyday and away from political inferences.

The two main characters reflected two ethically distinct personalities and wove their differences into the stories, something that the Lebanese show did not do. Al-Haddad distinguishes the two characters based on their affective relationship: 'Zumba is sensible and compassionate, while Grande tries to sell illusions and dreams'. The episodes' structure consists of two men regularly bumping into each other and having a couple of mini-conversations (see image 10.2). Most of the plots centre on Grande spotting a gap in people's existential realities and, to Zumba's dismay, trying to profit from it. After common sense fails, all still ends well and they take leave of each other until next time.

The graphics and narratives also reflected Libya's changing times. When Season One was launched in summer 2010, the characters were set on an empty street with their backs to a wall and the skyline of an indeterminate

10.2 Still from *Boq'at Jaw*, directed by Mohamed Karwad (2010)

city. Some random and basic graffiti tagged the wall. Two street signs were visible. One read Al-Shari' (the street), and the second Al-Shari' Illi Ba'du (the next street) in an allusion to everyday stultifying uniformity under the regime.

The shorthand in Season One skilfully evaded the regime's volatile censorship with mundane narratives, yet it was filled with muted allusions to deep national traumas. For example, in one episode entitled 'Kamira khafiya' ('Candid Camera'), Grande suggests an idea for an episode of Candid Camera, which Zumba welcomes since it is a popular show during the Ramadan season.[31] Grande's idea consists of an arrest stunt perpetrated against any youngster on the street, including their lock up, torture, sentencing and then execution. Worried about the youngster's fate, Zumba asks Grande at which point the hidden camera will be revealed to the youngster. Grande brushes off his worries with a brisk 'We will figure it out later'.

The shorthand of this episode hints at Gaddafi's gruesome and repeated violation of citizens' bodies and his ruthless stifling of dissidence. Mesrati recounts his father's recollections of the time: 'In the 1980s, during the month of Ramadan, families gathered to break the fast while watching the festive TV programming. As an opening, they would be greeted with daily live transmission of prisoners' executions.'[32] Random and unannounced, such mediated scenes terrified families at the cruel prospect of watching their loved ones being lynched on their festive screens.

The shorthand thus unfolds a serial history of gruesome bodily violation established by Gaddafi from the 1970s on as part of his crackdown on fellow revolutionaries and groups of dissidents.[33] The most infamous incident took place on 7 April 1976. In response to university student protests, Gaddafi and his most ruthless top commanders orchestrated a public festival inviting school kids to the Tripoli University campus to celebrate the so-called Students' Revolution. As pupils were ushered to public arenas, they were met with live public hangings of dissident students and army officers. This bloody show of force spiralled into systemic public executions of activists, students and artists. From then on, until 2011, school children were forced to participate every year in the 'Week of Culture' commemorating these horrific hangings as yet another revolutionary triumph. Sibai and many other contributors remember how, during this week, they were herded from schools to pour onto the streets repeating chants glorifying 'Baba Moammar.'[34] Over the years, as the regime stifled freedom of expression, it shoved compliance and self-censorship down the population's throat, turning them, as Mesrati describes, into 'a lumpen mass saturated with a fear of death and indiscriminate murder [...] ruled by a bunch of militias and gangs [in] a land that knew no law [...] nor difference or diversity of opinion.'[35]

With every season, the show's set reflected an evolving street scene. In the second season, more graffiti became visible on the wall, reading *Al-Thawra* (Revolution) and *Yasqot Al-Nitham* (Down with the Regime). The street name changed to Shari` Al-Shuhada (Martyrs' Street). The backdrop evolved throughout the season to include the frontline and bombed buildings. By that time, Misrata was liberated and the artists came back from the frontline and headed straight into the studio. Season Two aired in Summer 2011 on Misrata Al-Horra (Free Misrata), a channel run by the dissidents of Misrata. For the first time, the team launched overt satire of Gaddafi. As Karwad explains, 'In the second season, we went overboard with the revolution (*sar fih infilat*), and we do not regret this. It was part of the propaganda of the revolutionary tide. *Boq`at Jaw* was one of Misrata's tools for confrontation with Gaddafi'.

The narrative followed political and visual progressions. The tone was direct, with un-nuanced support for the dissidents, attacking Gaddafi, his followers and the sceptics who jumped on the bandwagon of the revolution. One episode, 'Salluum' (Ladders), features Grande frantically looking to buy a ladder to climb to the top of the revolution.[36] Zumba does not have one since revolutionary climbers have used them all and now outnumber the fighters on the frontline. Grande then comes up with a money-spinning idea to learn from the best and organise 'climbing protection workshops', attracting top revolutionary climbers who want to prevent anyone else from getting there.

The shows' creators testify to their growing disappointment with the co-opting of the revolution at the expense of activists who sparked it. As Shahin, a member of the scriptwriting team, mentioned:

> Now anyone and everyone claims to be a rebel. And you know them, their background, how they used to jump from one seat to another within the regime, how they were locking up

protesters, and now you see them branding the rebels' flag and
speaking on behalf of the revolution.[37]

The shorthand thus evoked the then dominant moral division of the Libyan
street between *tahaleb* ('regime scum' with a literal meaning of 'green
algae'), and the *thuwwar* ('rebels', a term later used to refer to Misrata's
militant groups). Political climbing took on another meaning in Gaddafi's
Libya, merging a 42-year violent ban on any political activity with a swol-
len public sector. It meant a progression from regular administrative public
sector jobs to top positions in Popular and Revolutionary Committees that
straightjacketed citizens' everyday life. During the revolution, many former regime affiliates of all ranks defected to the dissidents' side, blurring
the moral revolutionary lines between 'scum' and 'rebels'.

The Ladders episode exposed bitter, yet unspoken national anxieties
resulting from the self-realisation that many citizens were involved, at some
point, in one way or another, in the regime's apparatus. At the time, the
National Transitional Council (TNC) was debating a transitional justice bill
that was to be issued in 2013 as 'The Isolation Code'. The code banned anyone
who had held any formal posts within the regime from taking up a public
position. This law affected most of the population, with the exception of those
Islamists who were locked up at Bu Sliim, the regime's notorious prison.

The code thus served to favour Islamists in accessing political leadership, while it lacked any meaningful measures to address the affective
blurring between repressor and repressed in everyday life. Many people
grieved at seeing former regime operators known for their arrests, torture,
and killings, walking out free from any punishment, and scaling the revolutionary ranks.[38] Others quietly remembered how some former regime
members had helped them escape detention and torture at the start of the
revolution.[39] On the Libyan street, people struggled with reconciling the
conflicting discourses of repression and revolutionary ideals.

The third season of *Boq`at Jaw* renamed the street Al-Intiqali
(Transitional) and added diverse colourful outdoor settings and some shel-
tered ones. By then, the narrative had turned to critique the rebels and post-
revolutionary public actors. Two episodes in particular, 'Dhol'[40] (Shadow)
and 'Ajindat' (Agendas), sum up the contradictions in the changing post-
regime environment:[41] 'Dhol' skilfully denounced the TNC's decision to

Animating Libya in Shorthand

reinstate Islamic family law and the Mufti position (the religious authority over national and personal affairs); 'Ajindat' exposed the political economy of post-revolutionary governance exemplified by the proliferation of Islamist (Qatar, Saudi Arabia) and Western (US, EU) political funding, and the consequent mushrooming of new militant factions. Crucially, the shorthands within 'Dhol' and 'Ajindat' revealed how the revolutionary forces brought in a new Islamist order through affective economies tying personal politics with Islamist governance agendas. For one, in its first ever post-revolutionary directive, the TNC reinstated the official position of the Mufti (after Gaddafi banned it in the 1980s) and appointed a powerful Islamist cleric Sadiq Al-Ghariani, who used to be an aide to Saif Al-Islam. Secondly, the TNC also reinstated Shari'a law as the national legal code for marriage, reversing Gaddafi's long ban on polygyny.

This shorthand in *Boq'at Jaw* hit at the untold controversies behind Gaddafi's often-cited version of feminism. Gaddafi's feminism manifested as a ban on polygyny and encouraging women to military service, which he still interpreted within an Islamic framework.[42] Between 1973 and 1980, Gaddafi established the Jihad Fund, sourcing fighters and ammunition to the Taliban, among others. He also declared himself the legitimate source of Shari'a law, wresting control from religious leaders. As a result, the Mufti was made redundant and his position discontinued. Gaddafi issued several laws based on his own reinterpretation of gender equity, laws in which women were equal, but biologically different to men. Polygyny was banned except with written consent from the wife, and military education and army service opened for both boys and girls. Gaddafi's fondness for his all-woman security squad *Al-Rahibat Al-Thawriyat* (Revolutionary Nuns or RN) is chilling to many Libyans. The RN leader, Huda Bin Amer, was known to willingly handle Gaddafi's public executions and sexual whims. Among the many stories were her unannounced visits to schools, selecting schoolgirls to escort to Gaddafi's residence. Sibai's father, Ibrahim, a painter and a teacher, witnessed first-hand the deep affective impact these measures had on girls' education and public presence:

> It was terrible. You know we are a conservative society. And these measures terrified people. You could see how families deregistered their daughters in scores in fear of rape. It resulted

233

in a whole generation of women missing out on education and pushed behind closed doors.[43]

In that generally conservative society, these measures produced a deep contraction in the gendered socio-cultural reflex.[44] *Boq`at Jaw* evoked the double loop of everyday gender discrimination, first by Gaddafi's military/sexual politics, and the second by the Islamisation of family law in post-revolutionary Libya.

This line of critique aimed at the rebels was carried over in Season Three, as cracks within the revolutionary landscape were starting to show, as Karwad explains:

> Last year, we were rebels, now we realise there are many weak spots in the revolution, and we need to talk about the ill-practices that are happening. As an artist I need to highlight the weak points: secret prisons with torture inside [...] There are various visions for Libya: a military state, Islamic, civil, something that lacks democracy.[45]

Critique of rebel corruption and abuse of power were central to Season Three. Yet, these episodes were subject to multiple lines of censorship that were new to the creators. As Al-Haddad reflects:

> In the past we had experience with one censor, now we have got more than one, each to their own mood of censorship. We lost count now. We are disoriented. It will take years to fix.[46]

At this stage, they were trying to make sense of the escalating repertoire of dissonance and embodied violations. In the demo episode of Season Four, the street sign reads Tasqot Ayy Haja (Down with Anything). It opens with new absurdist highs by turning the critique upon the characters in the episode, aptly entitled 'Jahawiya' ('Dogmatism'). Grande and Zumba are very proud of their city. They boast about belonging to the best city in the country. Next they carry on boasting about their neighbourhood and then their street being the best, until they end up fighting about who between them is the best. This episode sums up the times to come.

The positioning of *Boq`at Jaw* became increasingly difficult in the changing political, security and media landscapes, and especially within the growing clout and controversy of Misrata as the 'City of Rebels'. The main channel in Misrata, *Misrata Al-Horra*, which aired the series, shut down, but the team had big dreams to launch the fourth season nationally. They sought sponsorship through private sector advertising and were promised two major contracts. However, as the climate became more uncertain, the appetite for overt satirical animation dropped and the contracts were pulled. The demo episode, the last to come out from the *Boq`at Jaw* team, was released on YouTube.[47]

Conclusion: Documenting Libya through Animated Strings of Shorthand

As the Arab Uprisings unfolded, animated visual art emerged as a popular medium among dissidents all over the region, hinting at questions about the emergence, survival and use of visual dissident art under repressive regimes. Its revolutionary potential was explored through intense conceptual debates drawn from various contexts with minimal exploration for the conditions surrounding its emergence and persistence. Taking the case of dissident animated satire in Libya, the chapter aimed to redirect the question towards the usefulness of dissident satire as a chronicle of the unspoken violations towards the repressed body. The experiences of animation artists in creating political satire series, *Boq`at Jaw* between 2010 and 2013 presented the potential for chronicling of everyday socio-political conditions in Libya during its transition from a dictatorship to a precarious post-revolutionary climate. The show symbolised the value of dissident visual cultural production in making sense of the turbulent state of affairs in post-revolutionary Libya.

By tracing the local and regional influences on these artists and activists, their accounts are seen to point to a rich heritage of visually-articulated dissent through the 'shorthand' illustrations of cartoonist Zwawi. The *Boq`at Jaw* team found inspiration in these productions in their post-revolutionary times. Each generation of artists lived under Gaddafi's regime, practiced their craft and produced visual satire by walking the tightrope of sanctioned dissent. They both also opened up affective localities that escaped the regime's control, either around comic books in the privacy of their homes or in the convoluted conduits of the internet. Both generations of artists began revolutions leading respectively to the start and end of the 42-year long Gaddafi regime. Through their artwork transpired a creative skill for dodging tight censorship policies and repression in order to evoke the traumas buried deeply within the population.

As *Boq'at Jaw* animated the three crucial years of regime change, its value, and that of visual animation art as 'embodied shorthands' emerges. Such shorthands serve to crystallise an intense situation, while trimming away the bulk of explanations and questioning of the legitimacy of the regime via self-censorship. Instead of looking for elements of subversion within illustration, it can be more useful to direct attention to the conditions (histories, practices, discourses, economies) that enable the production of such sanctioned dissent and the discursive implications of its content.

Hence, another way of understanding political satire in Libya is not only by asking what made the audiences laugh for 42 years in terms of the actual 'shorthand'; it is fruitful, too, and perhaps more so, to unpack these embodied shorthands and piece them together to form an embodied timeline, a chronicle of everyday repression. By omitting the compressed and censored contextual discourses behind the laughter, the shorthand retrieves the long-standing traumas under the Gaddafi regime and post-revolutionary actors. The shorthand corresponds to Opondo's call to examine affective regimes for any chance to understand post-revolutionary Libya. The embodied shorthands created by *Boq'at Jaw* represent a continuing timeline of a repressed Libyan body. A gruesome stream of direct, repeated and randomly embodied violations by Gaddafi's torturous security apparatus, economic appropriation and gender violence, emerged from the series. It also revealed new open wounds from the transitional period in relation to justice and retribution, collective and individual trauma, equitable distribution, and reconciliation. Over the course of its three-year lifespan, *Boq'at Jaw* adapted to the historical changes in contemporary Libya and reworked its narrative to accommodate the changing margins of censorship and sanctioned dissent. As its narrative became overtly political, though, it struggled with the politics of positioning and the challenge of producing the shorthand of unspoken allusions.

Notes

1. *Boq'at Jaw* is on YouTube. Available at https://www.youtube.com/user/BuqaatJaw/videos (accessed 23 March 2014).

2. Information on *The Morganti Rebels* can be found online. Available at https://www.facebook.com/MorgantiRebels (accessed 23 March 2014).

3. Sam Okoth Opondo, 'Libya's "Black" Market Diplomacies: Opacity and Entanglement in the Face of Hope and Horror', *Globalizations*, 8, 5, pp. 661–8: p. 663.

4. Lina Khatib, *Image Politics* (New York, 2013); Marwan Kraidy, 'The body as medium in the digital age: Challenges and opportunities', *Communication and Critical/Cultural Studies*, 10, 2–3 (2013), pp. 285–90; Farida Makar, 'Let them have some fun: Political and artistic forms of expression in the Egyptian Revolution', *Mediterranean Politics*, 16, 2 (2011), pp. 307–12; Nour Sacranie, 'Image politics and the art of resistance in Syria', *State Crime Journal*, 2, 2 (Autumn 2013), pp. 135–48.

5. Victoria Bernal, 'Please forget democracy and justice: Eritrean politics and the power of humour', *American Ethnologist*, 40, 2 (2013), pp. 300–309.

6. Oring, Elliot, 'Risky business: Political jokes under repressive regimes', *Western Folklore*, 63, 3 (Summer 2004), p. 229.

7. Annie Rogers, Mary Casey, Jennifer Ekert, Jim Holland, 'Interviewing children using an interpretive poetics', S. Green and D. Hogan (eds), *Researching Children's Experience: Approaches and Methods* (London, 2005), p. 160.

8. Nisrine Mansour and Tarik Sabry, '(Mis)trust, access and the poetics of self-reflexivity: Arab diasporic children in London and media consumption', T. Sabry, N. Sakr and J. Steemers (eds), *Children's TV and Digital Media in the Arab World* (London, 2017).

9. Victoria Bernal, 'Please forget democracy and justice', p. 308.

10. Oriol Pi-Sunyer, 'Political humor in a dictatorial state: The case of Spain', *Ethnohistory*, 24 (1977), pp. 179–90.

11. Brian Massumi, *Parables For The Virtual – Movement, Affect, Sensation* (New York, 2002), p. 30.

12. Marwan Kraidy, 'The body as medium in the digital age: Challenges and opportunities', *Communication and Critical/Cultural Studies*, 10, 2–3 (2013), p. 289.

13. Opondo, 'Libya's "Black" Market Diplomacy', p. 667.

14. Interview with Mohammad Karwad, 10 June 2011.

15. The legacy of the independence was built around Omar Al-Mukhtar, an Islamic scholar who resisted the Italians for 22 years until his capture and execution by the Italian colonials in 1931.

16. Zwawi named in particular Cairo-based Greek illustrator Barny, who published his editorial cartoons in the Egyptian magazine *Al-Ithnayn*.

17. Fatima El-Issawi, 'Libya media transition: Heading to the unknown', *mediapolicy.org* (July 2013). Available at http://eprints.lse.ac.uk/59906/1/El-Issawi_Libya-media-transition_2013_pub.pdf (accessed 13 July 2014).

Animation in the Middle East

18. Lisa Anderson, 'Assessing Libya's Qaddafi', *Current History*, 84, 502 (1 May 1985), pp. 197–227.
19. Hans-Christian Mahnke, 'On Film and Cinema in Libya – Interview with Libyan film critic and festival director Ramadan Salim', *AfricAvenir*. Available at http://www.africavenir.org/nc/news-details/article/on-film-and-cinema-in-libya-interview-with-libyan-film-critic-and-festival-director-ramadan-sali.html (accessed September 2015).
20. Oliver Leaman. *Companion Encyclopedia of Middle Eastern and North African Film* (London: 2001).
21. Only the Eastern parts of Libya managed to escape it by relying on satellite connection.
22. Interview with Mohammad Karwad, 10 June 2011.
23. *Boq`at Daw (Spotlight)*, a Syrian comedy show created in 2001 by Ayman Rida and Bassem Yakhur, produced by Syrian International Productions, was aired on several pan-Arab satellite channels. SAPITV channel is on YouTube. Available at https://www.youtube.com/playlist?list=PLOpvfjrLz9uelWroM2C UuzBHOi4WJTZBN (accessed 15 March 2014).
24. Asteris Huliaras, 'Qadhafi's comeback: Libya and Sub-Saharan Africa in the 1990s', *African Affairs*, 100 (2001), pp. 5–25.
25. Larbi Sadiki, 'In-formalized polity and the politics of dynasty in Egypt and Libya', L. Anceschi, G. Gennaro and T. Andrea (eds), *Informal Power in the Greater Middle East: Hidden Geographies* (Oxford, 2014), pp. 11–23.
26. Fatima El-Issawi, 'Libya media transition: Heading to the unknown.'
27. Interview with Mohammad Karwad, 10 June 2011.
28. El-Issawi reports, for instance, that the cultural supplement of Libyan newspaper *Sabah Eoa* at the time was not subject to censorship.
29. Interview with Mohamed Karwad, 10 June 2013.
30. Interview with Abdulwahab Al-Haddad, 13 June 2013.
31. *Boq`at Jaw*, Season 1 Episode 10 'Kamira Khafiya' is on YouTube. Available at https://www.youtube.com/watch?v=fQhdqgzHdtU (accessed 2 March 2015).
32. Interview with Mo Mesrati, 26 July 2013.
33. Mohamed Mesrati, 'Bayou and Laila', M. Cassel, L. Al-Zubaidi, C. R. Nemonie (eds), *Writing Revolution: The Voices from Tunis to Damascus* (London, 2013), p. 86.
34. Interview with Jamal Sibai, 3 June 2013.
35. Mohamed Mesrati, 'Bayou and Laila.'
36. *Boq`at Jaw*, Season 2 Episode 1 'Salluum' (Ladders) is on YouTube. Available at https://www.youtube.com/watch?v=BfDUI05vJBA&list=PLuVc63nQ5rUpT97u-l0Vkapt-A5-qNa3G&index=1 (accessed 2 March 2014).
37. Interview with Ali Shahin, 20 June 2013.
38. For instance, stories abounded about mothers of inmates who used to commute weekly from Bengazi to Bu Sliim in Tripoli to visit their sons and bring

them food. Every week the prison guards would take the food from them and deny them the visits. Years of this weekly routine went by until the late 2000s. Only then did these women realise that their sons had long before been killed under torture by the same prison guards who ate their food for years. Within Saif Al-Islam's permissive climate, these women held weekly sit-ins asking for information about their sons' fates. On 15 February, the lawyer representing them was jailed. Civilian protests broke out sparking the start of the Libyan revolution.

39. Some accounts mentioned former officers who concealed the activists' files from the regime's security apparatus during the civilian protests and secretly opened prison doors for them to escape and join the revolution.

40. The episode entitled 'Dhol' (Shadow) skillfully tied the personal with the political. Trying to explain the concept of shadow cabinet to Grande, his interlocutor likens its relationship to the cabinet as that of *darayer* (up to four women married to the same man according to Islamic law). Grande objects that for the comparison to fully match, each cabinet needs three more shadow cabinets, as the 'Sheikh' ordered.

41. *Boq`at Jaw*, Season 3 Episode 4, 'Dhol' (Shadow) is on YouTube. Available at https://www.youtube.com/watch?v=d6AYUCJb6KI&index=9&list=PLuVc63n Q5rUpT97u-l0Vkapt-A5-qNa3G (accessed 2 March 2014). *Boq`at Jaw*, Season 3, Episode 24, 'Ajindat' (Agendas) is on YouTube. Available at https://www.youtube.com/watch?v=EKB40Ov2L1U (accessed 2 March 2014).

42. Andrea Khalil, *Crowds and Politics in North Africa: Tunisia, Algeria and Libya* (Oxford, 2014).

43. Interview with Ibrahim Sibai, 7 June 2013.

44. Hakan Seckinelgin, 'Contradictions of a sociocultural reflex: civil society in Turkey', M. Glasius and D. Lewis (eds), *Exploring Civil Society: Political and Cultural Contexts* (London, 2004), pp. 173–80.

45. Interview with Mohamed Karwad, 10 June 2013.

46. Interview with Abdulwahab Al-Haddad, 13 June 2013.

47. *Boq`at Jaw*, Season 4, Demo Episode 'Jahawiya' is on YouTube. Available at https://www.youtube.com/watch?v=FMtin1pP1sw (accessed on 21 May 2014).

Filmography

Boq`at Daw, directed by Ayman Rida and Bassem Yakhur (2001).

Boq`at Jaw (Chilling Spot), directed by Mohamad Karwad (2010).

Rusum Mutaharrira (Liberated Illustrations), directed by George Khoury, Lina Ghaibeh, Edgar Aaho (1993).

The Morganti Rebels, directed by Nisrine Mansour and Mohamed Mesrati (forthcoming).

11

Cinema Against an Authoritarian Backdrop: A History of Tunisian Animation

Maya Ben Ayed
Translated by Cristina Johnston

Animated Cinema in Tunisia: 'Terra Incognita'

Tunisian animated cinema remains neglected as much beyond its own national borders as within them. Since production is limited to short formats, animation suffers from the same screening problems faced by non-animated Tunisian short films. And the latter have almost entirely disappeared from screens, with the exception of the Carthage Film Festival (Journées Cinématographiques de Carthage) or in some 'art house' cinemas. So, short films in general, and animated films in particular, are only ever seen by large audiences during film festivals, specific cultural events or in film-clubs. Animated cinema in Tunisia, as is the case everywhere else, is still subject to prejudice.

Considered purely as entertainment and deemed to be aimed exclusively at children, Tunisian animated cinema has been neglected by both critics and researchers. Specialist works dealing with this form of cinema are almost non-existent. Certainly, rare and brief passages making reference to a particular film or *auteur* within larger studies of cinema in Tunisia do occur, but, to the best of my knowledge, the only work to dedicate an entire chapter to animation in Tunisia is Victor Bachy's *Le Cinéma de Tunisie* (*Tunisian Cinema*, 1972). Its author offers a catalogue of directors and films that ends at the beginning of the 1970s.

240

Samir Besbes, a Tunisian director of four animated films (released in 1985, 1990, 1995 and 2008), undertook postgraduate studies in Paris and graduate-level research on animated cinema. His 1998 doctoral thesis examining the evolution of the universal art of animation from its origins in the magic lantern to its 'electronic' manifestations, dedicates its third and final section to the topic of Tunisian animated cinema and the beginnings of animation in the Arab world (Egypt, Algeria, etc.).[1] However, he was, in effect, merely continuing the cataloguing task initiated by Victor Bachy, introducing a generation of filmmakers from the birth of the movement to the middle of the 1990s, by way of historical overview. Unfortunately, too, certain (production) dates in the work do not match up and have had to be verified both with the filmmakers and via press archives.[2]

Bachy begins his work on animated cinema in Tunisia with an insight that remains relevant: 'Introducing Tunisian animated cinema is an undertaking that demands the patience and the intuition of an archaeologist. These few lines can only bring together disparate fragments'. And so it is with this study: I have had to undertake both archival research and an investigation involving filmmakers (those still alive) and the different agents of the cinematographic landscape, in order to reconstruct the context of the movement's origins, as well as the evolution of this art form in the Tunisian context.

It is not only the lack of written works, but even that of a focussed discourse on animated cinema, that underlies the continuing speculation surrounding the origins of this movement – and even the date of the first ever Tunisian animated film. Indeed, something of an obsession with the start of animation, rather than its developments, is revealed: not only in the press but also in more specialist publications, through the prevalent use of the same catchy phrases which appear and reappear on numerous occasions, right up to the 2000s: 'the first Tunisian animation'; 'the first experiments in animation', etc. In some works of film history,[3] the date given is the start of the 1970s, and 1972 in particular, marking the release of Nacer Khemir's *Le Mulet* (*The Mule*).[4,5]

The Origins of Animated Cinema in Tunisia

The year 1964–5 marks the beginning of the history of animated cinema in Tunisia. In that year, Mongi Sancho, initiator and pioneer of this art form in Tunisia, who was at the time a young amateur filmmaker, made his first object animation film, *La Rentrée des classes* (*Back to School*). The film was produced under the auspices of the Association of Young Tunisian Filmmakers (AJCT) that would later transform into the very important Tunisian Federation of Amateur Filmmakers (FTCA).

Born in 1935, Sancho was introduced to cinema and particularly burlesque films (Charlie Chaplin, Buster Keaton, Max Linder, *et al.*) at a very early age by his maternal uncle Slouma Ben Abderrazak, who had installed a basic screening room in a warehouse next to his house. Cinema had to co-exist alongside other pre-existing forms of popular entertainment in Tunisia, such as *Karakouz* shadow theatre (considered by many a forerunner of cinema),[6] singing cafés (or caféchanta), puppet theatre, 'fdaoui' or Meddah performances (troubadour storytelling), etc. And it was in the old town that these performances established themselves, especially in the neighbourhood of Halfaouine.

Cinema made its appearance in Tunisia at almost the same moment as it did in France. While art forms associated with popular spectacle took over the medina, the cinema – a symbol of modernity – established itself essentially in the European sector of the town. According to historian Habib Belaid, in 'colonial Tunisia [cinema was] a French monopoly, notably in terms of production, distribution and political and administrative control,[7] thereby confirming modernity as the founding myth of colonialism. And cinema was the vehicle of colonial propaganda, *par excellence*. Belaid, a historian specialising in the colonial period, also states that 'Tunisians remained outside the domain of cinematic production, at least until independence.[8] This would also provide an explanation for the lack of Tunisian cinematic productions prior to independence in 1956, be it in terms of either live-action or animation.[9] Still, the first screenings in Tunisia had taken place in 1896 'when a certain "photographer Albert" (was it Albert Semama Chikly?) introduced the cinematograph for the first time for paid public screenings, organised from 1 November in Bénévent Passage, at the corner of Amilcar Street, in the modern – or European – town.[10]

The cultural policies of the state authorities at the dawn of independence were favourable to the development of cinema and its associated trades and professions, most notably that of newsreel cameramen. At the same time, from the creation of the cinephile movement in Tunisia under the occupation in 1950 onwards, a certain cinephilic elite that had taken shape through film-clubs began to see cinema as a tool for working towards liberation, for combating imperialism and as an instrument of 'decolonisation'. These two elites – a political elite associated with the regime, and a (left-wing) cinephile elite – although not usually driven by the same motivations, nevertheless shared one common goal: the desire to found a national cinema. As a result, since independence on 20 March 1956, the development of cinephile life and activities has been extremely rich.

In 1957, the Society for the Production and Expansion of Cinema in Tunisia (SATPEC) was created by the new independent state. Ten years later, in 1967, and in a very specific political context,[11] SATPEC 'formed the Gammarth cinema complex where numerous films from across the continent were to be filmed and/or entered into post-production'.[12] In 1962, the Association for Young Tunisian Filmmakers (AJCT) was founded by a group of young amateur filmmakers, becoming the Tunisian Federation for Amateur Filmmakers (FTCA) in 1968. Two film festivals saw the light of day: Kélibia International Festival of Amateur Films (FIFAK) and the Carthage International Film Festival, in 1964 and 1966 respectively. The sixties was a hugely important decade in Tunisian cinema, and also, as I show here, for Tunisian animation.

The Pioneers: The 1960s Generation

It was in the mid-1960s that Mongi Sancho, a professional photographer with a gift for drawing, made his first forays into animation. He had joined the AJCT and, while his peers were fascinated by live-action fiction, by reportage and particularly by *Actualités* reporting, Sancho decided to try his hand at animation.[13] As an accomplished autodidact, he created in his 'sub-artisanal' style, without celluloid, a first attempt that he entitled *La Vieille et l'ogre* (*The Old Woman and the Ogre*) by reworking the characters and backdrops for each drawing, and also by drawing the movements of the camera, producing tracking shots and even optical effects like the 'fade to black'. It was in this way, and by becoming part of the AJCT, that he was able to make title sequences for films in 1964. In 1965, he made his first object animation film, *Back to School* and was given charge of animation for the film *Caprices de poupons* (*Dolls' Whims*), a film featuring animated dolls, made by the amateur filmmaker Belcadi. Both works won prizes at the Kélibia International Festival for Amateur Films and attracted the attention of the Tunisian press. In 1966, Sancho made his first animated short film, *Le Chien Intelligent* (*The Intelligent Dog*), which was to win the First Prize at the Kairouan Festival of Engaged Cinema.

It is worth noting that the AJCT, which had by then become the Tunisian Federation for Amateur Filmmakers (FTCA), represented a breeding ground for young talent. Many professional Tunisian filmmakers started their careers within this association. The FTCA and the Tunisian Federation of Film-Clubs (FTCC) constituted something of a film school, where a younger generation learned to 'watch' and to make films. Tunisia is, in fact, considered something of an exception in the Arab and African worlds in terms of the originality of its creation of cinephile associations. Indeed, another young amateur filmmaker from the Kairouan club, the late Habib Masrouki, made *Notre Monde* (*Our World*) in 1967, a short object animation film that sought to 'denounce war by representing the warring factions as cigarette packets'.[14]

In the same year, 1967, Sancho, whose first attempts at animation had gained some visibility, won a bursary to the National Centre for Cinematography in Sofia, Bulgaria. He began his training in animation under the guidance of Todor Dinov, the father of Bulgarian animation, and his graduation film, *Le Marchand de Fez* (*The Fez Seller*), won a special mention from the jury at the International Festival for Animated Films in Mamaia, Romania, in 1968. On his return to Tunisia, caught up in the excitement of his Bulgarian experience and perceiving favourable cultural politics, Sancho submitted a full application to SATPEC in order to create a specialist animation production unit. The request, however, received no response.[15] Ten years later, Zouhair Mahjoub experienced the same thing.

Another decade later, in 1980, Samir Besbes, just back from his film studies in France, was to pick up on the idea again and submitted an application to Tunisian television for the creation of an animation unit (animation, dubbing and puppet shows). Besbes makes reference to the outcome in his doctoral thesis: 'But television, which should in principle have encouraged us in this initiative, didn't even respond to our sugges-tion'.[16] A repeated neglect of these calls for an animation unit, whether with SATPEC or Tunisian TV, discouraged artists from trying, and bears

Cinema Against an Authoritarian Backdrop

consequences up until today, as animation is still a marginal art form within an otherwise very productive film culture in Tunisia. If, as Florence Martin has noted, cultural policies under the two regimes of independent Tunisia have encouraged the development of a national cinema supported by the state (although also kept under its control), it has principally been live-action cinema that has been the beneficiary. Animated cinema has remained at the margins.[17]

Ahmed Bennys, director of the animated film *Mohammedia* and cameraman for the Tunisian news, gave me an indication of the production context for his film in 1973–4. When I asked him whether SATPEC encouraged filmmakers, he replied:

> No, there was no encouragement. SATPEC is a State company. But there was a dedicated budget, given annually by the State: we had to do something with it. The lab had originally been created to produce weekly newsreels, but now, since SATPEC had a budget, I was told 'ok, you can make news magazines. The current affairs shows, we don't need them anymore, it's not political anymore'.[18]

And it was in this format, under this umbrella term of 'news magazine', that Bennys produced his mixed technique film *Mohammedia* (paper cutouts and live-action shots). Bennys' comments regarding the choices and direction taken by SATPEC give a clear indication of this state institution's priorities with regards to cinema. Primacy was given to the Tunisian *Actualités* news coverage that was screened in all cinemas until the beginning of the 1970s, before switching exclusively to television with the expansion of that medium across Tunisian households. In this way, and despite the fact that almost all Tunisian cinematic production (including animated films) was funded and produced by SATPEC, until the latter was dissolved in 1992, the state's cinema policy privileged newsreel and reportage as a genre. Training bursaries were allocated to young Tunisians to help them learn the various professions associated with cinema and to come back to work within the domain of *Actualités* newsreel coverage. The overall aim was to support the ruling regime's propaganda. 'Until television became common-place, newsreel represented a means of communication that was privileged by Bourguiba's regime as he sought to build the nation'.[19]

245

Founding Myths of the Nation and the Post-Collectivist Crisis (1960s and 1970s)

The first Tunisian animated films (those made by Sancho and Masrouki in the 1960s[20]) were made during the first period of President Bourguiba's rule, that of nation-building. This period was characterised by a nationalistic tendency with the new authorities seeking to affirm a supposed Tunisian identity by means of 'Tunisification', with the nationalisation of State institutions alongside the early stages of the national modernisation project. Modernisation and 'Tunisian-ness' were the two key pillars of post-independence Tunisia, Bourguiba's Tunisia. And Bourguiba, in his own right, was seen as the personification of this founding myth of the independent nation. He was the national hero of the struggle for independence, seen as having taken the best that the West had to offer (thanks to his training in France) while preserving his Tunisian identity.

Auteurs use the *mises-en-scène* of political power (both regimes that have ruled Tunisia) in their films, in a subversive way, to criticise abuses committed by the authoritarian system. For president Bourguiba, the *mise-en-scène* is constructed as if for a monarchy, based on the image of the leader: first through photos, stamps and busts, then through cinema and television. The leader used cinematic and pro-filmic tricks to stage himself. His successor based his own *mise-en-scène* on signs (colours, numbers etc.), banning the image of the president (at least initially). Ben Ali tried to embody the democracy by using modern vocabulary of political power performance.

Sancho's first films from this amateur period bear witness to this initial post-independence enthusiasm soon followed by disappointment, something reflected subtly in the *mise-en-scène* in his films. The didactic nature of his first film *Return to School* fits perfectly with the central pillars of Bourguiba's modernisation project: the democratisation of education, emancipation of women and the secularisation of society. Education became free and compulsory following independence. So, the film, telling the story of a child who tries to escape first day of school by defying a policeman who then proceeds to chase him around town, can be viewed as an illustration of this policy. The film – a 4-minute short – is an animation featuring penicillin bottles of different sizes that Sancho painted and

Cinema Against an Authoritarian Backdrop

transformed into characters with moustaches, wearing fezzes and twisting in a movement that is at once mechanical and fluid. Bachy confirms Sancho's pedagogical leanings, observing how 'Sancho sets out to write his animation with a specific moral intention. He aims for social improvement via animation cinema and chooses his gags in virtue of their educational impact'.[21]

The animated short *The Intelligent Dog* follows the same didactic trajectory as his first film. It tells the story of an old man who, when he gets home from work, hides his money in a purse. He falls asleep, cigarette in hand, thus starting a fire. It is the dog of the title that we see at the end of the film, purse in paw, at the counter of a branch of the Société Tunisienne de Banque (STB) to pay in his master's money. Although the director claims that the film was not commissioned by the STB, this consciousness-raising work was made at the same time as an advertising campaign led by the bank.[22] In *The Intelligent Dog*, the setting is the medina, which the dog crosses to reach the bank. We can see in Sancho's first films evidence of the director's engagement in favour of the regime's policy of modernisation, as well as his adherence to the national *mise-en-scène* and story. In terms of its visuals, in *Return to School*, the clothing is typically Tunisian with moustaches and traditional hats (the fez) painted on all of the penicillin bottles, including those representing the children and their parents, as well as those representing the forces of law and order; in *The Intelligent Dog*, besides the moustache and the traditional hat, the old man is wearing baggy trousers (the *sarouel*), a traditional shirt, as well as traditional slippers (*babouches*). The emphasis is on Tunisian identity with the backdrop, in *Return to School*, of a blackboard behind the schoolmaster on which the first letters of both the Arabic and the French alphabets have been written, beneath the date of the first day of school (1 October) which is also given in both languages.

The Fez Seller, made in Sofia in 1967, differs from the two films made during Sancho's amateur period, as much in terms of the style of drawing, which is much purer and more minimalist, almost abstract, as in its themes, which take it more into the territory of allegory than illustration. The filmmaker said about his film that 'the idea is that it is important not to just blindly imitate',[23] what is, again, a very didactic tale.

In 1962, President Bourguiba announced a policy of collectivism. The experiment meant the nationalisation of lands previously owned

247

by colonisers, followed by the expropriation of peasant-owned lands by the state. By 1967, when *The Fez Seller* was made, collectivism was in full swing; but this economic policy and, above all, its enforced implementation, produced great resistance, first from the small *fellahin* who refused to be dispossessed of their land, then by bigger landowners who had initially been spared; and thus ended Tunisia's experiment with economic socialism. The legacy of this period for the country was a single-party state and a deep economic crisis. Frederic Jameson, in his famous 1986 work, *Third-World Literature in the Era of Multinational Capitalism*, states that works produced by the Third World are, on the whole, necessarily allegorical, insofar as they translate social and political concerns. Thus, those that seem to tell a tale of individual destiny finally become nothing more than an allegory of the circumstances of social and cultural oppression in the Third World.[24] Just so, *The Fez Seller*, made in Sofia in 1967, can be viewed and interpreted as an allegory of this contemporary economic policy of cooperatives, borrowed from the communist regime. The monkeys who want to imitate the smallholder, in Sancho's film, by stealing his fezzes in order to wear them, lose not only the fezzes but also their own food (coconuts).

Allegory is even more explicit in Sancho's film *Le Pain* (*Bread*), a first (black and white) version of which was made in 1972, referencing a Tunisian expression, which translates literally as 'running after bread' and means that times are hard. It shows the tale of a peasant who chases after a loaf of bread trying to catch it, coming up with a new strategy at every attempt. In the final scene, we see the bread metamorphose into a cannibalistic monster, spitting out the bones of the peasant, which land on a pile of other bones, conveying to the audience that this is not the monster's first victim. The plot, based on chase sequences between the two characters and repeated gags in the style of the American running gags we might find in *Roadrunner* or *Tom and Jerry* cartoons, differs from such animation because of its climax confirming the symbolism of the character of the loaf of bread. The peasant's death cannot be undone as is the case with Wile E. Coyote or Tom and Jerry who are resuscitated after each gag. Yet Sancho's film is far from an exception. The 1970s saw the advent of a new generation of animation directors whose films embody a strand of resistance and political allegory in line with Jameson's analysis.

Nacer Khemir, a multifaceted artist – both storyteller and visual artist – started his cinematic career in the field of animation at the beginning of the 1970s, in Paris, where he frequented Otero's workshop, meeting the Polish Piotr Kamler and other figures from world animation. He made his first films in 1970 (*La Fleur* / *The Flower*), 1971 (*L'Homme qui dort* / *The Sleeping Man*) and in 1972 (*The Mule*).[25] This last one was selected for the 'non-competition' strand at the 1973 Annecy Festival and recounts the tale of a carter who lost his job because he was diverted by his dreams of better life. The film is a mixture of drawings and cut-outs, in sepia-tinged monochrome, and the graphic characteristics are reminiscent of the *Tale of Tales* by Yuri Norstein.[26]

The film develops around an alternation between close-ups and extreme close-ups, in succession, of the mule, the wheel of the cart and the worker. The further we get into the film, the more the camera zooms in on the characters, from close-up to extreme close-up. By means of metamorphosis, the head of the mule blurs with that of the worker and that of the worker with that of the mule. The soundtrack, with its repetitive mechanical noises, working in tandem with the long close-ups on the cart's wheel, creates a sense of oppression in the viewer. When asked what story he sought to tell via the tale of the carter and his mule, Khemir replied:

> There was a desire to be on the side of the people, in a sense. Later, I understood that being on the side of the people means helping to build a future for the country and not only for one social class. It's much more complicated, it's not simply a case of being on the side of the workers.[27]

In 1973, Ahmed Bennys, cameraman and director of photography, joined forces with Mohammed Abdennadher, who was responsible for the animation of title sequences and in documentaries produced by RTT (Radiodiffusion Télévision Tunisienne), to make *Mohammedia*, a mixed media film (cut-outs and live-action), which went on to win the Bronze Tanit at the Carthage Film Festival in 1974. *Mohammedia*, whose political protest is much more evident than that to be found in the films of Sancho or Bennys, tells the story of one of the Beys of Tunis, Ahmed Bey I, who reigned from 1837 to 1855. The film is structured around parallel editing of sequences with animated paper cut-outs and live-action footage. The animated sequences recount the story of the building of Mohammedia's palace, and the megalomania of Ahmed Bey who, due to poor financial management and the guidance of a corrupt court, embarked on reforms that had not been properly examined and who ultimately led the country into debt and a deep economic crisis. The consequence of the crisis was the annexation of Tunisia by the French empire a few years later under the reign of Ahmed Bey I's successor. The live-action footage is shot in documentary style or in the manner of a reportage, showing daily life in the village of Mohammedia a century later; in contemporary Tunisia. The animated sequences are filmed in the style of the *Actualités* by Ahmed Bennys. The allusion to President Bourguiba and his political choices is all too clear. Both he and Ahmed Bey undertook modernising reforms whose implementation was a failure and that ultimately led to political and economic crisis.

Bennys' film was made at the start of the 1970s, at the height of the post-collectivist crisis and a time of toughening policies. The decade also saw the arrival of another animation pioneer in Zouhair Mahjoub, who, having studied cinema at the in Conservatoire Indépendant du Cinéma Français in Paris, returned to Tunisia and began working for Tunisian television as an assistant director. After his failed attempt to establish a structure for the production of animation within Tunisian TV, he obtained a bursary to study animation at AnimaFilm in Bucharest. Mahjoub left for Romania where, in 1971, he made his first animated film, *Hajji dans sa mille et deuxième nuit* (*Hajji in his 1002nd Night*), a 2-minute film with animated puppets.

Still, from this generation of pioneers in the 1960s and 1970s, it was only Sancho and Mahjoub who, driven by their passion for the art form, truly embraced it. They specialised in animation, making it their life's work, despite the difficulties they encountered and the marginalisation of the art form by official structures. Mohamed Charbaji, cinephile and amateur filmmaker (member of AJCT) only made one animated film, *Une petite histoire d'oeuf* (*A Little Story of an Egg*) in 1976. Nacer Khemir was to switch to live-action filmmaking, and neither Ahmed Bennys nor Habib Masrouki continued with their experiments in animation. The former left Tunisian television and dedicated himself to his work as director of photography working in cinema, and the latter expanded his field of interest to cinema more generally before becoming consumed by theatre.[28]

250

The Zaïm and the 'War' of Succession

At the beginning of the 1980s, the country was undergoing its third major political and social crisis, following those of the 1960s and of 1978 (when a general strike by the trade unions was ended through bloody repression). It was a crisis characterised by the popular uprising of January 1984, known as the 'bread riots'. This third crisis ultimately undermined the regime, which was, furthermore, based upon the figure of a single man, the ageing President Bourguiba, also called the 'Zaïm' or 'leader'. The war to succeed the Zaïm only intensified the political crisis throughout the decade, right up to the *coup d'état* in 1987.

At the same time, that is, at the start of the 1980s, Zouhair Mahjoub left for Czechoslovakia in order to hone his skills in puppet animation. There he made *Le petit hibou* (*The Little Owl*), and in 1984 his film *Guerbaji* (*The Water Seller*) with animated puppets was screened in competition at the Annecy Festival. In 1984, *The Water Seller* represented the end of Bourguiba's regime onscreen. It is the story of a *guerbaji* (a water seller) in a Tunis under French occupation, who, thanks both to his particular position as a blind old man and to his job, has access to the interior of people's houses (something that was forbidden to strangers at the time). He takes advantage of this privilege to spy on collaborators and to help the revolutionaries of the nationalist movement by distributing leaflets. Through this character, Mahjoub undid one of the founding myths of post-independence Tunisia: that of the supreme leader, *Al-Moujahid Al-Akbar*, saviour of the nation. Guerbaji is a man of the people, placed centre stage, and although a voiceover recounts the official version of the national story, making reference to Bourguiba, the latter remains unseen. This is particularly significant insofar as Bourguiba's communication strategy was based exclusively on the use of his image in general, and on cinematic and televisual images in particular.

The 1980s also saw the arrival of new animation filmmakers, including Mustapha Taieb, a young amateur filmmaker (member of the Tunis club), and gifted, self-taught illustrator, who plays a role in Salah Khélifi's film project *L'Enfant et l'avion* (*The Child and the Aeroplane*). This animated film was made in 1983, just after Israel's military action in Lebanon in 1982 and the PLO's headquarters being moved to Tunisia. The film serves as an illustration

Animation in the Middle East

of Marcel Khalifé's protest song of the same name and as homage to the victims of Sabra and Shatila. Taieb continued his experiments in animation in the films *Jahjouh 1* and *La cigale* (*The Cicada*), directed by Samir Besbes in 1985 and Ezzedine Harbaoui in 1986, respectively. From 1987 until 1994, he directed his own animated films, in which the recurring theme is that of the status and problems of the artist in society in the face of new technology (*Lemalif*, 1989), of censorship and of religious fanaticism (*Secourez la, elle est en danger / Save Her, She's in Danger*, 1987 and *Le Déluge / The Flood*, 1994).

But others were also at work. Samir Besbes studied cinema at the Louis Lumière School in Paris where his 1978 graduation film was an animated work, *Joha et les fantômes de la nuit* (*Joha and the Ghosts of the Night*). On his return to Tunisia, he imagined the continuation of Joha's adventures through an animated series (two works), which centred on Jahjouh, Joha's godson, in *Jahjouh 1* and *Jahjouh 2*. The first work, made in 1985, critiqued of the star system and the alienation of the general population via advertising and propaganda. The second, made in 1990, focused on environmental problems. Ezzedine Harbaoui, a TV director, made two forays into animation: *The Cicada* in 1986, with Mustapha Taieb, and *Il était une fois, notre monde* (*Once Upon a Time, Our World*), with young animators from the Tunis School of Fine Arts in 1989. While the former, like Taieb's other films, deals with the problems faced by the artist (in this instance, the status of the artist and of art in society), the latter can be seen as an anti-militarist and anti-imperialist film.

1987 *Coup d'état*: The Promise of Change and Disillusionment

On 7 November 1987, Zine El-Abidine Ben Ali put an end to three decades of Bourguiba's rule. In his speech of 7 November, the new president promised the population that there would be change and this notion of change was to become the label attached to his regime until his overthrow in 2011. While Ben Ali's initial rise to power was welcomed unanimously across all sections of civil society, as well as by the different political movements, the disenchantment that followed was just as rapid. Steffen Erdle[29] has broken up the Ben Ali era into three key stages: The Tunisian Spring between 1987 and 1990, the Authoritarian Turnaround from 1991 to 1995 and finally the third period, from 1995 to 2004, the Authoritarian Reconfiguration.

No significant production of animated films took place during the first stage. Only Taieb's *Lemalif*, made in 1989, could really be considered as belonging to this period. The old calligrapher, who is the hero of this film, is threatened by new technology: typewriters, television, computers, etc. His old hut is surrounded on all sides by high buildings. The final shot shows a bulldozer demolishing the calligrapher's hut while he shouts 'No' (in Arabic letters: ﻻ). While the place of the artist in society, faced with the advent of new technology, is certainly the film's central theme, we can also read between the lines the image of a past era chased away by the new.

In the 1990s, the period of the Authoritarian Turnaround, the resistance fighters of animation returned with Sancho and the colour version of his film *Bread* in 1994, Taieb and his two works *The Flood* and *La chaussure* (*The Shoe*) in 1994, and Besbes' and his animated doll film *Les ficelles* (*The Threads*) in 1995. At the same time Mahjoub, as well as making short films, was embarking on a full-length feature with the help of new technology and a team of young illustrators. Due to a lack of time and funding, the project only got as far as becoming a medium-length animated film *Le sous-marin de Carthage* (*The Carthage Submarine*, 1999). Nadia Rais, a graphic designer trained at the Tunis School of Fine Arts and a filmmaker of the 'generation 2000', was part of the project. *The Threads* is a work that centres on Tunisian history, that of the Beys. Unlike Bennys, Besbes does not choose a specific period, event or sovereign, but, rather, critiques the entire dynastic system established by the Beys, with its many similarities to that installed by Ben Ali at the start of the decade.

However, in spite of this apparent upturn in animation, SATPEC's liquidation in 1992 meant that filmmakers found it increasingly difficult to get their films made. At the start of the 2000s, a new project, Euromédiatoon, which sought to set up a production structure for animation in a country of the global South, was started up in Tunis, on the premises of the late Ahmed Bahadin Attia's production company *Cinétéléfilm*. This project was funded by Euromed Audiovisuel and its aim, in addition to a desire to create an animated film industry in the Mediterranean region, was to train youngsters after art school in the various roles associated with animation. Young Tunisians and Algerians participated in the project to make a series of animated films entitled *Viva Cartago*, while following different forms of training in Tunis. As far as I am aware, the project did not succeed in achieving its ultimate aim of producing 26x26-minute episodes. However, 13x26-minute episodes were produced, in 2003 and in 2006, and were screened as a full-length format on cinema screens under the title *Cartago 1 & 2*.

Boubaker Boukhari, a graduate of the Algiers School of Fine Arts, and a group of young animators who had taken part in the *Viva Cartago* project, founded their own production society 5D and, under Boukhari's direction, made the animated film *Dedi wa Doudi* (*Dedi and Doudi*) in 2006. Lotfi Mahfoudh, who studied at the School of Fine Arts in Tunis before specialising in animation at ENSAD (School of Decorative Arts) in Paris, made his first animated short, *La noce du loup* (*The Wolf's Wedding*) in 2001. In 2002, he participated in the animation of the film *Fish Never Sleep* by Gaëlle Denis, a BAFTA winner.[30] In 2004, he started his own production company and made *Ryeh* in 2008, followed by *Hoffili*, a mixed media work (using 2D animation and CGI) in 2012. The latter was selected for screening and won prizes at numerous festivals, including in Brussels, Zagreb and Lima.

Following her experience working on Mahjoub's *The Carthage Submarine* in 1999, Nadia Rais, a graduate of the Tunis School of Fine Arts, made *Lambouba* in 2009, prize-winner at the Meknès Festival in 2010, and *L'mrayet* (*The Glasses*) in 2011, a film that combined animation with rotoscoping (see image 11.1), which was screened in the official selection at Annecy in 2012 and won prizes at festivals in Italy, Mexico and Egypt.[31] Alaedine Boutaleb, visual artist and author of graphic novels, made an animated film entitled *Coma* in 2009 which went on to be selected in the Panorama section of the 2010 Carthage Film Festival and was picked up in Sweden, Germany, France, etc. Boutaleb had preceded *Coma* with a number of animated works, including *Mazamir* in 2005.

In terms of experimental animation, filmmakers such as myself, another graduate of the Tunis School of Fine Arts, made two first attempts at animated films. My first one came out in 2001: *In and On* was pre-selected for the Oberhausen Short Film Festival, and *Kashf* in 2003, a mixed media film (2D Flash animation and live-action footage), was among the prizewinners at Kélibia and attracted attention in Tallinn and Prague. Cinephile and amateur filmmaker Rafik Omrani made *Kharmouj*, his first animated film, in 2008. This work also did the rounds of the festival circuit and was followed by *Amour névrosé* (*Neurotic Love*) in the same year and by *La*

Cinema Against an Authoritarian Backdrop

11.1 Still from *L'mrayet* (*The Glasses*), directed by Nadia Rais (2011)

poule de Sabaa (*The Hen from Saaba*) in 2010. In 2007, *L'Enfant roi* (*The Child King*) (shadow theatre and animated shadows), a hybrid animated film, was made by the actor Mohamed Grayaa.

But the 2000s also saw the return of the pioneers, with *Ruse par ruse* (*Cunning Craftiness*) by Sancho in 2006, screened and picked up by several festivals; Besbes' puppet film *Jahjouh et la sirène* (*Jahjouh and the Mermaid*) in 2008; Mahjoub's *La goutte miraculeuse* (*The Miraculous Droplet*) in 2009; and finally Taieb's *Châteaux de sable* (*Sandcastles*) in 2010. Parallel to this trend of the 'return' of the pioneers, I note an increased audience and curators' interest in animated cinema from the end of the 2000s onwards, which saw the organisation of a special animated selection, 'Animated Cinema of the Maghreb', on the fringes of the Film Festival of Carthage in 2006. In addition, there were several events exclusively dedicated to animated films organised by the Tunisian Federation of Film Clubs, and by the French Institute for Cooperation. Finally, and of great importance for Tunisia, was the inauguration in 2014 of the Tahrik festival, an international festival of animation in Tunis.[32]

For the most part, these films offer a subversive slant on the regime. Particularly notable in this regard are Nadia Rais' *The Glasses* and *Coma* by Boutaleb, clear allegories of the third period of Ben Ali's authoritarian regime. Although it was only released in 2011, after the revolution, work on *The Glasses* had started in 2010. In an interview I conducted with the film-maker, she revealed that the film was written in 2010, with the exception of the final section that is an illustration of the January 2011 Revolution.[33] The film depicts a character, Boumrayet, born with glasses like all the people in his universe until the day he decides to remove them.

It is through the use of symbols that became part of the regime's label, such as the number 7, the colour purple, etc., that Rais constructs her allegory. For example, at the start of the film and during the sequence depicting Boumrayet's birth, a close-up of the monitor attached to the mother's stomach shows the date of 7 November 1987 and the time 6.12 am, thus making clear to the viewer that we are on the day of Ben Ali's coup. The glasses the child is forced to wear from birth are an allusion to the short-sightedness imposed on the people by the regime. The number 7 is also to be seen in another close-up of a clock on the wall where the hands of the clock, as they go mad, make all the numbers fall except for the number 7. Time stops on the 7 of Ben Ali. The clock also reminds us of the great clock on Habib Bourguiba Avenue, built by Ben Ali's regime a few years after the putsch. As Siino notes, 'the careful observer could note that it was probably the only clock where the 7 was where the 6 would normally be on the clock-face. A subtle way to suggest that it was a period – officially known as the 'new era' ('ahd jedîd) – that was already marked by this digit that was to become the trademark or logo of the regime'.[34]

Coma is likewise politically inspired. It depicts skeletons who try to escape death and come back to life, driven on by an irresistible nostalgia for the feeling of existence. One of the film's first sequences shows a mass of human skeletons, with one trying to wake up and get to its feet. It is crushed by the boot of a black-suited monster upon whose head there is a sort of blue light (a radar perhaps) that keeps a close watch. The monster will ultimately be beaten by the same skeleton that manages to grow wings and to neutralise the blue light of the monster's motion sensor by turning it against the monster. The monster ends up drowned and in the last shot we see all the skeletons, on their feet, floating in the air. The parallel between this film and the Tunisian political context is all the more stark since it was made in 2009–10, just one year after the 2008 revolt in the mining region of Gafsa that was violently repressed by the regime. The film got its cinema release in October 2010 and the filmmaker has stated that the question often posed by the audience was 'who is the authoritarian figure in the black suit?' When I asked him whether he thought the audience understood the parallel with the regime, the director suggested that many understood the symbolism without daring to name it.[35]

Conclusion: The Trajectories of Subtle Political Content

As we have seen, the 'firsts' in Tunisian animation are highly contested, but I have attempted to show that perhaps it is more fruitful to follow the trajectories of these first artists, and to see how their subject matter evolved over time under the two totalitarian regimes in Tunisian politics. It must also be admitted that this historical overview is far from exhaustive. Directors of animated series for television, as well as awareness-raising animation, advertising, video clips or film school works do not feature here, and neither do the complete filmographies of those filmmakers who are cited.

After tenuous initial experiments with film in Tunisia, most animators learned their craft abroad or from masters in the field, that is to say in France and Eastern Europe, and on their return to Tunisia were supported a little by the amateur film-clubs. The Eastern European influence then is to be seen perhaps most interestingly in the subtle political content of many of these films. Likewise, it is noticeable how the pioneers make a return. The art of animation is not old enough in Tunisia for these pioneers to be forgotten or neglected.

Many of the films discussed here ended up on the national and international festival circuit, attracting attention and prizes, as well as being screened during other events. Moreover, animation's profile has been on the rise since the revolution of 14 January 2014, particularly in the context of amateur and film school cinema. The political dimension and the subversive content remain present in these films albeit in a more direct and satirical form than in those allegorical forms mentioned here. Animation is a powerful tool in the aftermath of the Revolutions in Tunisia, and many other Arab nations. Might we say, then, that the future looks bright?

Notes

1. Samir Besbes, *Regard Sur L'évolution Du Cinema D'animation Depuis Ses Origines. Le Cas Du Film Tunisien* (doctoral thesis, University Paris 1 Panthéon-Sorbonne, 1998).
2. The production date does not feature in the title sequences of some films, most notably those of the first period (1960s and 1970s).
3. The following extract from Robert Vrielynck's *Le Cinéma d'animation avant et après Walt Disney* (*Animated Cinema Before and After Disney*, 1981) is worth noting here: 'In order to complete our overview, we should note that the birth of national movements in the context of animated cinema, as we have observed since the 1950s beyond the USA, would still appear to have far-reaching repercussions, sometimes in the most unexpected of times and locations. For example, 1972 saw the production of both *The Mule*, probably the first Tunisian animated film, using paper cut-outs, made by Med Nacer Khemir'.
4. *The Mule*, an animated short film by the Tunisian director, was cited by Vrielynck as 'probably' the first Tunisian animated film (see Note 5) but it is also the only animated film mentioned by Vieyra in his 1975 work *African Cinema, from its origins to 1973*, in the section that centres on cinema in Tunisia.
5. Victor Bachy makes reference to the first forays into animation by Amor Ben Mahmoud, illustrator and professor at the Tunis School of Fine Arts, and dates these to the early 1960s, that is to say a decade before Nacer Khemir's film.
6. [Editor's note] *Karakouz* has an obvious (and not merely linguistic) relation to the Karagoz shadow theatre discussed in the chapter on Turkish animation in this volume.
7. Belaid, 'Aperçu sur le cinéma en Tunisie à l'époque coloniale', *Rawafid ISHMN*, 4, (1998), pp. 85–106; p. 85.
8. Ibid.
9. The only exception being the two films (one short and one full-length) made by Albert Samama Chikly in 1922 and 1924 respectively, which is hailed as the earliest cinematographic work on the African and Arab continents, the work of a naturalised French Tunisian who was an operator of the film section of the French army during World War I. For more information, see Laurent Véray, *Les films d'actualité français de la Grande Guerre* (Paris, 1995).
10. Translated from : 'Lorsque le photographe Albert (S'agit-il d'Albert Semama Chikly?) introduit pour la première fois le cinématographe lors de séances publiques payantes, organisées à partir du premier novembre au passage Bénévent, au coin de la rue Amilcar', taken from Habib Belaid, 'Aperçu sur le cinéma en Tunisie à l'époque coloniale', p. 87. In fact, according to Morgan

Corriou, the 'Albert' mentioned here by Belaid is another photographer whose last name was Albert, not the famous Albert Samama Chikly. Morgan Corriou, 'Tunis et les "temps modernes": les débuts du cinématographe dans la régence (1896–1908)', *Publics et spectacle cinématographique en situation coloniale* (Tunis, 2012), pp. 95–133.

11. The idea that this cinema complex in Gammarth should be created followed the diplomatic break with France after the battle of Bizerte in July 1961. SATPEC was not yet able to ensure the production of a weekly news bulletin: part of the material filmed by the Tunisian news (during the war in Bizerte), whose post-production and development were carried out in France, never made it back to Tunisia. For this reason, in order to distance itself from dependence on, and the supervision of, French newsreel footage and to establish its own propaganda, the regime decided to create this complex.

12. *Cinémas africains d'aujourd'hui. Guide des cinématographies d'Afrique* (Paris, 2007), p. 12.

13. I base my assertions here on the interview I conducted with the author on 12 September 2012 in Tunis.

14. 'Hommage: Habib Masrouki. Jeune cinéaste tunisien', *Revue Adhoua*, 3 (January, February, March 1981), *Lumière de cinéma, revue de culture cinématographique*, edited by the Cercle d'études et de recherches cinématographiques, p. 16.

15. Interview with the author (12 September 2012), as well as a reference in Victor Bachy, *Le Cinéma de Tunisie* (Paris, 1978), p. 335.

16. Besbes, 1998, p. 348.

17. Florence Martin, 'Tunisia', Mette Hjort & Duncan Petrie (eds), *The Cinema of Small Nations* (Edinburgh, 2007), p. 214.

18. Interview with Ahmed Bennys, 28 March 2014, in Tunis.

19. Ikbal Zalila, 'Des mises en scène du pouvoir à la fiction du pouvoir. Bourguiba au prisme des actualités cinématographiques tunisiennes', Camau & Geisser (eds), *Habib Bourguiba. La trace et l'héritage* (Tunis, 2004), p. 289.

20. I was not able to see Masrouki's short film as no copy of it exists in the Culture Ministry's Cinemathèque and it no longer exists in FTCA's film archives. I asked one of the leading figures of the Federation, amateur filmmaker Ridha Ben Halima, about the film and was told that the only copy the Federation had owned was lost when it was screened at a film festival in Algiers.

21. Victor Bachy, *Le cinéma de Tunisie* (Tunis, 1978), p. 335.

22. Interview with Mongi Sancho on 12 September 2012 in Tunis.

23. Ibid.

24. Frederic Jameson, 'Third-World Literature in the Era of Multinational Capitalism', *Social Text*, 15 (1986), pp. 65–88; p. 6.

25. Victor Bachy, and later Besbes in his doctoral thesis, refer to *L'homme qui dort*. The filmmaker himself states that he does not recall how many films he made during this short period at the start of his career. The only film I have been

Animation in the Middle East

able to see is *The Mule*, which is also the only one of Khemir's films for which the synopsis and themes are known (descriptions of these exist in the work of Bachy [1978] and Vieyra [1975]).

26. This film is available online https://www.youtube.com/watch?v=dFSc7aaj2JM (accessed 25 November 2015).
27. Interview with Nacer Khemir, 27 November 2012 in Paris.
28. Habib Masrouki committed suicide later on in life (in the 1980s).
29. Steffen Erdle, *Ben Ali's 'New Tunisia': A Case Study of Authoritarian Transformation*, PhD thesis in Political Science, Humboldt University of Berlin, October, 2006.
30. This film is on YouTube. Available at: https://vimeo.com/23379449 (accessed 12 November 2015).
31. This film is on YouTube. Available at: https://www.youtube.com/watch?v=fM5oi9f4oLM (accessed 12 November 2015).
32. More information on the festival is available at http://www.tahrik.tn (accessed 15 November 2015).
33. Interview with Nadia Rais, 3 December 2012 in Paris.
34. François Siino, 'Insupportables successions', *Temporalités* (6 June 2012). Available online http://temporalites.revues.org/2138 (accessed 25 February 2013).
35. Interview with Alaedine Boutaleb, 29 May 2013 in Tunis.

Filmography

Amour névrosé (*Neurotic Love*), directed by Rafih Omrani (2008).
Caprices de poupons (*Dolls' Whims*), directed by Mongi Sancho (1965).
Coma, directed by Alaedine Boutaleb (2009).
Dedi et Doudi (*Dedi and Doudi*), directed by Boubakar Boukhari (2006).
Fish Never Sleep, directed by Gaëlle Denis (2002).
Guerbaji (*The Water Seller*), directed by Zouhair Mahjoub (1984).
Hajji dans sa mille et deuxième nuit (*Hajji in his 1002nd Night*), directed by Zouhair Mahjoub (1971).
Hoffili, directed by Lotfi Mahfoud (2012).
Il était une fois, notre monde (*Once Upon a Time, Our World*), directed by Ezzedine Harbaoui (1989).
In and On, directed by Maya Ben Ayed (2001).
Jahjouh 1 & Jahjouh 2, directed by Samir Besbes (1983–5).
Jahjouh et la Sirène (*Jahjouh and the Mermaid*), directed by Samir Besbes (2008).
Joha et les fantômes de la nuit (*Joha and the Ghosts of the Night*), directed by Samir Besbes (1978).
Kharmouj, directed by Rafih Omrani (2008).

Cinema Against an Authoritarian Backdrop

L'Enfant et l'avion (*The Child and the Aeroplane*), directed by Salah Khélifi (1983).

L'Enfant roi (*The Child King*), directed by Mohamed Grayaa (2007).

L'Homme qui dort (*The Sleeping Man*), directed by Nacer Khemir (1971).

L'mrayet (*The Glasses*), directed by Nadia Rais (2011).

La Chaussure (*The Shoe*), directed by Mustapha Taieb (1994).

La Cigale (*The Cicada*), directed by Ezzedine Harbaoui (1986).

La Fleur (*The Flower*), directed by Nacer Khemir (1970).

La Goutte miraculeuse (*The Miraculous Droplet*), directed by Zouhair Mahjoub (2009).

La Noce du loup (*The Wolf's Wedding*), directed by Lotfi Mahfoud (2001).

La Poule de Saaba (*The Hen from Saaba*), directed by Rafih Omrani (2010).

La Rentrée des classes (*Back to School*), directed by Mongi Sancho (1965).

La Vieille et l'ogre (*The Old Woman and the Ogre*), directed by Mongi Sancho (1964).

Lambouba, directed by Nadia Rais (2009).

Le Chien intelligent (*The Intelligent Dog*), directed by Mongi Sancho (1966).

Le Déluge (*The Flood*), directed by Mustapha Taieb (1994).

Le Marchand de Fez (*The Fez Seller*), directed by Mongi Sancho (1967).

Le Mulet (*The Mule*), directed by Nacer Khemir (1972).

Le Pain (*The Bread*), directed by Mongi Sancho (1972).

Le petit hibou (*The Little Owl*), directed by Zouhair Mahjoub (1984).

Le Sous-marin de Carthage (*The Carthage Submarine*), directed by Zouhair Mahjoub (1999).

Lemalif, directed by Mustapha Taieb (1989).

Les Ficelles (*The Threads*), directed by Samir Besbes (1995).

Mazamir, directed by Alaedine Boutaleb (2005).

Mohammedia, directed by Ahmed Bennys (1974).

Notre Monde (*Our World*), directed by Habib Masrouki (1967).

Ruse par ruse (*Cunning Craftiness*), directed by Mongi Sancho (2006).

Ryeh, directed by Lotfi Mahfoud (2008).

Sécourez-la, elle est en danger (*Save Her, She's in Danger*), directed by Mustapha Taieb (1987).

Tale of Tales, directed by Yuri Norstein (1979).

Une petite histoire d'oeuf (*A Little Story of an Egg*), directed by Mohamed Charbaji (1976).

Viva Cartago, directed by Abdel Belhadi (2000s).

12

Animation in Morocco: New Generations and Emerging Communities

Paula Callus

While it is possible to catch a glimpse of animation in the 2000 Moroccan production *Ali Zaoua: Prince of the Streets* by Nabil Ayouch, the popularity this film garnered with international audiences is not there for most of contemporary Moroccan animation. Although attention and discussion has been directed towards Moroccan cinema,[1] it is hard to come by evidence of specific discourses addressing Moroccan animation in the academic literature.[2]

Filmmaking in Morocco began as far back as the early 1900s, and was consolidated with the establishment of the Centre Cinématographique Marocain (CCM) in 1944 and the production of the first Moroccan postcolonial feature-length films.[3] This history has contributed to the visibility of, and support for, Moroccan cinema on local and international platforms, although it is a history that has presented its own unique set of problematic topographies.[4] Nevertheless, the same attention has not been paid to animation, resulting in an irregular collection of accounts that do not shape a gratifying narrative of the form's existence and development. As other nations' accounts of animated film have demonstrated, this peripheral status is not unique to Moroccan animation. The outlying position of animation in its relation to cinema has resulted in the tardy establishment of the field of animation studies even within European and American discourses on the moving image.[5] In the case of animation produced outside of these geographies, for example in the African and Arab worlds, the condition is further compounded, and animation studies scholars have offered only piecemeal narratives and brief glimpses of animation production. There are a few scholars, however, who provide notable exceptions, who offer important, if somewhat sporadic accounts of African animation with various emphases on specific countries or regions, among them, Morocco.[6]

Bazzoli's *African Cartoon* provides one of the first examples of an attempt at wider discussion of animation on the African continent, and includes case studies from Algeria and Egypt.[7] It is in such a context that this chapter attempts to bring light to the history of animation in Morocco. It is suggested that, whilst appearing to be peripheral to the cultural space that film occupies in Morocco, animation has historically circulated within different spaces: on television and, more recently, on the internet and mobile platforms. As artists adopt new technologies within their practices, they are able to produce digital animations that extend across and pervade different genres. At times these practices can serve to subvert official institutional barriers that may be in place to control the dissemination and exhibition of mass media. This can be seen with the case of digital animators who contribute to the fields of games and visual effects, and who mobilise their work through online distribution.

Other Moving Images

The establishment in 1944 of the CCM suggests a long historical engagement with film practices and film culture in Morocco. The organisation acted as one of the key local institutional bodies seeking to actively promote and preserve Moroccan film, specifically through the establishment of a film library and an affiliation with bodies such as the International Federation of Film Archives (IFFA) and UNESCO. In the 1980s, CCM established a public film fund (initially funded by a 10 per cent tax on cinema tickets sales) to support local productions, and whilst this model was subsequently changed, CCM continued its support through investments, amassing a portfolio of 124 feature-length films between 2004 and 2012.[8] Even so, Moroccan animation was not produced with a similar vigour to that of live-action film, and rarely benefited from any active investment.

Where cinema and the arts have been framed and contextualised within discussions of patronage and cultural heritage, the marginalisation of animation from these categories suggests that animation was not considered or recognised as carrying the same cultural value.[9] Moreover, while Morocco is not short of film festivals, animation festivals are much less prominent. The CCM identified a total of eighteen different film festivals running across various cities in Morocco, but only one of these was listed as a festival for animation: the Meknès International Animation Festival (FICAM).[10]

FICAM has a long-standing presence in Morocco. The festival was launched in 2000 and has since showcased a range of animations from the international circuit. Mohammed Beyoud, FICAM's creative director from 2000 until 2014, inaugurated the festival with an eye on the promotion of the art of animation, both through animated film screenings as well as via educational workshops. Beyoud invited animators and filmmakers from both commercial and independent backgrounds to showcase their work and provide, as speakers, valuable knowledge of a range of animation practices; such figures as Bill Plympton, Michel Ocelot, Peter Lord and Isao Takahata. Typically, FICAM ran over five days at the French Institute in Meknès, screening a range of animations on the international platform, presented within thematic segments. On occasion, this would also include screenings of local productions; for example, in 2002 Hamid Semlali's *L'oiseau de l'Atlas* (*The Bird of the Atlas*, 2002).[11] At the time, Semlali's ten-minute film was exceptional on two counts: firstly as a rare example of a local animation screened at an international festival, and secondly as a case of a Moroccan animation receiving funding from the CCM (100,000 dinars).[12] As the Moroccan newspaper *Liberation* reported in 2010:

> The professionals are unanimous: The development of a national animation is penalised by the lack of financial and technical resources as well as by the lack of adequate training. 'We greatly lack the funds and an animated film requires huge budgets. Worse, few Moroccan producers are willing to invest in this sector. They show little interest in this kind of cinema. I think that in Morocco we have not yet grasped the economic and social challenges of such a film', said Rachid Zakie, critic and journalist for 2M.[13]

Pioneers: Individuals and Organisations

Semlali is, in fact, one of the pioneers of Moroccan animation and regarded as an auteur in the field. In 1984, he created *Didi, la poule* (*Didi, the Chicken*) and later, the animations *Bobo, le sauveur* (*Bobo, the Saviour*, 1988) and *Bobo et le fromage* (*Bobo and the Cheese*, 1990).[14] Semlali's background in filmmaking and fine art – as a graduate in sculpture from Baghdad's École des Beaux Arts – informed his passion for animation. On his return to Morocco in 1978, he briefly taught sculpture in Kenitra before attending film production workshops in Prague at the Kratiki Institute, and began to produce films and commercials by 1985.[15] However, these were the contributions of a single auteur and it was not until the early 1990s that a collective of artists emerged to form one of the earliest Moroccan animation studios, noted for both its animated productions and its didactic outlook within a community of emergent animation artists. In 2010, Semlali participated in FICAM as part of a roundtable discussion on Animation in the Maghreb, alongside the Tunisian animator Zouhair Mahjoub. As Aziz Maaqoul says:

> It is important to note that there was a pioneering organisation [FICAM], the first organisation in Morocco to work with animation in spite of the lack of means and materials. This did not stop artists from trying their best and expressing their various artistic sensibilities motivated by their love of the field, individually.[16]

Another important pioneer in the foregrounding of animation has been Casablanca's CASAPremière; set up in 1996, it is one of the earliest Moroccan organisations to focus on animation, and was founded by four key figures, all fine art graduates of Casablanca's École Nationale Supérieure des Beaux-Arts: Said Bouftass, Lachguar Mohamed, Said Bouchmar and Khalid Ghalib.[17] All shared a keen interest in painting, design, and the graphic and plastic arts, but lacked a formal education in animation, and therefore taught themselves the practices and processes required to produce animated shorts whilst taking on live projects. The group are often cited by their peers as seminal figures in Moroccan 2D animation, whose entrepreneurial efforts subsequently inspired a range of artists. In 1998, the company began taking on new artists who would continue to work in the field, including Aziz Maaqoul, Youssef El-Aakouchi and Youssef Boukany. CASAPremière was responsible for the foundational education of Morocco's nascent animators, and is described by its members as a key formative aspect of their professional development.[18] While it was commissioned to work on various commercial projects (most notably in television advertising) the association also had a wider educational impact on the artistic community. As Said Bouftass recollects, CASAPremière was created to 'offer an intellectual and artistic space for young people who wished to make animation', and this was exemplified by the association's weekly Saturday morning animation workshops, offered free to the general public.[19] In 1998 and 1999, it was also responsible for the production and publication of three issues of *BOOM-Magazine*, a comic magazine aimed at children, drawing on the skills of various local cartoonists and including a treatment of the Persian fables of *Kalila and Dimna*.

At first, the artists at CASAPremière studio used the traditional method of celluloid strip and gouache paint, but later adapted their methods to the employment of new technologies in the form of the scanner and computer. In a 'hacker-maker' approach to animation, they aligned their images by fixing their peg-bars to the scanner.[20] A lack of proprietary animation software meant that the scanned images were retouched using digital image editing software and then composited in digital video editing software. This multi-layered approach to the animation process, while not unique to the digital format, does display the versatility of artistic practice that the animated form invites: artists are adopting and adapting computer software originally designed for digital image manipulation or compositing, rather than for animation *per se*. It was only in 2006 that the company transitioned to using the proprietary animation software Toonz, employing vectors rather than bitmapped images. This early exposure to the innovative use of different tools can be seen as pre-emptive and enabling for the movement of these artists across different fields of image-making practices.

Although it pitched many ideas for animated series, CASAPremière only managed to bring two series, each comprising 26 episodes, to fruition for broadcast in 2002, entitled *Allo Mamman Bobo* (2002). Aimed at an audience of children and incorporating predominantly educational content, the minute-long animations were broadcast on state-owned television station 2M TV. The series was co-directed by Said Bouchmar and Kalid Ghalib.

The company worked on early 2D animated shorts, chiefly as advertising for broadcast television. In 2002, Said Bouftass sold his share of the company and left to pursue a career in fine art education and philosophy, focusing on the phenomenology of anatomy in artistic practice, while Youssef Boukany left to become artistic director for another budding company, Osmose Studio. By the end of 2006, CASAPremière was dissolved, and the early practitioners moved on to further their professional careers across different fields. This movement and mobility was extensive: Youssef El-Aakouchi, for example, secured a job with Montreal's successful games company Ubisoft. This transfer of talent was symptomatic of the growing transnational industries of computer-generated animation and the rise of computer games as a separate sector. Ubisoft has excelled on the international market for games development, establishing 29 studios in 19 countries across Europe, Asia and America by 2014. Ubisoft Casablanca was setup in 1998 and became a prime recruiter of Moroccan animators interested in computer animation, offering in-house training and international career prospects.

The Impact of Digital Technology

The transition from traditional 2D to 3D computer animation is a result of a wider cinematic engagement with computer-related technologies. In Morocco, the use of computers and the internet not only changed the ideas and practices around production, but also the means of exhibition, dissemination and viewership. Moroccan animation artists who shifted into these digital practices were able to move across different genres of animation through their professional interactions with related industries, such as games development and (with limitations) visual effects for film. Aziz Maaqoul, originally a cel animator for CASAPremière in 1998, moved on to a range of related professions, including graphic designer, storyboard artist for Ubisoft Casablanca, and post-production matte-painter for SIGMA Technologies by 2013. Maaqoul's professional trajectory across these disparate strands is testament to the variety of skills that animation offers to the versatile artist. An animation artist with such experience has the ability to draw upon a range of different artistic practices, whether painterly, photographic, dramatic or sculptural, and to apply combinations of these in the animated form. This, alongside the use of additional tools made available by the computer, facilitates a blending of techniques across different media. Maaqoul was able to move seamlessly from animating cartoons to creating animated images in the service of cinema, in the form of computer-generated imagery (CGI), visual effects and games. His portfolio of digital paintings and matte-paintings spans different genres, from science fiction to fantasy, and provides evidence of the pervasive practices present within the animation sphere. He recounts how his 'passion for matte painting began with my discovery on the internet of different artists in the digital painting domain [...] Their exceptional work opened the door for me to the art of matte painting.'[21] In 2007, Maaqoul's co-worker at CASAPremière, Youssef Boukany, joined SIGMA Technologies, also moving across different animation practices. Boukany made a similar transition from traditional 2D animation to produce a portfolio of work that includes 3D computer animation, thus enabling him to work on a range of projects as a 3D animator for SIGMA-Toons.

Simultaneously, these digital artists were independently promoting their own animated work (now in digital format) through online platforms. Through Vimeo profiles, YouTube Channels, personal websites and various profile pages on social networking sites, they both showcased their work and increased their online visibility. These animations are presented alongside the artists' own documentation of their techniques and production practices, and are accompanied by comments from fellow practitioners and feedback and suggestions from within interested communities. Such digital traces all suggest the presence of a growing Moroccan online audience. In 2008, El-Aakouchi, for example, created a blog dedicated to animation and published in Arabic with a view to presenting his work across different animation techniques. The blog, Harakatoon,[22] hosts embedded YouTube videos linked from the artist's own channel, and demonstrates a range of animation techniques, from traditional drawn animation to 3D computer-generated images. Among the videos are demonstrations of his own custom-built zoetropes illustrating an animated cycle of a running anthropomorphised Tagine character (see image 12.1). Other experiments – with clay,[23] with small flipbooks of the same character jumping – are

12.1 Sketch for the Tagine Character on Harakatoon (2008)

accompanied by informative videos on 3D clay modelling of the characters for stop-motion; tutorials for various techniques within 3D computer animation software in Arabic can also be found there.

Even though the pioneering Moroccan artist Said Bouftass developed his career in a different field, his contribution to Moroccan animation continues through involvement on social networking sites, distribution platforms such as YouTube, and in blogs. Among other things, Bouftass has created a YouTube channel incorporating documentation of his work in art pedagogy, with examples of earlier animations made while he was still involved with CASAPremière. Bouftass has also digitised and uploaded a collection of commercial shorts and examples from CASAPremière. In this selection he includes an experimental surrealist animation entitled *J'ai bu un café dans un café* (*I Had a Coffee in the Café*, 2005).[24] This short was screened at FICAM in 2005 and depicts a series of metamorphic transitions of, and musings on, a simple black and white line drawing of a man sipping his coffee.

Any discussion of computer animation in Morocco must also include the exceptional cases of animators who, although they did not share the same background in fine art, nonetheless furthered more specialised studies in the field of 3D computer animation outside of Morocco. Abdallah El-Fakir, a prominent Moroccan animator with a string of short computer generated animations, is one such artist. His introduction to this field was via his education in the arts for three years at the Casablanca School of Design and Communication, Art'COM. In 1998, he obtained his diploma from the school, before furthering his studies in Ghent, Belgium, in 2000, where he obtained a specialised certification in character animation for Maya, a 3D software package, from the software's developers Alias Wavefront. He continued his Maya training in Toronto in 2002, obtaining certification for dynamics (the simulation of systems such as crowds, smoke, particles, fluids, etc.).[25] Fakir also undertook various training internships in visual effects,[26] lighting and compositing in US studios such as DreamWorks and A52. In large-scale productions the specialised nature of computer animation is reflected in the demarcation of duties and departments. However, in Fakir's case, he personally took on all these different roles, so although he has made commercial work for the advertising industry while in employment at SIGMA Technologies from 1998, his own processes reflect those of an independent animator more than those of a practitioner from a large-scale commercial or industrial pipeline following a strict division of labour. Between 2001 and 2009, Fakir produced personal and commercial 3D computer animations that were screened at FICAM and the MultiClic Festival in Casablanca, as well as on television. Fakir's interest in computing was thus not limited to CGI and animation, and by February 2014 he had created a YouTube channel entitled ABTech to host his webcasts. Between February and November 2014, Fakir uploaded over 40 short videos, ranging from his reviews of computer games and instructional computing advice to explanations of topical computing themes, such as the Bitcoin currency, Big Data, the Oculus Rift (a 3D virtual reality headset for gaming), various mobile phone technologies and games conventions.

Fakir was notably the subject of a number of interviews on Moroccan television and online articles covering the news of the launch of the 3D computer animated feature film *The Companions of the Elephants*.[27] The film went into production in 2009, aiming to be completed for 2016 as the first feature-length 3D computer-generated animation entirely produced in Morocco. Based on an adaptation of a story in the Quran, the film concerns a south Arabian King who assembled 60,000 troops and 13 elephants to destroy the holy city of Mecca. When the King gives the order to attack, a cloud of birds appears in the sky, which defeats the opposing troops by pelting them with thousands of little stones. The narrative calls for a production of ambitious proportions and scale, and seemingly requires a large team and budget to match. The concept art, developed for the film by Aziz Maaqoul, Abdelhamid Benali and Michael Paolinetti, illustrates large armies with a range of characters in environments evocative of Moroccan landscapes. These images conjure a sense of epic narrative boasting an impressive cast of characters. Typically, the scale of the proposed scenes presented in the concept art would necessitate substantial production resources and labour to see the film to the screen. However, contrary to conventional industrial practice in Europe or the US, Fakir's entire production team consists of only 15 people: two matte-painters, ten 3D computer animators and three programmers. The film is self-financed by the director together with the animation and postproduction company SIGMA Technologies. Whilst the company works across a range of fields, including documentary, broadcast programmes and commercial work, it also includes an animation department with a team of fifteen 3D computer animation artists.[28]

SIGMA-Toons, an ancillary studio and part of SIGMA Technologies, has also been responsible for a portfolio of other productions and co-productions in computer animation, such as Eveline Fouche and Abdelhamid Benali's *Ramzi and Adam* (2007, 2008, 2009). Featuring the adventures of two young brothers, each of these three series of 30 three-minute episodes was planned so that its didactic content could be aired for children every day over the period of Ramadan. Production and distribution rights were purchased by Al-Jazeera Children, but it was never aired on Moroccan television.The collaboration between Fouche and Benali, nurtured at SIGMA-Toons between 2006 and 2009, resulted in the development of other pilot animations to be developed as children's series: *Les Aventures de ZeZe Le Bourdon*, *Casa Street* and *La Boîte à Histoires*, can all be viewed online on the website of their production company, SK Productions.[29]

SIGMA Technologies was also responsible for the successes of animator Rachid Jadir, the creator of the popular 3D computer animation series *Rass Derb* (2008–10). Jadir, like his contemporaries, is mostly self-taught in animation after having undertaken a basic two-year training course in computer graphics and design from InfoDesign in 2005. By 2014, the same educational facility had grown its portfolio to include professional and accredited training in multi-media, web design, computer-generated animation and related fields. In 2007, Jadir joined SIGMA Technology as a pre-production artist and producer, and over the next three years

271

12.2 Still from *Rass Derb*, directed by Rachid Jadir (2010)

developed the widespread viral video *Rass Derb* series (2008–10) from concept to production. *Rass Derb* translates as *The Corner of the Street*, and this is where most of the action for these animations takes place. It reflects the daily routines of Moroccan youth in the city, as they loiter on the corner of the street (see image 12.2), 'watching the girls walk by, playing football, smoking or taking drugs'.[30] The animations consist of a series of three-minute shorts depicting three central characters, Mchaabat, Snina and Rqia Lhawla.

The popularity of *Rass Derb* can be attributed to its sincere and realistic depiction of disaffected Moroccan youth. It is presented humorously and resonates with a younger audience now digitally connected and largely watching content online. The animation and characters were adopted and further developed as a series of adverts for the telecommunications company Maroc Telecom. This commercial context did not stop Jadir from continuing his socio-political approach, albeit humorously, to the series, so that in one episode, *Recharge Moi STP* (*Recharge Me, Please*), Jadir alludes to the exploitation of young Moroccan girls by foreign Arab men. The animation proved to be so successful that in 2010 Jadir began a Kickstarter project to develop the shorts into a feature-length production. Although the project never came to fruition, it garnered considerable online interest. Jadir promoted his venture through social media with a Rass Derb Facebook page, a RassDerb.tv webpage and his own personal YouTube Channel. He was able to tap into this online viewership and continued to make animations, including a humorous political short on the elections in 2012. The film was reported in *Telquel* as having been viewed 120,000 times in less than 48 hours.[31] The animation presented a political party announcement by the speaker for the Sabon el'Beldi Party, and consisted of an odd-looking 'talking-head' character, Kote7a, giving the speech. In 2012, Jadir left Morocco to work for an advertising agency in Qatar, and a year later found employment as a senior artist in Al-Dawri, Al-Kass Sports TV Channel, also in Qatar.

The popular technical director and computer animator Farid Khadiri-Yazami also began his career at SIGMA Technologies.[32] Although a star of Morrocoan CGI, strictly speaking his work does not consist of animation, but includes aspects of the specialisms surrounding computer animation practices, such as modelling, lighting and compositing. Khadiri-Yazami migrated from Morocco to France in 2003, moving later to the US. Having begun his career in Casablanca, he eventually worked for a range of international visual effects and animation companies such as Digital Domain and Sony Picture Works. He has worked on blockbuster films and animations such as Disney's *Frozen* (2014), DreamWorks' *Shrek Forever After* (2010), *The Amazing Spiderman* (2012), *Guardians of the Galaxy* (2014) and others, and is considered a hugely successful technical director on the international circuit. Unlike the other artists mentioned in this context, Khadiri-Yazami's work as an auteurist filmmaker within Morocco or as an independent digital artist is not overtly visible. Instead he has secured leading roles in high-profile production teams in the US, working predominantly on Hollywood films. Nonetheless, his case provides an important example of the cross-medium versatility afforded by CGI and digital animation techniques. In a climate where the lines between digital film and animation are becoming increasingly blurred, these practices allow the artist to move freely across live-action film, animation and games.

Although Bouftass and his contemporaries transitioned from fine arts education to digital media, it is notable that the more recent Moroccan computer animators have not necessarily shared the same background in the 'traditional' arts. The opportunities that these digital technologies afford animators who do not have a formal education in the arts (or animation), but who are able to acquire knowledge of these techniques through the internet, has significantly changed the discourse on animation within Morocco. In turn, the communities that were forged online have mobilised new generations of Moroccan talent.

New Talent, Emerging Communities

From 2000 onwards, both the presence of animation in Morocco and its visibility galvanised and gained momentum. This can be attributed to the combined efforts of FICAM, the early pioneers and the rising popularity of animation on new viewing devices such as mobile phones. Each and all of these factors gave rise to a new community of young talented Moroccan animators who were making strides in the field of computer animation and related media through their online interactions. The innovator and polymath Amine Beckoury, for example, has skills in graphic design, stop-motion and both 2D and 3D animation. Beckoury graduated from Casablanca's Académie des Beaux Arts in 2007, followed by a further three years in animation at the prestigious French school, École George Méliès.[33] Beckoury is distinctive in that his experimentation with animation began in stop-motion, inspired by a workshop conducted by Chilean animator Luis Briceno that he attended at the 2006 FICAM festival. In 2007, he produced a short animated music video called *Blad Skizo* (2007) as his Académie graduate film, and has since won awards and garnered international support and grants. *Blad Skizo* is a combination of stop-motion Plasticine characters within composited environments. The animation follows typical music video conventions, eschewing linear narrative in favour of intercuts between Plasticine characters of the band playing music, the central character, Reda, locked in a padded cell, and the band travelling in model cars through a cut-out mobile cityscape. Reda is a recurring character who tries to escape the metaphorical mental asylum (actually a representation of contemporary Morocco), but who tragically dies before making it through a doorway serving as a metaphor for the national border. The animation was produced over a period of four months, with the apartment of his colleague's sister serving as a makeshift studio, just in time for FICAM 2007 where it received its first screening. The following year *Blad Skizo* (2007) won the First Prize for the Best African Short film at FICAM 2008 and was also shown at festivals in Spain and Portugal, as well as screening on local television. Beckoury's next short animation was his graduate piece from École George Méliès, *Cuisine Jap* (2010), made in collaboration with David Fernandez and François Dumoulin. The animation is a combination of 2D drawn animation alongside 3D computer animation. It was during his time at the École George Méliès that Beckoury was introduced to computer animation and switched his focus to CGI. These films were uploaded to his Vimeo channel in 2010.[34] In 2012, Beckoury attended the Maarifa Animation Lab in Valence, France and in 2013 he received a grant, courtesy of Maarifa, an organisation promoting the creation of audio-visual productions for educational purposes, and Canal France (CFI), to travel to France and work as an intern at Folimage animation studio. Recently Beckoury has been developing the conceptual work for his short film *Achour*, which has not yet (2014) gone into production: Beckoury reported that 'notwithstanding the aid I received from CFI and Folimage, the development is still insufficient to go into production which will require another year of work and about 3 to 5 people at least'.[35] Beckoury's influence and achievements in the field have extended beyond his personal and commercial work. Having acquired a reputation, he has contributed educationally as a guest speaker at various events and has provided workshops at both FICAM and the more recent animation festival CASANIM.

Whilst FICAM has made some important contributions to the distribution and exhibition of animation, its international remit has had the inevitable consequence of side-lining, to an extent, the community of local artists and their productions. The CASANIM festival was setup in 2010 in Casablanca in response. Younes Mouslih, the director of the festival and chair of the Moroccan Association for Animated Film and Games (Animaroc), positions the event as an opportunity to showcase Moroccan animation, with an emphasis on digital animation and specific training activities. The festival offers a range of workshops and master classes in animation techniques with a focus on the digital. In 2014, for example, the CASANIM festival ran a series of workshops showcasing the open-source 3D animation software Blender. It also curated an exhibition of computer art, including matte-painting and pixel art: *Digit'Art*.[36] This exhibition was an important achievement as it reflected a shift in discourses surrounding

275

artistic practice associated with computer animation and related fields, such that contemporary digital images moved from virtual and peripheral spaces of exhibition and dissemination to physical exhibition spaces in galleries associated with 'fine art'.[37] The collaborative list of the new generation of animation artists, such as Salim Ljabli, a freelance Moroccan 3D CGI character artist, Rachid Jadir of *Rass Derb* fame, Abdelkader Behloul from games company UbiSoft (Casablanca), Basti Salaheddine and Abdelah El-Fakir from SIGMA, Amine Beckoury and others, illustrates the sudden surge in collaboration within Moroccan computer animation. These emerging communities of Moroccan computer animation enthusiasts, who were previously chiefly visible online, through interest groups set-up on social networking sites or blogs, were coming together to showcase their work and share their knowledge of different computer animation techniques.

In 2014, Facebook listed a range of Moroccan animation interest groups: L'Association Marocaine du Cinema d'Animation (AMCA, 154 members), ArtCom Sup, ZMorocco[38] (247 members), La 3D au Maroc (1,033 members), La 3D Marocaine (876 members), Institut National des Beaux-Arts de Tétouan and 3D Marocaine (7,535 members). These internet 'prod-users', while not necessarily experts in their execution of animation, were nonetheless able to capture vast amounts of views; Mohammed Nassib's YouTube animations[39] received three million hits for one short upload. In addition, a range of new webpages, such as fousdanim.org, has provided a useful resource to Moroccan animators by including multiple postings addressing Moroccan animation and the various animation festivals.[40]

Conclusion: Converging Networks and Communities in Moroccan Animation

These emergent Moroccan animators provide examples of a new type of dexterous artist able to capitalise on the use of the computer to create moving images that straddle different aesthetic practices. They mobilise themselves through an expert use of web-related technologies, applying their skills beyond animation as understood in its traditional sense, towards a range of practices in the realm of digital imagery. This chapter has shown how most of the pioneering Morrocan animators have a background in the fine arts and how, after honing their skills in other areas, becoming established, innovative digital animators, they return to their fine arts roots. As such, they are the perfect examples of how a 'new' art form can develop a coherent internal discourse that confirms its space among the established arts. As demonstrated through the cases presented here, the artists have moved across diverse fields encompassed by the form during the short spans of their careers. This is indicative of the versatility that the animated form itself presents, as the artists draw upon a range of artistic practices that constitutes an assemblage of representational methods that at times can appear painterly, pictorial, performative, sculptural and photographic. This has been catalysed by, and has itself further inspired their use of the computer, the necessary accompaniment to contemporary media convergences. Such convergence is nowhere more visible than in the case of Issam Mohammed Hanine's film *Al-Hikma* (2010), a film with over half of its scenes being computer-generated and with the integration of computer-animated characters. Hanine's script combines fantastical characters composited with footage and actors filmed on blue-screen. The locations move between real and imaginary landscapes, combining the village of Imlil in the Atlas Mountains with a fabricated world of spirits. Hanine's immersion in all aspects of production, from script and concept art to the shooting of footage, direction, animation and compositing, illustrates the convergences of practices in contemporary digital moving images and the efficiencies afforded by the use of the computer. Like other Moroccan animators, Hanine has also been employed by Ubisoft since 2004 as a lead CGI modeller for computer games, displaying his ability to apply himself across games, film and animation. Hanine is also able to use the computer and the internet to promote his films, embedding segments of *Al-Hikma* on his Vimeo channel.[41]

In its earliest stages, in the mid-1990s, Moroccan animation was produced by a handful of artists and mostly limited to the production of commercials for local broadcasting; but this context of restricted production and exhibition has been transformed significantly over the last decade. The popularisation of the computer and the onset of digital media have dramatically changed the previously limited and limiting conditions, ushering in a lively interest in, and favoured attention for, animation and its related techniques and practices.[42] The impact of digital technologies is felt through the economy in the production, dissemination and distribution that they have offered to countries on the African continent, circumventing traditional costly methods associated with animation. Whilst Moroccan animation has been barely visible at European animation festivals, its online presence, the fan-following it has garnered and the number of specialist web-based social networking groups for Moroccan animation artists would suggest that a new generation of digital artists is afoot.

Notes

1. Valerie Orlando, 'Mean streets, bad boys, drugs and rock'n'roll: Morocco's urban legends of the 21st century', *South Central Review*, 28, 1 (2011), pp. 52–73; Valerie Orlando, 'Being-in-the-world: the Afropolitan Moroccan author's worldview in the new millennium', *Journal of African Cultural Studies*, 25, 3 (2013), pp. 275–91; Sandra Carter, *What Moroccan Cinema? A Historical and Critical Study* (Plymouth, 2009); Kevin Dwyer, 'Moroccan Cinema and the Promotion of Culture', *The Journal of North African* Studies, 12, 3 (2007), pp. 277–86; Guy Hennebelle, 'Arab Cinema', *MERIP* Reports, 52 (1976), pp. 4–12.
2. For example Bendazzi's historical overview of world animation in *Cartoons; One Hundred Years of Cinema Animation* (Bloomington, IN, 1994) does not include Morocco within the section on African Animation.
3. Sandra Carter, *What Moroccan Cinema? A Historical and Critical Study* (Plymouth, 2009); Dwyer, 'Moroccan Cinema', pp. 277–86.
4. For a discussion of the particular moments in Moroccan film history and the socio-political contexts that informed the development in Morocco see Carter, *What Moroccan Cinema?*
5. Paul Wells, *Understanding Animation* (London, 1997); Jayne Pilling, *A Reader in Animation Studies* (London, 1998).
6. See for example, Guido Convents, *Images & Animation: Le Cinema d'animation en Afrique Centrale* (Brussels, 2014); Paula Callus, 'Reading animation through the eyes of anthropology: A case study of sub-Saharan African Animation', *Animation: an interdisciplinary journal*, 7, 2 (2012), pp. 113–30; Giannalberto Bendazzi, *Cartoons; One Hundred Years of Cinema Animation* (London, 2004); Maria Silvia Bazzoli, *African Cartoon* (Milano, 2002); Bruno Edera, *À La Découverte d'un Cinéma Méconnu; Le Cinéma D'Animation Africain* (Annecy, 1993).
7. Bazzoli, *African Cartoon*.
8. Said Graiouid and Taieb Belghazi, 'Cultural production and cultural patronage in Morocco: the state, the Islamists, and the field of culture', *Journal of African Cultural Studies*, 25, 3 (2013), pp. 261–74; Mohammed Bakrim, 'Public funding

for eilm, a Moroccan experience: The history of Moroccan public funding for cinema', *EuroMed Audiovisual* (24 January 2013). Available at http://euromedaudiovisuel.net/p.aspx?t=news&mid=21&l=en&did=1174 (accessed 4 April 2015).

9. Graiouid and Belghazi, 'Cultural production', p. 265.

10. FICAM is listed on the CCM website, however another animation festival, Animaroc, that has been running in Casablanca since 2010, was not included in the official listing.

11. Kenza Alaoui, 'Le cinéma d'animation en fête à Meknès', *L'economiste*, 1191 (23 January 2002). Available at http://www.leconomiste.com/article/le-cinema-danimation-en-fete-meknes (accessed 4 April 2015).

12. Centre Cinématographique Marocain Division de la Production Service Fonds d'Aide, *primes, aides et avances sur recettes octroyées de 1988 au16 octobre 2014* (16 October 2014). Available at http://www.ccm.ma/pdf/SITFA.pdf (accessed 4 April 2015).

13. Hassan Bentaleb, 'Journée mondiale de cinéma d'animation: Un art qui peine à trouver son chemin au Maroc', *Liberation* (28 October 2010). Available at http://m.libe.ma/Journee-mondiale-de-cinema-d-animation-Un-art-qui-peine-a-trouver-son-chemin-au-Maroc_a14875.html (accessed 4 April 2015).

14. Ramon Sender, 'La Fête des Images' *Maroc-Hebdo International*, 494 2(4 January 2002), p. 35. Available at http://www.maroc-hebdo.press.ma/archive/files/494/494.pdf (accessed 4 April 2015).

15. Kenza Alaoui, 'Le cinéma d'animation en fête à Meknès', *L'economiste*, 1191 (23 January 2002). Available at http://www.leconomiste.com/article/le-cinema-danimation-en-fete-meknes (accessed 4 April 2015).

16. Personal Communication, Aziz Maaqoul, 19 August 2014.

17. Personal Communication, Said Bouchmar, 16 March 2014.

18. Personal Communication, Youssef Boukany, 19 April 2014.

19. Personal Communication, Said Bouftass, 7 August 2014.

20. Personal Communication, Said Bouchmar, 7 August 2014.

21. Personal Communication, Aziz Maaqoul, 12 October 2013.

22. Hamid El-Aakouchi, *Harakatoon Blog*. Available at http://7arakatoon.blogspot.co.uk/ (accessed 4 April 2015).

23. The film is available at https://www.youtube.com/watch?v=wcbKYufGsCY#t=226 (accessed 4 April 2015).

24. The film is available at https://www.youtube.com/watch?v=0pvLFgw5FUs (accessed 4 April 2015).

25. It is worth noting that each of these processes requires a degree of specialisation that would typically be reflected in a production pipeline with the inclusion of separate departments responsible for the character animation and the simulations and dynamics, amongst others, such as modelling or rendering and lighting.

26. The term 'visual effects' is used to refer to processes that involve creating or manipulating a range of digital imaging outside of live-action. These practices can involve significant crossover with computer animation techniques such as modelling, lighting, rigging, animating, etc.

27. Amin Rboub, 'Au cœur de la "DreamWorks" marocaine; Des jeunes marocains talentueux apprivoisent la 3D, les images de synthèse', L'economiste, 2727 (4 March 2008). Available at http://www.leconomiste.com/article/au-coeur-de-la-dreamworks-marocaine#sthash.yZ0sSgIs.dpuf (accessed 4 April 2015).

28. Personal Communication, Abdallah El-Fakir, 8 August 2014.

29. SK-Production. Available at http://www.sk-production.com/eveline/index.html (accessed 4 April 2015).

30. Personal Communication, Rachid Jadir, 24 June 2014.

31. Telquel, 'Humour electorial', Telquel, 1279 (21 February 2012). Available at http://telquel.ma/2012/02/21/humour-electoral_1279 (accessed 4 April 2015).

32. Alexia Colette, 'Animation. Bienvenue dans la 3ème dimension', Telquel, 252 (5 December 2006). Available at http://w.telquel-online.com/archives/252/arts2_252.shtml (accessed 4 April 2015).

33. Personal Communication, Amine Beckoury, 19 December 2013.

34. Amine Beckoury, Vimeo Channel. Available at http://vimeo.com/aminebeckoury (accessed 4 April 2015).

35. Ibid.

36. H.O.M., 'Casanim, la grande-messe du film d'animation de retour a Casa', Medias24: L'information Economique Marocaine en Continu (23 October 2014). Available at http://www.medias24.com/CULTURE-LOISIRS/150084-Casanim-la-grand-messe-du-film-d-animation-de-retour-a-Casa.html# (accessed 4 April 2015).

37. Agoumi, 'L'arte numerique' (11 October 2012).

38. The use of the letter 'Z' is a reference to the 3D modelling software called Z-Brush.

39. Mohammed Nassib's YouTube channel. Available at https://www.youtube.com/user/NassibMohammed (accessed 4 April 2015).

40. Cobayanim, 'Meknes 2010', Fousdanim (12 May 2010). Available at http://www.fousdanim.org/festivals/index.php?Meknes-2010 and 'La création marocaine', Fousdanim (12 May 2010). Available at http://www.fousdanim.org/festivals/index.php?2010/05/12/142-la-creation-marocaine (accessed 4 April 2015).

41. The Al-Hikma (2010) trailer can be viewed at https://vimeo.com/28980350 (accessed 2 January 2014).

42. Lev Manovich, The Language of New Media (Massachusetts, 2002); Will Merrin, Media Studies 2.0 (Oxford, 2014).

Filmography

Al-Hikma, directed by Issam Mohammed Hanine (2010).

Ali Zaoua: Prince of the Streets, directed by Nabil Ayouch (2000).

Allo Mamman Bobo, directed by Said Bouchmar and Kalid Ghalib (2002).

Blad Skizo, directed by Amin Beckoury (2007).

Bobo et le fromage (Bobo and the Cheese), directed by Hamid Semlali (1990).

Bobo, le sauveur (Bobo the Saviour), directed by Hamid Semlali (1988)

Casa Street, directed by Eveline Fouche and Abdelhamid Benali (2008).

Didi, la poule (Didi, the chicken), directed by Hamid Semlali (1984)

Frozen, directed by Chris Buck and Jennifer Lee (2013).

Guardians of the Galaxy, directed by James Gunn (2014).

J'ai bu un café dans un café (I Had a Coffee in the Café), directed by Said Bouftass (2005).

L'oiseau de l'Atlas (The Bird of the Atlas), directed by Hamid Semlali (2002).

La Boite à Histoires (The Box of Histories), directed by Eveline Fouche and Abdelhamid Benali (2009).

Les Aventures De ZeZe Le Bourdon (The Adventures of ZeZe Le Bourdon), directed by Eveline Fouche and Abdelhamid Benali (2007).

Ramzi and Adam, directed by Eveline Fouche and Abdelhamid Benali (2007–09).

Rass Derb, directed by Rachid Jadir (2008–10).

Shrek Forever After, directed by Adam Adamson and Vicky Jenson (2010).

The Amazing Spiderman, directed by Mark Webb (2012).

The Companions of the Elephants, directed by Abdallah El-Fakir (2016).

Bibliography

Agoumi, Karim, 'L'arte numerique gagne ses lettres de noblesse', *L'economiste*, 3886, 11 October 2012.

Ahmed, Sara, *The Promise of Happiness* (Durham, NC, 2010).

al Ali, Nadje and Nicola Pratt, 'Between nationalism and women's rights: The Kurdish women's movement in Iraq', *Middle East Journal of Culture and Communication*, 4 (2011), pp. 339–55.

Al Banay, 'abd Al-Muhsin, 'Jadeeduna Al-Musalsal Al-Kartouniyy "Ahmad wa Kan'aan"', Al-*Qabas* (25 December 2009). Available at http://www.alqabas.com.kw/node/562436_9 (accessed 20 November 2014).

Al-Jamil, Furat, 'Furat Al-Jamil'. Available at http://furataljamil.webs.com/ (accessed 3 July 2014).

—— ' "Baghdad Night" Press Folder' (2013).

al Najjar, Muhammad Rajab 'Contemporary trends in the study of Folklore in the Arab Gulf States', Eric Davis and Nicholas Gavrielides (eds), *Statecraft in the Middle East: Oil, Historical Memory, and Popular Culture* (Miami, FL, 1991).

al-Qassemi, Sultan Sood, 'Our cartoon heroes: now that they are really our own', *Arab News* (7 September 2009). Available at http://www.arabnews.com/node/327794 (accessed 20 November 2014).

Alaoui, Kenza, 'Le cinéma d'animation en fête à Meknès', *L'economiste*, 1191 (23 January 2002). Available at http://www.leconomiste.com/article/le-cinema-danimation-en-fete-meknes (accessed 4 April 2015).

Alexander, Livia, 'Is there a Palestinian cinema? The national and transnational in Palestinian film production', R. Stein (ed.), *Palestine, Israel, and the Politics of Popular Culture* (Durham, NC, 2005), pp. 150–72.

And, Metin, 'An important cultural heritage: Karagöz', S. Koz (ed.), *Torn is the Curtain, Shattered is the Screen, the Stage all in Ruins* (Istanbul, 2004).

—— *Karagöz: Turkish Shadow Theatre* (Istanbul, 1987).

Anderson, Lisa, 'Assessing Libya's Qaddafi', *Current History*, 84, 502 (1 May 1985), pp. 197–227.

'Arab world's first animation film fest held in Algiers', *Euromed Audiovisual* (27 December 2012). Available at http://euromedaudiovisuel.net/p.aspx?t=news&mid=21&l=en&did=1125 (accessed 24 March 2015).

Arango, Tim and Michael R. Gordon, 'Next leader may echo Maliki, but Iraqis hope for new results', *The New York Times* (20 August 2014). Available at

Bibliography

http://mobile.nytimes.com/2014/08/20/world/middleeast/sectarian-grudges-color-record-of-man-who-may-lead-iraq.html?emc=edit_th_20140820&nl=todaysheadlines&nlid=55610143&_r=1&referrer (accessed 20 August 2014).

Arieli-Horowitz, Dana, 'Alive and kicking: Israeli animation – a conversation with Roni Oren, Head of the Screen Arts Department, Bezalel', *Bezalel – Proceedings on History and Theory*, 8 (2008). Available at https://bezalel.secured.co.il/zope/home/he/1209439536 (accessed 20 February 2015) (Hebrew).

Armbrust, Walter, 'New cinema, commercial cinema, and the modernist tradition in Egypt', *Alif: Journal of Comparative Poetics*, 15 (1995), pp. 81–129.

Armes, Roy, *African Filmmaking: North and South of the Sahara* (Bloomington, IN, 2006).

—— *Arab Filmmakers of the Middle East: A Dictionary* (Bloomington IN, 2010).

Arraf, Jane, 'Iraq film directors look to build "Baghdadwood"', *Christian Science Monitor* (2010). Available at http://www.csmonitor.com/World/Middle-East/2010/0728/Iraq-film-directors-look-to-build-Baghdadwood (accessed 1 December 2014).

Atkinson, Paul, and Simon Cooper, 'Untimely animations: Waltz with Bashir and the incorporation of historical difference', *Screening the Past*, 34 (2012), pp. 257–76.

Austin, Guy, *Algerian National Cinema* (Manchester, 2012).

Aysan, Yilmaz, *Let's Go Postering, 1963–1980: The Turkish Left's Visual Adventure*, Iletisim Publication (Istanbul, 2013).

Bachy, Victor, *Le Cinéma de Tunisie* (Tunis, 1978).

Baghdad International Film Festival, Official site. Available at http://www.baghdadfilmfest.com/ (accessed 29 July 2014).

'"Baghdad Night" keeps alive folk tales of the dead', *Al-Arabiya News*. Available at http://english.alarabiya.net/en/life-style/art-and-culture/2013/09/05/-Baghdad-Night-keeps-alive-folk-tales-of-the-dead.html (accessed 5 March 2014).

Bakrim, Mohammed, 'Public funding for film, a Moroccan experience: the history of Moroccan public funding for cinema', *EuroMed Audiovisual* (24 January 2013). Available at http://euromedaudiovisuel.net/p.aspx?t=news&mid=21&l=en&did=1174 (accessed 4 April 2015).

Balan, Canan, 'Transience, absurdity, dreams and other illusions: Turkish shadow play', *Early Popular Visual Culture*, 6, 2 (July 2008), pp. 171–85.

Balázs, Béla, 'The spirit of film', in Erica Carter (ed.), *Béla Balázs: Early Film Theory*, trans. Rodney Livingstone (New York, NY, 2010).

Basbukey, Hakki, *Association of Turkey Cinematheque* (Istanbul, 2008).

Bazzoli, Maria Silvia, *African cartoon. Il cinema di animazione in Africa* (Milan, 2003).

Beck, Jerry, 'Mish-Mish in national defense', *Cartoon Brew* (November 2013). Available at http://www.cartoonbrew.com/classic/mish-mish-in-national-defense-18442.html (accessed 15 March 2015).

Bibliography

Beckman, Karen (ed.), *Animating Film Theory* (Durham, NC, 2014).

Belaid, Habib, 'Aperçu sur le cinéma en Tunisie à l'époque coloniale,' *Rawafid ISHMN*, 4, (1998), pp. 85–106.

Bendazzi, Giannalberto, 'African cinema animation', *Enter Text: An Interdisciplinary Humanities e-Journal*, 4, 1 (2004), pp. 10–26.

—— *Cartoons; One Hundred Years of Cinema Animation* (London, 2004).

Bendazzi, Giannalberto, *Cartoons: Le cinéma d'animation. 1892–1992* (Paris, 1991).

—— *Animation – A World History* (Oxford, 2015).

Bentaleb Hassan, 'Journée mondiale de cinéma d'animation: Un art qui peine à trouver son chemin au Maroc', *Liberation* (28 October 2010). Available at http://m.libe.ma/Journee-mondiale-de-cinema-d-animation-Un-art-qui-peine-a-trouver-son-chemin-au-Maroc_a14875.html (accessed 4 April 2015).

Bernal, Victoria, 'Please forget democracy and justice: Eritrean politics and the power of humour', *American Ethnologist*, 40, 2 (2013), pp. 300–309.

Besbes, Samir, *Regard sur l'evolution du cinema d'animation depuis ses origines. Le cas du film Tunisien* (Doctoral Thesis, University Pantheon-Sorbonne, Paris, 1998).

Bocco, Riccardo and Jordi Tejel, 'Introduction', Riccardo Bocco, Hamit Bozarslan, Peter Sluglett, and Jordi Tejel (eds), *Writing the Modern History of Iraq: Historiographical and Political Challenges* (Singapore, 2012), pp. xi–xvii.

Boulos, Jean-Claude, *La Télé Quelle Histoire!* (Beirut, 1997).

Boym, Svetlana, *The Future of Nostalgia* (New York, NY, 2001).

Brockelmann, Carl, 'Kalila wa-Dimna', B. Lewis, Ch. Pellat and J. Schacht (eds), *The Encyclopaedia of Islam IV* (Leiden, 1978), pp. 503–506.

Brode, Douglas, *Multiculturalism and the Mouse. Race and Sex in Disney Entertainment* (Texas, 2005).

Buchan, Suzanne, 'Animation, in theory', Karen Beckman (ed.), *Animating Film Theory* (Durham, NC, 2014), pp. 111–30.

Buchan, Suzanne, *Pervasive Animation* (London, 2013).

Callus, Paula, 'Creative comment and critique: Animation filmmaking in Africa', Africa in Motion Blog (2008). Available at http://www.africa-in-motion.org.uk/2008/animation.html (accessed 15 March 2015).

—— 'Reading animation through the eyes of anthropology: a case study of sub-Saharan African animation', *Animation: An Interdisciplinary Journal*, 7, 2 (2012), pp. 113–30.

Cambié, Silvia, 'Lessons from the front line: The Arab Spring demonstrated the power of people and social media', *Communication World* (January–February 2012), pp. 28–32.

Carter, Sandra, *What Moroccan Cinema? A Historical and Critical Study* (Plymouth, MA, 2009).

Bibliography

Caryl, Christian, Michael Hastings, Scott Johnson, Ayad Obeidi, Ahmed Obeidi, Mohammed Sadeq, Christopher Dickey, and Karen Fragala Smith (eds), 'Iraq's young blood', *Newsweek*, 149, 4 (2007), pp. 24–34.

Cavalier, Steven (ed.), *The World History of Animation* (London, 2011).

Centre Cinématographique Marocain Division de la Production Service Fonds d'Aide, *Primes, aides et avances sur recettes octroyées de 1988 au16 octobre 2014* (16 October 2014). Available at http://www.ccm.ma/pdf/SITFA.pdf (accessed 4 April 2015).

Cercle d'études et de recherches cinématographiques, 'Hommage: Habib Masrouki. Jeune cinéaste tunisien', *Revue Adhoua*, 3 (Spring 1981).

Cetin, Yalcin, 'Pessimists about our animation', *Miliyet Art Magazine*, 42, (Istanbul, 1973).

Ceviker, Turgut, 'Caricature and Karagöz', S. Koz (ed.), *Torn is the Curtain, Shattered is the Screen, the Stage all in Ruins* (Istanbul, 2004).

—— 'Outline of Turkey animation', *Gül Diken Humor Culture Magazine*, 8 (Autumn 1995).

—— *The Turkish Animation Cinema* (Istanbul, 1995).

Chute, Hillary, 'The texture of retracing in Marjane Satrapi's *Persepolis*', *WSQ: Women's Studies Quarterly*, 36, 1 (2008), pp. 92–110.

Ciecko, Anne, 'Digital Territories and States of Independence: Jordan's Film Scenes', *Afterimage: The Journal of Media Arts and Cultural Criticism*, 36, 5 (March/ April, 2009), pp. 3–6.

Cinemaye Azad, 'Karnameh', *Cinemaye Azad*. Available at http://www.cinemaye-azad.com/karnameh/karnameh.html (accessed January 2008, link inactive).

Cobayanim, 'La création marocaine', *Fousdanim* (12 May 2010). Available at http://www.fousdanim.org/festivals/index.php?2010/05/12/142-la-creation-marocaine (accessed 4 April 2015).

—— 'Meknès 2010', *Fousdanim* (12 May 2010). Available at http://www.fousdanim.org/festivals/index.php?Meknes-2010 (accessed 4 April 2015).

Cole, Alexander, 'Distant neighbours: the new geography of animated film production in Europe', *Regional Studies*, 42 (2008), pp. 891–904.

Colette, Alexia, 'Animation. Bienvenue dans la 3ème dimension', *Telquel*, 252 (5 December 2006). Available at http://w.telquel-online.com/archives/252/arts2_252.shtml (accessed 4 April 2015).

Comic4Syria, 'Cocktail', M. Halasa, Z. Omareen and N. Mahfoud (eds), *Syria Speaks. Art and Culture from the Frontline* (London, 2014), pp. 181–91.

Contadini, Anna, *Arab Painting: Text and Image in Illustrated Arabic Manuscripts* (Leiden, 2007).

Convents, Guido, *Images & Animation: Le Cinema d'animation en Afrique Centrale* (Brussels, 2014).

Cooke, Miriam, *Dissident Syria: Making Oppositional Arts Official* (Durham, NC, 2007).

Bibliography

Corriou, Morgan, 'Tunis et les "temps modernes": les débuts du cinématographe dans la régence (1896–1908)', *Publics et spectacle cinématographique en situation coloniale* (Tunis, 2012), pp. 95–133.

Costantino, Manuela, 'Marji: Popular commix heroine breathing life into the writing of history', *Canadian Review of American Studies*, 38, 3 (2008), pp. 429–47.

Coward, Martin *Urbicide: The Politics of Urban Destruction* (London, 2008).

Dabashi, Hamid (ed), *Dreams of a Nation. On Palestinian Cinema* (London, 2007).

—— *Close-up: Iranian Cinema: Past, Present and Future* (London, 2001).

—— *Mohsen Makhmalbaf at Large: The Making of a Rebel Filmmaker* (London, 2007).

Darwish, Mustafa, *Dream Makers on the Nile* (Cairo, 1998).

Davis, Eric, *Memories of State: Politics, History, and Collective Identity in Modern Iraq* (Berkeley, CA, 2005).

Davis, Eric and Nicholas Gavrielides, 'Statecraft, historical memory, and popular culture in Iraq and Kuwait', *Statecraft in the Middle East: Oil, Historical Memory, and Popular Culture* (Miami, FL, 1991).

Davis, Rocío G., 'A Graphic Self: Comics as Autobiography in Marjane Satrapi's *Persepolis*', *Prose Studies*, 27, 3 (2005), pp. 264–79.

Denieuil, Pierre-Noël (ed.), *Socio-Anthropologie de l'image au Maghreb* (Paris, 2009–10).

Diawara, Manthia, *African Cinema, Politics & Culture* (Bloomington, IN, 1992).

DOHA Film Institute, 'People in film: Sulafa Hijazi', DOHA Film Institute blog (17 January 2012). Available at http://www.dohafilminstitute.com/blog/people-in-film-sulafa-hijazi (accessed 3 May 2015).

Dubai Press Club, *Arab Media Outlook 2009–2013*, (Dubai, 2010), p. 178. Available at http://fas.org/irp/eprint/arabmedia.pdf (accessed 2 April 2015)

Dumont, René, *Paysanneries aux abois. Ceylan, Tunisie, Sénégal* (Paris, 1972).

Dwyer, Kevin, 'Moroccan cinema and the promotion of culture', *The Journal of North African* Studie, 12, 3 (2007), pp. 277–86

Edera, Bruno, 'African animation', in J. Greene and D. Reber (eds), *Drawing Insight: Communicating Development through Animation* (Malaysia, 1996), p. 111.

El Aakouchi, Hamid, *Harakatoon Blog*. Available at http://7arakatoon.blogspot.co.uk/ (accessed 4 April 2015).

El-Issawi, Fatima, 'Libya media transition: Heading to the unknown', *mediapolicy.org* (July 2013). Available at http://eprints.lse.ac.uk/59906/1/El-Issawi_Libya-media-transition_2013_pub.pdf (accessed 13 July 2014).

Elahi, Babak, 'Frames and Mirrors in Marjane Satrapi's *Persepolis*', *symploke*, 15, 1 (2007), pp. 312–25.

Elkayal, Heba, 'The musician artist', *Daily News Egypt* (18 March 2009). Available at http://www.masress.com/en/dailynews/108204 (accessed 1 September 2014).

Encyclopaedia Iranica, 'Kamāl-al-molk, Moḥammad Gaffāri', *Iranica Online*. Available at http://www.iranicaonline.org/articles/kamal-al-molk-mohammad-gaffari (accessed 3 March 2015).

Bibliography

—— 'Noḵostin festivāl-e bayn-al-melali-e filmhā-ye kudakān o nowjavānān', *Iranica Online*. Available at http://www.iranicaonline.org/articles/kanun-e-parvares-e-fekri-e-kudakan-va-nowjavanan-international-film-festival (accessed 3 March 2015).

Engin, Aydin, *This is the Title of the Book, Tan Oral book* (Istanbul, 2006).

Erdle, Steffen, *Ben Ali's 'New Tunisia': A Case Study of Authoritarian Transformation* (Doctoral thesis, Humboldt University of Berlin, October, 2006).

Feldestein, Ariel L., *Cinema and Zionism: The Development of Nation through Film* (Portland, OR, 2012).

Fertek Raki, *Encyclopedia of Raki* (Istanbul, 2010).

Ferzat, Ali, 'Two cartoons', M. Halasa, Z. Omareen and N. Mahfoud (eds), *Syria Speaks. Art and Culture from the Frontline* (London, 2014), pp. 169–70.

Festival Dei Popoli, 'Interview with Hala Alabdallah' on YouTube. Available at https://www.youtube.com/watch?v=bvLWcvENQdU (accessed 3 May 2015).

Filmer, Cemil, *Memories* (Istanbul, 1984).

Foster, Lisa 'The Rhetoric of heavy metal resistance: musical modalities in Iraqi public life', *Middle East Journal of Culture and Communication*, 4 (2011), pp. 320–38.

Furniss, Maureen, *Art in Motion: Animation Aesthetics* (London, 1999).

Gertz, Nurith and George Khleifi, *Palestinian Cinema: Landscape, Trauma, and Memory* (Bloomington, IN, 2008).

Ghazala, Mohamed, *Animation in the Arab World: A Glance on the Arabian Animated Film Since 1936* (Saarbrücken, 2011).

Ginsberg, Terri, 'Radical rationalism as cinema aesthetics: the Palestinian-Israeli conflict in North American documentary and experimental film', *Situations: Project of the Radical Imagination*, 4, 1 (2011), pp. 92–3.

Goren, Michal, 'This is the Land: Zionism, man and land – cinematic aspects and poetic devices in the service of Zionism', *Slil – Online Journal for History, Film and Television*, 5 (2011), pp. 40–50.

Görgün, Ege, 'Cici Can'. Available at www.tersninja.com (accessed 22 April 2014).

Graiouid, Said and Taieb Belghazi, 'Cultural production and cultural patronage in Morocco: the state, the Islamists, and the field of culture', *Journal of African Cultural Studies* (2013), pp. 261–74.

Gross, Nathan, *The Hebrew Film: Chapters in the History of Israeli Cinema 1869–1999* (Tel Aviv, 1991) (Hebrew).

Güdükbay Ugur, Fatih Erol and Nezih Erdogan, 'Beyond Tradition and Modernity: Digital Shadow Theater', *Leonardo*, 33, 4 (2000), pp. 264–5.

H.O.M., 'Casanim, la grande-messe du film d'animation de retour a Casa', *Medias24: L'information Economique Marocaine en Continu* (23 October 2014). Available at http://www.medias24.com/CULTURE-LOISIRS/150084-Casanim-la-grand-messe-du-film-d-animation-de-retour-a-Casa.html# (accessed 4 April 2015).

287

Bibliography

Hakem, Tewfik, 'La fabuleuse histoire des momies animées du cinéma égyptien. Rétrospective de dessins animés égyptiens,' Liberation (1 June 1996). Available at http://www.liberation.fr/culture/1996/06/01/la-fabuleuse-histoire-des-momies-animees-du-cinema-egyptien-retrospective-de-dessins-animes-egyptien_175533 (accessed 15 March 2015).

Halasa, Malu, Zaher Omareen, and Nawara Mahfoud, *Syria Speaks: Art and Culture from the Frontline* (London, 2014).

Halberstam, Judith/Jack, *The Queer Art of Failure* (Durham, NC, 2011).

Halbwachs, Maurice, *On Collective Memory* (Chicago, IL, 1992).

Harris, William, *Lebanon: A History 600–2011* (New York, NY, 2012).

Harsin, Jayson, 'The Responsible Dream On Ari Folman's *Waltz with Bashir*', *Bright Lights Film Journal*, 63 (2009). Available at http://brightlightsfilm.com/the-responsible-dream-on-ari-folmans-waltz-with-bashir/#.VVBW8GCHfww (accessed 10 May 2015).

Hennebelle, Guy, 'Arab cinema', *MERIP Reports*, 52 (1976), pp. 4–12.

Higbee, Will and Song Hwee Lim, 'Concepts of transnational cinema: towards a critical transnationalism in film studies,' *Transnational Cinema*, 1, 1 (2010).

Higson, Andrew, 'The limiting imagination of national cinema,' E. Ezra and T. Rowden (eds), *Transnational Cinema: The Film Reader* (London, 2006), pp. 15–25.

Hijazi, Sulafa, 'Arabic identity in Arab animation', *AniFest Lecture in Czech Republic* (April 2012). Available at https://www.youtube.com/watch?v=kcC0SdL8qh0 (accessed 3 May 2015).

—— 'Biography' [Sulafa Hijazi Webpage.] Available at http://sulafahijazi.com/index.html (accessed 12 February 2015).

——'People in film', *Doha Film Institute Blog* (17 January 2012). Available at http://www.dohafilminstitute.com/blog/people-in-film-sulafa-hijazi (accessed 3 May 2015).

Historical Society of Jews from Egypt, 'Frenkel animated cartoons' (n.d.), [Historical Society of Jews from Egypt.] Available at http://www.hsje.org/mish_mish%20in_1935_files/mishmish.pdf (accessed 25August 2014).

Hobsbawm, Eric, 'Introduction: Inventing traditions', Eric Hobsbawm and Terence Ranger (eds), *The Invention of Tradition* (Cambridge, 1983).

Hodgkin, Katharine and Susannah Radstone, 'Introduction: Contested pasts', *Contested Pasts: The Politics of Memory* (London, 2003).

Honess Roe, Annabelle, 'Absence, excess and epistemological expansion: Towards a framework for the study of animated documentary', *Animation: An Interdisciplinary Journal*, 6, 3 (2011), pp. 307–23.

—— *Animated Documentary* (Basingstoke, 2013).

Honour, Hugh and Fleming, John, *The Visual Arts: A History* (Trenton, NJ, 1992).

Horak, Jan-Christopher, 'Animation symposium at FIAF', UCLA Film & Television Archive (May 2012). Available at https://www.cinema.ucla.edu/blogs/archival-spaces/2012/05/04/animation-symposium-fiaf (accessed 26 August 2014).

Bibliography

Hoy, Norman Emberson, 'Report on mission in Iraq, December 26th 1968 to February 24th 1969,' *UNESCO Document Archive*. Available at http://unesdoc. unesco.org/images/0015/001582/158205eb.pdf (accessed 2 February 2015).

Huliaras, Asteris, 'Qadhafi's comeback: Libya and sub-Saharan Africa in the 1990s', *African Affairs*, 100 (2001), pp. 5–25.

Hunerli, Selcuk, *About Animation Cinema* (Istanbul, 2005).

Hunot, Alexis, 'FICAM 2013', *Zewebanim: Webzine sur le cinema d'animation* (7 September 2013). Available at http://www.zewebanim.com/blog/index. php?2013/09/07/4359-ficam-2013 (accessed 4 April 2015).

Ilk, Berat, 'The Canlandiranlar Association', Available at www.canlandiranlar.com (accessed 11 May 2014).

Inanc, Demet Deger, 'Animation cinema section', *Sanat Olayi Magazine*, 4 (Istanbul, 1981).

Independent Film & Television College, Official site. Available at http://www.iftvc. org/index.php (accessed 1 December 2014).

Irving, Sarah, 'Israel's movie-funders ban recipients from calling themselves Palestinian', *The Electronic Intefada* (30 January 2015). Available at http://electronicintifada.net/blogs/sarah-irving/israels-movie-funders-ban-recipients-calling-themselves-palestinian (accessed 23 February 2015).

Isakhan, Benjamin, 'Targeting the symbolic dimension of Baathist Iraq: cultural destruction, historical memory, and national identity', *Middle East Journal of Culture and Communication*, 4 (2011), pp. 257–81.

Ismael, Tareq Y. and Max Fuller, 'The disintegration of Iraq: the manufacturing and politicization of sectarianism', *International Journal of Contemporary Iraqi Studies*, 2, 3 (2008), pp. 443–73.

Issari, Mohammad Ali, *Cinema in Iran, 1900–1979* (New York, NY, 1990).

Jameson, Frederic, 'Third World Literature in the Era of Multi-National Capitalism,' *Social Text*, 15 (Autumn, 1986), pp. 65–88.

Javaharian, Mahin, *Short History of Animation in Iran* (Tehran, 1999).

Jensen, Eric, 'Mediating social change in authoritarian and democratic states – irony, hybridity and corporate censorship', B. Wagoner, E. Jensen and J. A. Oldmeadow (eds), *Culture and Social Change: Transforming Society Through the Power of Ideas* (Charlotte, NC, 2012), pp. 212–17.

Joint Program Production Institution (JPPI), *Gulf Cooperation Joint Program Institution* (2013), website. Available at http://www.gccopen.com/institution. html (accessed 3 April 2015).

Kaba, Fethi, 'Department of Animation'. Available at www.anadolu.edu.tr/tr/akademik (accessed 27 May 2014).

Kaphafe, Assaddollah, *The Background of Animation in Iran, Vision of Wakefulness* (Tehran, 1999).

Kaplan, Nese, *The year of Family Films 1960s* (Istanbul, 2004).

Bibliography

Karimi Saremi, Mohamma Reza, 'History of Tehran International Animation Festival', *Tehran International Animation Festival*. Available at http://tehran-animafest.ir/first_fest/about_pg/about_history_first_fest_en.htm (accessed 25 February 2015).

Kassir, Samir, *Beirut* (Berkley, CA, 2010).

Khalil, Andrea, *Crowds and Politics in North Africa: Tunisia, Algeria and Libya* (Oxford, 2014).

Khalil, Joe and Marwan M. Kraidy, *Arab Television Industries* (London, 2009).

Khallaf, Rania, 'One boy and his goat', *Al-Ahram Weekly Online*, 562 (29 November 2001). Available at http://weekly.ahram.org.eg/2001/562/fe3.htm (accessed 13 March 2015).

Khatib, Lina, 'Iraq: between the present and the future', *Middle East Journal of Culture and Communication* 4 (2011), pp. 253–5.

Khatib, Lina, *Image Politics in the Middle East. The Role of the Visual in Political Struggle* (New York, NY, 2013).

King, C. Richard, Carmen R. Lugo-Lugo and Mary K. Bloodsworth-Lugo, *Animating Difference: Race, Gender and Sexuality in Contemporary Films for Children* (Lanham, MD, 2010).

Kononenko, Natalie. 'The Politics of innocence: Soviet and Post-Soviet animation on folklore topics', *Journal of American Folklore*, 124, 494 (2011), pp. 272–94.

Kraidy, Marwan, 'The body as medium in the digital age: Challenges and opportunities', *Communication and Critical/Cultural Studies*, 10, 2–3 (2013), pp. 285–90.

Kruks, Sergei 'The Latvian epic "Lāčplēsis: Passe-Partout" ideology, traumatic imagination of community', *Journal of Folklore Research*, 41, 1 (2004), pp. 1–32.

Kurtulus, Mehmet, 'Anima İstanbul'. Available at www.animaistanbul.com (accessed 30 June 2014).

Lahlali, Al-Mustapha, *Contemporary Arab Broadcast Media* (Edinburgh, 2011).

Landesman, Ohad, and Roy Bendor, 'Animated Recollection and Spectatorial Experience in *Waltz with Bashir*', *Animation* 6, 3 (2011), pp. 353–70.

Lent, John A. and Asli Tunç (1999) 'In a man's world: Turkish women animators,' *Animation World Magazine*, 3, 11 (February 1999). Available at http://www.awn.com/mag/issue3.11/3.11pages/lentturkey.php3 (accessed 11 May 2014).

Leservot, Typhaine, 'Occidentalism: Rewriting the West in Marjane Satrapi's *Persepolis*', *French Forum*, 36, 1 (2011), pp. 115–30.

Livingston, David, 'Lebanese Cinema,' *Film Quarterly*, 62, 2 (2008), pp. 34–43.

Lord, Peter and Brian Sibley, *Cracking Animation, The Aardman Book of 3-D Animation* (London, 1998).

Loshitzky, Yosefa, *Identity Politics on the Israeli Screen* (Austin, 2001).

Bibliography

Luleci, Yalcin, *Turkish Cinema and Religion* (Istanbul, 2008).

Makar, Farida, 'Let them have some fun: Political and artistic forms of expression in the Egyptian Revolution', *Mediterranean Politics*, 16, 2 (2011), pp. 307–12.

Malek, Amy, 'Memoir as Iranian exile cultural production: A case study of Marjane Satrapi's *Persepolis* series', *Iranian Studies*, 39, 3 (2006), pp. 353–80.

Manovich, Lev, *The Language of New Media* (Massachusetts, MA, 2002).

Mansfield, Natasha Jane, 'Loss and Mourning: Cinema's' Language'of Trauma in *Waltz with Bashir*', *Wide Screen* 2, 1 (2010), pp. 1–13.

Mansour, Nisrine and Sabry, Tarik, '(Mis)trust, access and the poetics of self-reflexivity: Arab diasporic children in London and media consumption', in T. Sabry, N. Sakr and J. Steemers (eds), *Arab Children's Digital Media: Breakthroughs and Setbacks* (London, forthcoming).

Marks, Laura, 'Calligraphic Animation: Documenting the Invisible', *Animation: An Interdisciplinary Journal*, 6, 3 (2011), pp. 307–23.

—— *Enfoldment and Infinity. An Islamic Genealogy of New Media Art* (Cambridge, MA, 2010).

Martin, Florence, 'Tunisia,' Hjort Mette & Petrie Duncan (eds), *The Cinema of Small Nations* (Edinburgh, 2007), pp. 213–28.

Masliyah, Sadok, 'The Folk songs of Iraqi children: part one', *Journal of Semitic Studies*, L/VII (2010), pp. 183–235.

Massad, Joseph, 'The weapon of culture: cinema in the Palestinian liberation struggle', Hamid Dabashi (ed.), *Dreams of a Nation: On Palestinian Cinema* (London, 2007).

Masson, Nicolas, 'War, crimes and video tapes: conflicting memories in films on Iraq', Riccardo Bocco, Hamit Bozarslan, Peter Sluglett, and Jordi Tejel (eds), *Writing the Modern History of Iraq: Historiographical and Political Challenges* (Singapore, 2012), pp. 445–58.

Massumi, Brian, *Parables For The Virtual – Movement, Affect, Sensation* (New York, NY, 2002).

Matar, Amer, 'Art & freedom', M. Halasa, Z. Omareen and N. Mahfoud (eds), *Syria Speaks. Art and Culture from the Frontline* (London, 2014), p. 241.

McGlennon, David, 'Building Research Capacity in the Gulf Cooperation Council Countries: Strategy, Funding and Engagement', Zayed University Dubai, UAE. Available at http://portal.unesco.org/education/es/files/51665/11634953625McGlennon-EN.pdf/McGlennon-EN.pdf (accessed 20 November 2014).

McKernan, Luke, 'Albert Samama Chikly, Tunisian film pioneer', *Victorian Cinema*, available at http://www.victorian-cinema.net/samama (accessed 25 November 2015)

Mehrabi, Masoud, *Tarikh-i sinima-yi Iran, az aghaz ta sal-i 1357* (Tehran, 1984).

Merrin, Will, *Media Studies 2.0* (Oxford, 2014).

Bibliography

Mesrati, Mohamed, 'Bayou and Laila', M. Cassel, L. Al-Zubaidi and C. R. Nemonie (eds), *Writing Revolution: The Voices from Tunis to Damascus* (London, 2013).

Miller, Nancy K., 'Out of the Family: Generations of Women in Marjane Satrapi's *Persepolis*', *Life Writing*, 4, 1 (2007), pp. 13–29.

Mir-Hosseini, Ziba, 'Iranian cinema: Art, society and the state', *Middle East Report*, 219 (2001).

Mirbakhtyar, Shahla, *Iranian Cinema and the Islamic Revolution* (Jefferson, NC, 2006).

Mirsepassi, Ali, *Intellectual Discourse and Politics of Modernization* (Cambridge, 2000).

Morag, Raya, *Waltzing with Bashir: Perpetrator Trauma and Cinema* (London, 2013).

Muhanna, Elias, 'Translating *Frozen* into Arabic', *The New Yorker* (30 May 2014). Available at http://www.newyorker.com/books/page-turner/translating-frozen-into-arabic (accessed 15 November 2014).

Munk, Yael, *Israeli Cinema at the Turn of the Millennium* (Israel, 2012) (Hebrew).

Naghibi, Nima and Andrew O'Malley, 'Estranging the Familiar: "East" and "West" in Satrapi's *Persepolis*', *ESC: English Studies in Canada*, 31, 2–3 (2005), pp. 223–47.

Nagm "al-baltouk" fil-sa'udiyya yakshif ismuhu wa waghuhu ba'd sanawat min al-ghumud (11 June 2011). Available at http://www.alarabiya.net/articles/2011/06/11/152835.html (accessed 20 November 2014).

Neidhardt, Irit, 'Egyptian cinema-industry. A brief historical overview', *MEC Film* (2011). Available at http://www.mecfilm.com/de/media/z_regie/EgyptianCinemaIndustry_BriefHistory.pdf (accessed 13 March 2015).

Newbould, Chris, 'Middle East animation on the map at Postman Pat's London premiere', *The National* (21 May 2014). Available at http://www.thenational.ae/blogs/scene-heard/middle-east-animation-on-the-map-at-postman-pats-london-premiere (accessed 22 March 2015).

News, 'Live pictures', *The New Cinema Magazine*, 14 (Istanbul, 1968), p. 6.

Niedermüller, Péter, 'Ethnicity, nationality, and the myth of cultural heritage: a European view', *Journal of Folklore Research*, 36, 2/3 (1999), pp. 243–53.

Nouri, Shakir, 'Social criticism in Iraqi cinema', *Alif: Journal of Comparative Poetics*, 15 (1995), pp. 202–207.

Omar, Hasan, 'Entrepreneurial spirit and small businesses in Palestine: what is missing?', *This Week in Palestine*, 80 (April 2013). Available at http://archive.thisweekinpalestine.com/details.php?id=3990&ed=217&edid=217 (accessed 23 January 2015).

Onaran, A. Serif, *Turkish Cinema* (Istanbul, 1999).

Opondo, Sam Okoth, 'Libya's "black" market diplomacies: Opacity and entanglement in the face of hope and horror', *Globalizations*, 8, 5 (2011), pp. 661–8.

Bibliography

Oral, Zeynep, 'Interview: Yalcin Cetin', *Miliyet Art Magazine*, 1, (Istanbul, 1973), p. 3.

Oren, Zvika 'Animation in Israel – Summary 1982', *Cinematheque: Cinema Journal*, 13 (1983), pp. 18–19. (Hebrew).

—— '100 Years of Animation', *Cinematheque: Cinema Journal*, 101 (1999), pp. 13–22. (Hebrew).

—— 'Animation in Israel', *Bezalel – Proceedings on History and Theory* 8 (2008). Available at https://bezalel.secured.co.il/zope/home/he/1209439536 (accessed 20 February 2015). (Hebrew).

Oring, Elliot, 'Risky business: Political jokes under repressive regimes', *Western Folklore*, 63, 3 (Summer 2004), pp. 209–36.

Orlando, Valerie, 'Being-in-the-world: the Afropolitan Moroccan author's worldview in the new millennium', *Journal of African Cultural Studies*, 25, 3 (2013), pp. 275–91.

—— 'Mean street, Bad boys, drugs and rock'n'roll: Morocco's urban legends of the 21st century', *South Central Review*, 28, 1 (2011), pp. 52–73

Pay, Ayse, *Director Cinema: Ahmet Ulucay* (Istanbul, 2010).

Payne, Jessica M., 'The Politicization of culture in applied folklore', *Journal of Folklore Research*, 35, 3 (1998), pp. 251–77.

'Persian epic animation to go on US, UAE screens', *Press TV*, 13 April 2013. Available at http://www.presstv.com/detail/2013/04/13/297984/us-uae-to-host-iran-3d-animation/ (accessed 3 March 2015).

Pi-Sunyer, Oriol, 'Political humor in a dictatorial state: The case of Spain', *Ethnohistory*, 24 (1977), pp. 179–90.

Pilling, Jayne, *A Reader in Animation Studies* (London, 1998).

Prince Claus Award Committee, 'Ali Farzat. Political cartoons of an Arab master', 20 & 28, 'Leaders and Workers'. Available at http://creativesyria.com/farzat.htm (accessed 3 May 2015).

Rakha, Youssef, 'Inventing the wheel: Ihab Shaker profile', *Al-Ahram Weekly* (16 June 1999). Available at http://www.ihabshaker.com/news/Alahram/InvintingTheWeelF.html (accessed 13 March 2015).

Rastegar, Kamran, *Surviving Images: Cinema, War, and Cultural Memory in the Middle East* (Oxford, 2015).

Raya, Morag, *Waltzing with Bashir: Perpetrator Trauma and Cinema* (London, 2013).

Rboub, Amin, 'Au cœur de la "DreamWorks" marocaine; Des jeunes marocains talentueux apprivoisent la 3D, les images de synthèse', *L'economiste*, 2727 (4 March 2008). Available at http://www.leconomiste.com/article/au-coeur-de-la-dreamworks-marocaine#sthash.yZ0sSgIs.dpuf (accessed 4 April 2015).

Renov, Michael, 'Toward a poetics of documentary', *Theorizing Documentary* (New York, 1993), pp. 12–36.

—— *The Subject of Documentary* (Minneapolis, MN, 2004).

Bibliography

Reuters, 'Syrian director Razam Hijazi produces an award-winning animated film for Syrian and Arab children', *ITN Source* (2 September 2007). Available at http://www.itnsource.com/en/shotlist/RTV/2007/09/12/RTV1353807/?v=1 (accessed 3 May 2015).

RFI, *Cinémas africains d'aujourd'hui. Guide des cinématographies d'Afrique* (Paris, 2007).

Rimawi, Tariq, 'The Arab animation spring: How have Arab animation artists used the power of YouTube and social media in response to the recent Arab revolution?' Conference paper presented at CONFIA, Second International Conference on Illustration and Animation in Porto, Portugal (December 2013). Available at http://www.uop.edu.jo/download/Research/members/901_3179_T_Al.pdf (accessed 13 March 2015).

Rogers, Annie, Mary Casey, Jennifer Ekert and Jim Holland, 'Interviewing children using an interpretive poetics', S. Green and D. Hogan (eds), *Researching Children's Experience: Approaches and Methods* (London, 2005).

Ruya Foundation, Official site. Available at http://www.ruyafoundation.org/ (accessed 29 July 2014).

Sacranie, Nour, 'Image politics and the art of resistance in Syria', *State Crime Journal*, 2, 2 (Autumn 2013), pp. 135–48.

Sadiki, Larbi, 'In-formalized polity and the politics of dynasty in Egypt and Libya', L. Anceschi, G. Gennaro and T. Andrea (eds), *Informal Power in the Greater Middle East: Hidden Geographies* (Oxford, 2014), pp. 11–23.

Sadr, Hamid Reza, *Iranian Cinema: A Political History* (London, 2006).

Saeed-Vafa, Mehrnaz, 'Ebrahim Golestan: Treasure of pre-revolutionary Iranian cinema', *Rouge* (2007). Available at http://www.rouge.com.au/11/golestan.html (accessed January 2012).

Safar Khan Art Gallery, 'Ihab Shaker profile' (n.d.) [Safar Khan Art Gallery]. Available at http://safarkhan.com/Ex-ArtWork.aspx?artistid=161&Year=2009 &isartist=1&type=past&exid=296 (accessed 13 March 2015).

Said, Edward, 'Preface', H. Dabashi, *Dreams of a Nation: On Palestinian Cinema* (London, 2007).

—— *After the Last Sky: Palestinian Lives* (New York, NY, 1986).

Salem, Badar, 'Experts worry over high regional costs of animation production', *Variety Arabia* (September 2012). Previously available at http://www.varietyarabia.com/Docs.Viewer/1ce464b6-8869-4eec-bc80-b151781e5a7b/default.aspx (accessed 8 December 2012).

Salibi, Kamal, *Histoire du LIBAN du 18ème siècle à nos jours* (Paris, 1988).

Salti, Rasha, *Insights into Syrian Cinema: Essays and Conversations with Contemporary Filmmakers* (New York, NY, 2006).

Samuel, Sigal, 'Netanyahu: Hamas wants to pile up "telegenically dead Palestinians"', *The Jewish Daily Forward* (20 January 2014). Available at http://forward.com/articles/202436/netanyahu-hamas-wants-to-pile-up-telegenically/#ixzz3QjN-w8kFg (accessed 23 February 2015).

Bibliography

Sayfo, Omar, 'Arab animation: between business and politics', T. Sabry, N. Sakr and J. Steemers (eds), *Children's Television and Digital Media in the Arab World* (London, 2015).

—— 'Arab sitcom animations as platforms of satire', S. de Leeuw (ed.), *The Power of Satire* (Amsterdam, 2015).

—— 'The emergence of Arab children's televisions and animation industry in the Gulf States', M. Al-zo'oby and B. Baskan (eds), *State-society Relations in the Arab Gulf States* (Berlin, 2014), pp. 77–101.

Schäuble, Michaela, '"All Filmmaking is a Form of Therapy": Visualizing Memories of War Violence in the Animation Film *Waltz with Bashir*', Six-Hohenbalken, Maria and Nerina Weiss (eds), *Violence Expressed: An Anthropological Approach* (Farnham, 2011), pp. 203–22.

Scognamillo, Giovanni, *The History of Turkish Cinema* (Istanbul, 1990).

Sebag, Paul, *Tunis, Histoire d'une ville* (Paris, 1998).

Seckinelgin, Hakan, 'Contradictions of a sociocultural reflex: civil society in Turkey', M. Glasius and D. Lewis (eds), *Exploring Civil Society: Political and Cultural Contexts* (London, 2004), pp. 173–80.

Sender, Ramon, 'La fete des images' *Maroc-Hebdo International*, 494 (24 January 2002), p. 35. Available at http://www.maroc-hebdo.press.ma/archive/files/494/494.pdf (accessed 4 April 2015).

Shafik, Viola, *Arab Cinema. History and Cultural Identity* (Cairo, 2005 [1988]).

—— *Popular Egyptian Cinema. Gender, Class and Nation* (Cairo, 2007).

Shohat, Ella, *Israeli Cinema: East/West and the Politics of Representation* (London, 2010).

Shomali, Amer, 'Pixelated Intifada', website (2012). Available at http://www.amer-shomali.info/pixelated-intifada/ (accessed 23 February 2015).

Siino, François, 'Insupportables successions: Le temps politique en Tunisie de Bourguiba à la révolution,' *Temporalités*, 15 (2012). Available at http://temporalites.revues.org/2138 (accessed 25 February 2013).

Siraj, Mounir, 'Le 3D en Maroc; en jeune industrie en plein essor', *Aujourd'hui au Maroc* (4 January 2009).

Sobchack, Vivian, 'The line and the animorph: or travel is more than just A to B', *Animation: an Interdisciplinary Journal*, 3, 3 (2008), pp. 251–65.

Sorbera, Lucia. 'History and fiction in the new Iraqi cinema', Riccardo Bocco, Hamit Bozarslan, Peter Sluglett, and Jordi Tejel (eds), *Writing the Modern History of Iraq: Historiographical and Political Challenges* (Singapore, 2012), pp. 423–44.

Stelfox, Dave, 'Ali Ferzat, Cartoonist in exile', *The Guardian* (19 August 2013). Available at http://www.theguardian.com/world/2013/aug/19/ali-ferzat-cartoonist-exile-syria (accessed 3 May 2015).

Stewart, Garrett, 'Screen memory in Waltz with Bashir' *Film Quarterly*, 63, 3 (Spring 2010), pp. 58–62.

Strøm, Gunnar, 'Animated documentary', *Studies in Documentary Film*, 9, 1 (2015), pp. 92–4.

Bibliography

Sturken, Marita. *Tangled Memories: The Vietnam War, the Aids Epidemic, and the Politics of Remembering* (London, 1997).

Syria Untold, 'Animated films in the face of oppression', *Syria Untold* (28 March 2014). Available at http://www.syriauntold.com/en/2014/04/animated-films-in-the-face-of-oppression/ (accessed 3 May 2015).

Tapper, Richard (ed.), 'Introduction', *The New Iranian Cinema: Politics, Representation and Identity* (London, 2002).

Tawil-Souri, Helga, 'Digital occupation: Gaza's high-tech enclosure', *Journal of Palestine Studies*, 41, 2 (2012), pp. 27–43.

Telquel, 'Humour electorial', *Telquel* (21 February 2012). Available at http://telquel.ma/2012/02/21/humour-electoral_1279 (accessed 4 April 2015).

Tensuan, Theresa M., 'Comic visions and revisions in the work of Lynda Barry and Marjane Satrapi', *MFS Modern Fiction Studies*, 52, 4 (2006), pp. 947–64.

The Heritage Trust, 'World's oldest animation?' (25 July 2012), [*The Heritage Trust*.] Available at http://theheritagetrust.wordpress.com/2012/07/25/worlds-oldest-animation/ (accessed 3 March 2015).

The Iraq Pavilion at the 55th International Art Exhibition – la Biennale di Venezia 'Welcome to Iraq'. Available at http://www.theiraqpavilion.com/ (accessed 8 May 2014).

Todorova, Maria, 'Introduction: Learning Memory, Remembering Identity', Maria Todorova (ed.), *Balkan Identities: Nation and Memory* (London, 2004), pp. 1–24.

Tryster, Hillel, *Israel Before Israel: Silent Cinema in the Holy Land* (Jerusalem, 1995). (Hebrew).

Tunc, Ertan, *Economic Structure of Turkish Cinema 1896–2005* (Istanbul, 2012).

Turun, Cemil, 'Animation cinema', *Ve Sinema Magazine*, 7 (Istanbul, 1989).

twofour54, Official site, Available at http://twofour54.com/en (accessed 22 August 2014).

United Nations' Department of Economic and Social Affairs, *World Population Prospects: The 2012 Revision*. Available at http://esa.un.org/wpp/unpp/p2k0data.asp (accessed 9 August 2014).

Van de Peer, Stefanie, 'Fragments of War and Animation: Dahna Abourahme's *Kingdom of Women* and Soudade Kaadan's *Damascus Roofs: Tales of Paradise*', *Middle East Journal of Culture and Communication*, 6, 2 (2013), pp. 151–77.

—— 'National animation in Syria', *Animation Studies 2.0* [Blog]. Available at http://blog.animationstudies.org/?p=779 (accessed 3 May 2015).

Véray, Laurent, *Les films d'actualité français de la Grande Guerre* (Paris, 1995).

Vrielinck, Robert, *Le Cinéma d'animation avant et après Walt Disney / Animated Cinema Before and After Disney)* (Brussels, 1981).

Ward, Paul, 'Animated realities: the animated film, documentary, realism', *Reconstruction: Studies in Contemporary Culture*, 8, 2 (2008), pp. 1–28.

Bibliography

Weber-Feve, Stacey, 'Framing the "Minor" in Marjane Satrapi and Vincent Paronnaud's Persepolis', *Contemporary French and Francophone Studies*, 15, 3 (2011), pp. 321–8.

Wedeen, Lisa, 'Tolerated parodies of politics in Syria', J. Gugler (ed.), *Film in the Middle East and North Africa: Creative Dissidence* (Austin, TX, 2011 [1999]).

Wells, Paul, *Understanding Animation* (London, 1998).

——*Animation: Genre and Authorship* (London, 2002).

——'The language of animation', J. Nelmes (ed.), *Introduction to Film Studies* (5th Edition) (London, 2011), pp. 230–58.

WHO Office for West Bank and Gaza, 'Breast cancer in the Gaza Strip: the struggle for survival of Fatma Bargouth' (December 2005), [Israel's Occupation]. Available at http://www.israelsoccupation.info/sites/default/files/Breast%20 Cancer.pdf (accessed 23 February 2015).

Wiedermann, Julius (ed.), *Animation Now!* (Köln, 2007).

Winnicott, D. W., *Playing and Reality* (London, 1991).

Wood, Ramsay, *Kalila and Dimna, Fables of Friendship and Betrayal* (London, 2008).

Worth, Jennifer, 'Unveiling: *Persepolis* as Embodied Performance', *Theatre Research International* 32, 2 (2007), pp. 143–60.

Yetkiner, Ayhan, *Nasreddin Hodja's Children* (Istanbul, 1973).

Yoon, Hyejin and Edward J Malecki, 'Cartoon planet: worlds of production and global production networks in the animation industry', *Industrial and Corporate Change*, 19, 1 (2009), p. 240.

Yosef, Raz, 'War fantasies: memory, trauma and ethics in Ari Folman's Waltz with Bashir', *Journal of Modern Jewish Studies*, 9, 3 (2010), pp. 311–26.

Zaitoon, 'Gaza university student animation: *The Return* – video', *The Guardian* (28 June 2012). Available at http://www.theguardian.com/global-development/video/2012/jun/08/gaza-university-student-animation-return-video (accessed 23 February 2015).

Zalila, Ikbal, 'Des mises en scène du pouvoir à la fiction du pouvoir. Bourguiba au prisme des actualités cinématographiques tunisiennes', Camau & Geisser (eds), *Habib Bouguiba. La trace et l'héritage* (Paris, 2004).

Zarrinkelk, Noureddin, 'History of animation' (n.d.) [Noureddin Zarrinkelk]. Available at http://www.zarrinkelk.com/eng/animation.html (accessed July 2014).

Zeydabadi-Nejad, Saeed, 'Iranian intellectuals and contact with the West: The case of Iranian cinema', *British Journal of Middle Eastern Studies*, 34, 3 (2007).

Zipes, Jack, *The Enchanted Screen: The Unknown History of Fairy-tale Films* (London, 2011).

Ziraoui Youssef, 'Animation: Monsieur 3D', *Telquel*, 303 (28 December 2007). Available at http://ykzxlck.telquel-online.com/archives/303/maroc6_303.shtml (accessed 4 April 2015).

Index

$9.99 (2007), 182
1001 Arabian Nights (1959), 9
1001 Days (2000), 133
16 Hours in Baghdad (2004), 43
16mm Bolex camera, 55
2D animation, 39, 60, 79, 98–99, 117, 133, 136–38, 140, 142, 152–53, 161–62, 200, 207–8, 254, 265, 267–68, 274–75
3D animation, 18, 37, 39–40, 49n40, 60, 64, 65n1, 67n36, 71, 73, 75–76, 80, 98, 100, 102, 136–37, 140–42, 153–54, 156–57, 160–62, 167, 168n1, 178, 181, 207, 267–71, 274–76, 280n27, 280n38
5D, 254
7 Days a Week (2000), 133
9/11, 1, 99

'Abid, Qasim, 43
A Little Story of an Egg (1976), 250
A Tale of Two Nails (1991), 111, 115, 124n15
A Wonderful Land (2003), 183
A+ Cartoon, 207
A52, 270
Abbas, Reine, 136, 146n29
ABC, 130
Abd El-Hameed, Fahmy, 203
Abd El-Hameed, Raouf, 203
Abdennadher, Mohammed, 249
Abdulwahed, Khaled, 121
Abi-Samra, Fadi, 132, 146n20, 146n31
Abid, Kasim, 44

Abourahme, Dahna, 125n25, 137, 168n2, 193n29
absurd, 103n5, 159, 161, 186, 188, 234
ABTech, 270
Abu Al-Nasr, Mona, 206–7, 212
Abu Dhabi, 11, 26n24, 49n40, 72, 145n10, 164, 169n10
Abu Hashash, Mahmoud, 154–55, 160–65
Abu Sayf, Salah, 32
Abusharif, Mohammad, 13
Adaimy, Emile, 136, 141, 146n27, 147n33
Adaimy Studios, 136, 141, 146n27, 147n33
Adeyes Animation Studio, 79–80
Adventures of Sinbad (1978), 131, 146n15
affect, 218
African Cartoon, 27n32, 214n23, 263, 278n6, 278n7
African Movie Academy Awards, 209
Agadati, Baruch, 174
Agha, Akram, 114–15, 121, 123, 126n33, 126n35
Ahmad wa Kannan (2009), 73, 81n14
Ahmadieh, Esfandiar, 55–56
Ahmed Bey I, 249–50
Ahmed and Salim, 183
Aho, Edgar, 132, 135, 147n33
Ajans Bulu, 90, 95
Akaçik, Turgut, 100
Akad, Lütfi, 89
AKP, 100

Index

Aksam, 86
Akşehir Nasreddin Hodja Aminated Film Competition, 93
Al-A'raj, Ali, 79
Al-Ahram Studios, 198
Al-Ahram, 198–99
Al-Akkad, Mostafa, 225
Al-Ali, Naji, 137, 150–1, 168n2
Al-Aqsa TV, 156
Al-Assad, Bashar, 109
Al-Badri, Nasser, 79
Al-Borgainy, Abdel-Haleem, 203
Al-Daradji, Mohamud, 43, 48n13
Al-e Ahmad, Jalal-e, 54
Al-Ghad Media Group, 207
Al-Gomhouriya, 204
Al-Haddad, Abdulwahab, 228, 238n30, 239n46
Al-Hikma (2010), 277, 280n41
Al-Ibrahim, Waleed, 79
Al-Ibrahimi, Faysal, 73, 78
Al-Jaahiziyya, 14
Al-Jamil, Furat, 17–18, 29, 30–47, 47n2, 47n10, 48n19
Al-Jazeera Children's Channel, 117, 271
Al-Malki, Fayez, 79
Al-Munis Media Production and Distribution, 279
Al-Qadisiya (1981), 32
Al-Sahar Studio, 207
Al-Sahy, Njla, 78
Al-Sakia Animation Festival, 208
Al-Shorbaji, Ammar, 114
Al-Soud, Abdul-Mouein Oyaun, 113
Al-Watan TV, 77–78
Al-Yassiri, Faisal, 33
Al-Zaidi, Thamer, 30, 72–73
Al-Zaman, 79
Alabdallah, Hala, 123, 124n10, 127n56, 128, 287
Aladdin (1991), 8–9

Aleppo, 108
Alexandria, 6, 196–97, 201, 208
Alexandria Film Festival, 208
Algeria, 3, 14–16, 26n27, 241, 253, 263
Algiers, 15, 27n28, 27n30, 254, 259n20
Algiers School of Fine Arts, 254
Ali Baba and the 40 Thieves (1996), 75
Ali Zaoua: Prince of the Streets, 262
Alias Wavefront, 270
Alkabetz, Gil, 179
Alkaç, Bahattin, 96
allegory, 108, 247–48, 256
Allo Mamman Bobo (2002), 266
Alter, Sagi, 188
Altin Koza Film Festival, 93
amateur, 93, 242–44, 246–47, 250–51, 254, 257, 259n20
Amcabey, 86
American University of Beirut (AUB), 136
Amir, Aziza, 198
An Eye for an Eye (1979), 94
Anadolu University, 91, 99
ANAP, 96
Anatolia, 86, 98–100
Anbar, Hassan, 203
ANC, 225
ancient, 2–3, 5, 8–9, 46, 104n20, 111, 114, 196
And Film Production Company, 89
Andoni, Saed, 160
Angelman, Mayan, 189
Anigraf, 99
Anima Film, 178
Anima Istanbul, 98, 104n22
Animal Treasure Island (1979), 131
Animaroc, 275, 279n10
Animatek, 95
Animation Association, 178, 208
Animation Home, 181
Animax Animation Studios, 100
Anime, 70, 81n6, 116, 126n37, 212

299

Index

animism, 176

Animix, 24, 180, 182, 191n2, 193n32

Ankara Advertising Agency, 92

Annecy, 23, 65, 94, 100, 249, 251, 254, 278n6

Another Year (2008), 137

Anti-Discrimination Committee (ADC), 9

anti-realist, 151

Anwar, Adel 203

Aoun, Chadi, 137–38

Applied Industrial Arts Vocational College, 94

Arab Spring, 24, 114, 121, 123, 140, 210–12, 215n37

Arab Uprising, 157, 235

Arabani, Ahmad, 62, 65

arabesque films, 94

Arabian Nights, 9, 75, 206; *see also One Thousand and One Nights*; *1001 Arabian Nights*

Arabic Centre for Animation Films, 33

Aral, Oğuz, 88, 90, 92

Aram, Mohamed, 15–16, 27n32

Arasoft, 73

Arch of the Garden, 52

archaeology, 3, 5, 24

architecture, 13, 134, 156–57, 164

archive, 24, 47n3, 57, 89, 93, 125n24, 184, 189, 192n6, 213n10, 241, 259n20, 263

Art'COM, 269

Artnet, 90, 95

As If We Were Catching a Cobra (2012), 123, 124n10

Ashekman, 138

Ashkenazi, 174, 186, 192n10

ASIFA, 23–24, 27n26, 57, 102, 178, 180, 191n2, 205, 208–9, 212

Association Marocaine du Cinema d'Animation (AMCA), 23, 276

Association of Young Tunisian Filmmakers (AJCT), 243–45, 250

Asterix (1994), 97

Astroganga (1979), 131

Ata (1997), 133

Atlas, 264, 277

Attention (2005), 114–15, 121

Attia, Ahmed Bahadin, 253

audio-bridge, 164

auteur, 4, 10–16, 18, 137–38, 140, 240, 246, 265, 273

authorship, 71

autocracy, 30, 109

autodidact, 15, 243

avant-garde, 129

Ayouch, Nabil, 262

Aziza and Youness (1938), 201

Azzeh, Dia', 20, 150–51, 154, 156–57, 160, 167, 168n3, 169n15, 170n26

Baath Party, 30, 32–3, 36, 107–9

Bachy, Victor, 240–41, 247, 258n5, 259n15, 259n21, 259n25

Back to School (1965), 242–43

Back, Frédéric, 57

Badrakhan, Ahmed, 198

BAFTA, 254

Baghdad Night (2013), 17, 29, 31, 32, 36–37, 39–40, 42, 44–47

Baghdad Studio, 30

Bakar, 206–7

Balázs, Béla, 160

Bali, Nihat, 91

Bargouth, Fatma, 162

bas-reliefs, 52

Battle of the Kings (2012), 64–65, 67n36

Bau, Joseph, 175

Bayyumi, Mohamed, 197

Bazzoli, Maria Silvia, 27n32, 263, 278n6

Beckoury, Amine, 274–76, 280n33, 280n34

300

Index

Bedouin, 197, 223
Behloul, Abdelkader, 276
Beirut Animated, 139–43, 147n34
Beit Avi Chai, 187
Beit Sahour, 165–66
Beizai, Bahram, 56
Belgium, 57, 269
Belinco, Ariel, 188
Belluzzo, Coi, 182
Ben Ali, Zine El-Abedine, 246, 252–53,
    256, 260n29
Ben Ami, Dafna, 183
Ben Dor, Eli, 183
Benali, Abdelhamid, 270–71
Bendazzi, Giannalberto, 27n33,
    200, 202, 204, 213n6, 213n13,
    278n2, 278n6
Benghazi, 217, 224, 228
Benice, Ateş, 95–96
Bennys, Ahmed, 245, 249–50,
    253, 259n18
Besbes, Samir, 241, 244, 252–53, 255,
    258n1, 259n16, 259n25
Bethlehem, 164–65
Betty Boop, 201
Beyoud, Mohammed, 264
Bezalel School of Art, 179,
    191n2, 192n22
biblical stories, 174–77
Bibliotheca Alexandrina, 208
Big Data, 270
Big Yusuf (1966), 90–91
Bin Amer, Huda, 233
Bina Film, 63
Bitcoin, 270
Bitzbutz (1985), 179
black market, 225–26, 237n3
Black Tape (2014), 189
Blad Skizo (2007), 274
Blender, 275
Blue.Dar, 116, 125n30
Bobo and the Cheese (1990), 265

Bobo, the Saviour (1988), 265
Boğaç Khan (1988), 95
Bon Appétit (1947), 201
Book of Dede Korkut, 95, 104n20
book illustrator, 57
BOOM-Magazine, 266
Boq'at Jaw, 22, 218, 221–23,
    225–29, 231–36
Bosphorus University Cinema
    Club, 93
Bouchmar, Said, 265, 267,
    279n17, 279n20
Bouftass, Said, 265–67, 269,
    273, 279n19
Boukany, Youssef, 266–68
Boukhari, Boubaker, 254
Bourekas, 175, 192n10
Bourguiba, Habib, 245–47, 250–52,
    256, 259n19
Bousa, Khousa, 78
Boutaleb, Alaedine, 254, 260n35
Boycott, Divestment and Sanction of
    Israel (BDS), 155, 166
Boym, Svetlana, 34
Bozzetto, Bruno, 57
Bread (1972), 248
bread riots, 251
Brenas, Alain, 136
Briceno, Luis, 274
British Council, 155
British mandate, 47n6
Broken Branches (2014), 182,
    187–88
Buchan, Suzanne, 162, 164, 169n9
Bugs Bunny, 130
Buka, Mabuka and Mabulka
    (2014), 186
Bullet (2014), 121
Burj El-Mur: Tower of Bitterness
    (2012), 134
burlesque films, 242
Büyükdoğan, Orhan, 88, 104n10

301

Index

Cable Vision, 73
Café Babel (2013), 183
Cairo Cartoon, 206–7
Cairo International Film Festival for Children, 208
Çakaralmas Detective, 89
calligraphy, 3, 8, 93, 117
Canadian Islamic Congress, 74
Canli Karikatür, 90
Capitole Theatre, 129
Captain Abu Raed (2008), 12
caption, 174–75, 223
caricature, 19, 84, 86, 88–89, 92–93, 119, 125n18, 178, 204, 212
Caricature Advertising, 92
Carioca, Taheya, 200
Cartago 1 (2003), 254
Cartago 2 (2006), 254
Carthage Film Festival (JCC), 22, 124n16, 169n10, 240, 249, 254
cartoon film festival, 94
Cartoon Network Studios Arabia, 11
Cartoon of Neighbourhoods, 78
Cartoonile, 207
Casa Street, 271
Casablanca School of Design and Communication, 269
CASANIM, 275
CASAPremière, 265–69
Caustic, 141
cave walls, 52
CBS, 130
Cedar Revolution, 133
cel animation, 60–63, 65, 133, 137–38, 140, 153, 267
censorship, 3, 4, 19, 22, 25n3, 32, 53, 82n30, 87, 94, 108–10, 114, 118–19, 121–22, 133, 144, 197, 201, 204, 210–13, 217, 220–24, 227–28, 230–31, 234, 236, 238n28, 252
Censorship (1969), 93, 102

Central Army Cinema Office, 85
Centre Cinématographique Marocain (CCM), 262–4, 279n10
Centre National du Cinéma, 15, 205
Çetin, Yalçin, 90–92, 96
CG, 12
CGI, 70–1, 76, 81n7, 98, 136, 146n25, 254, 268, 270, 273, 275–77
Chahine, Youssef, 74, 202
Chaplin, Charlie, 242
Charbaji, Mohamed, 250
Cherrycherry Animation, 102
Chikly, Albert Samama, 242, 258n9, 258n10
Children of the Aristocracy (1932), 198
Chilling Spot, 218
CHP, 100
Christian, 32
Cici Can (1962), 91
CIDCYA, 52
Cinderella (1950), 129
cinéma vérité, 158, 169n18
Cinemaye Azad, 54
Cinétéléfilm, 253
civil war, 19, 46, 107, 130–31, 134–35, 137–38, 140–41, 145n12
Çizgi Advertising, 95
Claw (1917), 86
claymation, 133, 164, 207
Cleanliness is a Sign of Faith, 59
Clearing the Mind (1974), 177
co-production, 2, 11, 18–20, 24, 33, 72, 75, 79, 110, 112, 116–17, 123, 154–5, 181, 207, 271
Coalition forces, 33, 43, 46, 48n20
Codsi, Fulvio, 132
collaboration, 12, 20–21, 110, 113, 123, 136, 142, 157, 180, 206, 208, 271, 275–76
collage, 93

Index

collective identity, 32, 34, 45, 47n5, 151, 183, 186–87
collectivism, 247–48
College of Television and Cinema (Iran), 57, 59
Coma (2009), 254–56
comic book, 91, 235
comic hero, 150
Commodore 63, 64
Compagnie Libanaise de Télévision (CLT), 130
competitions, 12, 13, 24, 93, 95, 98, 177, 180, 208, 249, 251
compositing, 29, 98, 137, 144, 205, 209, 220, 266, 270, 273, 277
computer game, 39, 267, 277
computer graphics, 60, 81n7, 136, 146n25, 157, 271
Concrete (2007), 188
consciousness, 6, 21, 48n14, 165, 247
Conservatoire Indépendent du Cinema Français, 250
Cordoba Animation Studios, 102
cosmopolitanism, 45
Costi, Anat, 183
Council of Ministers, 92
coup d'état, 90, 95, 251
Cowan, Paul, 154, 165
Cube, 141
Cuisine Jap (2010), 275
Cumhuriyet, 86
Cunning Craftiness (2006), 255
Cut Me Off (2013), 183
cut-out animation, 77, 249, 258n3, 274
Czechoslovakia, 38, 56, 251

Dabashi, Hamid, 53, 66n7, 76n27, 158, 170n19, 170n20, 170n24, 291
DAD Studio, 178
Dalvand, Kianoush, 64, 67n36
Damascus, 6, 109–11, 113, 116–17, 124, 125n22, 238n33

Damascus Spring, 109
Damla Animation, 96
DANA Film Studio, 72–73
DAR Films, 161
Data City (2004), 117
Day and Day (2011), 78
Dead Flowers (1918), 197
Dead Sea, 178
Debate Between Yeshayahu Leibowitz and Israel Eldad 1980 (2013), 189
Dedi and Doudi (2006), 254
Dekel, Yael, 187
Deli Dumrul (1988), 96
Demirağ, Turgut, 89
Demolition of the Russian Monument in Ayastefanos (1914), 85
Denis, Gaëlle, 254
DePatie-Freleng, 201
Diaries of the Lazy, 78
Diary of a Chair (2004), 133
diaspora, 53
dictator, 3, 43, 115, 135, 217, 219, 223, 235
didactic, 14, 72, 124n2, 207, 211, 246–7, 265, 271
Didi, the Chicken (1984), 265
Die Abenteuer des Prinzen Achmed (1926), 8
DigiPen, 136
Digit'Art, 275
digital, 2–5, 7, 10–11, 17, 19–20, 22–24, 25n13, 26n21, 85, 107, 120, 136, 150, 154, 157, 172, 180–81, 208–9, 211–12, 237n4, 263, 266–68, 272–73, 275–78, 280n26
Dimensions Studio, 156
Dinov, Todor, 244
Direklerarasi (1968), 92
Disney, 8–9, 11, 70, 76, 86, 91, 97, 104n21, 129, 144, 162, 199–200, 258n3, 273

303

Index

dissent, 4, 19, 116, 123, 184, 210, 218, 220–22, 225, 227–28, 235–36

distribution, 1, 5–7, 45, 67n36, 75, 79, 108, 111, 131, 145n4, 152, 156, 167, 181, 201, 204, 236, 242, 251, 263, 269, 271, 275, 278

Divine Intervention (2002), 188

documentary, 18, 22, 25n2, 38, 48n20, 55, 72, 86, 92, 123, 124n10, 126n41, 137, 150, 154, 158–67, 169n10, 170n18, 172, 187, 189, 191n1, 192n8, 194n37, 197, 202, 208, 218, 250, 271

Doğan, Ferruh, 88, 90, 92

Dokdok (1940), 201

Dolls' Whims (1965), 243

Don Quixote in Jerusalem (2005), 189

Doron, Yigal, 178

Dovnikovic, Bordo, 57

Dragon FX, 156

Drawing the War (2002), 137

Dream of the Olives (2009), 75–76

DreamWorks, 270, 273, 280n27

Dubai Film Festival, 45

dubbing, 126n37, 130–31, 144, 225, 244

Dümbüllü, Ismail, 92

Dumoulin, François, 275

Düşyeri Animation Studio, 102

École George Méliès, 274–75

École Nationale Supérieure des Beaux Arts, 265

Edelbaum, Gali, 181, 183

edutainment, 5, 7, 11, 73, 116–18, 152

Efeoğlu, Efe, 100

Egg (1980), 179

Egyptian Animation Association, 208

Egyptoon, 212

Ein El-Hilweh: Kingdom of Women (2010), 137, 168n2

Ein Gedi Studios, 178

El-Aakouchi, Youssef, 266–68

El-Deen, Hossam, 202

El-Fakir, Abdallah, 269, 280n27

El-Islam, Saif, 227

El-Rahabani, Elias, 76

El-Sadat, Anwar, 203

El-Toro Azul (2008), 135

Elad, Reut, 188

Eli (2014), 188

EmariToons, 114, 125n28, 126n30

Emberson, Norman Hoy, 30, 47n3

empowerment, 4, 122, 210, 218

enfold/unfold, 2–4, 30, 55, 134, 221–22, 230, 235

Enjaaz Film Fund, 45

Enough (2006), 133

ENSAD School of Decorative Arts, 254

entrepreneur, 1, 4–5, 7–8, 10–12, 14, 16, 19, 21, 87, 143, 177, 180–81, 197, 203, 265

Erez, Meral, 95

Erez crossing, 162

Erkoç, Eflâtun Nuri, 88–89, 92

escapist, 151, 172–3, 175, 182, 186–87, 190, 204

Estayqazat, 122

ethnography, 220–22

Euromed Audiovisuel, 27n28, 253, 279n8

Euromédiatoon, 253

Evliya Çelebi, 91

exhibition, 1, 6–7, 11, 89, 108, 152–53, 155, 167, 180, 263, 267, 275–77

experiment, 1, 5–7, 11, 14, 18, 20–22, 25n11, 55–56, 60, 63, 91, 93–95, 110, 113, 116, 119, 123, 129, 138, 142–45, 157, 167, 170n18, 175–77, 179, 181, 202, 204–6, 208, 211–12, 226, 241, 247–48, 252, 254, 257, 268–69, 274

export, 2, 107, 112, 122, 130, 206

304

Index

Face. Day. Memory (2012-13), 187–88

fairy tale, 33, 36, 38, 201, 206

Family Guy, 77

fantasy, 151, 163, 182, 268

Farabi Cinema Foundation, 60

Farabi University of Arts, 57, 59

Faraj, Bassam, 72

Farooha Media Productions, 77

Fatenah (2009), 20, 154–55, 160–64, 167

Faust, Michael, 188

Feghali, Ziad, 136

Felix the Cat, 198

feminism, 122, 233

Fenari, Yasmeen, 123

Ferber, Tzahi, 177

Fernandez, David, 275

Ferzat, Ali, 109, 123, 124n11, 124n12, 124n13, 127n45

festival, 1, 5–6, 10–15, 17, 20, 22–24, 25n2, 26n24, 27n29, 44–45, 56, 59–60, 65, 69, 93–95, 99–100, 112–13, 124n15, 125n16, 125n22, 135, 139–41, 143, 146n22, 146n30, 154, 164, 169n10, 176–78, 180, 187, 191n2, 193n32, 208–9, 214n25, 230, 238n19, 240, 243, 249, 251, 254–55, 257, 259n20, 260n32, 264, 270, 274–76, 278, 279n10, 280n40

FICAM, 23, 264–5, 269–70, 274–5, 279n10

figurative, 196

film farsi, 53

FILMALI Production SAL, 131, 146n16

Filmar Studios, 88, 90

finance, 44

Fine Arts Academy, 88

Fine Media Group, 114

Fischinger, Oskar, 176

Fish Never Sleep (2002), 254

Fleisher, 9, 200

FLN government, 14

Folimage, 275

folk music, 117

folklore, 8, 10, 16–18, 29, 31–32, 34–37, 46, 48n24, 49n25, 49n29, 88, 95, 100, 117, 132, 203, 206, 237n6

Folman, Ari, 2, 21, 25n1, 172, 182, 189, 191n1

Fouad (2013), 138

Fouche, Eveline, 271

fousdanim.org, 276

Frame by Frame Studio, 178

frame-by-frame, 187

Free Cinema, 54

Freed Drawings (2001), 132

freedom of expression, 12, 43, 95, 114, 121, 143–44, 231

French Institute, 255, 264

French mandate, 108, 129

Frenkel Brothers, 6, 8, 21, 141, 199–03, 208, 212, 213n5

Fried, Shaul, 183

Frozen (2014), 273

funding, 7, 16, 20, 49n41, 58, 70, 77, 81n24, 98, 101, 126n35, 138, 143, 145, 154–56, 161, 163, 167, 169n10, 181–82, 193n31, 203, 206, 225, 233, 253, 264, 278n8

Future Boy Conan (1979), 131

Future Television, 20, 132–33, 135, 141, 146n17, 146n18, 147n41, 148n52, 168n3

Ga'ash, Alon, 183

Gaddafi, Moammar, 22, 212, 217–25, 227–28, 230–36

Gaddafi International Prize for Human Rights, 225

gags, 174–75, 247–48

gamification, 136

gaming, 270

305

Index

Gaza, 151, 155–58, 161–62, 168n5, 169n16, 170n27

Gaza College of Applied Science, 151, 155

General Foundation for Cinema (GFC), 224

Gentlemen Visuals, 102

Gerber, Nir, 181, 183

Gergeadam (1975), 94

Gezi Park Resistance, 102

Ghaibeh, Lina, 132–34, 136, 147n33

Ghalib, Khalid, 265, 267

Ghazala, Mohamed, 10, 21, 23–24, 25n13, 111, 196

Ghorbankarimi, Hosseinali, 63–65, 67n28, 68

ghost story, 91

Ghotbi Gilani, Reza, 57–58

Gibraltar (2005), 137

God's Loyal Subject (2011), 101

God on Our Side (2005), 189

Godard, Jean-Luc, 159, 170n23

Gogo's (1959), 89

Goubran, Redha, 203

Gözen, Erim, 94, 99

graffiti, 151, 217, 230–31

Grafika Advertising Agency, 92

Grandizer (1979), 131, 140

graphic design, 23, 135–36, 139, 146n26, 147n32, 164, 204, 221, 226, 253, 267, 274

graphic novel, 51, 164–65, 254

Gravity, 181

Grayaa, Mohamed, 255

Green Book, 224

Grimault, Paul, 24, 205

Gross, Yoram, 175, 177, 179, 192n13

Growing (2013), 12

Guardian Angel, 59

Guardians of the Galaxy (2014), 273

Guild of Egyptian Animators, 23, 208

Güler, Cemal Nadir, 86

Gulf Cooperation Council (GCC), 19, 72, 81n24, 117

Gulf States, 10, 44, 69, 71–72, 79, 81n21, 122, 126n30, 143

Gulf War, 9, 187

Gun (1976), 94

Guweta, Sason, 178

Ha' Srutonim, 183

Habash, Ahmed, 20, 154–55, 160–63, 165

Habchi, David, 138

hacker-maker, 266

Haidar, Mohamed, 78

Hajji in His 1002nd Night (1971), 250, 260

Hakem, Hassan, 202, 203, 215, 216

Halas, John, 89, 104n12

Halbwachs, Maurice, 35, 48n17

Halutz, 174, 176

Halwani, Ghassan, 137

Hamas, 157–58, 169n17, 294

Hamdi, Ashraf, 212

Handalah, 150, 167

hand-drawn, 137, 153

Hani Bayoun Studio, 141

Hanine, Issam Mohammed, 277, 281

Hanna-Barbera Studio, 201

Harakatoon, 268–69, 279, 286

Harb, Talaat, 197–98

Harbaoui, Ezzedine, 252

Harib, Mohammed Saeed, 77

Hashim, Tarek, 43

Hasidic, 176

Hassib, Mohammed, 203

Hava Nagilah (1955), 176, 192n13, 195

He and She (1995), 113, 128

Heckle and Jeckle, 130

Hedayat, Sadegh, 54

Hedgehog, 141

Hercules (1999), 97, 104n21

Index

heritage, 20, 22, 29, 31–33, 35–36, 38, 40, 45–46, 48n18, 59, 65n3, 70, 104n20, 131, 137, 155, 176, 235, 259n19, 264, 283, 292, 296–97

Herzl, Theodor, 186

Hide and Seek, 150, 170

Hijazi, Mannaa, 113, 116

Hijazi, Razam, 116, 126n40

Hijazi, Sulafa, 20, 107, 113, 116–21, 123, 126n36, 126n29, 127n46, 127n48

Hindawi, Mahmoud, 13–14, 26n25

hip-hop, 138

Hiroshima International Film Festival, 100, 125n22

Hisar Short Film Competition, 93

Hoffili (2012), 254, 260

Hollow Land (2013), 183–84, 195

Hollywood, 53, 90, 98–99, 177, 225, 273

Holy Land, 174, 177, 192n4, 296

homegrown, 9, 11–12, 19, 57, 71, 112, 117, 199, 218

Homs, 113

Honour the Bedouin (1918), 197

Honyan's Shoe (2010), 209

How the Ship of Creed Sailed (1960s) 3, 8, 27, 93, 105

Hungry (2005), 208

Hussein, Fayza, 203

Hussein, Habib, 73

Hussein, Mostafa, 202–3

Hussein, Saddam, 33

hyper-realism, 142, 151, 175

I Had a Coffee in the Café (2005), 269, 281

I Wish (2013), 138, 149

IAC, 23, 180

Ibrahim, Antoine Selim, 201–2

identity, xv, 1, 4–5, 8, 14, 19, 21, 26n27, 31–38, 41, 44–47, 47n5, 47n7, 47n9,

47n11, 48n14, 54, 67n30, 76, 78, 80n4, 84, 111, 115–18, 122–23, 133, 143, 151, 183, 186–88, 192n14, 213n2, 246–47, 286, 288–89, 291, 295–96

ideology, 54, 58, 86, 97, 102, 108–09, 156, 173, 186, 190, 290

idiosyncrasies, 174, 176, 179, 189, 221, 223, 225

Idriss I, king of Libya, 223

Ilk, Berat, 102

illustration, xiii, 22, 36, 38, 60, 69, 119, 121, 123, 125n24, 135, 139–40, 147n32, 150, 153, 164, 167, 215n35, 220, 222–23, 225–26, 235–36, 239, 246–47, 251, 256, 282

import, 18–19, 51, 53, 70, 90, 96, 112, 130–31, 206, 226

In Clear Mind (2010), 183, 194

In the Name of the Law (1952), 89, 105

In and On (2001), xiii, 254, 260

Independence '05 (2005), 133, 148

Independent Film and Television College, 43, 289

India, 26n24, 78–80

Indian cinema, Bollywood, 53

industry, 5, 9–10, 12, 14, 21, 26n19, 30, 33, 44–45, 51–53, 55–58, 63, 65, 66n19, 69, 74, 81n21, 87, 94–95, 98–100, 102–3, 107–8, 115, 117, 126n34, 131, 141, 143–44, 148n50, 152, 154, 156–57, 160, 173, 175, 177–78, 180–82, 189, 193n31, 196–98, 201–2, 206, 210, 214n34, 253, 270, 292, 295, 297

InfoDesign, 271

Information Office, 175

infrastructure, 3, 7–8, 11, 30, 44, 51, 69, 71–72, 80, 98, 122, 135 , 146, 164, 174–75, 197, 223

innovation, 6, 60, 92, 138

307

Index

Insel Film, 91
institutions, 11, 18–20, 23, 39, 43–46, 51–54, 56, 60, 63, 65, 73–74, 93, 97–98, 136, 141, 143, 155, 173, 181–82, 224, 226, 246
International Animation Day, 23, 208, 212
International Animation Festival Tehran, 67n22, 67n32, 290
International Children's Film Festival New York, 100
International Federation of Film Archives (IFFA), 263
International Festival of Animated Films in Mamaia, 244
International Festival for Children and Young Adults, 59
Intifada, vii, 20, 150–51, 153, 155, 157, 159, 161, 163–65, 167, 167n1, 169n11, 180
Iran–Iraq War, 59, 62
Iranian New Wave, 18, 53–54, 58
Iraqi Independent Film Production Centre, 43
IRIB, 59–60, 63–64, 68
Isabelle (2010), 135, 148
ISIS, 122
Iskandar, Noshi, 203
Islamic Republic, 58–59
Islamic Revolution, 53–54, 63, 65n4, 292
Islamists, 78, 224, 226, 232–33, 278n8, 288
Islamoğlu, Barış, 100
Ismailia International Film Festival, 208
Israeli Animation Centre (IAC), 23, 180
Israeli Broadcast Authority (IBA), 177
Israeli Film Centre, 179, 193n25
Israeli Film Fund, 182

Israeli War, 133
Istanbul Advertising Agency, 88
Istanbul Animation Festival, 100
Istanbul Reklam, 90
ITC, 130

Jabr, Samir, 112, 119, 125n19
Jack TML, 184–85, 195
Jadir, Rachid, 271–72, 276
Jaffa, 178, 199
Jahjouh 1 (1985), 252, 260
Jahjouh 2 (1990), 252, 260
Jahjouh and the Mermaid (2008), 255
Jalal, Rashid, 108
Jameson, Frederic, 248
Jamil, Muhammad Shurki, 33
Japan, 70, 72, 81n6, 125n22, 131, 140, 146n15
Jaroudi, Bahij, 132
Jihad Fund, 233
JoAnimate, 12–15, 26n26, 27n29
Joha and the Ghosts of the Night (1978), 252
Johatoon, 252
Jordan, 8, 12–15, 26n20, 26n22, 125n21, 145n10, 156, 212
Joseph the Dreamer (1962), 176–77
JPPI, 72, 81n10
Juha at Court (1985), 111

Kaffafi, Asadollah, 55
Kairouan Festival of Engaged Cinema, 244
Kalil wa Dimn (1993), 132, 266
Kaminski, Hanan, 178–79, 195
Kamler, Piotr, 249
Kanun, 52, 56–57, 59–60, 62, 64–65
Kapal, Liran, 187
Karaali, Lamia, 99
Karagöz, 84–87, 91, 103, 258n6
Karagöz and Hacivat, 85–86
Karakouz, 242, 258n6

308

Index

Karameesh TV, 156
Kare Ajans, 90
Karikatür Ajans, 90
Karim, Mohamed, 197–98
Karimi, Nosratollah, 56, 66n17
Karshouny, Michel, 138
Kartal, Ayce, 102–3
Karwad, Mohammed, 221–22, 226–29, 231, 234, 237n14, 238n22, 238n27, 238n29, 239n45
Kashf (2003), 254
Katt, Mwafaq, 111–12, 115, 119, 124n16, 125n18
Keaton, Buster, 242
Kelibia International Festival of Amateur Film (FIFAK), 243–44, 254
Kemal Film, 86
Keslasi, Sariel, 186
Khadiri-Yazami, Farid, 273
Khalifa, Shweikar, 203
Khalifa, Usama Ahmad, 74–76, 81n15
Khalifé, Marcel, 252
Kharabeesh, 156, 212
Kharmouj (2008), 254
Khatib, Lina, 31, 36, 47n4, 50n43, 237n4
Khélifi, Salah, 251
Khemir, Nacer, 241, 249–50, 258n3, 258n5, 260n25
Khitruk, Fyodor, 57
Khomeini, Ayatollah, 58
Kiarostami, Abbas, 56
kibbutz, 164, 166, 176, 178
Kickstarter, 272
Kilani, Mustafa, 15
Kimiai, Masud, 56
King Ghazi (1993), 33
Kobliner, Ofra, 183
Koraman, Bedri, 90–92
Kranot, Michelle, 183–84, 188–89, 191n2

Kranot, Uri, 183–84, 188–89, 191n2
Kratiki Institute, 265
Kuwait, 19, 30, 33, 73, 77–78, 81n5, 113, 125n23

L'Association Marocaine du Cinema d'Animation (AMCA), 23, 276
La Boîte à Histoires (2009), 271
Lambouba (2009), 254
Lamia, Michel, 136
Lammtara Pictures, 77
Lang, Andrew, 8
Laval Decree, 197
Lawrence of Arabia in Soup and Vinegar (2011), 79
Lebanese Academy of Art (ALBA), 136
Lebanese American University (LAU), 136
Lebanese Broadcasting Company (LBC), 131
Lemalif (1989), 252–53
Liberated Illustrations (n.d.), 226
Libya Al-Ghad, 227
Libyan Broadcasting Division, 224
Life After the Fall (2008), 43
Light and Darkness (1947), 108
Lighthouse Visual Effects, 102
Lights: The Story of Chanuka (1982), 179
Linder, Max, 242
Line (1970s), 93
live-action, 21, 60n17, 92, 117–18, 142, 150, 159, 163–64, 166, 174–77, 180, 187–78, 190, 200–4, 242–43, 245, 249–50, 254, 263, 273, 280n26
Ljabli, Salim, 276
Lockerbie, 225–26
Loneliness (2011), 138
Loof (2011), 188
Looney Tunes, 130
Lord, Peter, 264
Louis Lumière School, 252

309

Index

Lumière Brothers, 84–85, 196
Luxor African Film Festival, 208
Lye, Len, 176

Maaqoul, Aziz, 265–68, 270
Maarifa Animation Lab, 275
magic lantern, 241
Mahfoudh, Lotfi, 254
Mahjoub, Zuhair, 244, 250–51, 253–55, 265
Malsoun.org (2012), 117
Mamluks, 75
Manaki Brothers, 85
Mandela, Nelson, 225, 227
Marco Monkey, 199
Marks, Laura U., 2–4, 25n4, 25n5, 25n7, 25n9
Maroc Telecom, 272
Marxist, 54
Mary Le Roi Short Film Festival, 95
Masrouki, Habib, 224, 250, 259n14, 260n28, 261, 285
Masrur on the Pearl Island (1998), 75
Masturbation, 199
Matalqa, Amin, 12
Matar, Luna, 183
Matchsticks and Maggots (1967), 93
Maya the Honey Bee (1978), 131
Mazamir (2005), 254
MBC, 11, 79
MCIG, 58, 60
McLaren, Norman, 57, 176, 204
media zone, 77
Medya, Arca, 102
Mehmet II, sultan, 74
Meknès Festival, 254, 264, 279n11, 279n15, 280n40
melodrama, 36, 94, 204
Menderes, Adnan, 88, 90
Merhej, Lena, 137, 146n31
Mesghali, Farshid, 56–57

Meshulam, Noam, 178, 182, 191n2, 193n27
Mesrati, Mo (Mohamed), 217, 221–22, 230–31, 238n32, 238n33, 238n35
metaphor, 22, 62–3, 108–11, 113, 115, 122, 166, 189, 220, 274
Metropolis Association, 139
Mezher, Fouad, 138
Mickey Mouse, 199–200
Mighty Mouse, 130
military coup, 19
Mimar Sinan University, 94
Mimiche, 201
Minia University, 207–8
Minotti, Carlo, 204
Mint and Lemon (2008), 102
Mish-Mish Effendi (1936), 199–201
Misr Bank, 197
Misrata, 218, 221, 228–30
Missing (2010), 12
Mister Magoo, 9
Mitry, Jean, 162
Mizrahim, 175, 186, 192n10
Mohamed, Lachguar, 265
Mohammad the Conqueror (1995), 74
Mohammedia (1973), 245, 249–50
Moheeb, Ali, 202, 204
Moheeb Brothers, 6, 21, 202–4
Molla Nasreddin (1957), 55
Monty Python's Flying Circus (1969), 178
Moroccan Association for Animated Film and Games, 275
Moscow, 99, 111–12
motion graphics, 136
Mouslih, Younes, 275
Mroué, Rabih, 132, 146n20
Mubarak, Hosni, 206, 212
Muhammad: The Last Prophet (2002), 8, 125n27
MultiClic Festival, 270
multimedia, 99, 136, 160

310

Index

Munk, Yael, 187
music videos, 98, 137–38, 274
Mut (2013), 187–88
Muznah and Fami (2007), 79
My Arab House, 117, 126n41, 127n43
My Lord (2008), 185
My Son (2006), 134
Mysh and Moshko, 186
Mzaik, Tahsin, 114

Naasani, Nasser, 113
Nakba, 150, 159
Nasser, Gamal Abdel, 79, 201, 203–4, 223–24
Nassib, Mohammed, 276, 280n39
Nathan, Merav, 181
Nathan, Yuval, 181
National Centre for Cinema Sofia, 244
National Defence (1939), 200
National Egyptian Animation Festival, 208
National Film Organisation, 19, 108
National Iranian Radio and Television, 52, 65
NBC, 130
Neilson Hordell Ltd, 112
Netanyahu, Benjamin, 159
Neurotic Love (2008), 254
New Jew, 174
new media, 3, 31, 39, 46, 77, 110, 157, 172
Newport Film School, 12
newsreel, 86, 174, 197–98, 242, 245, 259n11
NFO, 108, 110–14, 116–17, 119, 122–3, 124n2, 125n24
NGO, 20, 31, 97, 99, 102, 117, 155, 158, 160, 162–63, 167, 187, 209, 221
Nippon Animation, 131, 146n14, 146n15

No Difference (2014), 121–22
noir, 30, 41
Norstein, Yuri, 249
Nothing to Do (1939), 200
Notre Dame University (NDU), 136
Notre Musique (2004), 159
Nourallah, Sawsan, 140
Nursi, Said, 101
Nyosha (2012), 187–88

occupation, 20, 53, 133, 150–67, 169n16, 170n27, 188–89, 200, 223, 243, 251
Ocelot, Michel, 264
Oculus Rift, 270
Oh, If He Knew How to Read (1964), 15
oil revenue, 48n24, 51
OK Toon, 74
Oman, 19, 71–72, 78–79, 81n5
Omar, Hassan, 156
Omrani, Rafik, 254
On My Door Step (2010), 183
Once Upon a Time - Nasreddin Hodja, Kalaghban and Gülderen Sultan (1950), 89, 93
Once Upon a Time, Our World (1989), 252
One (1998), 99
One Battle Too Many (n.d.), 188
One Hand (2010), 121
One Pound Only (1964), 177
One Thousand and One Nights, 8–9, 29, 40, 131, 133; *see also* 1001 Nights; Arabian Nights
One, Two, Three (1973), 205
One, Two, Three… (1980), 61
Open Sesame (1979), 72
optical effects, 243
Oral, Tan, 93–94, 102
Oren, Roni, 178–79, 191n2
Oren, Tsvika, 23
Orhan, Esin, 101

311

Index

Orientalism, 8–9, 175, 186, 201
Osanlu, Parviz, 56
Oslo Accords, 153, 155, 157, 163, 187
Osmose Studio, 267
Otero, 249
Ottoman Empire, 8, 47n6, 74, 85–86, 91, 93, 97, 108, 209
Our World (1967), 244
outsourcing, 7–8, 77, 80, 145
Özdemir, Orhan, 90
Özgür, Tahsin, 97
Özkinay, Fuat, 85
Ozsinay, Yael, 182, 186, 191n2

Pachachi, Maysoon, 18, 43–44
Palestinian Authority, 157
PALTEL Palestine Telecom Communication, 157
pan-Arab, 30, 75, 130–32, 136, 144, 146n18, 222–24, 226, 238n23
Paolinetti, Michael, 270
Pardon Me, Mr. X (1993), 113
Paronnaud, Vincent, 25n1, 51
Pasin, Dervis, 75
Pasin-Benice Studio, 96
Paz, Or, 183
performance art, 85, 146n20
performativity, 4, 219
Persepolis (2007), 6, 25n1, 25n11, 51–52, 63, 65
Persian fables, 266
Pertev, Kerem, 87
Petting Corner (2014), 183
Physicians for Human Rights (PHR), 161–62
PICTI, 156–7
pilot, 72, 271
pioneer, 11, 14, 22, 24, 52, 55, 65, 72, 79, 87, 119, 123, 137, 138, 173–74, 196, 205, 208, 241, 243, 250, 255, 257, 265, 269, 274, 276
pipeline, 114, 270, 279n25

PitchiPoy, 178, 181–82, 191n2, 193n30
Pixelated Intifada (2012), 165, 167n1
Plasticine, 274
Plympton, Bill, 264
poetry, 3
Pojar, Břetislav, 257
political satire, 21, 79, 154, 156, 177, 218–20, 235–36
Popeye the Saylor meets Sinbad the Sailor (1936), 9
pornography, 94
post-production, 45, 98, 141, 243, 259n11, 267
Postman Pat (2014), 8, 13, 26n14
propaganda, 86, 173–76, 192n6, 200, 220, 224, 231, 242, 245, 252, 259n11
protest, 22, 102, 218, 228, 230, 232, 239n38, 249, 252
psychedelic, 178
PTSD, 37
puppet animation, 8–9, 56, 85, 87, 91, 117, 138–39, 176, 242, 244, 250–51, 255

Qarantina (2010), 43
Qattan Foundation, 155
Quran, 75, 93, 148n52, 270

Raatsiz Animation Studio, 102
Rabin, Yitzhak, 187
Rabinovich, Michal, 183
racism, 153
Radar Reklam, 90
Radiodiffusion Télévision Tunisienne, 249
Radyolin, 87
Rahnama, Feryedoon, 54
Rais, Nadia, 253–55
Raki, Fertek, 87, 104n9
Ramadan, 140, 145, 148n52, 206, 227, 230, 271

Index

Ramadan, Ibrahim, 140
Ramallah, 6, 150, 156
Ramzi and Adam (2009), 271
Rasheed, Oday, 43, 48n13
Rass Derb (2010), 271–73, 276
reconciliation, 31, 35, 46, 226, 236
refugee, 137, 150–51, 159, 161,
  165, 167
Reiniger, Lotte, 8
relic, 31, 189
Reşat, sultan, 85
resistance, 50n42, 102, 121–22, 151,
  154, 157–58, 160, 164, 166–67,
  170n24, 237n4, 248, 253
Return to the Land of Wonders
  (2004), 43
Revolutionary Nuns, 233
revolutions, 1, 4–6, 96, 115, 121, 217–
  18, 235, 257
Rich Animation Studios, 8
RichCrest, 8
Right of Return, 151
Rimawi, Tariq, 12, 13, 25n2, 25n3,
  26n23, 211, 215n35, 215n36
Rimon, Ada, 186, 189
Rita Saab Mukarzel, 147n33
Roadrunner, 248
Robot Grandizer Raids (1979),
  131, 140
Robotika Films, 102
Ropes (1981), 95
Rosenberg, Dani, 189
Rostam and Esfandiar (2002), 55
Rotana, 69
Rotoscope, 133
Royal Academy of Fine Arts, 57
Royal Film Commission (RFC), 12
Rozental, Tatia, 182
Roznov, Michael, 183
Rubicon Group Holding
  Entertainment, 8
Rubin, David, 188

Ruya Foundation for Contemporary
  Culture, 44
Ryeh (2008), 254

Saad, Ahmed, 203
Saba Art and Culture Company, 60
Sabah El-Kheir, 204
Sabra and Shatila, 189, 252
Sabreen Association for Artistic
  Development, 161
Sad Man (2002), 134
Sadeghi, Ali Akbar, 56–57, 62, 65
Said, Edward, 158, 170n20
Salaheddine, Basti, 276
Sama Dubai, 77–78
Samandal, 139
Sancho, Mongi, 241–44, 246–50, 253
Sandcastles (2010), 255
Sarout, Jad, 137, 149
Sasanians, 32
Sasson, Daniel, 188, 191n2
satellite, 77, 79, 107, 116, 132, 147n41,
  151, 154, 156, 205–6, 222, 226,
  238n21, 238n23
satire, 21, 79–80, 81n20, 86, 154, 156,
  177–78, 183, 218–20, 222, 226,
  231, 235–36
SATPEC, 243–5, 253, 259n11
Satrapi, Marjane, 25n1, 51
SATRBC, 111
Save Her, She's in Danger (1987), 252
Scarecrow, 152, 161
Screen Gems, 130
sculpture, 164–65, 167, 168n1, 265
secret police, 133
sectarian, 33–34, 37, 46, 132,
  144, 147n41
secular, 3, 32, 174, 186, 246
self-censorship, 8, 11, 16, 79, 102, 119,
  210, 220, 227, 231, 236
Semlali, Hamid, 264, 281
Senan, Emre, 94

313

Index

Separation Barrier, 152
Serafettin the Bad Cat (2016)
Servais, Raoul, 57
service centre, 152
Seyhan, Ayla, 91
shadow theatre, 19, 84, 242, 255, 258n6
Shah, 52, 54
Shahbandar, Nazih, 108
Shahin, Ali, 221, 238n37
Shaker, Ihab, 21, 24, 204, 212, 214, 216, 293–94
Shakhabeet Avatar, 156
Shalita, David, 177–79, 191n2, 192n20, 193n25, 193n27
Sham'un, Baz, 43
Shariati, Ali, 54
Sharif, Omar, 202
Sharon, Ariel, 189
Sharon, Yoel, 188
Sharott, Ayala, 182
Shekin, Barak, 175
Shemer, Ofek, 186, 189
Shiite, 32, 46, 54
Shomali, Amer, 150, 154, 156, 164–67, 168n1, 170n32
Shortcut Playground, 181
Showqi, Ghaith Mohammed, 39
Shrek Forever After (2010), 273
Sibai, Jamal, 221, 228, 230, 233, 238n34
SIGMA Technologies, 267, 268, 270–71, 273, 276
SIGMA Toons, 268, 271
Sigorta, Güven, 87
Sima Film, 59–60
Simavi, Sedat, 86
Sinbad, 9, 75, 131, 146n15, 206
Sinefekt, 98–99
Sinematek Society, 92–93
Sinevizyon, 90
Sintel Film, 92
sitcoms, 71, 76–79
SK Productions, 271

Sketches from Munich (2013), 184–85
slapstick, 177
Snowballs, 181
Sobchack, Vivian, 190, 194n43
social media, 22, 143, 181, 211–12, 215n35, 218, 273
software, 3, 74, 85, 135, 141, 168n1, 180, 212, 226, 266, 269–70, 275, 280n38
solidarity, 110, 121, 137, 160, 169n18
Soliman, Ido, 185, 194
Son of the Forest (2006), 73
Songs Without Words (1958), 176
Sony Picture Works, 273
sound design, 111, 135
South Park, 77, 122
Soviet Union, 49n29, 108, 203, 219
SpaceToon, 116, 126n41
special effects, 98, 142
SPGIL, 23, 139, 147n33
Spotlight, 226, 238n23
Star Animation, 113–14, 123, 126n30
Stereo (1980), 95
stereotypes, 9, 13, 45, 78–79
stop-motion, 12, 88, 91, 93, 98, 126n41, 137–38, 153, 156, 164, 166–76, 176, 269, 274
Stories of the Wise Uncle (1999), 75
street art, 220
Studio Baalbek, 131, 146n16
Studio Misr, 197–98
Stüdyo Çizgi, 90
subsidy, 155
subtitles, 130
subversion, 4, 122–23, 172, 236
Suleiman, Elia, 159, 188
Sultan, Abdel Wahab, 73
Sunni, 32, 46, 127n46
Super Powers (1987), 62
Superman, 150
Suriano, Shlomo, 179

314

Index

Syrian Arab TV, 112
Syrian Youth (2008), 123

taboo, 93–94, 100, 109, 123, 201, 217
Taghvai, Naser, 56
Tahrik Festival, 255, 260n32
Taieb, Mustapha, 251–53, 255
Taish Eyal (2012), 79
Takahata, Isao, 264
Tale of Tales (1979), 249
Taliban, 233
Tansuğ, Sezer, 93
Tarek Rashed Studio, 78–79, 207
Tarzan (1997), 97
Tash ma Tash, 79–80
Tawfiq, Salih, 33
Tawit-Souri, Helga, 157, 169n16, 296
technologies, 5, 15, 23, 51, 70, 76, 80,
    99, 144, 172, 180–81, 207, 212, 263,
    266–68, 270–71, 273, 276–77
Tehrani, Mahvash, 63–65, 67n28
Tejaratchi, Jafar, 56
Tekin Aral, 90, 92
Tel Aviv, 174–75, 177–78, 180, 191n2,
    192n22, 193n26, 193n27, 194n35
Tele Çizgi, 90, 95
Télé-Liban, 130, 146n16
Télé-Orient, 130
Ternoirio, Joao, 182
terrorism, 80
The Adventures of Gadi Ben Sussi
    (1932), 173–74
The Adventures of ZeZe le Bourdon
    (2009), 271
The Amazing Spiderman (2012), 273
The Animated Hagada (1984), 179
The Arabian Nights, 75
The Axe (1981), 179
The Bat and the Robin (2004), 133
The Baton (1994), 113, 125n24
The Bird of the Atlas (2002), 264
The Blue Fairy Book (1889), 8

The Book of Kings, 55, 64
The Book of Travels, 91
The Bottle (1968), 204
The Boy and the King (1996), 75
The Burnt City, 52
The Cabinet Decision (2014), 189
The Carthage Submarine
    (1999), 253–54
The Cat (1978), 95
The Child and the Aeroplane
    (1983), 251
The Child King (2007), 255
The Cicada (1986), 252
The Common Room Animation Project
    (2014), 182, 186
The Companions of Elephants, 270
The Conquest of Andolusia-Tareq ibn
    Ziyad (1999), 75
The Daily Comment (1995), 132
The Deception (1982), 63–4, 67n35
The Diaries of Mnahy (2006), 79–80
The Diary of Bou Qatada and Bou
    Nabeel (2007), 78
The Dictator (2003), 135
The Dinosaur and the Ant
    (1962), 203
The Dream of the Beautiful Blue
    Danube (1964), 201
The Eleventh Commandment
    (2011), 112
The Ella Endowment for Art
    Production, 74
The Empty Room (1964), 105
The Enchanted Forest (1974), 179
The Facts in the Case of Mr. Valdemar
    (2009), 135
The Festival of the Tree (1963), 15
The Fez Seller (1968), 244, 247–48
The Flintstones, 130
The Flood (1994), 252–53
The Flower (1970), 249
The Foxy Rabbit, 116, 118–19

315

Index

The General's Boot (2008), 114–15, 121, 126n34
The Glasses (2011), 254–56
The Good Soldier Schweik, 93
The Heart of Amos Klein (2008), 188
The Hen from Saaba (2010), 255
The Innocent Suspect (1928), 108
The Intelligent Dog (1966), 244, 247
The Israel Machine (2011), 186
The Jar: A Tale from the East (1999), 114
The Jasmine Birds (2009), 114, 116–18
The Jungle Kid (2005), 30
The Jungle of Dreams (1991), 64
The Knight and the Princess (1988), 207
The Lamp Lighter (newspaper), 109
The Line, 160, 167
The Lion of the Desert (1980), 225
The Little Owl, (1984), 251
The Long Days (1980), 33
The Mad Mad Mad World (1975), 61
The Makers of Civilisation (2005), 73
The Man Who Discovered the Curved Line for the Very First Time (1976), 94
The Martyr of the World (2003), 75
The Message (1976), 225
The Minivan and its Driver, 88
The Miraculous Droplet (2009), 255
The Morganti Rebels, 22, 218, 221, 237n2
The Mule (1972), 241, 249, 258n3, 260n25
The Neighbourhood (2006), 77
The New Cinema Magazine, 93
The Old New Land (2012), 186
The Old Woman and the Ogre (1964), 243
The Parliament's Monsters, 183
The Pirates and the Gold Treasure (1998), 75

The Post Office, 141
The Princess and the River (1982), 33, 44
The Red Suitcase (2008), 183
The Revolution (newspaper), 231
The Rook (1974), 62
The Sand Castle (n.d.), 182
The Shoe (1994), 253
The Simpsons, 77
The Sleeping Man (1971), 249
The Street Artist (2015), 13, 26n25
The Survival (1988), 206
The Thief and the Cobbler (1993), 9
The Thread of Life (2005), 116
The Threads (1995), 253
The Traffic Signal (1987), 112
The Victorious Saladin (1996), 74
The Wanted 18 (2014), 20, 150, 153–55, 164–67, 168n1, 169n10
The Water Seller (1984), 251
The White Rose (1933), 198
The Wolf's Wedding (2001), 254
The Zeybek Dance (1947), 88
theatre, 19, 30, 84–85, 87, 90, 92, 98, 113, 129–31, 201, 204, 224–25, 242, 250, 255, 258n6
therapy, 121–22
They Have Children (2014), 121–22
This City of Istanbul (1968), 90
Thrashing (2009), 137
Tiger Production, 113, 116–17, 121, 125n30, 126n41
Titi and Rashwan (1962), 203
TNC National Transitional Council, 232–33
TOEI Animation, 146n14
Tom and Jerry, 151, 248
Toonz, 266
Tornistan (2014), 102–3
Toronto International Film Festival, 164, 169n10
Toubaji, Wael, 121

316

Index

Toufyl, Hon, 31
tourism, 175
Toval, Sharon, 182
Toy Story (1995), 76
tracking shot, 243
Trade Union for the Animating
  Professions, 180
Trager, Tom, 183
training, 7, 11–12, 20, 24, 40, 44,
  55–57, 97, 99, 102, 110, 112–13,
  135–37, 144, 154, 156, 162, 180–81,
  208–9, 224, 244–46, 253, 264, 267,
  270–71, 275
transnational, 1–2, 5–11, 17–21, 23–4,
  30, 45, 65, 69, 72, 76, 96, 119, 122–23,
  142, 152, 168n6, 168n7, 181–82,
  186, 267
trauma, 108, 119, 122, 185, 187–88,
  191n1, 230, 236
Trilogy of Voice (2014), 122
Tripoli, 221, 224, 226–27, 230, 238n38
TRT, 93–94, 96–97, 100, 102
TRT Çocuk, 100
True Love Hotel (2008), 183
Tunç Izberk Studio, 95
Tunis School of Fine Arts,
  252–4, 258n5
Tunisian Federation of Amateur
  Filmmakers (FTCA), 242–44
Tunisian Federation of Film-Clubs
  (FTCC), 244, 255
Turkish Commercial Bank, 92
Turkish Film Archive, 93
Turkish Radio and Television
  Culture, Arts and Science Awards
  Short Film Competition, 93
Tüzecan, Yalçin, 92
Two Boys (2012), 182

UAE, 19, 26n24, 67n36, 72, 78
Ubisoft, 267, 276–77
Ülken, Mehmet Celal, 93

Ulvi, Ali, 90, 92
Umay, Ridvan, 87
Umm Kalthoum, 198
Underexposure (2005), 43,
  48n13
UNESCO, 30, 47n3, 204, 263
Unilever, 92
United Kingdom of Libya, 223
Université Saint Esprit Kaslik
  (USEK), 136
University of South Wales, 13
Ünsal, Yüksel, 89, 91–92
UPA, 9
USSR, 38
Ustudio, 73

Vatan, 89
Vedat Ar, 88, 91
Venus Studio, 74, 116
Veto (1991), 113
VFX, 99
VGIK, 111–12
VHS, 74, 131
Victory (1987), 179
Viruses in Bins (1964), 15
Viva Cartago, 253–54
Vog-Bali, 91

wall painting, 52
Walt Disney, 76, 91, 97, 129, 199
Waltz with Bashir (2008), 2, 6, 21,
  25n1, 25n11, 172–73, 179, 182,
  187–89, 191n1
War of Independence, 15, 86
Waraq, 139, 146n28, 146n32
We Shall Never Die (1950s), 176
West Bank, 152, 155–57
Westoxication, 54
Where is Iraq? (2005), 43
White Tape (2010), 189
WHO, 161–62, 170n27
Why? (2013), 152

Index

Widad (1936), 198
Wile E. Coyote, 248
Williams, Richard, 9
Wind (2007), 138
Wixel Studios, 136
workshops, 12, 23–24, 43–44, 55, 70, 102, 138–40, 209, 231, 264–66, 275
World War I, 85, 199, 258n9
World War II, 53, 86, 88
wrestling, 62, 91

Yaşar, Tonguç, 3, 8, 88, 92–94
Yassir, Haidder Abdul Rahim, 39
Yelostudio, 137
Yishuv, 173–75
Yoresh, Yithak, 175, 177
Youth Rally Against Oppression, 121
Youth Salon festival, 208
YouTube, 6, 10, 115, 156, 183, 211–12, 215n35, 235, 268–70, 273, 276
Yushij, Nima, 54

Zaatari, Hashim, 73, 83
Zaghlul, Saad, 198
Zagreb Animation Film Festival, 65, 95
Zagreb, 65, 95, 203, 254
Zaim, 251
Zaitoon Studio, 151–52, 155–56, 168n5
Zaki, Abdellaim, 203
Zamzam, 207
Zan Studio, 150, 156, 165
Zarrinkelk, Noureddin, 23–24, 56–7, 60–61, 65, 67n23, 67n24, 67n25, 67n31, 67n33
Za'toor (1993), 73
Zeid and Leila (2009), 137
Zionism, 174–76, 186, 192n4, 192n7, 201
Zionist cinema, 174
zoetropes, 268
Zwawi, Mohamed, 22, 222–25, 235, 237n16

TAURIS WORLD CINEMA SERIES

Series Editors:
Lúcia Nagib, *Professor of Film at the University of Reading*
Julian Ross, *Research Fellow at the University of Westminster*

Advisory Board: Laura Mulvey (UK), Robert Stam (USA), Ismail Xavier (Brazil), Dudley Andrew (USA)

The *Tauris World Cinema Series* aims to reveal and celebrate the richness and complexi of film art across the globe, exploring a wide variety of cinemas set within their own cu tures and as they interconnect in a global context. The books in the series will represen innovative scholarship, in tune with the multicultural character of contemporary audiences. Drawing upon an international authorship, they will challenge outdated conceptions of world cinema, and provide new ways of understanding a field at the centre of film studies in an era of transnational networks.

Published and forthcoming in the World Cinema series:

Animation in the Middle East: Practice and Aesthetics from Baghdad to Casablanca
Edited by Stefanie Van de Peer

Basque Cinema: A Cultural and Political History
By Rob Stone and María Pilar Rodriguez

Brazil on Screen: Cinema Novo, New Cinema, Utopia
By Lúcia Nagib

The Cinema of Sri Lanka: South Asian Film in Texts and Contexts
By Ian Conrich and Vilasnee Tampoe-Hautin

Contemporary New Zealand Cinema: Fro New Wave to Blockbuster
Edited by Ian Conrich and Stuart Murray

Contemporary Portuguese Cinema: Globalising the Nation
Edited by Mariana Liz

Cosmopolitan Cinema: Cross-cultural Encounters in East Asian Film
By Felicia Chan

Documentary Cinema: Contemporary Non-fiction Film and Video Worldwide
By Keith Beattie

East Asian Cinemas: Exploring Transnational Connections on Film
Edited by Leon Hunt and Leung Wing-Fai

East Asian Film Noir: Transnational Encounters and Intercultural Dialogue
Edited by Chi-Yun Shin and Mark Gallagher

Film Genres and African Cinema: Postcolonial Encounters
By Rachael Langford

Impure Cinema: Intermedial and Intercultural Approaches to Film
Edited by Lúcia Nagib and Anne Jerslev

Latin American Women Filmmakers: Production, Politics, Poetics
Edited by Deborah Martin and Deborah Shaw

Lebanese Cinema: Imagining the Civil War and Beyond
By Lina Khatib

New Argentine Cinema
By Jens Andermann

New Directions in German Cinema
Edited by Paul Cooke and Chris Homewood

New Turkish Cinema: Belonging, Identity and Memory
By Asuman Suner

On Cinema
By Glauber Rocha
Edited by Ismail Xavier

Palestinian Filmmaking in Israel: Narratives of Place and Identity
By Yael Freidman

Paulo Emílio Salles Gomes: On Brazil and Global Cinema
Edited by Maite Conde and Stephanie Dennison

Performing Authorship: Self-inscription and Corporeality in the Cinema
By Cecilia Sayad

Queer Masculinities in Latin American Cinema: Male Bodies and Narrative Representations
By Gustavo Subero

Realism in Greek Cinema: From the Post-war Period to the Present
By Vrasidas Karalis

Realism of the Senses in World Cinema: The Experience of Physical Reality
By Tiago de Luca

The Spanish Fantastic: Contemporary Filmmaking in Horror, Fantasy and Sci-fi
By Shelagh-Rowan Legg

Stars in World Cinema: Screen Icons and Star Systems Across Cultures
Edited by Andrea Bandhauer and Michelle Royer

Theorizing World Cinema
Edited by Lúcia Nagib, Chris Perriam and Rajinder Dudrah

Viewing Film
By Donald Richie

Queries, ideas and submissions to:

Series Editor: Professor Lúcia Nagib – l.nagib@reading.ac.uk

Series Editor: Dr. Julian Ross – rossj@westminster.ac.uk

Cinema Editor at I.B.Tauris, Maddy Hamey-Thomas – mhamey-thomas@ibtauris.com

CPSIA information can be obtained
at www.ICGtesting.com
Printed in the USA
LVHW020325050921
696998LV00012B/1164